D0816716

*Machiavelli and
the Discourse of Literature*

MACHIAVELLI

AND THE DISCOURSE
OF LITERATURE

EDITED BY

Albert Russell Ascoli

AND

Victoria Kahn

CORNELL UNIVERSITY PRESS
Ithaca and London

First published 1993 by Cornell University Press.

International Standard Book Number 0-8014-2870-x (cloth)
International Standard Book Number 0-8014-8109-0 (paper)
Library of Congress Catalog Card Number 93-11804

Printed in the United States of America

*Librarians: Library of Congress cataloging information appears
on the last page of the book.*

⊛ The paper in this book meets the minimum requirements of the American
National Standard for Information Sciences—Permanence of Paper for
Printed Library Materials, ANSI Z39.48-1984.

In Memoriam

Giulio Ascoli, 1922–1992

Doris W. Kahn, 1921–1991

CONTENTS

Contents

ACKNOWLEDGMENTS

WE are grateful to our contributors for their patience in the long, drawn-out process of editing this collection and to our translators, Michael Moore, Ronald L. Martinez, and Olivia Holmes for their fine work. We also thank David Quint for reading a draft of the Introduction, Eileen Reeves for help with the illustrations, Robert Ultimo for assistance with a number of translations from the Latin, and Bernhard Kendler for shepherding this volume through the Press. Thanks are due as well to our readers, Samuel Cohn, Jr., and Jon R. Snyder, for their endorsement and for their helpful suggestions. Northwestern University's Research Grants Committee and the Princeton University Committee on Research in the Humanities and the Social Sciences provided financial assistance for the translations.

Carlo Dionisotti's "Machiavelli letterato" originally appeared in the *Notiziario culturale dell'Istituto Italiano di Cultura di Parigi* 4 (1969): 15–26, and was republished in *Machiavellerie* (Turin: Einaudi, 1980), 227–66. Ezio Raimondi's "Il politico e il centauro" first appeared in his *Politica e commedia dal Beroaldo al Machiavelli* (Bologna: Il Mulino, 1972), 265–86. Giulio Ferroni's "Mutazione e riscontro nel teatro di Machiavelli" first appeared in *Mutazione e riscontro nel teatro di Machiavelli e altri saggi sulla commedia del Cinquecento* (Rome: Bulzoni, 1972), 19–137. We are grateful to the respective publishers for permission to reprint. We are also grateful to Nancy S. Struever and the University of Chicago Press for permission to reprint "Purity as Danger: Gramsci's Machiavelli, Croce's Vico" from *Theory as Practice: Ethical Inquiry in the Renaissance* (Chicago: University of Chicago Press, 1992), 210–24, copyright © 1992 by the University of Chicago; and to the University of

Acknowledgments

California Press for permission to reprint Victoria Kahn's "*Virtù* and the Example of Agathocles in Machiavelli's *Prince*," which originally appeared in *Representations* 13 (Winter 1986): 63–83, copyright © 1986 by the Regents of the University of California. Unless otherwise noted translations of *Il Principe* are reprinted from *The Prince* by Niccolò Machiavelli. Translated and edited by Robert M. Adams. A Norton Critical Edition. With the permission of W.W. Norton & Company, Inc. Copyright © 1977 by W.W. Norton & Company, Inc.

A. R. A. and V. K.

Machiavelli and
the Discourse of Literature

INTRODUCTION

*Albert Russell Ascoli
and Victoria Kahn*

LATE in the winter of 1517, in the period we usually suppose marked the completion of *The Prince* and *The Discourses*, Machiavelli wrote to his friend Lodovico Alamanni about his reading of the recently published *Orlando furioso*: "Io ho letto a questi dí *Orlando furioso* dello Ariosto, et veramente il poema è bello tutto. . . . Se si truova costí, raccomandatemi a lui, et ditegli che io mi dolgo solo che, havendo ricordato tanti poeti, che m'habbi lasciato indietro come un cazzo" (I have just read *Orlando furioso* by Ariosto, and truly the poem is beautiful throughout. . . . If you run into him, give him my regards and tell him that I am only sorry that, having spoken of so many poets, he left me out like a prick).[1] The letter, as has often been noted, tells us both that Machiavelli thinks of himself as a poet worthy of inclusion among the significant authors of his age and that he is intensely aware of its great literary events, in particular of the work that was to become most emblematic of the pleasures of literature during the sixteenth century in Italy and throughout Europe. There is, however, more to be said of these few words as representative of Machiavelli's sense both of himself as poet and of poetry as a mode of discourse.

Machiavelli's letter refers to a particular section of Ariosto's text, the celebrated return of the poet from the sea of writing to a shore of reading, where his readers, the courtly literati of his day, "donne e cavallieri" alike, await him, offering encouragement and welcome (canto 46, stanzas 1–19). From this list the name of Machiavelli is ostentatiously omitted, although critics are now recognizing that Ariosto

1. Niccolò Machiavelli, *Lettere*, ed. Franco Gaeta (Milan, 1961), letter no. 170 (December 17, 1517), 383; translated by the authors.

did not leave the "segretario fiorentino" behind entirely, for traces of his presence were persistently suggested in a series of allusive echoings.[2] The characteristic, and scandalous, directness of Machiavelli's reaction—registering the beauty of the poem and its world beside a bitter sense of exclusion from them—in many ways is sufficient explanation of why Ariosto did not mention Machiavelli and why, for all his attempts at conciliation, Machiavelli would remain fundamentally excluded from the courtly world of Ariosto, Castiglione, and the Medici family.[3]

What is perhaps not so apparent is that the exclusion Machiavelli feels so keenly is in fact double. We know from the famous letter of December 10, 1513, to Francesco Vettori, from the dedications to *The Prince* and *The Discourses*, and from the prologue to *Mandragola* (among many other sources) that Machiavelli felt a radical ambivalence about the humanistic, literary pursuits of his exile in the Tuscan countryside. On the one hand, they were a redemptive sanctuary from the squalor of a life of enforced *otium* or idleness; on the other, they were a means whose end was their own abolition, an offering of appeasement explicitly meant to return him to the world of political activity from which he had been so abruptly banished with the fall of the Florentine republic in 1512. On the one hand, they were "quel cibo, che solum è mio" (that food, which alone is mine); on the other, they were "questi van' pensieri" (these vain thoughts), a degraded substitute for better avenues of expressing one's *virtù* and talent.

In other words, to be included among the poets, from Machiavelli's perspective, is already to be excluded from the world of political action and historical reality. An intellectual itinerary from the early part of the decade to its end, from *The Prince* through *The Discourses* to *Mandragola*, suggests a deepening sense of his own exclusion, coupled with a growing awareness that the pursuits of literature are, contrary to humanistic

2. On the Machiavellian presence in Ariosto, see G. B. Salinari, "Ariosto fra Machiavelli e Erasmo," *Rassegna di cultura e vita scolastica* 21 (1957); Charles Klopp, "The Centaur and the Magpie," in *Ariosto 1974 in America*, ed. Aldo Scaglione (Ravenna, 1976), 69–84; and Peter DeSa Wiggins's note in his translation of *The Satires of Ludovico Ariosto: A Renaissance Autobiography* (Athens, Ohio, 1976), 112, n. 12. For a more recent and more suggestive (though still brief) analysis, see Sergio Zatti, *Il furioso fra epos e romanzo* (Lucca, 1990), 60, 67–68n., 143, 153. The subject still awaits a systematic treatment, however.

3. Ironically, Ariosto would come to feel himself increasingly excluded from this world as well since, like Machiavelli, he would never receive the sought-for preferment of Leo X and since, quite unlike Machiavelli, he would deeply resent the role of political functionary in which he was cast by Duke Alfonso, which kept him from the *otium* of the professional poet's courtly life.

myth, do not complement but are antithetical to the life of the polis. An active attempt to teach a real prince how to deal "not with what should be, but with what is" gives way to the resigned attempt to show political truths not to those who are princes, but to those who are not but should be (as in the dedication to *The Discourses*). This reduced effort at political education in turn cedes to the composition of an entertainment for the stage, where one travels hypothetically to Rome one day, to Pisa the next, "cosa da smascellarsi dalle risa" ([a] setting [that] will tickle you till your sides are splitting) and where political strategy is sublimated into a degraded art of adultery.[4] Without ever abandoning his basic preoccupation with the knowledgeable deployment of power, Machiavelli slides grudgingly from pursuit of the humanistic dream of an activist use of *litterae*, to a clearly utopian politics of Roman exemplarity, to a mode of writing that openly declares its alienation from reality—not simply *litterae* now but literature in a tendentiously modern sense.

The letter to Alamanni on the reading of Ariosto comes just before the final turning point in this process, between the two political-historical treatises and the composition of *Mandragola*. One might speculate that in Ariosto's great poem of crisis and evasion Machiavelli could have read the fate of literature overtly resigned to its relegation to the aesthetic margin, the historical sidelines, as well as the myth of the poet's final reintegration into society that so obviously captures his imagination. (The two moments, clearly, are part of the same experience.) Whether or not he was such an astute reader of *Orlando furioso*, Machiavelli's own image of exclusion certainly betrays an ambivalence that at once distances itself from Ariosto's poetics and refigures them. For Ariosto's *amplificatio* of the boat of poetry/sea of writing trope Machiavelli substitutes a brief and violent "realism": as Ariosto nears his shore, Machiavelli is left behind "like a prick." The image suggests two readings, both applicable to Machiavelli in this and other contexts. First is the image of castrated humiliation: severed from the republic of letters as well as from the polis itself, Machiavelli is now doubly unmanned. Second and just as important, however, Machiavelli's rough, direct style suggests its own phallic potency in contrast to the maternal, oceanic periphrasis of Ariosto's image. For Machiavelli, the dream of inclusion among the poets is thus powerful but ambivalent: to become part of the community, any community, is to be reempowered, but to

4. The phrase is from the prologue to *Mandragola*. The Italian and the English translation are from Niccolò Machiavelli, *The Comedies of Machiavelli*, ed. and trans. David Sices and James B. Atkinson (Hanover, N.H., 1985), 157.

be acknowledged as a poet is to be openly exposed as disempowered. Hence a language, like that of the letter we have just scrutinized, that speaks of exclusion and violation with its own intrusive violence.

Machiavelli's ambivalence about literature can be traced in part to his humanistic education. It is a commonplace of Renaissance scholarship, and of Machiavelli studies in particular, that the liberal arts, the *studia humanitatis* or *litterae humaniores*, were much more closely bound together in the early sixteenth century than they are today. Although in theory the humanistic subjects—grammar, rhetoric, poetry, history, and moral philosophy—were studied sequentially, in practice the boundaries between them were often blurred.[5] For example, the student of grammar or literature would learn about rhetorical figures of speech and would assimilate as well the view that literature had the rhetorical power to persuade the reader to moral action. Similarly, the student of history learned moral precepts from the examples of ancient heroes, a lesson that for the humanists was inseparable from the pedagogical goal of rhetoric.

From the *Ricordi* of his father, Bernardo, and from his own work, we know that Machiavelli received just such an education in the *studia humanitatis*. He learned Latin from the standard Latin grammar of the day, the *Donatello*. In his father's library he would have had access to, among other classical works, Cicero's *De officiis* and a printed copy of Livy's *Histories*, as well as to Flavio Biondo's humanist history, the *Decades*. His correspondence is full of references to his reading in the classics and in contemporary literature: in the letter about his life of forced retirement after the fall of the Florentine republic, he tells us that he carries on his walks "un libro sotto, o Dante o Petrarca, o un di questi poeti minori, come Tibullo, Ovvidio et simili" (a book in his pocket, either Dante or Petrarch, or one of the lesser poets, such as Tibullus, Ovid, and the like).[6] The influence of the classics and of contemporary literature is evident not only in the Dantean terza rima of his unfinished poems, the *Decennali*, and in his imitation of Plautus's

5. Paul Oskar Kristeller discusses the *studia humanitatis* in terms of these subjects in "Humanist Learning in the Italian Renaissance," in *Renaissance Thought and the Arts* (Princeton, N.J., 1990), an expanded edition of *Renaissance Thought II* (New York, 1964). In the following paragraph we have drawn on Allan H. Gilbert's introduction to Niccolò Machiavelli, *The Letters of Machiavelli*, reprint ed. (Chicago, 1988), as well as Myron P. Gilmore's introduction to *Machiavelli, The History of Florence and Other Selections* (New York, 1970). On Machiavelli's education, see Roberto Ridolfi, *The Life of Niccolò Machiavelli*, trans. Cecil Grayson (Chicago, 1963), as well as the bibliographical essay in Felix Gilbert, *Machiavelli and Guicciardini: Politics and History in Sixteenth-Century Florence* (Princeton, N.J., 1965).

6. Machiavelli, *Lettere*, ed. Gaeta, letter no. 140 (December 10, 1513), 303; translated by the authors.

Casina in *Clizia*, but also in his references to the histories of his humanist predecessors Leonardo Bruni and Poggio Bracciolini in his *Florentine Histories* and his extended commentary on Livy in *The Discourses*.[7]

Yet, although the *studia humanitatis* seemed to promise a harmonious relationship between its several disciplines, at times this relationship was strained. From our modern perspective, this strain is particularly evident between poetry and rhetoric. For, as our brief outline of humanist education has already suggested, poetry or imaginative literature in the Renaissance is a category that is both related to and distinct from humanist rhetoric. On the one hand, literature is identified with epideictic, the rhetoric of praise and blame, and shares with it both the means of persuasion—figures of speech, illustrative examples, narrative techniques—and the goal of teaching moral behavior by literary example. On the other hand, to the extent that literature is equated with epideictic, it is distinguished from the political and legal uses of rhetoric and begins to claim an autonomous realm of aesthetic pleasure for its own. Thus, for example, in *De copia* Erasmus recommends fluency of expression as much for the pleasure it gives as for its use as a vehicle of moral instruction. And Castelvetro argues in his 1570 commentary on Aristotle's *Poetics* that the chief effect of literature is delight rather than instruction.[8] The relationship between rhetoric and literature is further complicated by the fact that a humanist rhetoric that was judged to be too idealistic might be ridiculed as merely literary; the humanist ideal of the active life might be derisively conflated with the life of *otium* and the consolations of literature.

In Machiavelli's lifetime the strains in the humanist pedagogical program coincided with and were aggravated by the political crisis in Italy precipitated by the French invasion at the end of the fifteenth century. In the early part of the sixteenth century, the machinations of the Spaniards and Pope Julius II combined with Piero Soderini's temporizing and the Florentines' lack of military strength to cause the downfall of the Florentine republic in 1512. As Felix Gilbert has argued, these

7. Quentin Skinner conjectures that this humanist education helped Machiavelli gain the post of second chancellor of Florence: "The prevalence of these [humanist] ideals [in Florence] helps to explain how Machiavelli came to be appointed at a relatively early age to a position of considerable responsibility in the administration of the republic. For his family, though neither rich nor highly aristocratic, was closely connected with some of the city's most exalted humanist circles. . . . It is also evident from Bernardo's *Diary* that, in spite of the large expense involved—which he anxiously itemised—he was careful to provide his son with an excellent grounding in the *studia humanitatis*" (*Machiavelli* [New York, 1981], 4, 5).

8. Desiderius Erasmus, *De copia*, bk. 1, sec. 8 [*Collected Works of Erasmus*, ed. Craig R. Thompson (Toronto, 1974–), 24 (1978): 301–2]; Lodovico Castelvetro, *Poetica d'Aristotele vulgarizzata e sposta*, ed. Werther Romani, 2 vols. (Bari, 1978), 1:46.

events precipitated a crisis in the assumptions of political thinking and of humanist historiography, both of which had proved incapable of encompassing recent events or of helping to preserve the republic.[9] In this climate of political crisis, the failure of the humanist ideal of the *vita activa* (active life) was acutely felt not only by Machiavelli but by many of his contemporaries.

Machiavelli's own ambivalent attitude toward literature reflects the tensions both within the humanist tradition and between humanist ideals and contemporary political events. Thus he both incorporates the literary strategies of humanist rhetoric in his political work and disparages humanist rhetoric as merely literary and ineffective. From one Machiavellian perspective, Machiavelli's political works can still be read as part of an ongoing humanist project to educate by literary example, even as these works revise the humanist notion of the exemplary. For, although Machiavelli often takes issue with the idealist tendencies of his predecessors, he shares with them, as Guicciardini noted with disapproval, the humanist belief in the persistent usefulness and exemplarity of classical literature, as well as in the use of rhetoric to persuade the reader of the advantages of imitation and effective political action.[10] In this light Machiavelli's work is rhetorical because persuasion is an art that is relevant to politics as well as to literature. And if Machiavelli at times disparages the merely literary uses of rhetoric, he does so in order to highlight the strategic use of rhetoric in the realm of politics.[11]

From another Machiavellian perspective, however, rhetoric serves as a paradigm for the failure of humanist knowledge, and literature emerges both as a consolation for and an ironic comment on this failure. We can see this process of privileging and scapegoating literature

9. See Gilbert, *Machiavelli and Guicciardini,* chaps. 3 and 6.

10. See Francesco Guicciardini, *Ricordi* (Milan, 1975), series C, nos. 110, 117.

11. In addition to the works of Dionisotti, Ferroni, and Raimondi reprinted here, pioneering studies on the literary dimension of Machiavelli's work have been conducted by Joseph Anthony Mazzeo, *Renaissance and Seventeenth-Century Studies* (New York, 1964), chaps. 5 and 6; Giorgio Bárberi Squarotti, *La forma tragica del "Principe" e altri saggi sul Machiavelli* (Florence, 1966); Michael McCanles, *The Discourse of "Il Principe,"* vol. 8 of *Humana Civilitas,* Studies and Sources Relating to the Middle Ages and Renaissance (Malibu, Calif., 1983); Mark Hulliung, *Citizen Machiavelli* (Princeton, N.J., 1983); Thomas M. Greene, "The End of Discourse in Machiavelli's *Prince*" in *Literary Theory/Renaissance Texts,* ed. Patricia Parker and David Quint (Baltimore, 1986) and Wayne A. Rebhorn, *Foxes and Lions: Machiavelli's Confidence Men* (Ithaca, N.Y., 1988). Felix Gilbert is also attentive to the literary Machiavelli in chap. 4 of *Machiavelli and Guicciardini,* esp. 162–70. Although the focus of his work is not literary, Eugene Garver's *Machiavelli and the History of Prudence* (Madison, Wis., 1987) is an important contribution to the study of Machiavelli's rhetoric.

at work already in the famous passage from the *The Prince* in which Machiavelli attacks the tradition of political utopias with obvious reference to Plato's *Republic*: "molti si sono immaginati repubbliche e principati, che non si sono mai visti né conosciuti essere in vero." (A great many men have imagined states and princedoms such as nobody ever saw or knew in the real world.)[12]

The dramatic force of this passage lies in the fact that Machiavelli attacks Platonic idealism by reducing it to the same level that poetry occupies for Plato himself. That is, for Machiavelli, Plato's great rational synthesis of knowledge and power in the "philosopher-king" can be shown to be a merely literary fiction. And Machiavelli's impersonal, methodological critique of the humanist tradition as hopelessly literary is matched by his personal sense that literature (in the restricted sense of drama, poetry) is an idle pastime, one to which he finds himself unfortunately and unhappily relegated after the return of the Medici and his exclusion from the Florentine political scene in 1512. This attitude finds unambiguous expression in the following lines from the author's prologue to *Mandragola*:

> E, se questa materia non è degna,
> per esser pur leggieri,
> d'un uom, che voglia parer saggio e grave,
> scusatelo con questo, che s'ingegna
> con questi van' pensieri
> fare il suo tristo tempo più suave,
> perché altrove non have
> dove voltare el viso,
> ché gli è stato interciso
> mostrar con altre imprese altra virtùe,
> non sendo premio alle fatiche sue.

If this material, because it is frivolous, is unworthy of a man who wants to appear wise and serious, excuse him thus: that he is striving with these vain thoughts to make his sad time sweeter. He has nowhere else to turn, since he has been cut off from showing with other enterprises other virtues, there being no reward for such labors.[13]

---

12. Niccolò Machiavelli, *Il Principe* in *Il Principe e Discorsi*, ed. Sergio Bertelli (Milan, 1960), 65; Niccolò Machiavelli, *The Prince*, trans. and ed. Robert M. Adams (New York, 1977), 44.

13. Italian text from Machiavelli, *The Comedies of Machiavelli*, ed. Sices and Atkinson, 159; translation by the authors.

Machiavelli's complaint echoes those of classical figures such as Cicero, who turned to the literary activities associated with the contemplative life only because they had been excluded from the realm of politics.[14] But Machiavelli goes considerably beyond the humanistic use of yet another classical topos to air his personal disappointments. His problems with literature have an obvious epistemological dimension as well. As we have begun to see, he clearly links the domain of the literary and the imaginary to the failures of an idealist, antiempirical rationalism. He thus anticipates the new science's critique of the humanistic division and ordering of human knowledge that emerged during the late sixteenth and the seventeenth centuries. In this sense, Machiavelli's work foreshadows the gradual emargination not only of literature itself, but of all the *studia humanitatis* (rhetoric, history, in the end even philosophy) in the intellectual economy of the West.[15]

Machiavelli's ambivalence regarding the uses of rhetoric and of literature may thus be seen as emblematic of the gradual changes in the disciplinary divisions of knowledge over a two-century (or longer) period. In schematic terms, there were two major changes. First, there was an increasingly strict separation of one field of knowledge from another, evidenced, for example, in the development of specific academies for specific fields in the latter part of the sixteenth century, and in the increasing skepticism about the proposition that history, philosophy, poetry, law, and the other disciplines of the *studia humanitatis* could all be included under the same rubric, with the shared pedagogical goal of providing powerful examples for imitation by readers. This amounted to a crisis of humanist rhetoric, which had been the common thread that bound together the various fields of knowledge. Second, the humanities generally, if gradually, lost their primacy in the hierarchy of knowledge, ceding pride of place to the natural sciences. We suggest that the limit case of this dual process was the field we now know as literature, which was separated from and excluded by its former companions in the *humanae litterae* on the grounds that it could not be said to be a vehicle for knowledge at all. At the same time

14. See Marcia L. Colish, "Cicero's *De officiis* and Machiavelli's *Prince*," *Sixteenth Century Journal* 9 (1978): 85–86 and 93, on the parallels between Cicero's and Machiavelli's responses to a life of enforced *otium*.

15. On Machiavelli's anticipation of some aspects of Enlightenment thought, see J. G. A. Pocock, *The Machiavellian Moment: Florentine Political Thought and the Atlantic Republican Tradition* (Princeton, N.J., 1975), 85; Albert O. Hirschman, *The Passions and the Interests* (Princeton, N.J., 1977), 13–14; Jürgen Habermas, "The Classical Doctrine of Politics in Relation to Social Philosophy," in *Theory and Practice*, trans. John Viertel (Boston, 1974), 41–81. In the introduction to *Machiavelli and the History of Prudence*, Garver draws an analogy between Machiavelli and Enlightenment thinkers, arguing that Machiavelli does for practical reason what Descartes does for theoretical reason.

literature became representative of all the humanities in its failure to satisfy the new concerns of rationalism and the scientific method. One reason for this situation, which culminated in Kant's relegation of art of all kinds to the status of "purposive objects without purpose," is not far to seek. From the time of the Homeric allegorists, the claims of literature to the status of knowledge lay in its ability to offer representations of reality that approximated completeness and in some cases totality. In Machiavelli's own time and shortly before, Neoplatonists commonly identified poetry as the vehicle of a total, theologically complete knowledge, the so-called poetic theology (in the process overlooking Plato's repeated attacks on poetry as a false image of total knowledge and therefore quite dangerous). By contrast, the critiques of the humanities by the new sciences, including Machiavelli's own critique of theological politics and historiography, were directed precisely at the delusive power of the human intellect to construct ideal images of total coherence that failed to account fully or satisfactorily for stubborn particulars. Literature in this sense is emblematic of all humanistic disciplines because it consistently subordinates empirical reality to ideal schemes while consistently representing those schemes as images of particular realities.

If Machiavelli can be seen as prescientific, however, it is only in the sense of initiating empiricist and secularizing trends, whose implications would then be systematically explored later on.[16] As *Mandragola* itself eloquently testifies, Machiavelli's ambivalence toward the utopian ideals of literature and the rhetorical arsenal of humanism does not prevent his taking from both a range of formal and persuasive techniques. And although literature represents all that Machiavelli opposes in his intellectual and political life, in works such as *Mandragola* we see that it is also an alternative vocation for him, one to which he is constrained but for which he has obvious talents and affinities. To speak of Machiavelli and the discourse of literature, then, is not simply to examine an isolable and neglected aspect of his career. It is to understand literature as a fundamental and integral category of Machiavelli's thought and writing—one that he alternately rejects and embraces and through which he attempts to define, by negation, the other disciplines, above all the historiographical and political, to which he is primarily dedicated. To speak of Machiavelli and the discourse of literature is to resituate him, once more, at a pivotal and an ambiguous moment in the history of the sociopolitical organization of knowledge.

In editing this collection of essays, our overarching concern was thus

---

16. Rebhorn takes issue with the scientific interpretation of Machiavelli in *Foxes and Lions*, 3–4.

twofold: to situate the literary within the range of cultural discourses available to Machiavelli and to locate Machiavelli in an evolving history of disciplines and modes of writing during the early modern period. Although all the essays included here were solicited or chosen because they reflect a distinctively literary Machiavelli—either in the sense that they explore Machiavelli's literary works and his concept of the literary, or in the sense that they adopt a literary and rhetorical approach to the reading of Machiavelli's works—disciplinary questions are most openly at issue in the first and last pairs of essays. Carlo Dionisotti and John M. Najemy focus on Machiavelli's understanding of what it means to be a man of letters in the wake of Quattrocento humanism and in the context of the Italian crisis of the early Cinquecento. Giuseppe Mazzotta and Nancy S. Struever adopt a historical perspective that views Machiavelli in relation to the traditional terminus of Italian humanism, Giambattista Vico, in whose own special variant of the new science, poetic knowledge is understood precisely as the foundation upon which the earliest human societies developed, although its "certainties" have largely given way to the "truth" of a rationalizing age. In addition, many of the other essays in the collection show a keen awareness of how Machiavelli negotiates the shifting boundaries between literature in the relatively specialized and exclusive modern sense, and "litterae" in the more general terms of rhetorical humanism.

Within this general perspective, we have chosen essays that take a wide variety of approaches to defining the literary dimension of Machiavelli's work. We have tried to balance Italian scholarship with American, previously published "classics" with new work by younger scholars. Taken together, the essays show that Machiavelli's work is haunted in a variety of complex and conflicted ways both by the idea of literature as a distinct mode of writing (to be compared and contrasted with history, philosophy, and so on) and by the general rhetorical practices of narration, figuration, and so on. They explore Machiavelli's ambivalence about his humanistic education, his stigmatizing of it as merely literary and unrelated to the political realities of his day; they also show his use of a variety of humanist literary and rhetorical strategies to antihumanist ends. Precisely because the literary Machiavelli encompasses more than Machiavelli the poet, dramatist, or letter writer, we have included only two essays on works that are, strictly speaking, literary (*Mandragola* and *Clizia*). Most of the essays on the treatises, however, are clearly literary in emphasis, whether in the use of techniques of rhetorical analysis, or in stressing the poetic elements of Machiavelli's political-historical writings.

In the first of the two essays that focus on Machiavelli's understanding of himself as a man of letters and of what it means to write literature in early sixteenth-century Florence, Carlo Dionisotti offers a richly detailed picture of the Tuscan literary and political traditions available to Machiavelli at that time. He traces Machiavelli's borrowings from and ultimate rejection of the dominant Florentine literary tradition—the Hellenizing humanism of Ficino, Pico, and Poliziano. The Neoplatonic otherworldliness of this literature promoted the interests of the Medici and it found quixotic political expression during the period of Savonarola's greatest influence, but it was incapable of regenerating the Florentine republic during the ensuing political crisis. In contrast to his Neoplatonic contemporaries, Machiavelli drew on the Florentine vernacular achievements of the fifteenth century, as well as on his own humanist education, to create a committed literature capable of responding to the political and literary crisis in Florence after the fall of Savonarola: a literature that found its first full expression in Machiavelli's prose masterpiece, *The Discourses*. In the later sixteenth century, this literature would prove to be an isolated but still powerful model for the preservation of a distinctively Florentine literary voice in the face of the powerfully homogenizing "Italianization" of prose in this period.

John Najemy also locates Machiavelli at the heart of a literary and political crisis of Florentine humanism. For Najemy, Machiavelli displays his ambivalent relation to this tradition and his own negotiations with it in the famous letter to Francesco Vettori on the composition of *The Prince*. Najemy proposes a new interpretation of the letter, in which Machiavelli's self-presentation as a humanist *uomo letterato* conversing with the ancients is counterbalanced by an acute sense of the dangers of dependence on both political patrons and ancient authorities. Tracing a reference to "Geta" back to a fifteenth-century Tuscan verse novella and its classical antecedents, Najemy argues that Machiavelli satirized his own intellectual and literary pretensions in the figure of Geta, the foolish slave. The Machiavelli who emerges here is far less confident of his abilities to transform the literary tradition and to recall Florence to its republican first principles than is the Machiavelli of Dionisotti's essay.

The next two essays consider Machiavelli's literary production, specifically *Mandragola* and *Clizia* and the ways they continue under different colors the thematics of historical change and political power that are at the center of Machiavelli's great treatises. Giulio Ferroni argues that *Mandragola* articulates an anthropology of continual change and adaptation to fortune that destabilizes the hierarchy between the low subject matter of comedy and the high seriousness of political theory. Machiavelli's comedy, in this analysis, is not the minor work of an otherwise serious political thinker, for in addition to amusing its audience, it offers a polemical look at the corruption of contemporary Florence, in which slander is both the reward for *virtù* and the only available response to that corruption. If in *The Prince*, fortune (*Fortuna*) is a woman, in *Mandragola* Lucrezia represents wisdom and political *virtù* in consciously accepting the corruption that has been her "fortune."

In "Benefit of Absence," Ronald L. Martinez reads Machiavelli's late play, *Clizia*, as an autobiographical reflection of his failure as a lover and a man of action, as well as on the themes of temporal decline and renewal that are central to his political works. Like *Mandragola*, *Clizia* is set in the period shortly after Charles VIII's invasion of Italy and, like the earlier play, *Clizia* draws on plautine comedy to present a gendered exploration of the conflict between male *virtù* and female temperance and of the cyclicality of nature (symbolized by Sofronia and Clizia). Yet, in contrast to *Mandragola*'s combination of "disenchanted inventiveness" and "republican idealism," *Clizia* offers a pessimistic view of the possibilities of change and renewal. Literature here serves a compensatory function: it is the vehicle of Machiavelli's valediction to republican Florence and of his fictional self-recreation as man of letters. The author of this play is much closer to Najemy's portrait of Machiavelli as ironist concerning his own literary and political ambitions than he is to Dionisotti's confident revisionist of the humanist tradition.

The essays that follow consider the literary aspects of the nonliterary works from two different perspectives: from the perspective of their use of what we now take to be the tools of literature per se—myth, figure, narrative—or from that of the humanist understanding of "litterae," which gathered several diverse modes (among others, poetry and history) under the larger umbrella of an epideictic rhetoric that teaches by offering persuasive examples for imitation.

In "The Politician and the Centaur," Ezio Raimondi analyzes chapter 18 of *The Prince* as an exemplary instance of the binary logic of Machiavelli's thought. In this chapter, Machiavelli notoriously subverts Cicero's recommendations regarding political action in *De officiis*, by restoring Cicero's antithesis between reason and force/fraud to the world of the fable, in which force and fraud are not the exception but the rule. Raimondi traces Machiavelli's interest in the fable, here and in his other works, to popular authors such as Luigi Pulci and Domenico Burchiello; at the same time, he shows how Machiavelli's Chiron (the teacher who advises princes on the necessity of a dual nature, half man, half beast) revises humanistic, moralizing interpretations of the teacher from Boccaccio to Cristoforo Landino and Coluccio Salutati. Like Xenophon, Machiavelli reads the centaur as a symbol of an ancient, nonmoralistic anthropology, a figure of the warrior-politician, such as Romulus. Yet, in Raimondi's analysis, Chiron may also symbolize Machiavelli's own ambivalence as a would-be instructor of princes, an author whose book has only an imaginary interlocutor.

John Freccero also explores Machiavelli's mythmaking power by analyzing the ways in which the figure of the body politic in *The Prince* and *The Discourses* invites us to see a homology between sexual politics and political sexuality. In Machiavelli's deliberate violation of rhetorical decorum and his demystification of political myth, this body may appear as a Dantesque spectacle, as in the case of Remirro de'Orco in chapter 7 of *The Prince;* but more often it appears as a female body, which is the object of rape and of struggle between social classes. Taking issue with those who have reduced Machiavelli's gendered analysis of politics to his private sexual fantasies, Freccero argues that Machiavelli's images of sexual violence must be seen in their proper historical and political contexts: precisely because rape in Machiavelli's culture was less a violation of a woman's consent than of her father's, Machiavelli's myth of the rape of the courtly Lady Fortune in chapter 25 of *The Prince* should be construed as an invitation to defy the social order. If the state appears as a battered woman in *The Prince,* in *The Discourses* the state as a female body has an energy of its own. Drawing on Freud's analysis of the Medusa, Freccero shows how Machiavelli turned the historical Caterina Sforza into a myth of political agency: her body is no longer a passive object of political struggle but is rather the source of reproductive and thus political power.

In "Politics on the Warpath," Barbara Spackman explores the analogies between military strategy and Machiavelli's strategic rhetoric in *The Art of War.* Rather than seeing war as an alternative to rhetorical persuasion, Spackman argues, Machiavelli treats military strategy as a rhetoric. In Spackman's analysis, Machiavelli is less interested in the exercise of brute force (hence his well-known aversion to firearms) than he is in the deployment of appearances to create the illusion of force. And just as Machiavelli turns the battlefield into a semantic field, so *The Art of War* is designed to create a new "semiotic sensibility" in the reader, one that will enable him to invent new military strategies of signification.

In "*Virtù* and the Example of Agathocles," Victoria Kahn is also concerned with Machiavelli's strategic rhetoric; like John Freccero, she focuses on Machiavelli's deliberate violations of rhetorical decorum, his shocking examples of spectacular violence. But rather than dissecting Machiavelli's new myths of political agency, she analyzes his ironic revision of humanist doctrines of imitation and rhetoric. If *virtù* includes a flexible faculty of judgment or discretion, Machiavelli in *The Prince* does not simply describe this faculty but also intends to inculcate it in the reader. In chapter 8, the example of Agathocles' effective brutality is a test of the reader's *virtù*, his capacity for political discrimination uncontaminated by sentimental moralism.

In "Machiavelli's Gift of Counsel," Albert Russell Ascoli takes issue both with those readers who have sought a republican or absolutist content in *The Prince* and with those who have analyzed the rhetoric of this work in a tendentiously modern sense, according to which the play of figuration subverts political efficacy. Rather, according to Ascoli, the rhetoric of *The Prince* is verbal action, whose logical contradictions are strategically designed to secure employment for Machiavelli as counselor to the Medici. Yet, although Machiavelli aims to reconcile the counselor's prudent foresight with the ruler's *virtù*, to present himself as the unthreatening cognitive supplement to the prince's force, the treatise shows the strains of this attempt. The rhetoric of prophecy in chapter 26 of *The Prince* registers Machiavelli's recognition that pragmatism has itself become a utopian position. Like Raimondi's centaur, Machiavelli is a would-be counselor, whose gift may remain in the realm of the imagination.

Two meditations on the relationship of Machiavelli and Vico, the two great early modern Italian theorists of human society, complete the collection. Though Giuseppe Mazzotta and Nancy S. Struever take very different positions, their essays have been chosen for inclusion in the volume because the pairing of Machiavelli and Vico inevitably brings into focus the relevance of the latter's broad valorization of poetic knowledge as a founding category of human culture to the former's equivocal, and far less openly theorized, understanding of the place of poetry—of literature—in human experience.

Nancy S. Struever shows that what Machiavelli and Vico share is an abstract investigative mode combined with the impure object of investigation, that is, politics. Both repudiate humanist historiography, and the humanist pedagogy of teaching morality by examples. As Vico and, later, Gramsci realized, the key to Machiavelli is not the tradition of civic humanism but the consideration of historical necessity. Giuseppe Mazzotta also argues that Vico understood Machiavelli's critique of moralistic politics. But, whereas Struever's Machiavelli is in some ways more radical than Vico, Mazzotta's Vico criticizes Machiavelli's humanistic assumption that "man is the measure of all things," as well as his ahistorical, Epicurean conception of human nature. And whereas Struever argues that *The Prince* rejects humanistic pedagogy and the assumption that a unified meaning can be extracted from historical events, for Mazzotta *The Prince* is still very much part of the rhetorical genre of the educational treatise, whose epistemology Vico himself rejects in *The New Science*. Language, for Vico, is not simply a tool of persuasion; rather, it is constitutive of human subjectivity, experience, and knowledge. In contrast to the Renaissance cult of individualism, very much alive in Machiavelli's prince, Vico proposes an intersubjective and interdisciplinary paradigm rooted in language itself.

The Machiavelli who emerges in these essays has certain recognizable features, despite the variety of interpretations of particular works. He is familiar with the classics of humanist education, as well as with the popular literature of the fifteenth and sixteenth centuries. He has read Petrarch, Dante, and Ariosto, and he alludes to them in his negotiations both with the literary tradition and with the rhetorical and fictive dimension of politics. He thinks enough of his literary talents to want to be included among the poets, yet recognizes in this inclusion a sign of his exclusion from the active life. He is the centaur whose mythic status is both a sign of the inextricability of politics and the imagination, and an emblem of Machiavelli's fantastic, and ultimately futile, attempt to acquire, through writing, the position of counselor to the Medici. The literary dimension of Machiavelli's work is the locus of these fertile and frustrating conflicts, the terrain upon which Machiavelli played out his changing views of the role of poetry in civic life.

CHAPTER ONE

MACHIAVELLI, MAN OF LETTERS

Carlo Dionisotti

T HE subject of this essay is Machiavelli, the Florentine man of letters, rather than Machiavelli, the world-famous writer. When I speak of Machiavelli as a "man of letters," I am referring to the concept he may have had of literature, which was certainly different from ours, and to the part that he played in "Tuscan-Italian" literature at the turn of the sixteenth century. I am *not* referring to the role he is now universally recognized as having played in the wider history of "European-Italian" literature. This preliminary definition of my subject has been determined by my own methodological criteria and personal preferences, and with consideration to the probable limits of my competence and the brief time available for this study. In the first half of the twentieth century, it was not easy for Italian scholars of my generation to overcome our disgust with the superstitions and fanaticism imposed on the texts of Machiavelli and Dante by the fashionable ideology of that time. Back then one needed at least the moral courage of Federico Chabod, who was a historian rather than a literary critic. For our safety and comfort we dwelt long in the company of Petrarch, rather than of Dante; in that of Ludovico Ariosto, and even Francesco Guicciardini, rather than of Machiavelli. When we could finally breathe more freely, it was getting late for us and there was not much time left for such

The title and gist of this paper repeat a talk with this title that I gave in the fall of 1969 at the Villa I Tatti in Florence in honor of the fifth centennial of Machiavelli's birth, which has been published various times in various forms: in the *Notiziario culturale dell'Istituto Italiano di Cultura di Parigi* 4 (1969): 15–26; in *Studies on Machiavelli*, ed. Myron P. Gilmore (Florence, 1972), 101–43; and in *Machiavelli nel quinto centenario della nascita* (Bologna, 1973), 93–109. [Editors' note: The essay appeared most recently in the author's *Machiavellerie* (Turin, 1980), 227–66. This is the first time it has been translated into English.]

studies. And probably, deep down inside, we were moved by an abiding resentment against all the nonsense—sometimes innocent, but more often harmful—that had been written about those texts by people who were disrespectful of both the past and the present, and who cared only about grinding their own axes. Moreover, as controversial as Machiavelli's work has been since the sixteenth century, there is always the risk that the discussion will slip past the actual content of the texts into the realm of pretentious effusions and personal preferences. All things considered, then, I find it more useful and more prudent to limit my discussion to his literary career.

If we want to start with certainties, we must begin with the composition in 1504, and publication in 1506, of Machiavelli's first *Decennale*. I have already spoken of this subject on another occasion, and as there is nothing I wish to change after the objections raised by Gennaro Sasso and Roberto Ridolfi, I will not repeat myself here.[1] Ridolfi believes that the now familiar picture we have of Tuscan-Italian literature in Machiavelli's age, and especially the notoriously unresolved question of the connections between popular poetry and high literary art, are explained by the "evidence of the things themselves." Allow me to believe that the matter should be reviewed, since there is the risk now and again that such evidence might turn out to be illusory, like the emperor's new clothes.

I believe that new investigations are indispensable, and although there is nothing to be changed in what I wrote before concerning the *Decennale,* there *is* something to be added to it. Years ago, my late, lamented friend Tammaro de Marinis introduced me to Pier Andrea da Verrazzano, an unpublished fifteenth-century writer from an illustrious Florentine family, generally supposed to have been father of the famous navigator. De Marinis and I wrote an article about him in 1967.[2] I would now like to point out that there is an anonymous manuscript in St. Mark's Library (Venice) with a different redaction of the text described in that article. Yet another Venetian manuscript, which once belonged to the monastery of San Michele di Murano and has been described by Giovanni Mittarelli, contains a work by Verrazzano

---

1. [Editor's note: Professor Dionisotti refers to the essay "Machiavelli, Cesare Borgia, e Don Micheletto," first published in *Rivista storica italiana* 79 (1967): 960–75, and republished in *Machiavellerie*, 3–59, along with a reply to the objections of Gennaro Sasso and Roberto Ridolfi, itself previously published in *Rivista storica italiana* 82 (1970): 308–34. For the opposition, see Gennaro Sasso, "Ancora su Machiavelli e Cesare Borgia," *La cultura* 7 (1969): 1–36, and Roberto Ridolfi, *Vita di Niccolò Machiavelli*, 3d ed. (Florence, 1969), 457, 567–68.]

2. See Tammaro de Marinis and Carlo Dionisotti, "Un opuscolo di Pier Andrea da Verrazzano per Beatrice d'Aragona," *Italia medioevale e umanistica* 10 (1967): 321–43.

that proves to be closer to Machiavelli's *Decennale* than any other that I know of. This work, entitled *Specchio circa le occorrentie d'Italia* (Mirror of the Events in Italy), consists of a preface in prose and forty-four chapters in terza rima, just under five thousand lines. The *occorrentie* are the historical events that took place in Italy in the author's lifetime. The first chapter briefly sums up the events in the period of Paul II and Sixtus IV, from 1466 to 1484. The narrative passes immediately in chapter 2 to the War of the Barons, then proceeds more slowly and in greater detail. It focuses on Charles VIII's invasion of Italy in chapter 23, about halfway through the work. From then on the subject matter coincides with that of the *Decennale* until 1503–4, when Verrazzano interrupts his narrative, just as Machiavelli does, although in a different way and for different motives. The interest that this coincidence in subject matter and in meter of works by two contemporary Florentine writers excites among scholars is self-evident. The differences between the two works—in their size and in the ages of the two authors—are obvious, but of secondary importance. The comparison of the two has clearly become essential for every scholar of the *Decennale;* because of the "evidence of things" uncovered to date, no more appropriate basis of comparison has been found.

Verrazzano was not a writer of popular literature. It was not in his nature, except inasmuch as he had been born and raised in Florence and belonged, both personally and through family ties, to the Florentine people. This feeling of attachment could not be eradicated from him or from others at the time, not even from Lorenzo the Magnificent, by any experience of or attraction to courtly life and literature. In the *Specchio* of his old age, Verrazzano shows off his theological, astrological-scientific, and mythological learning, just as he had in his youthful *Specchietto* (Little Mirror), written for Beatrice d'Aragona. The titles themselves, *Specchio* and *Specchietto,* reflect a prehumanist Scholastic tradition that was already anachronistic in Italy. It was still alive elsewhere, but it could not be considered "popular" in any case. What strikes one right away is the older Verrazzano's continuous care to disguise and conceal reality by means of a complicated allegory (almost as if he thought that this alone was the secret key to historical interpretation), compared with the young Machiavelli's concreteness, incisiveness, and political engagement in the *Decennale*. A selection from the prose preface is illustrative:

> We have represented the Church Militant by the Supreme Pontiff;
> and His Most Christian King of France, by . . . the quintessence,
> when it is necessary; we have represented the happy and
> immortal memory of King Ferdinand I, in the name of Jove, by the

element of fire; and the state of Milan, in the name of the goddess Juno, by the element of air; we have made Neptune, the god of the sea, and the element of water stand for the most illustrious and serene Dominion of Venice; and we have represented the element of earth by the divinity Latona who gave birth in Delos to Phoebus and Diana, that is, to the sun and the moon, and have taken them to stand for our own magnificent and excellent municipality of Florence; and the aforesaid Phoebus, in the name of the sun, stands for the immortal memory of Lorenzo the Magnificent of the Medici.

Better than any commentary could, this long quotation exposes the unbridgeable gap between the two authors and their texts, despite the agreement in subject matter. Not that we should, for this reason, throw Verrazzano's text on the ash heap. It is their very divergence that matters, because, individual differences aside, this divergence is evidence of the preexistence and persistence in Florence of a literary tradition in political matters. Machiavelli doubtlessly rejected this tradition, for his own good reasons, but he was probably aware of it, and it may have played a role in that primary (and for us, mysterious) tangle of considerations, refusals, and choices out of which arose his vocation for writing, and in this case, writing poetry.

If we must start with the *Decennale* as a fixed point of reference, that does not exempt us from conjecturing back from it in time. By comparison with the elder Verrazzano, who died in 1507 when he was over seventy years of age, the Machiavelli of the *Decennale* was indeed a young man, if not exactly in his salad days. At the time of its composition, in November 1504, he was already thirty-five years old and had crossed over what Dante considered the middle point of life's journey. Of course, Dante had in mind an ideal life span, much longer than the one that fate actually had in store for him, or for Machiavelli, or for so many others. Without knowing it, Machiavelli had reached the middle of his life's journey in 1498, when he was appointed chancellor. At that time and because of that appointment, his political position appears clear to us. He had never been, nor was he then, a *pallesco* (a Medici partisan) and still less was he a *piagnone* (a Savonarolian). He had come of age as part of the opposition party and of the civic minority, not only during the Medici regime but also, and even more so, during the hegemony of Savonarola. History shows that he never changed his original political position. It is true that, after the failure of the Soderini regime and the return of the Medici, his condition forced him to make a virtue of necessity and stoop to begging fruitlessly for Medici preferment in any old post. Nonetheless, all his works, even those dedicated to the Medici, are proof of his untamed and untamable independence. Nor can his exclusion in the last months of his life from the new regime of 1527 (in which ex-*piagnoni* played such a large part) be blamed exclusively on the suspicions aroused by an offer of collaboration that had never been fully accepted. In Florence in those days, and not in Florence alone, people had good memories, excellent when such an ability served the spirit of partisanship.

Machiavelli's literary position, in 1498 and afterward, is not quite as clear as his political position, however. Considering the qualifications of Alessandro Braccesi, his immediate predecessor in the post of secretary, as well as those of his superior, the chancellor of Florence, Marcello Virgilio, we might suppose that Machiavelli was appointed primarily because he had already distinguished himself as a man with a good humanistic education and potential literary ability. And if we were obliged to skip from 1498 directly to 1513, and to wait for the moment when Machiavelli, expelled from his post and reduced to impotence and desperation, should suddenly, in his forced inactivity, become a writer, finding comfort and ultimately vindication in literature, we would have to content ourselves with this cautious hypothesis. Fortunately for us, the first *Decennale* shows that Machiavelli did not wait until he fell into political disfavor before discovering in himself the vocation of writer, and even of poet. Machiavelli put into verse his intense experience as a man who took part in the events of his day, and viewed such participation not as a game or diversion among a group of friends, but as a serious occupation. He addressed his fellow citizens in print, and authorized a friend and colleague from his office to present the publication as a prelude to and the promise of a literary work of greater import. Nor is it likely that Machiavelli had suddenly discovered in himself a poetic calling in the midst of his activity as secretary of Florence, when his head was full of so many other things. Rather it is more likely that precisely the success of his political career as secretary and counselor to the government encouraged him to make public at that particular moment a vocation and a talent that he had been carrying around inside him for quite a while.

The verses of the *Decennale* are not those of a beginner. They do not reach the summits of poetry, but they do show an uncommon mastery of poetic language. One is led to believe that Machiavelli's poetic apprenticeship had begun some time earlier. It would not be a good idea, however, to suppose that he was already seriously engaged in a literary career, or had already composed works in prose or in poetry that have not come down to us. Such a hypothesis is improbable and awkward. It is improbable because even if something by Machiavelli—such as occasional poems and letters—had been lost or had escaped our notice, those which remain prove that after his death, his heirs and successors did their best to collect and preserve his writings, not only the obviously important ones but also those that, rightly or wrongly, might have seemed negligible, such as his poetry. But the hypothesis is also awkward, inasmuch as it would put us on the wrong track. If Machiavelli had died when he was forty, like Angelo Poliziano, or at forty-three, like Lorenzo the Magnificent, his name, despite the *Decennale,* would perhaps be known today only by collectors of archival and bibliographical rarities. The masterpieces that have made Machiavelli's name survive in the history of civilization were crowded into the space of the twelve years from 1513 to 1525, from about his forty-fifth year on. It was a period of creative output that was exceptional, not only for its intensity and concentration but also and above all because he started so late, at the tail end of the period in which most men of letters are productive. Any hypothetical reconstruction of Machiavelli's literary career that attempted to put this effort earlier in time, and in doing so to dilute it, would not only be illusory but would be a falsification of what is most characteristic of Machiavelli's work: the intensity, and revolutionary novelty, which exploded in his forties.

Having said this, I must still explain his late-blooming, which was already noteworthy in 1504, that is, explain why the young Machiavelli might have objected to becoming a part of the open and flourishing literary climate of Florence in the late fifteenth century. It is clear that this aversion cannot be attributed to a lack of interest or to laziness. We must imagine, rather, the reluctance of a young man, dissatisfied and in disagreement with that literature, who secretly desired a completely different kind of literature, just as he perhaps already desired and planned for a completely different kind of politics than the politics that first the Medici and then Savonarola had imposed on Florence, with so much literary support and to such applause. The connection between literature and politics, so tight and so obvious in Machiavelli's later creative efforts, may have already existed as a negative polemical reaction during the long incubation period that preceded his writing. One must therefore set up an objective comparison between the Florentine literature with which the young Machiavelli was acquainted, and that which he himself brought into being in his more mature years. It is obvious that, as this comparison proceeds, it will be necessary to take into account the developments not only in the Florentine literature of Machiavelli's day but also in Italy as a whole. We must begin with Florence, however, and with the last years of the life of Lorenzo the Magnificent (1449–1492)—as far back as 1489 at least, when the twenty-year-old Machiavelli must have been capable of looking around and distinguishing what he liked from what he did not.

The year 1489 is, or should be, memorable in the history of Italian literature for the publication in Florence of Poliziano's *Miscellanea*. This masterpiece marked a decisive turning point in the history of Italian and European philology, that is to say, in the history of humanism. The immediate effect of the *Miscellanea*, and the teaching on which it was based, was that Florence became, in the eyes of Italy and of Europe, the center of a new humanism, able to rival the Greek tradition. This was the humanism of Aldo Manuzio, of Erasmus, of Guillaume Budé, and—if you will indulge me a little—of Marcello Virgilio, Machiavelli's superior. Thanks to Poliziano, Florence was recognized as the "Athens of Italy," an epithet that it had already merited as the center of the new Neoplatonic philosophy. Also in the year 1489, Marsilio Ficino published his treatise *De triplici vita* (Of the Threefold Life) in Florence, showing himself to be still very much alive, and still fighting the battle he began when he published the *Theologia platonica* in 1482—in the vanguard of a speculative philosophical movement that had also emerged from Florence to shake up Italy and Europe. We hardly need to be reminded that Giovanni Pico della Mirandola had only recently added his presence to the school of Ficino, and that in the same year, 1489, he had published one of his most important and extravagant works, the *Heptaplus*. Because he was of noble origin and had given up his claim to rule, because of his sensational clash with the official Roman theology and philosophy, and because of the extraordinary power of his intellect, the youthful Pico seemed perfectly suited to guide the new philosophy to the achievement of its revolutionary goals in the near future. In the same way, the equally young Poliziano seemed destined to guide the new philology and literature. And the close friendship and collaboration of the two, Poliziano and Pico, reinforced these bold expectations.

This was the shape of Florentine culture at its highest level at that time, and this was approximately how it must have appeared to the twenty-year-old Machiavelli. But the picture did not necessarily seem as attractive to him as it does to modern scholars. Certainly not everyone in Florence then was happy with it. Indeed, one of the three works I mentioned as having been published in Florence in 1489 seems to suggest dark spots in the background of the picture. It is the elderly Ficino, of course, who sounded the alarm: a warning cry at the end of *De triplici vita* against the malevolent enemies and slanderers of a work that had already been effectively defended by its dedication to Lorenzo the Magnificent. It should be of interest to us, if for no other reason than that Ficino called to his defense three Peters—Pier del Nero, Piero Guicciardini, and Piero Soderini—three names that make Machiavelli scholars prick up their ears. Ficino had acted as godfather at the confirmation of Guicciardini's son Francesco (whose baptismal godfather was Pier del Nero). Now he asked his boon companion to summon Poliziano, the herculean slayer of monsters (that is, the Poliziano of the *Miscellanea*) to join the battle on his side. He also asked Soderini to call on Pico, whom he had repeatedly mentioned and praised in the treatise qua author of the *Heptaplus*. This is not the moment to analyze the particulars of the "scientific" and theological question that concerned Ficino. One hopes that the young Machiavelli was only slightly interested in it and thus prefigured his mature self. But it is important to take into account the continued existence at that time in Florence of an irrepressible and unresigned, if not impotent, opposition to the Hellenizing philological-philosophical avant-garde sponsored by the Medici regime. And it is important to ask oneself why such an opposition existed, where it came from, and what nourished it.

As for where it came from, that is easy to determine, even if we only pay attention to the fifteenth century, the still recent past. For a school of Florentine literary tradition that was incompatible with Hellenizing humanism was quite pronounced and widely represented, from Domenico Burchiello to Luigi Pulci. One can also see how and why this school became less important in Tuscany in the last decades of the fifteenth century, moving with Bernardo Bellincioni and Il Pistoia [Antonio Cammelli] to the princely courts in the north. But this non-Hellenizing school survived in Florence. Traces, which are not merely linguistic, of readings of Burchiello and Pulci are evident in Machiavelli's work, and they cannot be attributed to a later rediscovery of these texts, but rather reflect a youthful familiarity with them. We must ask, however, what this tradition may have represented, in its undeniable decline, compared with the equally undeniable success of the opposing tradition, not to those who at the height or at the end of their lives indulged again the tastes of their youth, but to a young man like Machiavelli, potentially disposed to receive the lessons of the new masters.

In the case of Machiavelli, we cannot exclude a politically motivated distrust of and distaste for any literature so closely tied to the increasingly courtly context of the Medici regime. Nor can we exclude a nostalgia for a freer and less conventional literature, representative of a less servile way of life, more open to individual initiative and role playing. But the hypothesis of a political motive, even if legitimate, is too easy, and is in any case inadequate. The high level of accomplishment of the Hellenizing philological-philosophical avant-garde is incontestable: it is still measured on a European scale, rather than on an Italian one. For that very reason, it seems likely that at that time in Florence the gap between the avant-garde and the masses had widened dangerously; the common starting-point of an indeed diversified and discordant majority was broadly separated from the point of arrival reached by an elite few when that majority could not, or would not, follow them any longer. I have already mentioned that Ficino, in sounding the alarm, took care to gather around himself as many men who agreed with him as possible, calling to own defense authorities in every field except literature. But as different as Pico's *Heptaplus* and Ficino's *De triplici vita* are, anyone who reads these works today, and knows that they enjoyed much greater popularity in countries that would participate in the Reformation, cannot help but wonder why they were written in Italy at all. These works represent a philosophy that comes close to questioning the very foundations of the Christian biblical tradition, and to fomenting a radical religious revolution; it could not have been compatible with the general needs and capabilities of a country in which such a revolution was not possible.

This gives rise to the inevitable question of why Machiavelli's work is so far removed from the contemplative, religious, Neoplatonic philosophy that was typical of Florence during his lifetime, not only in the late fifteenth century but also, to a lesser degree, in the early sixteenth century. I will only mention this question, as its resolution is not within my competence. I would prefer to discuss now the literary question of Machiavelli's attitude toward the Florentine humanist tradition that was splendidly embodied by Poliziano in his youth, and afterward by Poliziano's pupils, such as Pietro Crinito and Marcello Virgilio. The conjunction of Rome and Athens seems obvious today, as if they were two branches of the same tree. But it must be remembered that it was not so obvious in the fifteenth century. In Machiavelli's time, one could not escape the awareness that the two branches had been kept apart for a long time, and that Athens looked up toward the heavens of contemplation, philosophy, and art, whereas Rome focused on the earthly concerns of action, law, and power, even after the Christian church had taken up residence there.

The Hellenizing trend that made Florence the "Athens of Italy" in the fifteenth century, and increasingly so in the latter half of the century under the Medici regime, implied a competitive, although not necessarily a hostile, attitude toward Rome. Lorenzo the Magnificent, after escaping the Pazzi conspiracy and extricating himself, luckily, from war with the Pope, always took care to entrap and neutralize Rome's opposing forces, since he could not defeat them. Florence was even more weak militarily than the feudal Rome of the Colonna and the Orsini; therefore, its survival depended on a politics of peace that would permit competition with the other Italian powers on the plane of intellectual and technical ability, wealth, and civic prestige. The expansion of literature and the arts in Florence during Lorenzo's life-time, or rather during Machiavelli's youth, suited this policy admira-bly. In the field of literature, the Hellenizing tendency doubtlessly contributed to questioning the preeminence of the Latin language, in both theory and practice, and to opening a space for the use of the vernacular, as well as conferring dignity upon it. The zeal of the young humanist Poliziano, who got the inspiration for his *Stanze per la giostra* (Stanzas for the Joust) and *Orfeo* (Orpheus) from Homer himself, was crucial in promoting the vernacular, in Florence and throughout Italy. Lorenzo the Magnificent, a mediocre poet whose excellence in politics lent a golden patina to an otherwise merely "silver" *mediocritas,* per-sisted for some time in the effort to effect a humanist rehabilitation of the Florentine-Tuscan literary tradition, making it subordinately com-petitive with the classical literatures. In the meantime, Florence could consider itself the Athens of Italy because it excelled in a form of literature of which the other regions of Italy were incapable. But for reasons that still elude us, the great poet Poliziano, disdainful of any easy undertaking and attracted by the mirage of an international hu-manist community, did not persevere along this path after his unfin-ished *Stanze* and his *Orfeo.* Lorenzo died in 1492, and both Florence and Italy found themselves at the precipice of a decisive political crisis. The new trilingual literature—in Greek, Latin, and Tuscan—was already unstable, given the lack of proportion between its experimental bold-ness and its limited cultural sway. So it ended up arriving unarmed, or at least ill-equipped, on the front lines of the battle for linguistic mod-ernity, in a crisis that was still more Florentine and Italian than Eu-ropean.

It is usually thought that a breach was opened in this, the weakest link in the defenses of linguistic modernity, by the apocalyptic preach-ing of a friar who was not even of Florentine origin—and that this breach was sufficient to unhinge the whole literary system that had been inaugurated under Lorenzo. It is said that this preaching also breached the defenses of a philosophical system that was already in the throes of an anxiety for religious reform, so that many of the most authoritative survivors of the Neoplatonic literature that had flour-ished in the times of peace and prosperity under the Medici now found themselves in agreement with Savonarola, and then were caught up in his ruin. But Savonarola's influence remained alive in Florentine litera-ture after his downfall and even after the founding of the Medicean duchy, well into the second half of the sixteenth century—not only among the exiles but also among the resident literati of the Medici state. The persistence of his influence cannot be accounted for solely in political and social terms—for example, by the tragic revival of the popular republic immediately after Machiavelli's death. It can be explained only by the fact that a large number of Savonarola's opponents and slanderers themselves aimed at a moral or religious object in their literary activity, and employed interpretative methods essentially similar to those that the monk had used so effectively. Among them were the previously mentioned Pier Andrea da Verrazzano, as well as Gabriele Biondo.[3] Such an explanation is also sufficient to account for the fact that Machiavelli as a writer was alive and thriving at the beginning of the sixteenth century. For even though the conditions for radical religious reform did not exist at that time either in Machiavelli's Florence or in Italy as a whole, we must admit that religious concerns were no less, and perhaps more, alive in Italy than in the rest of Europe. It is thus obvious why, confronted with the greater seriousness of the Italian political crisis, so many would search for an explanation and a refuge in theology and in the stars, and in a literature of Dantean stamp: doctrinaire, allegorical, and prophetic.

The nexus between politics and literature is strong, especially in the case of Machiavelli, but it cannot be asserted solely on the basis of his participation in practical politics and his literary success. Caution is even more necessary when dealing with a literary trend such as the Hellenizing philological humanism of Poliziano and his school, which, despite the Medici sponsorship it enjoyed and its close relations with Neoplatonic philosophy, avoided by its very nature any practical political engagement. This evasive tendency and its ostentatious display of an aristocratic indifference to "vulgarization" may be seen in Poliziano's increasing detachment from the vernacular and even from Latin rhetoric, along with his growing concern with apparently marginal questions that touched the extreme limits of technical specialization. This attitude must have instinctively repelled the young Machiavelli. But it is hard to imagine that he reacted in his youth against Poliziano's humanism as negatively as he did against the philosophy of Ficino and Pico and the religious results of that philosophy during the Savonarola crisis. Still, with the passage of time Machiavelli could not help but realize that the Hellenizing direction taken by Florentine humanism under Poliziano's patronage was incompatible with the "Roman" orientation, civic and military, which seemed to him ever more clearly necessary. This orientation was neither philosophical, nor scientific, nor religious. Nor do I think that he realized this only after the irreconcilability of the two tendencies appeared to him in the form of something that could not have been previously foreseen: a revival of

3. See Carlo Dionisotti, "Resoconto di una ricerca interrotta," *Annali della Scuola Normale Superiore di Pisa* 37 (1968): 259–69.

Florentine Hellenizing humanism in the Rome of Leo X, a Medici [editors' note: that is, after 1512]. That he would certainly have recognized the opposition to his own, "Roman" orientation at this late date, however, is suggested (indirectly) by the publication in Rome, in May 1518, of the *Oratio in laudem urbis Romae* (Oration in Praise of the City of Rome), by the Florentine Dominican Zanobi Acciaiuoli. This text coincides chronologically with Machiavelli's masterpieces, and it speaks eloquently to this point.

Acciaiuoli, born in 1461, was a student of Poliziano and specialized in Greek studies. Under the influence of Pico, and his nephew Giovanni Francesco Pico della Mirandola, he later turned to Greek patristic and Neoplatonic philosophy; fascinated by Savonarola, he entered the Dominican order. Finally, despite his previous skepticism (and that of his family), he was welcomed in Rome by Leo X, was appointed professor at the university, and later was made prefect of the Vatican Library. He died in that city in 1519. The oration in praise of Rome, which dates from the year before his death and may therefore be considered a kind of testament, is dedicated to Cardinal Giulio de'Medici. It is not surprising that the oration praises Christian Rome, or that only enough is said of classical Rome, "which we see knocked down and laid low,"[4] "to establish a comparison . . . showing how much this newer city exceeds the old one in nobility, power, and happiness."[5] But Acciaiuoli was aware of his own recklessness when he affirmed that those ruins of ancient Rome, "which we regard as some bones of a giant body,"[6] might seem a great thing to men who were "profane and gazed only on earthly things, . . . but to the wise, and to men reflecting on eternal things, they are undoubtedly small and childish."[7] Holding a belief "far from the common opinion,"[8] he took care to justify himself historically and theoretically by going back to Cain and Abel, representatives of the active and the contemplative life. The mania for robbery and conquest has come down to us from Cain: "Therefore those things which may not have been found within their own country's borders, but were pleasant and agreeable, they obtained by plunder. . . . Nor do I think they would have anything valuable even if they emptied the rest of the world of all goods—pillaging shrines and holy places simply in order to make their own city and country dwell-

4. "Quam disiectam prostratamque videmus."

5. "Quod ad instituendam comparationem sit satis ut . . . quantum recentior haec veterem illam superemineat nobilitate potentia felicitate omnibus plane constet."

6. "Quas veluti ossa quaedam gigantei corporis intuemur."

7. "Prophanis et terrena tantum spectantibus, . . . sapientibus autem viris aeternaque contuentibus, parva nimirum illa et puerilia."

8. "Procul ab opinione vulgi."

ings more elegant. If anyone asks me who should be included under the banner of Cain, I reply—the Assyrians, the Persians, the Chaldaeans, the Macedonians, and the Egyptians. Nor would I by any means exclude the Romans from this list, but rather would put them at the head of it, first among all mortals."[9] That by itself might have been enough, but Acciaiuoli went on to underline the suggestive correspondence between the fratricidal Romulus and the fratricidal Cain, and the contrast between the depth of human wickedness reached by ancient Rome and the heights providentially assigned to Christian Rome in the scheme of salvation. Thus the barbarian invasions and the destruction they wrought assume the character of a providential scourge: "Indeed, who would dare to deny that it was by the counsel of God and for the greater good that the fury of the Goths raged unchecked against Rome and that after that barbaric destruction, the parts of the city that had survived were struck repeatedly by lightning and burned, like Nimrod's tower."[10]

Despite its interest, I will not consider the rest of the oration here. This [negative] interpretation of ancient Rome was proposed in Rome itself by a Florentine humanist, Hellenist, Neoplatonist, follower of Savonarola, and Medicean courtier, at the same time that Machiavelli was offering his own [favorable] interpretation in *The Discourses* and in *The Art of War*. It teaches us something, not only about the mood of the moment but also a posteriori, about the nearly insoluble tangle that was the Florentine humanist tradition as the fifteenth century gave way to the sixteenth. This was the matrix in which Machiavelli pursued the reading that was "his alone," of ancient Rome. To summarize: the belated literary debut of Machiavelli can be explained by the difficulty he faced in locating himself within a tradition that, both at its moment of greatest splendor and in the wake of the crisis that shook it from 1494 onward, offered him teachers and models who were largely unacceptable, but that was too dominant to permit the easy expression of still tentative opposition.

9. "Ergo quae in patriae finibus inventa non fuerint, modo commoda et iucunda, intra urbis suae moenia domesticosque parietes rapiendo convectant. Neque vero pensi quicquam habent si coeteras orbis totius partes inanes rerum vacuasque relinquant, phana etiam et sacraria expilantes, modo sibi urbanas aedes ac villas cultiores efficiant. Horum in numero siquis me roget quos reponendos putem sub duce illo Cayn, Assirios equidem, Persas, Caldaeos, Macedonas, Aegyptios respondebo, ita tamen ut antiquos Quirites non modo a commemoratis gentibus non excludam, sed in eo genere hominum cunctis mortalibus anteponam."

10. "Quis enim negare ausit Dei consilio factum esse, boni potioris ergo, ut in te Gothorum rabies deseviret, cum post barbaricam illam cladem quae superfuerant urbis loca, crebris icta fulminibus, quasi turris Nebrotica conflagrarent?"

The crisis in Florentine literature, which had already begun with the premature death of Lorenzo the Magnificent, concluded before the turn of the century [even if the political crisis had not]. By that time, Machiavelli had already found in his political post the way of life that was most congenial to him and he could therefore avoid the risky business of a public literary debut. He had no reason to lament if the men and the affairs of a society that had never really been his went to rack and ruin all around him. And born as he was for comedy, he probably enjoyed the spectacle of the writers and philosophers who, having made merry with the Medici, now hastened to beat their breasts with Savonarola, and then were left high and dry, without a clue as to what to do next. But it was a short-lived entertainment. Machiavelli really had no reason to rejoice at a crisis that evidently left Florence poorer and weaker and magnified the shadows that now darkened the city's precarious political order.

From the very beginning of the crisis, the interventions of *Fortuna* were decisive—above all, with the sudden deaths in 1494 of the young and irreplaceable teachers, Poliziano and Pico. The deaths shortly thereafter of the older masters, Ficino (1499), Landino (1504), and Bartolomeo Scala (1497), though foreseeable, were nonetheless grievous, and in some ways marked an ending. Tragically, Michele Marullo, last of the great foreign humanists to have been drawn to Medicean Florence, died prematurely in 1500; he was Greek, but much more Latin and Italian than many of the Hellenizing Florentines. And, as if this were not enough, the Florentine Pietro Crinito died in 1507, when barely in his thirties.[11] He had been the most talented of Poliziano's pupils by far, the only one who had the courage and the versatility of his teacher, and the only one who had learned from the lessons of teachers hostile to Poliziano, such as Marullo. But even if the ranks of Florentine humanist literature had not been irreparably decimated by fate in those few years, the crisis would still have been grave. Crinito's works show clearly that the splendid literature of the Medici regime no longer found favorable conditions for growth under the new government. It isolated itself in its nostalgia for the past and in protest against the present, and sought sustenance outside Florence, especially in Venice. It had become a literature in opposition to the government for which Machiavelli worked. Crinito's testimony in this regard is important, because it is that of a young man who was less than twenty at the

11. Note that we do not call Pietro Crinito by his family name, Del Riccio Baldi, which is not used in literary histories. Crinito's major work, *De honesta disciplina* (On Honest Instruction), has been reedited by Carlo Angeleri (Rome, 1955). It is too bad that this useful edition was not followed by the critical profile that Angeleri had promised.

time of the Medici expulsion. The generous patronage of Lorenzo the Magnificent had been similar to that of other contemporary Italian princes and was suspected of reflecting his own princely ambition. In an understandably polemical reaction to these suspicions, patronage of this kind abandoned the field to the old Florentine mercantile tradition, which was averse to any ostentation or waste of time and money. Crinito had traveled throughout Italy and made friends with the literati of Venice, Ferrara, and Rome; when he returned to Florence, he showed his belief that this city was, in comparison, by far the deafest to the call of literature. He wrote that in Florence, conspiracy was proof of virtue; dishonesty was proof of moderation; and literary endeavors were proof of idleness.

Crinito was among Poliziano's youngest pupils. Marcello Virgilio and Carteromaco were older than he, and better suited personally to represent the school after their master's death.[12] Thus it will be useful to include their rather different testimony as well. Marcello Virgilio was Poliziano's successor at the university, and was then promoted to head of the chancellery shortly before Machiavelli was appointed secretary. It would therefore appear that he should have been the one to bring humanism to the new regime. The result, instead, was that he gave no further evidence of his original calling until the Medici were restored. At that time, however, he promptly recaptured the honors of the humanist world with his *Dioscoride,* a work that certainly does not make modern Machiavelli scholars lose any sleep, but that was the only worthwhile product of Florentine philology between the death of Poliziano and the debut of Pier Vettori (b. 1499).

It is not surprising that Carteromaco, who was from Pistoia, never worked in Florence; but it is significant that he became, early on, Aldo Manuzio's close collaborator in Venice. And it is also significant that Poliziano's collected works were edited and printed in 1498 by Manuzio in Venice, and not in Florence, for in the space of a few years the center of Greek studies and of Italian humanist literature generally had moved to Venice. Not that this shift had taken place without some resistance. Crinito fought hard against it, for as long as his brief life lasted. The establishment and growth in Florence of Filippo Giunta's publishing enterprise, almost exclusively humanist, cannot be ex-

12. Marcello Virgilio wanted to be known by this pair of classical names only, but today he bears the arbitrary last name Adriani, which was chosen by his son Giovan Battista. (They were, respectively, grandson and great-grandson of one Adriano Berti.) See the brief article about Marcello Virgilio in the *Dizionario biografico degli italiani,* 1: 310. He was born in 1465, not in 1464, if his epitaph is correct. Concerning Carteromaco (Scipione Forteguerri), 1466–1515, see Alfredo Chiti, *Scipione Forteguerri, Il Carteromaco* (Florence, 1902).

plained without reference to Crinito, although he acted indirectly, through his friend Benedetto Filologo.[13] But his enterprise almost always proved to be a servile Florentine replica of Manuzio's Venetian publishing house. It showed conclusively that the good intentions and activities of the surviving Florentine humanists could barely (and only with outside help) keep the flame lit until better times. Nor does the situation change when we turn from professional literary humanism to humanistic philosophy. It does no disservice to Francesco Diacceto, a far more authoritative teacher in the end than the minor humanists left on the Florentine scene after the death of Crinito and the "vacation" from scholarship of Marcello Virgilio,[14] to observe that in this field as well, the degradation of the school of Florence after the epoch of Ficino and Pico was both obvious and precipitous.

This is the historical background against which Machiavelli's literary vocation developed, his work having an important but ambiguous relation with the classical tradition, which was inseparable from the humanism of the day. Underlying the literary choices of a man tied to Florence's new government we must assume the awareness of a break between the new regime and the humanist literature of the previous era, and the recognition that this literature's consequent decline and disintegration left more space for new initiatives in the vernacular. Out of this awareness came Machiavelli's project, realized in the *Decennale:* a literature that today we would call "committed," one that participated in the new regime's effort to overcome the crisis it faced. Machiavelli was in a position to understand that the crisis was not only political and military; in Florence, especially after Savonarola's downfall, the crisis was also religious and spiritual, and hence theoretical and linguistic—in a word, "literary." The military reform he promoted had literary origins as well.

Whatever Machiavelli's intentions were, no literary initiative could be undertaken by him or by anyone else, even in the humble field of the vernacular, independent of the Florentine tradition in that tongue. I have already shown how the vanguard of Medicean trilingual literature had recently been weakened because of Poliziano's death. The example of Lorenzo the Magnificent had been enough to preserve the

13. A member of the Riccardini family, Benedetto Filologo was appointed master at the seminary of San Lorenzo in 1497 and promoted to canon in 1506. He died the following year. Despite what most bibliographers think, Filologo was never a printer; he is relevant to the history of printing because of his philological consultation and collaboration with printers.

14. On Diacceto (1466–1522), see Paul Oskar Kristeller, "Francesco da Diacceto and Florentine Platonism in the Sixteenth Century," *Studies in Renaissance Thought and Letters* (Rome, 1956), 287–336.

cult of the older, more illustrious vernacular literature and prevent humanistic predominance, as in the last of Poliziano's Latin *Sylvae*, the poem entitled *Nutricia*. His example had also kept the popular practice of writing vernacular poetry alive. However, it had not promoted the ambitious courtly vernacular literature, influenced by Petrarch and Boccaccio, that was making a name for itself elsewhere at the time. The popular tradition, which had reached its apex with Pulci's epic, had lost its glitter but it had not been replaced by anything else. After Lorenzo's death, the production of vernacular literature in Florence was spurred greatly, although fleetingly, by the Savonarola crisis. It was at that time that the poet Girolamo Benivieni, a surviving member of Lorenzo's circle, returned to the limelight. Born in 1453, he had been a friend of Pico's and was an ardent Neoplatonist who subsequently became a most fervent supporter of Savonarola. His verses, published in 1500 and again in 1519, were certainly the most interesting, and the most successful, vernacular poems produced in Florence during the period. But Benivieni was both sustained and hampered by his sense of possessing the definitive truth, a moral and religious certitude that did not admit discussion. Destined to live a very long life (he died in 1542 when he was nearly ninety), he spent it bearing witness to his loyalty to the past. His farewell to art, embodied in his translation of the penitential Psalms of David into terza rima (published in 1505), is noteworthy, even in comparison with Machiavelli's contemporary *Decennale*, although it is unreadable now except as a devotional book. It was dedicated "to the devout nuns of Murate in Florence."

It is hard to know whom to single out from among the other surviving lyric and narrative versifiers in Florence in those years. Recently, since the renewal of interest in *Nencia da Barberino*, Bernardo Giambullari has become popular again. I do not mean to sound averse to this or any other revival of ghosts, as my friend Maria Corti would call it, but I do not think Giambullari ever had much of a reputation outside a narrow circle, nor did he ever write anything in verse that was on the same level as Machiavelli's *Decennale*, let alone a higher one. Castellano Castellani, another poet-follower of Savonarola, has also been investigated recently; he was younger than Benivieni and Giambullari, and thus, like Antonio Alamanni, was closer in age to Machiavelli.[15] In

15. Bernardo Giambullari (1450–1529) was still writing verses and seeking alms at the time of Leo X; see the *Rime inedite o rare di Bernardo Giambullari*, ed. Italiano Marchetti (Florence, 1955). These verses, including an unpublished tercet attributed to him by E. Orvieto, "Un poemetto inedito di Bernardo Giambullari," *Bibliothèque d'Humanisme et Renaissance* 39 (1977): 531–44, add little or nothing of any importance to the texts published by the author himself or by Orvieto when he was alive. The revival of Castellano Castellani (1461–1519/20) is due to an exhaustive monograph of Giovanni Ponte, *Attor-*

short, the search is under way; we will have to reexamine each tree one by one, while trying not to lose sight of the forest. But to suggest a different way of proceeding, I will mention that in *Viridario*, a long poem by Giovanni Filoteo Achillini of Bologna (finished in 1504 but not printed until 1513), there is an interesting survey of contemporary Italian literati, geographically grouped. Achillini had promoted throughout Italy a collection of odes and verses commemorating the death of the poet Serafino Aquilano; he prided himself for being on friendly terms with men of letters from every region, and in fact he was well informed about them. The poets from Florence mentioned in his survey are Cristoforo Melanteo, Francesco Cei, Benivieni, and Piero de' Pazzi, to whom must be added, moving to Rome, the exiles who sided with the Medici: Giuliano de' Medici, Il Bibbiena [Bernardo Dovizi], and Nicola Grasso. No one else is mentioned; no one at the time had displayed such great abilities that a young Machiavelli could (I do not even say should) have taken note of him, with the exceptions of Benivieni and Cei.

Cei deserves particular mention, for although he has not attracted much attention in modern times (as far as I know), accurate information about him was brought to light in his own time by the excellent scholar Guglielmo Volpi (1471–1505). Volpi was just a little younger than Machiavelli; he published his collection *Sonecti, capituli, canzone, sextine, stanze, e strambocti in laude di Clitia* in 1503. This collection of verses was remarkably and deservedly popular, even outside Florence. Unless I am mistaken, it is the only important example produced in Florence of courtly lyric poetry in the style that was then fashionable all over Italy. During his lifetime, Cei had been an *arrabbiato* [Editors' note: literally "enraged one," term used of the factious anti-

---

no a Savonarola: *Castellano Castellani e la sacra rappresentazione a Firenze tra '400 e '500* (Genoa, 1969). Ponte has also published a collection of Castellani's verses (mostly religious), "Versi di Castellano Castellani," *Studi di filologia e letteratura* 1 (1970): 281–352. But Machiavelli scholars will have to go back to the collection of *Laude spirituali di Feo Belcari, di Lorenzo de' Medici, di Francesco d'Albizzo, di Castellano Castellani, e di altri,* ed. Gustavo Camillo Galletti (Florence, 1863), which includes Castellani's *Vangeli della Quaresima* (forty-two long ballads—over 3,000 lines—which were dedicated to "Madonna Argentina, wife of the most illustrious Gonfalonier of Justice for life, Piero Soderini, glorious protector of the city Florence"). On Antonio Alamanni (1464–1528), see the critical edition of his noteworthy *Commedia della conversione di Santa Maria Maddalena,* ed. Pierre Jodogne (Bologna, 1977). The verses of Machiavelli's friend and colleague Biagio Buonaccorsi have been edited twice by Denis Fachard: in *Studi di filologia italiana* 31 (1973): 157–206; and in *Biagio Buonaccorsi: Sa vie, son temps, son oeuvre* (Bologna, 1976). Both editions have conspicuous errors in language and meter; for example, the unexceptional word *merore* is mistakenly corrected to *memore; brama* is made to rhyme with *herede, fede,* and *vede* (having been exchanged with *chiede*).

Savonarolian partisans] both in the strict political meaning of that term in the Florentine context, and in the sense that he played an active role in the street violence of the final phase of the struggle against Savonarola. For this reason, and because of his surprisingly persistent and morbidly realistic degradation of the Petrarchan tradition of love poetry, he can be considered the exact opposite of the Neoplatonist piagnone, Benivieni. Cei's political position was not far from that of Machiavelli. His premature death helps to explain why his work, new and extravagant in the context of Florentine literature, never set a fashion. Confronted with the opposing examples set by Benivieni and Cei, Machiavelli entered once and for all a path diverging from that of Petrarchan love poetry, which represented the mainstream of the new Italian literature in the fifteenth and sixteenth centuries. Critics will reply that his path was naturally and necessarily a different one, that we could never imagine Machiavelli in the garb of a writer like Benivieni or Cei. I do not intend to answer this obvious objection, fostered as it is by an awareness of exactly who the "one and only" Machiavelli is. I maintain, instead, that a different method of investigation is more useful: one that considers the various possibilities that Machiavelli was offered but refused. Such a comparative method will help us to account for the unpredictable gestures, the startling inventiveness, the sudden flights, of the one and only Machiavelli.

In all its poverty and narrowness, the vernacular literary scene in Florence in the fifteenth and sixteenth centuries turns out to consist almost exclusively of poetry. And Machiavelli's own first literary works were poetic. Nothing strange so far—but it is worth noting that he remained faithful to this original notion of poetry as the principal form of literature for quite some time, even after he wrote *The Prince*. As far as we know, he still had confidence in his poetic calling in 1517. Then, in the last years of his life, just as Machiavelli seems to have dedicated himself more openly and intensely to literature (given the writing and performance of the plays, the publication of *The Art of War*, and the official commission to write the *Florentine Histories*), he seems to have lost all confidence in poetry. His poetic production may therefore be considered as a whole, setting aside for the time being its development in time, its influence on his prose, and the effect that his political disgrace of 1512 had on it (as on all of his activities).

In considering Machiavelli's poetic production as a whole, it is helpful to start with metrical analysis, which is the most straightforward and, within certain limits, the most immediately profitable kind. What stands out is the near absence of the sonnet, the standard metrical form at the time, and the prevalence of the *sonetto caudato*, or "tailed" sonnet, among the few examples that Machiavelli did compose. This form was common in the fifteenth century, but it was extraneous to the Petrarchan tradition and had recently been confined to the epistolary-humorous genre, as it was for Machiavelli as well. What also stands out is Machiavelli's unwavering preference for terza rima, significant in itself but also for its exclusion of the competing metrical form, ottava rima, which had become increasingly fashionable in narrative poetry. Luckily, a *serenata amorosa* (an autograph, to boot) has come down to us. It is the only known attempt at sustained ottava rima among Machiavelli's verses, and it reveals that Machiavelli was aware not only of the narrative application of that meter but also of the discursive and lyric uses to which he himself put it. Nevertheless, his preference for terza rima remains constant from the *Decennale* to *Asino*, from 1504 to 1517, both before and after the definitive crisis in his life and work.

If the examples of ottava rima produced by Poliziano, Lorenzo the Magnificent, and Benivieni in his short poem *Amore* had been as popular in Florence as they were elsewhere, the history of that meter would have been different. For reasons that I have already indicated in part, its new application to courtly aristocratic poetry had little success in Florence. Its success was greater in the north of Italy, so that the chivalric romance in ottava rima that Pulci, a Florentine, had redeemed from the anonymity of the *cantari* [Editors' note: composers and performers of popular narrative poems], ended up obtaining full citizenship in the republic of vernacular letters thanks exclusively to poets from Ferrara, such as Matteo Boiardo and Ludovico Ariosto. Machiavelli, the civil servant, could go down to the town square of Florence on his day off and listen to l'Altissimo [Cristoforo Fiorentino] recite the ottave of his *Reali di Francia* to great applause, just as Antonio di Guido's recitation of his own ottave had been applauded by Poliziano about fifty years earlier. Later, when Machiavelli had lost his post and was forced to seek the protection of the Medici, on the street he might have seen old Giambullari, who had stubbornly dedicated his continuation of Luca Pulci's *Ciriffo calvaneo* to Lorenzo de' Medici. And later still, after the publication of Ariosto's *Orlando furioso*, Machiavelli would see published in Rome in 1521 the dreadful epic in ottava rima, *Triompho magno nel qual si contiene le famose guerre d'Alexandro Magno Imperator di Grecia cominciando avanti sua natività, composto per Domenico Falugi Ancisano poeta laureato ad ill. signor Hippolito de' Medici* (The Great Triumph in Which is Contained the Famous Wars of Alexander the Great, Emperor of Greece, Beginning before his Birth, Composed by Domenico Falugi Ancisano, Poet Laureate, for his Highness, Sir Hippolito de' Medici), with an encomiastic papal authorization drafted by Pietro Bembo. Domenico Falugi died prematurely the same year. He had already merited a mocking and contemptuous poetic laurel from Leo X for his belief that he participated in the greatness of Petrarch through their common geographical origins, which had led to the publication at Rome in 1514 of his dreadful *Stella d'amore,* also in ottava rima and modeled on Boccaccio's *Ninfale.*[16] Also in 1521, a long poem in ottava rima (of a higher quality, to tell the truth), *La liberatione di terra santa per re Carlo Mano et Argentino figliuolo di Rinaldo di Montalbano* (The Liberation of the Holy Land by King Charlemagne and Argentino, Son of Rinaldo di Montalbano), was published in Venice by Machiavelli's fellow citizen Michele Bonsignori. Finally, in Florence itself, the *Libro appellato e nominato e' tradimenti di Gano di Maganza, composto in octava rima per Pandolfo de' Bonacossi habitante nella terra di Piombino e cameriere dello illustrissimo signore Iacopo Quinto de Aragonia de Appiano signore del Prefato Piombino, el qual volume decto Pandolfo a sua illustrissima signoria ha aplicato et titulato negli anni della salute MCCCCXVIII* (Book Called and Named the Betrayals of Gano di Maganza, Composed in Octaves by Pandolfo de' Bonacossi, Resident in the Region of Piombino, and Servant of his Highness Sir Iacopo the Fifth of Aragon, Lord of Appiano in the Prefect of Piombino, which Volume the Said Pandolfo Dedicated and Conferred to his Most Illustrious Lordship in the Year of the Lord 1518) appeared in 1525. This book was printed beautifully but was of very low quality in both form and content.

This, briefly, is the history of narrative poetry in Florence in the age of Machiavelli. If he had been willing to stoop to the level of that sort of poetry, he would have written the *Decennale* in ottava rima, the meter that was by then standard for the cantari and the sacred plays. But he chose the terza rima, the meter of an older and nobler tradition, with a more densely crafted structure, because as a versifier he was of a different mettle and had different objectives than Giambullari or Falugi. Of course, being Florentine, he *was* always ready to stoop to the level of folk literature, pleasantries, witticisms, *sonetti caudati,* and carnival songs. Lorenzo the Magnificent and Poliziano had enjoyed them as well, as did most of Machiavelli's contemporaries. This comic disposition is characteristic of Tuscans and their tongue and is very different from the laborious and harsh literature of the grotesque produced in other regions of Italy. But it should not be confused with artistic experi-

---

16. The blunders of Joachim Storost concerning Domenico Falugi in *Studien zur Alexandersage in der alteren italienischen Literatur* (Halle, 1935), 231–82, are memorable. In his introduction to Giovanni Falugi, *Canace* (Bologna, 1974), Riccardo Bruscagli describes the other Falugi's *Stella d'amore* as a "Petrarchan-style collection of poems," which at such an early date would be a rare thing, whether in Rome or in Florence. I will confirm that it is a poem in ottava rima, of exactly 300 octaves, about the love of the shepherd Domitio and the nymph Cyprea, who are transformed into the fountain in St. Peter's Square at the end; in short, it is a *Ninfale* transferred to the Rome of Leo X.

ments and intentions carried out on another level entirely. Nor do I think that Machiavelli's rejection of the ottava rima should be explained in purely literary terms. It seems to reflect, rather, a military theorist's aversion for a poetic form, celebrating the chivalric tradition, that developed in Italy in the age (which he detested) of mercenaries and condottieri. Machiavelli was surely more conscious of its origins than are we modern literary historians. To conclude this discussion of ottava rima, I should add that Machiavelli's famous letter to Lodovico Alamanni of December 17, 1517, about Ariosto's *Orlando furioso*, probably represents the turning point, or breaking point, in his poetic career. I do not believe in Machiavelli's steadfastness of intention, announced in that letter, to cite his friend Ariosto in *Asino*. I believe that when he thought it over again after reading *Orlando furioso*, a poem he described as "beautiful throughout and admirable in many passages," Machiavelli realized that ottava rima could be something else and something greater. Neither *Asino*, nor similar products of Tuscany, could bear the comparison. The competition remained open to him in the field of prose (and specifically in the field of prose drama, where he would take on Ariosto himself), but in the field of poetry he yielded the palm.

We now leap ahead to 1518. When he wrote the *Decennale*, in the first decade of the century, Machiavelli may not have realized that he had to compete with others outside Florence or Tuscany. He must have noticed that Tuscan literature was in decline but thought it was just a local matter. He probably looked for a solution to the political and literary crisis in the revival of an authentic Florentine tradition opposed to the developments in court culture that were common to the rest of Italy and that had also characterized the ephemeral splendor of the Medicean epoch. This continued to be Machiavelli's literary stance for the rest of his life, though it was tempered by inevitable and substantial variations attributable to a growing awareness that this was not merely an "internal" Florentine matter and that one had to compete, intensely, with the rest of the world.

At the beginning of the sixteenth century, a preference for terza rima in narrative works implied fidelity to the tradition of Dante. In spite of the great popularity of Petrarch's *Trionfi* in the fifteenth century, the original opposition between the works of Dante and Petrarch, the two supreme models of Italian poetry, had lately been reduced to a metrical opposition between long poems in terza rima influenced by Dante, and lyric poems influenced by Petrarch. The initial persistence in these lyrics of the *capitolo* [Editors' note: a facetious poem, usually in terza rima] is important, and was especially so for Machiavelli, but it does not adequately explain the preference for terza rima in his most serious poetic experiments. His rejection of Petrarchan lyric poetry, on which even Savonarola modeled his verses, represents an attachment to the older Florence and a distrust of the newer style typical of the younger, Medicean Florence and courtly Italy. Machiavelli's attitude was not merely personal but municipal and defensive; it was characteristic of Florentine culture in the critical years following the expulsion of the Medici.

In Florence, after the tragedy of Savonarola, events unfolded at a painfully slow pace, exemplified by the tragicomedy of the war with Pisa; an anxious sense of impending tragedy pervaded the city. With the literature of the Medici era out of the way, it was nonetheless unthinkable that the revival of a primarily comic and folkloric literature, rooted in the Florentine traditions of the early and middle fifteenth century, could adequately cope with the new and serious conditions of the present. It was necessary to go farther back—all the way back to Dante—and that is precisely what Machiavelli did in the *Decennale*. Its meter, its historical-political subject matter, its search for a rapid and incisive means of representation and characterization, its continuing series of textual echoes, all recall the Dantean model. But a return to Dante was too obvious a solution under these difficult conditions, and because it was obvious, it was not enough. In 1506, the same year in which the *Decennale* was published, an edition of the *Commedia* was also published in Florence. It was edited by Benivieni, a Neoplatonist who tried to confirm the traditional image of Dante as a "scientific" and theological poet, rather than as a political poet, by adding to the text his own *Dialogo di Antonio Manetti cittadino fiorentino circa el sito, forma, e misure dello Inferno* (Dialogue of Antonio Manetti, Florentine Citizen, Concerning the Location, Form, and Dimensions of Hell). As I have already mentioned, Benivieni had used Dante's meter for his translation of the penitential Psalms of David, which had come out the year before. Dante was still everyone's master in Florence, a man for all seasons, even for such conflicting purposes as the Savonarolian Benivieni's religious detachment and the anti-Savonarolian Machiavelli's political engagement. But it was just this conflicted return to the lessons of Father Dante that opened Florentine eyes to the fact that the crisis in their literature was no longer a local matter: like the political crisis, it was now an open question, subject to increasingly powerful initiatives and competition from the rest of Italy.

The 1506 Benivieni version of the *Commedia* did not appear by chance, or merely to satisfy Florentine demand; it was specifically intended as a defense of the traditional cult of Dante against its distortion elsewhere, and against the predominance of the cult of Petrarch outside Florence. The comparison of these two great poets had originally been established in Tuscany; it was proposed by Leonardo Bruni,

Landino, Lorenzo, and Poliziano repeatedly throughout the fifteenth century, without the poets' obvious differences ever throwing any doubt on their fundamental and peaceful complementarity, much less degenerating into the polemical denigration of one or the other. But the cult of Petrarch had become more and more exclusive and aggressive, accusing Dante, as if it were a flaw, of precisely that linguistic exuberance which was characteristic not only of his epoch but of the Florentine literary tradition, both then and now. The denigration of Dante thus turned into a denigration of Florence and its natural and proper linguistic excellence. Critical debate was grounded in the past, in the comparison of Dante and Petrarch, for a judgment of the past seemed a necessary premise for the new literature rapidly developing outside Florence.

Benivieni's edition of Dante was a response to the scandal produced in 1502 by an edition edited by the Venetian Bembo and printed in Aldo Manuzio's new italic type. In this edition, Dante's work had lost its traditional title, *Commedia,* and had acquired a new title, *Le terze rime di Dante,* more appropriate to a collection of lyrics than to a long poem. Dante's original text had also been radically restored, compared with previous editions, and freed from the accompaniment of Landino's 1481 commentary, which had become standard by that time and which had bespoken the glory of both Dante and Florence. In 1505, Aldo Manuzio had printed in Venice *Gli asolani,* a unique work in prose and verse by the same Bembo who had edited Dante's *Le terze rime* three years earlier. The work was immediately reprinted by Giunta in Florence. In it the discussion of love, which had played such a large part in Florentine Neoplatonic literature in the time of Lorenzo the Magnificent, reappeared in a language and style that was ostentatiously Tuscan, but completely different from anything recently written in Tuscany. The same could be said of another work, *Arcadia,* by the Neapolitan nobleman Jacopo Sannazaro, which had circulated for a few years before being published in Naples in 1504. *Arcadia* was destined to achieve even greater popularity in Italy and Europe than *Gli asolani.* It also revived a Tuscan-like form, yet was completely different from the pastoral style that had been explored and made fashionable by Tuscan writers in Lorenzo the Magnificent's time. Although its first Florentine edition did not come out until 1514–15, the work was probably known in Florence much earlier. It is, of course, true that hardly anyone in Florence could have known then that Ludovico Ariosto in Ferrara had undertaken the writing of *Orlando furioso.* Still less could anyone, there or elsewhere, predict its remarkable success. Because of the popularity of the *Orlando innamorato,* however, it was already perfectly clear that the leadership even in that kind of literature, so typically Tuscan, had already passed to others.

These non-Tuscan poets were all noblemen and not professional men of letters: from Matteo Boiardo and, more recently, Niccolò da Coreggio (to whom Benivieni had dedicated his little poem, *Amore*), to Bembo and Sannazaro, and soon thereafter to Ariosto and Baldassare Castiglione. Unlike the Florentine Pulci, they were also men who started out with a thoroughly humanistic education. And unlike Poliziano and the others in Florence who did have humanistic training, they carried over into the vernacular the same diligence and ambitiousness normally associated with Latin. They introduced a seriousness of method and nobility of purpose to the new vernacular literature, without thereby weakening the humanist vanguard but rather strengthening themselves in the process. Machiavelli, who had received humanistic training himself, was certainly acute enough to detect the special traits, both social and stylistic, of the new Italian courtly literature. He was heedful of the classical tradition, not only in literature, and was prepared by his political and diplomatic experiences to look outside Florence, and to grasp and measure differences. We must add to these entirely personal interests and commitments, however, the natural reluctance of any Florentine to take seriously the pretensions of people who barely knew the vernacular and spoke another language at home. It is hard to believe that when he was secretary, Machiavelli already clearly perceived that the question of a new vernacular literature no longer concerned only Tuscany but all of Italy.

Thus we arrive at the catastrophe of 1512, which overwhelmed Machiavelli but also inspired him. After his misfortunes, the relations between politics and literature, theory and practice, activity and inactivity changed radically. The nature of my argument, which has been until now uncontentious and concentrated largely on marginal considerations, ought to change as well, for I am approaching important and hotly debated issues. But I will stick to the margins and limit myself to a few comments. I do not intend to dispute matters of chronology or composition. The rhythm of Machiavelli's thought and language is varied, but his literary choices, the ones that matter here—concerning works that were all crowded into a little less than a decade—appear to be few and clear. With regard to questions of chronology in Machiavelli, or any other author, suffice it to say that the term *post quem* can never be substituted for *ante quem*, and that the term *ante quem*, which is probably valid for the work as a whole, is established by the date of publication, however late, or failing that, by the latest verifiable date in the text. It is established in *The Prince*, therefore, by the dedication to

Lorenzo [that is, it should be dated to 1517]. This does not mean that *The Prince* cannot have been conceived and drafted in 1513. But it does prevent one from attributing every word of the text that has come down to us to the year 1513, as if that word were an ante quem term. The same could be said of *The Discourses*. One speaks of an original version when one possesses a copy of that version. When a copy of the ur-*Discourses*, which preceded *The Prince*, or the copy of Livy that Machiavelli annotated in the margins comes to light, we will discuss it. I myself am not in a hurry, and since "life is short, and suffering is long," I must say that I rejoice at the idea that in the personal and general straits of 1512–13, Machiavelli's wonderful head for politics strained itself to produce an important treatise on republics, with or without Livy. I rejoice even more at the idea, which anyone can verify, that a revolutionary work like the *Discourses* might be traced back to an annotated copy of Livy. Of course, one would like to find that Livy, or Dante's Virgil, for that matter. There is no harm in looking. Maybe in that way we will manage to find out which of Livy's books Machiavelli was reading. There must be a text from that period, whether it is the ur-*Discourses* or Livy, and not just the hypothetical toy, ingenious or dull as it may be, of a modern scholar.

Although Machiavelli's work developed at a fast and unbroken pace, along a line of historical-political speculation, from *The Prince* to *The Discourses*, *The Art of War*, the *Life of Castruccio Castracani*, and the *Florentine Histories*, it included, in those few years, experiments that were entirely literary. At the end of 1517, Machiavelli was still absorbed in writing *Asino*, the long allegorical satire that he subsequently abandoned. This shows that his original (although illusory) poetic calling was still alive after the lightning-fast composition of *The Prince*, following a direction that was completely different from that of *The Discourses*. We now know that *Mandragola* is probably a later work, and that Machiavelli's daring engagement with the then-new genre of comic theater was closely tied to his political commitments. The lines along which Machiavelli's work developed diverge to some extent from every previous formal model in an absolutely original way, but in many respects they also follow closely the traditional models.

From the beginning of his greatest period (in which *The Prince* and *The Discourses* were written) until 1517, Machiavelli's truly literary experiments, such as his resumption of the *Decennale* and *Asino*, were only outlets for his escapism and desperate attempts to vindicate himself, and consequently they were left—thank God—unfinished. But there are important differences between *Asino* and the second *Decennale*. The second *Decennale* does not add anything, either in technique or in imaginative invention, to the first. It is merely a step backward into a past that consumes its political and autobiographical tinder without catching fire—without that fire which flares up in *The Prince* in the wind of a marvelous certainty. Machiavelli's resumption, after almost ten years, of a work that had been printed when he was secretary, was probably intended to suggest the author's availability for employment, just as *The Prince* had been. The old role of poet could serve as a cover for and—if worse came to worst—as an alternative to, the role of political adviser, on a more modest and secure plane. *Asino* is something else entirely: it marks the darkest, gloomiest, and most spiteful moment in the life and work of Machiavelli, a man whom not even prison and torture had managed to subdue. It was in the same period that he wrote the sonnet, "Io ho, Giuliano, in gamba un paio di geti" (I have jesses around my legs, Giuliano).[17] The writing of *Asino* had been prompted by the recent, still unbearable loss of the illusions that had accompanied the writing of *The Prince*. Literally, it was a step backward to an allegorical tradition that Machiavelli had already rejected at the time of writing the first *Decennale,* when he chose to confront historical reality directly. In this sense, *Asino* implied a kind of literary undertaking that was new for Machiavelli; it invoked literature as a discipline not only different from but in opposition to politics. In fact, if its conception has Machiavelli's characteristic nerve and eccentricity, its structure is uncertain and archaic, its execution unusually weak. One suspects an ingenious attempt on the part of Machiavelli to pass himself off as a man of letters who never practiced any other trade and who, even when writing in the humble vernacular, would want to show off his expertise in the classical and humanistic traditions: the fact that he had read not only Apuleius and his forebears, but also Giovanni Pontano's *Asinus.* To sum up, in *Asino* (and, in a very different way, in *The Discourses* as well) the image of a new Machiavelli appears, one who had left behind the disappointment of *The Prince,* at first inclining contemptuously to seek a reason for living in the militant literature of the day, then committing himself to it with increasing passion. In so doing, he seeks to detach himself from the expedient modernity of the *Decennale* and to pursue, in his own fashion, a middle way between the ancients and the moderns, one that rightly seems to him the road to success for that literature. I have already mentioned a possible reason why Machiavelli interrupted work on *Asino* and gave up poetry, namely, his reaction in 1517 to reading the just-published *Orlando furioso.* But the really decisive and positive reason for his doing so was that he had overcome the bitter loneliness and spiteful impotence of which *Asino*

17. [Translator's note: "jesses" are straps, usually of leather, attached to the legs of hunting falcons; see the essay by John Najemy that follows.]

was the direct result. He had also overcome the prophetic solitude of *The Prince,* which would have been impossible to sustain. Finally, he was spurred by the impetus of the new work, *The Discourses,* in the new environment, a Florence that was Medicean but princeless. That would continue to be Machiavelli's motive force for the rest of his life.

The Discourses show that at that moment, when Machiavelli reawoke from darkness to a new life, he was still wonderfully far from even a superficial obedience to the norms of contemporary literature, at least when the subject matter was really "his alone" and really absorbed him entirely. If we pay attention to the structure of *The Prince,* it is clear that it did not come out of thin air. It was influenced by the Latin and vernacular tradition of the theoretical-practice treatise, divided in chapters. Yet *The Discourses,* as far as we know, had no precedents, either in Latin or in the vernacular. Behind it there is no commentary of any kind on Livy, and no commentary like this one on any classical author. Of course, Machiavelli's work is unthinkable without the fifteenth-century humanist exegetical tradition, in general, and without the rupture in that tradition effected by Poliziano's *Miscellanea* and driven home for Machiavelli by Crinito's *De honesta disciplina.* From this tradition came, first, the subordination of the discourse on the quaestio to a base text, which was the normal procedure of lawyers and artists, not of the litterati. Second came the interpreter's disengagement from the continuous commentary on the base text and the isolation of freely chosen single passages. Finally came the superimposition upon those single passages of a commentary that goes beyond the base text and aims to elucidate general questions. This is certainly the prehistory of the literary structure of *The Discourses;* it is a prehistory that took place in Machiavelli's lifetime, and for the most part in Florence, under his very eyes. Yet for all this, the leap from the Scholastic and humanistic Latin tradition to a work in the vernacular, to a classical author who was marginal to that scholastic tradition, and to a subject that was so risky, but of such immediate general interest, still seems prodigious. This explains the popularity of this work, compared with *The Prince.* *The Prince,* which ended up being identified with the European legend of Machiavelli rather than with the Italian or Florentine one, was like a shipwrecked sailor's message in a bottle. It was wholly extraneous to the context of contemporary Italian literature, which could not accept it, except at a distance and surreptitiously. *The Discourses,* despite the absolute originality of their structure, were founded on a fundamental classical text and an interpretive method currently in use. They appealed to an audience of educated humanists and aimed to take by force their place and part in the contemporary literary scene.

The Machiavelli who writes *The Discourses* is not yet the one to write

The Art of War, but he is already the Machiavelli of the Orti Oricellari circle. A member of the common people, outcast, poor, and nearly fifty years old, he suddenly finds himself surrounded by a group of young men who belong to the aristocracy of Florence, to judge by their names and property. And these young men hang on his every word, in spite of the influence of their fathers (as often happens). This is not a mannerist painting, or an example of nineteenth-century historical portraiture. Anyone from my generation who had to read, as a professional duty, Machiavelli's dying words as recounted in *L'Assedio di Firenze* by Francesco Guerrazzi, is inoculated for life against those sorts of portraits, as if there were any need. These, instead, are the results of research only partially completed into Machiavelli's reception in his own time, among those that knew him, either directly or indirectly. It is a history very different from that of Machiavellianism and anti-Machiavellianism.

Machiavelli always had a lot of friends, in good times and bad, even friends much younger than he, such as Francesco Guicciardini, who played an important role in his life. But there is no proof that these friends had much influence on his work. On the other hand, there is no reason to doubt that at a certain point in his literary career, his spontaneous and candid teaching of young men who had grown up in the age of the Medicean papacy was the determining factor in his work. These young men communicated their various needs and hopes to Machiavelli, who may have been old but was still very much alive and had plenty of things to say. He was passionately eager for the future, if bitterly disappointed with the past. But because of tradition, their family rank, and their youth, the young Florentines could not take Machiavelli as their teacher and guide in any political undertaking aimed at reforming the state of Florence. And even if they had been tempted to, Machiavelli would not have fallen for it; he may have been an ingenuous and mediocre politician, but he was not a hack revolutionary devoid of class consciousness. He never did fall for it, in fact: not in 1522, or even in 1527. Yet the young men of the Orti Oricellari sensed that there was something extraordinary in Machiavelli's application of the lessons of the ancients to the problems of modern times, in the rigor and penetrating fantasy of his conversation and writing, and in his vitality.

This undertaking—that of seeing clearly and far—which these young men, champing at the bit, fresh from their studies, proposed and which Machiavelli performed for them was, yes, potentially a political enterprise; but at that moment it was also and above all a *literary* one. The Medicean papacy, with the Pope still young (younger than Machiavelli), and the members of the Medici family few but young also, was enough in itself to block change in Florence's political order for a long time, or so it seemed. But the papacy unblocked and put into crisis Florence's literary order by imposing on the city a new relation with Rome, and through Rome, with the rest of Italy. The defense of isolationism and of municipal autonomy had failed. Florence was already impoverished and diminished, compared with what it had been in the fifteenth century, and every day it lost more worthy, ambitious men to the Medici court in Rome. Florence found itself in the position of having to measure itself with the rest of Italy, not only in matters of politics and financial profit but in every other activity and skill as well. Consequently, it had to take notice of the growing freedom and power of the efforts of others. Subordination to Rome, which had certain economic and political advantages, meant a net loss in the field of vernacular literature and lessened the vigor of the municipal tradition.

Although their motives were different from his, the young men of the Orti Oricellari came to an understanding with Machiavelli. Both he and they yearned for Florence's political and literary revenge against Medicean Rome and Italy in general: especially against Rome, as can be seen from *The Discourses*, and later from *The Art of War*, where Machiavelli dared to present in print, as guest and teacher in Florence, a personage as alive and as well qualified as Fabrizio Colonna. Not that Machiavelli, "endowed with prophetic spirit," could already foresee at that date the role that Fabrizio Colonna's direct descendants would play in the second Medicean Pope's undoing shortly thereafter. For him it was enough to know (as everyone knew at the time) that he was dealing with a Roman member of the Colonna family who was a guest and teacher there, whereas because of Medici family ties, one would have expected to meet a man of the opposing party, an Orsini. But for Machiavelli and his friends at that point, what counted more than men, families, and parties were ideas, institutions, and *ordini* ("orders"), to use the term so comprehensively discussed by my friend J. H. Whitfield.[18] Against Christian and papal Rome, especially contemporary Medici Rome, which had distinguished itself from that of Julius II by waving the white flag of peace, they wished to set up a different Rome: ancient, republican, warlike. They wanted to revive, in the language of Florence, this ancient image with its precise, imperious features, in continuous polemical conflict with the present, and the proximate past, of the international humanism—decorative and evasive, Hellenizing and Ciceronian—that then triumphed in Rome.

18. [Editor's note: See J. H. Whitfield, "On Machiavelli's Use of 'Ordini,'" first in *Italian Studies* 10 (1955): 19–39; and then in *Discourses on Machiavelli* (Cambridge, 1969), 141–62.]

At this point, we move on to the issue of writing and language. The question of political theory was necessarily couched in literary terms—in the terms, that is, of a bilingual literature that was not proper to Rome, any more than it was to Venice, Ferrara, or Naples, but was, in fact, *Italian*. Machiavelli and his young friends were not willing to yield to the literary pretensions of those from Venice, Ferrara, and Naples, but they were becoming more and more aware every day of what Machiavelli would later write in his *Discorso o dialogo intorno alla nostra lingua* (Discourse or Dialogue Concerning Our Language): that non-Tuscans had begun to write well, and to produce "talents very suited to writing," and that it was therefore necessary to take them into account. In this encounter and conflict that centered around the new vernacular literature, in poetry and in prose, the agreement between Machiavelli, poet of *Asino,* and his friends could be neither easy nor complete. The young Florentines—Cosimo di Cosimo Rucellai, Luigi Alamanni, Niccolò Martelli, and Francesco Guidetti—were naturally inclined to poetry and influenced by the spreading fashion of Petrarchism. In his time, Machiavelli had also deluded himself that poetry was for him the winning card, and he had found it hard to give up that illusion. But in his old age, he was unwilling to submit to the discipline of Petrarch or adopt the fashionable style of courtly love lyrics, a style that not even Lorenzo the Magnificent had managed to impose on Florence when Machiavelli was young. Perhaps this insurmountable clash in taste and intention with young people who were so close to him in other ways helped to cure Machiavelli of his poetic ambition, and to make him recognize in vernacular prose (and to a certain extent in Latin prose) an artistic instrument that was equal to poetry, not merely a practical tool, was suited to the exposition of facts and ideas, and occasionally was capable of achieving striking rhetorical effect.

One need not be any better informed about the dominant trends in humanism than was Machiavelli to know that Cicero was currently much more talked about than Virgil. Circumstances were such as to allow a "barbarian" like Erasmus, utterly unsuited to poetry, to achieve first place in European humanism. In the other field, vernacular literature, the old masters of poetry, Dante and Petrarch, had always been much more authoritative than the prose writer Boccaccio, and for that reason the poetic tradition had dominated the new literature, leaving the field of prose writing largely open. But during Machiavelli's lifetime, from Naples to Venice, in *Arcadia* and *Gli asolani,* there had been clear signs of a desire to restore the prestige of prose, as had already happened in Latin literature. Such experiments repelled Machiavelli, both in form and in content; moreover, they revealed their continuing loyalty to poetry, and to the Petrarchan style of poetry in particular, which Machiavelli opposed. He did not live to see the publication of the very different work, much closer to his own sensibility and completely in prose, that the Lombard Castiglione was composing in those years. But even if he had been able to read the *Courtier*, he would not have had any reason to change his mind. On the contrary, the ideal courtly society of the Urbino duchy, into which the Florentine Medici exiles (the same ones who had ousted Machiavelli from office on their return to power) were introduced to tell witty stories and to describe the lady of court, was the embodiment of a political and literary situation that Machiavelli and his young friends could not accept for Florence. Certainly, in their proper place—that is, in the comic theater—Florentine witticisms would always be more piquant than those of the Lombard Ariosto. Proof of this superiority had already been given by Bibbiena, facetious interlocutor of the *Courtier*, in his one play, and Machiavelli was ready to give a decisive demonstration of it. But although important, this was only a secondary aspect of the new literature that aimed to appropriate the lesson of the ancients for the modern tongue, with modern subject matter. At stake was Florence's need to reaffirm its autonomy and preeminence with regard to the rest of Italy through an ambitious comparison of modern times to ancient.

Machiavelli was familiar—even obsessed—with the political and military comparison between the ancient and modern worlds—one that, in his eyes, inevitably implied a debasement of the modern world, and especially of Florence. But the comparison had to be elaborated in literary terms as well. In these terms, whatever the outcome of the political and military crisis that enveloped Italy, a margin for success would remain in which Florence, with its unique linguistic and literary tradition, would have a part to play—one larger than that of the rest of the peninsula. It was not necessary, or even desirable, that Florence should again become the Athens of Italy. It was enough that it should recognize, and be recognized for, what it had already been for centuries and still was. Such was the driving force behind Machiavelli's final commitment to the literature of his age. Starting with *The Discourses*, this commitment grew, and in doing so led him to assume a role different from his original one. Already in *The Discourses*, Machiavelli had found an audience that no longer consisted only, or necessarily, of the powerful men and professional politicians whom he had addressed in *The Prince*. A new way of life had opened up to him. It was not the path of employment that he yearned for, the one for which he had knocked, and would knock again fruitlessly, at the closed door of the Medici, and for which he would also call upon his high-placed friends, Francesco Vettori and Francesco Guicciardini, whose doors were left prudently ajar so that they could hear him without letting him in.

Machiavelli was not content with having only this one way open to him, yet he knew he was better suited to it than any of his Florentine contemporaries. In *The Discourses* it was still a solitary way, which accounts for that work's surprising structural originality. In *The Art of War,* in the *Life of Castruccio Castracani,* in the *Florentine Histories,* and ultimately in the plays, Machiavelli adhered to models authorized by classical humanist tradition. Especially noteworthy is the dialogue structure imposed on *The Art of War,* a work that signaled a decisive turning point, if only because it appeared in print under the direct supervision, and with the full responsibility, of its author. I say "imposed" on the work because a dialogue structure is evidently *not* required by the subject matter, or by the essentially "monological" development given to that material in the treatise. What also stands out is Machiavelli's passage from a personal discourse, in which the author is an actor or character on stage by himself, as in *The Prince* and *The Discourses,* to a representation of ideas and facts that the author promotes and directs from behind the scenes, participating only rarely, between one act and another, as in the proems to the individual books of the *Florentine Histories.* One can trace a dramatic development from monologue to dialogue, and from discourse to representation, which should be seen in the light of Machiavelli's contemporaneous involvement in the comic theater. More important, this development must be seen as the result of Machiavelli's growing commitment to the literature of his own age. The modern preference for monologue, my own included, is beside the point. The umpteenth reconfirmation of the supreme greatness and uniqueness of Machiavelli is irrelevant to the subject treated in this essay. Besides, everyone is willing by now to recognize that greatness in *Mandragola,* which certainly could not have emerged full-blown, like Athena, from the mind of the "political" Machiavelli. And if appreciation of the *Florentine Histories* has been more hesitant or qualified in modern studies, the fault lies in the modern studies, which are littered with the waste of a Byzantine Machiavellianism without temporal or geographical specificity and which are inadequately charged with historical interest in that Florence and that Italy, that is, in the temporal and geographical conditions in which Machiavelli lived and about which he wrote.

Machiavelli's commitment to the literature of his own age implied a choice. I have already suggested what he accepted in making that choice. I shall conclude by suggesting what it was that he rejected, particularly in drama. I would be neglecting the lessons of unforgettable teachers such as Ferdinando Neri and Fortunato Pintor, scholars of ancient Florentine theater, if I did not emphasize that the development of the dramatic verse form (namely, unrhymed hendecasyllabic verse) passed from Iacopo Nardi to Lorenzo Strozzi,[19] brushing by Machia-velli without actually touching him. From start to finish, from *Andria* to *Clizia*, Machiavelli wrote all his plays in prose. His theatrical develop-ment runs closely parallel to the Tuscan short-story writing tradition, although it is consistently marked by classical influences as well. He thus rejected grotesque and farcical drama in verse, even in the terza rima that was so dear to him but was nonetheless incompat-ible with the classical tradition. Thus one can observe an obvious historical opposition between *Mandragola* and the anonymous *Flori-ana*, which was printed in Florence in 1518.[20] But Machiavelli also rejected the opposite objective, which his friends pursued in those years, that of imitating the dramatic structure and technique of clas-sical comedy in blank verse. Machiavelli's polemical spirit seems just as evident here, although it is only implicit. We see, once more, that he assumed a middle-of-the-road position in approaching both the classical-humanistic and Tuscan traditions. He clearly perceived and rejected the risk, greater in poetry than in prose, of a pedantic, or merely Italian, adulteration of that which he felt to be the patrimony and strength of his city and language.

Machiavelli's polemic is made explicit, with regard to drama as well as other matters, in his *Discourse or Dialogue Concerning Our Language*. I will not dwell on this work, which would require extended discussion. I will limit myself to citing Carlo Lenzoni's fundamental *In difesa della lingua fiorentina e di Dante* (In Defense of the Florentine Language and of Dante), which was published posthumously in Florence in 1556. Oreste Tommasini, who considers the *Discourse* apocryphal, did not recognize the considerable importance of the later work either. Lenzoni presents "the argument which Niccolò Machiavelli had with a Mister Maffio from Venice when the prose-writing of Bembo came out, printed by Giunti" (26–27), as it was related to him by Giovan Battista Gelli. Even if this cannot be considered authentic documentation of Machiavelli's life and thought, it does contain, without a doubt, au-thentic documentation of the image that was still alive in Florence, twenty years later, of the elder Machiavelli's commitment to defending the language of Florence against the Vicentine Gian Giorgio Trissino and the Venetian Bembo, against anyone who might want to impose on it laws external to it in space or time. The image is of a Machiavelli who was "so lively and so ready by nature," who "always wanted to see things through with such people," and thus never gave a moment's

19. This was the title of Ferdinando Neri's fundamental essay on the subject in *Let-teratura e leggende* (Turin, 1951), 78–110.
20. See Neri, 111–17.

rest to his enemies as he pressed the attack—who, in short, "had very sharp wits." Under such changed literary and political conditions, this image would never have reemerged from the growing shadows of Machiavellianism and anti-Machiavellianism if it had not been sustained by a powerful legacy of sentiments, of ideas, and of works. The miracle is that this image returned so pure and so alive to Florence under the reign of the Medici, considering the caution and reserve displayed regarding the mention of Machiavelli by the exiles themselves, even though they had been close to him when young. But this miracle can be explained *historically,* in the terms of *literary history.* To Machiavelli, and to Machiavelli alone, is credit due for the sixteenth-century rebirth, starting with Francesco Guicciardini, of an autonomous Florentine literature primarily in prose. This municipal literature alone stood outside the otherwise homogenized and undifferentiated context of a new, princely, poetic, *Italian* literature that emerged between the time of Ariosto and that of Tasso. And it is from this perspective, finally, that we should view the fierce Florentine opposition, by the Crusca Academy, and by Galileo, to Tasso.

Translated by Olivia Holmes

CHAPTER TWO

MACHIAVELLI AND GETA: MEN OF LETTERS

John M. Najemy

B Y Machiavelli's time the relationship between literature and politics in the Renaissance was an old one, but hardly stable. The relationship had its origins in humanist convictions about the crucial role of rhetoric in the production of both good rulers and good citizens: "The science of speaking well and of governing people is the noblest art in the world," Brunetto Latini proclaimed in the thirteenth century.[1] Over the next two centuries, the convergences between a humanism that ennobled the political careers of notaries with doctrines of Ciceronian rhetoric and communal governments that similarly sought legitimation in Roman history, letters, and law consolidated the relationship of literature and politics, a development whose chief institutional manifestation was certainly the Florentine chancery with its long honor roll of chancellors trained in the *studia humanitatis*. There were, to be sure, some humanists who worried about too close a connection. Petrarch kept away from politics, and even when he got close to tyrants (as his critics called the Visconti of Milan), he defended himself by saying that he lived near them, not under them, and that they needed him more than he needed them.[2] Petrarch was willing enough to offer advice to rulers, and encouragement to revolutionaries, like Cola di Rienzo, who dreamed of old Rome reborn, but the poet, he insisted, could never get any closer to politics (or, for that matter, to citizenship) than such

---

1. Brunetto Latini, *Li Livres dou Tresor*, ed. Francis J. Carmody (Berkeley, 1948), 1.1.4, p. 17: "est la sience de bien parler et de governer gens plus noble de nul art du monde."

2. "Invectiva contra quendam magni status hominem sed nullius scientie aut virtutis," ed. P. G. Ricci, in Francesco Petrarca, *Prose*, ed. Guido Martellotti et al. (Milan, 1955), 694–709, esp. 698–705; partial English translation in *Petrarch: An Anthology*, ed. David Thompson (New York, 1971), 138–46.

occasional advice and exhortation. In the full flower of civic humanism, Leonardo Bruni rewrote Boccaccio's life of Dante to argue that
learned men and even poets could and should take their place in the
civic arena,[3] and the official culture of Florence in the first third or so of
the fifteenth century probably came closer to an unequivocal celebration of the ideal implicit in Brunetto Latini's dictum than did any other
moment of the Renaissance. Not so, as we shall see, the unofficial
culture of that age, which lampooned the pieties and complacencies of
a humanism that too easily trusted the honor that politics paid to
letters. In the second half of the century, literature was, if anything,
even more uncomfortably close to politics. The Italian literary world of
Machiavelli's youth was tied to the courts, and perhaps nowhere more
so than in the (still unofficial) court of the Medici, where poets and
learned humanists gratefully acknowledged the generosity of patrons,
chief among them Lorenzo, who both ruled the city and joined the
ranks of the poets: a world that, as Carlo Dionisotti has argued, fell
apart and into crisis following Lorenzo's death in 1492 and the political
upheavals that began in 1494.

We do not know what Machiavelli thought of the Laurentian calm in
the relationship between politics and literature, except that, having
been for a time just on the edges of its inner circle, he showed not much
nostalgia for it in the years after the storm broke, when none of the old
certitudes and platitudes of the relationship could be taken for granted.
Many illusions dear to the fifteenth century were crushed in this more
dangerous world, and literature discovered that it was far more precariously situated vis-à-vis politics than it had previously imagined. The
suddenly apparent vulnerability of letters was dramatically under-
scored by an event in Pesaro in 1504, the year in which Machiavelli
made his debut as a *letterato* and poet with the first *Decennale.* That
summer Pesaro's newly restored ruler, Giovanni Sforza, arrested and
executed the city's most famous literary native son, the humanist and
poet Pandolfo Collenuccio, for the treason of having recognized Cesare
Borgia as Pesaro's legitimate ruler when he conquered and entered the
city four years earlier, and for having supported his cause throughout
the Romagna. After the collapse of Borgia's little empire, Collenuccio

---

3. Leonardo Bruni's *Vita di Dante* is in Hans Baron, *Leonardo Bruni Aretino:
Humanistisch-philosophische Schriften* (Leipzig, 1928), 51–63; English translation by Alan F.
Nagel in *The Three Crowns of Florence*, ed. David Thompson and Alan F. Nagel (New
York, 1972), 57–73, reprinted in *The Humanism of Leonardo Bruni: Selected Texts*, ed. and
trans. Gordon Griffiths, James Hankins, and David Thompson (Binghamton, N.Y., 1987),
85–95.

petitioned Sforza for permission to return to Pesaro and fell into a trap set by the still angry prince, who wanted revenge.[4]

Collenuccio's career had assumed the compatibility and even the partnership of politics and letters.[5] In 1483 he had used his diplomatic skills to secure Giovanni Sforza's succession to the *signoria* of Pesaro, but some years later, for reasons that remain obscure, Sforza had Collenuccio imprisoned and sent into exile. Collenuccio gained the friendship and protection of Lorenzo de' Medici and in 1490 served a term as podestà in Florence, where he wrote poetry and a ceremonial oration in celebration of both the republic's civic and legal traditions and its literary culture. He idealized the Florentine world for its combination of political and literary virtues and lauded its humanist/poet/prince. Lorenzo became one of the models for Collenuccio's image (in the later apologues) of the ruler as the "true philosopher, because he not only understands the things of the philosophers, but, living the life of a true philosopher, he provides philosophers with the material for their writing." Claudio Varese has summarized Collenuccio's vision of the role of the prince in this marriage of culture and politics: "Only the prince, the cultured and enlightened sovereign, can understand the deep meaning and the public utility of culture and of literature; only he can accept its gift and make it bear fruit in civic society." And, on the other side of the partnership, Collenuccio insisted that the *virtù* of these great princes would be buried by time "if the prudence and diligence of *omini letterati* did not keep it alive and immortal."[6]

With such ideas, so typical of the Italian literary world of the second half of the fifteenth century, a world whose stunning naiveté was just about to be revealed, Pandolfo Collenuccio pursued his dual career in letters—as humanist, poet, and historian—and in politics—as podestà (in Florence and Mantua), ducal counselor to Ercole d'Este in Ferrara, and Ferrarese ambassador to both the imperial court of Maximilian and the papal court of Alexander VI. Respected and honored by the most powerful princes of his day, he was also admired by at least two of the already legendary men of letters of the time, Giovanni Pico and Angelo Poliziano. His sad end in 1504 stands as a kind of cautionary

---

4. Eduardo Melfi, "Pandolfo Collenuccio," *Dizionario biografico degli italiani*, 27:1–5.

5. On Collenuccio's humanism, see Claudio Varese, "Pandolfo Collenuccio umanista," in Varese, *Storia e politica nella prosa del Quattrocento* (Turin, 1961), 149–286; selections from his writings are included in *Prosatori volgari del Quattrocento*, ed. Claudio Varese (Milan, 1955), 593–720.

6. Passages quoted are from Varese, *Storia e politica*, 219–22.

tale for the new generation that would have to rethink the old connection of literature and politics.

As far as I know, Machiavelli never commented on Collenuccio's fate, but how could he not have taken sharp notice of it, in the very year in which he announced his own attempt to combine a political career with a literary calling, and especially in the light of Borgia's role in this story? Machiavelli knew that poets had often suffered exile with dignity and even with some advantage to poetry (if not to politics), but entrapment and execution (eerily reminiscent of Cesare Borgia's methods in dealing with his political enemies) were another matter altogether. It is even possible that Machiavelli knew Collenuccio from the latter's Florentine days.[7] But whether from this incident or from the general climate of the years after 1494, Machiavelli developed a certain skepticism about the relationship of literature and politics, a skepticism that suddenly intensified when, in 1512–13, he too was betrayed by politics. Machiavelli, even more—I think—than Dante, Petrarch, or Bruni, must be the locus classicus of the Renaissance linkage of literature and politics, partly because he took politics (as distinguished from political doctrine) more seriously than Dante or Petrarch, and literature more seriously than Bruni, and partly because, facing this complex tradition in its moment of crisis, he went on thematizing and revising the relationship as the old complacencies fell away, but without putting in their place some new declaration of its golden origins or noble ends.

A good place to begin is that hierarchy of famous and praised men with which Machiavelli opens the tenth chapter of the first book of *The Discourses.* Here he lists, first, the organizers of religions; second, the founders of republics and kingdoms; third, military leaders who have expanded their own or their countries' dominions; fourth, men of letters ("uomini litterati"); and, after them, the numberless men to whom some praise is given as a consequence of their different skills and professions. That was to put literary types in high company, just below the founders and wielders of political and religious power and ahead of everyone else. Implicit in this ranking is the notion that men of letters do something that merits high praise because it is more like what religious, political, and military leaders do than are the labors and exertions of all the other categories of men trained in professions or occupations. But curiously, although he designates each of the

---

7. A possibility that emerges from the friendships that the Florentine chancellor Bartolomeo Scala enjoyed with both Collenuccio and Machiavelli's father, Bernardo. On the former see Alison Brown, *Bartolomeo Scala, 1430–1497: Chancellor of Florence* (Princeton, N.J., 1979), 128–29; on the latter, see Felix Gilbert, *Machiavelli and Guicciardini: Politics and History in Sixteenth-Century Florence* (Princeton, N.J., 1965), 318–19.

other groups in terms of action, Machiavelli does not say what that praiseworthy activity of men of letters might be. Religious leaders are "ordinatori"; after them come those who have "fondato" or "ampliato" political entities. And even at the bottom of the list are men with some "arte" or "esercizio," skills they have learned and can perform. His "uomini litterati," however, are defined by nothing more than the passive condition of being lettered, or learned. We are not told what they do, or why they are praised. The uncertainties surrounding them are compounded by Machiavelli's comment that "because they are of so many kinds, they are celebrated each according to his rank."[8] The fates of literary men are thus more varied than those of men in the first three categories, being subject to distinctions and gradations that cause some to achieve fame surpassed only by that of founders and generals and others to fall short of that. But, again, Machiavelli does not reveal what those distinctions or "gradi" are, and we are left with the impression that "uomini litterati" exist in a condition of indeterminacy or unpredictability that subverts the very attempt to classify them. The only clue we get in this chapter comes a page or so later, where Machiavelli comments that no one should be deceived by the praise that ancient writers heaped on Caesar since imperial power did not allow writers to speak freely of him, and that if anyone wants to know what free writers ("scrittori liberi") would have said about Caesar, let him look at what they say about Catiline.[9]

Machiavelli often joked about his own unhappy fate as a literary man, and especially as a poet. In 1517 he wrote to Lodovico Alamanni that he had just finished reading Ariosto's *Orlando furioso*. He judged it "a fine poem throughout, and in many parts wonderful"; his only complaint was that its author, in recalling so many poets, "has left me out like some prick."[10] But poets could suffer even worse fates than neglect. In one of the prison sonnets addressed to Giuliano de' Medici, Machiavelli described his imprisonment and torture as the typical fate, not of defeated political figures, but of poets:

> Io ho, Giuliano, in gamba un paio di geti
> con sei tratti di fune in su le spalle:

---

8. *Discorsi sopra la prima deca di Tito Livio*, bk. 1, chap. 10, in Niccolò Machiavelli, *Il Principe e Discorsi*, ed. Sergio Bertelli (Milan, 1960), 156.

9. Machiavelli, *Il Principe e Discorsi*, 157.

10. Niccolò Machiavelli, *Tutte le opere*, ed. Mario Martelli (Florence, 1971), 1195: "et ditegli che io mi dolgo solo che, havendo ricordato tanti poeti, che m'habbi lasciato indreto come un cazo." I have used, but modified, Allan Gilbert's translation in *The Letters of Machiavelli* (Chicago, 1961; reprint ed., 1988), 192.

l'altre miserie mie non vo' contalle,
poiché così si trattano e' poeti![11]

I have, Giuliano, a pair of snares on my leg,
with six lashes of rope on my back:
I won't recount my other miseries,
since this is how poets are treated!

Machiavelli does not say *who* mistreats poets in this way, but the second of the paired sonnets to Giuliano locates the source of the danger in poetry itself. The imprisoned Machiavelli begs the muses to intercede with Giuliano on his behalf with their sweet music and songs. One of them appears to the prisoner and asks, "Who are you that dare to call me?" He tells her his name, but she strikes his face and shuts his mouth, saying: "You're not Niccolò, but il Dazzo, since you've got your legs and heels bound, and you lie there chained like a madman." By the end of the poem Machiavelli is asking Giuliano to testify to the muse "that I am not il Dazzo, but myself."[12] The poet/prisoner is helpless, trapped between the power of his imagined patron and the cruelty of poetry. At first he wants poetry to secure Giuliano's favor, but the muse does not recognize him and even repudiates and rebukes him for the impertinence of claiming his own identity. She forces him to reverse the direction of his dependence and to beg Giuliano to persuade her that he really is who he says he is. Betrayed by his poetry, the poet cannot even be himself without a political patron. And the particular irony of the appeal to Giuliano is that Machiavelli was acknowledging his dependence on the very family that had, if not caused, at least acquiesced in his humiliation. Was he in effect telling Giuliano that he felt betrayed by him too?

The same cluster of worries—the fate of literary men, dependence on political power, and the subversion of identity—underlies the most famous of Machiavelli's letters to Francesco Vettori. The letter of December 10, 1513, long ago became a canonical text for the reading and interpretation of Machiavelli. Even casual readers who may not remember the letter's date or recipient nod in recognition when reminded of its major themes: the account of the "exiled" former secretary's "day" *in villa*, his evening colloquies with the ancients, and the

---

11. Machiavelli, *Tutte le opere*, ed. Martelli, 1003.
12. Machiavelli, *Tutte le opere*, ed. Martelli, 1003–4. Here too the translation, with slight modifications of my own, is from Allan Gilbert in *Machiavelli: The Chief Works and Others*, 3 vols. (Durham, N.C., 1965; reprint ed., 1989), 2:1014.

announcement of the composition of his little treatise on principalities.[13] Perhaps more than any other text, this letter has organized
the interpretation of Machiavelli around a powerful story of becoming:
the existential drama of separation from his daily bread of politics, and
the discovery, in the solitude of his study, of "that food, which alone is
mine, and for which I was born"; the descent of the frustrated exile to
the vulgarity of games, shouts, and quarrels in order to "give vent to
the malice of this fate of mine"; followed by his ascent to the sublime
world of the "ancient courts of ancient men," where he feels no boredom, forgets every trouble, fears neither poverty nor death, and "transfers" himself totally into his ghostly interlocutors. Here, too, is the
Machiavelli who so hungered for his lost world of politics that he
imagined that the little book on principalities might reopen the door by
winning him the favor of the Medici, "even if they should begin by
having me roll a stone"—the book that would prove, "if only it were
read, that I have neither slept nor played away the fifteen years that I
have been studying the art of the state." To read the letter solely along
such lines, as an autobiographical account of a process of self-definition
in which Machiavelli ceased to be the victim of Fortune's malice and
became instead the theorist and possessor of a "scienza" worthy of a
prince's grateful attention, is, I think, to see only one part of the complex structure of the text. Such readings are invariably constructed
around the letter's central image and metaphor of the threshold: the
moment in which Machiavelli leaves behind the vulgarity of the world
of experience in the wood, on the road, and at the inn and, entering his
study, stops at the threshold to rid himself of his grimy everyday
clothes ("et entro nel mio scrittoio; et in su l'uscio mi spoglio quella
veste cotidiana, piena di fango et di loto"). Once past the threshold,
now dressed in new and appropriate robes, he enters the "ancient
courts of ancient men" as a new man liberated from his fears and ready
to converse with the ancients; from those conversations came *The
Prince,* and from *The Prince* the hope of pleasing Giuliano.

A whole mythology has grown up around this threshold moment,
grounded in the assumption that here we have, in Machiavelli's own
representation of the central transformation of his life and self, the
triumph of the man of letters over the unreason of politics, the humanist's emergence from the prison of dependence and the malice of For-

---

13. Machiavelli, *Tutte le opere,* ed. Martelli, 1158–60. See also the collection of Machiavelli's letters edited by Franco Gaeta in *Opere di Niccolò Machiavelli,* vol. 3: *Lettere* (Turin,
1984); the letter of December 10, 1513, is on 423–28.

tune into the sublime of a perfect and fearless understanding.[14] But if it was Machiavelli's purpose in this letter to tell a story of liberating self-discovery in the realm of letters, the notion of such a purpose must be tested against the text's several allusions to the changing, losing, or unhinging of identity, and, in particular, in the light of a little-noticed literary allusion that raises this problem precisely with reference to newly self-remade "uomini litterati."

The theme of indeterminate identity emerges, first of all, from the specular, mimetic quality of Machiavelli's response to Francesco Vettori. After a three-month interruption in their correspondence, Vettori, then Florentine ambassador to the court of Leo X, had written on November 23 to dissuade Machiavelli from any further discussions of politics. He urged him instead to come to Rome and gave a description of his own existence there ("qual sia la vita mia in Roma"): a life of quiet pleasures, a few good friends, dull formalities at the court, and evenings spent reading the historians of ancient Rome.[15] Machiavelli declined the invitation; but, "wishing to return equal favors," he could do nothing more than "tell you in this letter of mine what my life is like," thus repeating exactly Vettori's phrase "qual sia la vita mia." Machiavelli then added that "se voi giudichate che sia a barattarla con la vostra, io sarò contento mutarla" (if you judge that it [his life] is to be swapped for yours, I'll be happy to exchange it). The impossible hypothetical that they might "mutare" their lives hovers over Machiavelli's celebrated account of his life at Sant'Andrea and produces two comparisons. The first underscores the radical divergence of their lives: Vettori's proximity to power and to the Medici in the capital of European diplomacy contrasted with Machiavelli's marginalized existence in the countryside, removed from all contact with politics; and, despite this, Vettori's rejection of political discourse as always too late and perhaps pointless, given the power of fortune, contrasted with Machiavelli's insistent pursuit of a discourse capable of mastering events and their reasons, "dove io non mi vergogno parlare con loro, et domandarli della ragione delle loro actioni; et quelli per loro humanità mi rispondono" (where I am not ashamed to speak with them and to ask them the reason of their actions; and they, out of their humanity, answer me). The second level of comparison establishes elaborately articulated parallels between the two men's lives, through which

---

14. See, for example, Giorgio Bárberi Squarotti, "Narrazione e sublimazione: le lettere del Machiavelli," in his *Machiavelli o la scelta della letteratura* (Rome, 1987), 63–95; originally published in *Lettere italiane* 21 (1969): 129–54. Also the comments of Nino Borsellino in *Machiavelli*, Letteratura italiana Laterza no. 17 (Bari, 1986), 60–61.

15. Machiavelli, *Tutte le opere*, ed. Martelli, 1157–58.

Machiavelli presents his own "day" as the opposite double of Vettori's. Giulio Ferroni has shown how carefully Machiavelli's day is modeled on Vettori's, how it replicates the succession of segments of time (from morning to evening) and of particular activities (conversation with friends, meals, reading, and writing).[16] Reflecting Vettori's day in reverse, Machiavelli's day is simultaneously the same and diametrically opposed.

Halfway through the letter, at the culmination of his evening colloquy with the ancients, Machiavelli introduces another moment of indeterminate identity. After four hours of a *conversatione* that is also a kind of conversion banishing all boredom, anguish, poverty, and fear of death, he is completely "transferred" into his interlocutors ("tucto mi transferisco in loro") and thus is no longer himself. But at the end of the letter, pleading with Vettori that there ought to be no doubt about his good faith "because, having always kept faith, I cannot now learn to break it," Machiavelli insists on the immutable quality of his nature: "he who has been faithful and good for 43 years, as I have, must not be able to change his nature [*non debbe potere mutare natura*]."

Machiavelli's strategic purpose with regard to Francesco Vettori in the letter of December 10, 1513, had everything to do with his as yet undetermined identity as a "uomo litterato." For that purpose was, above all, to persuade Vettori to accept and to look with favor on the book Machiavelli had just written. He knew that Vettori was aware that he was writing a book, and he also knew that Vettori was highly skeptical of it (or of what he could anticipate of it on the basis of Machiavelli's letters of the previous summer). Vettori doubted that any book would get Machiavelli very far in winning the attention of the pope or of Giuliano, and he had warned Machiavelli repeatedly that he had nothing like the influence in Rome that Machiavelli ascribed to him. So Machiavelli's most immediate problem was how to present his book to Vettori, who was still his only link to the Medici in Rome. And it was precisely in the context of this political purpose and problem that Machiavelli had to present and legitimate himself as a "uomo litterato." But if, as he was later to write in *The Discourses*, there are many kinds of "uomini litterati," each praised "according to his rank," of what kind was he?

Two passages of the letter address this implicit question. Immediately after the lyrical description of his colloquy with the ancients culminating with the almost mystical transference, Machiavelli, as if waking from the reverie, explains the writing of *The Prince:*

16. Giulio Ferroni, "Le 'cose vane' nelle *Lettere* di Machiavelli," *La rassegna della letteratura italiana* 76 (1972): 215–64, esp. 231–37.

E perché Dante dice che non fa scienza sanza lo ritenere lo havere inteso, io ho notato quello di che per la loro conversatione ho fatto capitale, et composto uno opusculo *De principatibus,* dove io mi profondo quanto io posso nelle cogitationi di questo subbietto, disputando che cosa è principato, di quale spetie sono, come e' si acquistono, come e' si mantengono, perché e' si perdono. Et se vi piacque mai alcuno mio ghiribizo, questo non vi doverrebbe dispiacere; et a un principe, et maxime a un principe nuovo, doverrebbe essere accetto; però io lo indrizzo alla Magnificenza di Giuliano.

And because Dante says that, without retaining it, what has been learned doesn't amount to knowledge, I have noted those things in their conversation of which I have made use and composed a little book *De principatibus,* where I immerse myself as deeply as I can in thoughts on this subject, arguing what a princedom is, of what kinds they are, how they are acquired, how they are preserved, why they are lost. And if any of my whimsies ever pleased you, this one should not displease you. And it ought to be welcome to a prince, especially to a new prince; thus I am addressing it to His Magnificence Giuliano.

Here the task of definition and legitimation is entrusted to authorities. Machiavelli can write—indeed must write–because he has learned from the ancient men something worthy of being written. In this fiction he is little more than the bearer of their knowledge, the scribe who takes it upon himself—but authorized, we might say, by Dante's advice—to write down what they told him. He has learned ("inteso") something from them that becomes "scienza" when it is retained, or remembered. The thoughts he transmits ("cogitationi di questo sub-bietto") exist apart from him and prior to his contact with them, but once his "conversatione" with the ancients—actually their answers to his questions—makes this knowledge available to him, it becomes something that he can make use of ("di che . . . ho fatto capitale") and in which he can "sink" himself ("dove io mi profondo quanto io pos-so"). It is ordered and coherent knowledge about the essence of prince-ly rule and the processes that govern its acquisition, preservation, and loss. For all these reasons, it ought to be welcome to Francesco Vettori and to any prince, especially a new prince like Giuliano.

In this representation of Machiavelli's role and activity as a "uomo litterato," it is significant that the guarantee of legitimacy is also a link to power. The recourse to the authority of the ancients and of Dante underpins claims to systematic and secure knowledge about the forms of political power that, in turn, have some claim on the favorable judgment of those who represent or exercise that power (the ambassador, the new prince and his family). The "uomo litterato" is thus an intermediary between powerful authorities, transferring the wisdom of one set of authorities to another. (No wonder, then, that it was apparently so easy to lose oneself in that transference.) Machiavelli was here reproducing the humanist cosmos of knowledge and letters as the wisdom of antiquity about power transmitted to the powerful, and of the literary man doubly legitimated by the source and by the recipient of his discourse. But even as the fiction of his conversation with the ancients recalled the old humanist confidence in the power of letters to know and change the world, Machiavelli was simultaneously underscoring the dangers that "uomini litterati" face in this role: marginality and isolation, precarious dependence on patrons and masters, and the merging—or even loss—of self in the commanding voices of those ancient authorities. The dilemma of the "uomo litterato" was that his standing in relation to his contemporary political master depended on his success in reviving and representing the voices of his ancient masters: he existed in making them speak; but in becoming their voice he muted his own.

The second passage that alludes to these questions has not received the attention it deserves. At the beginning of the letter's second paragraph, just before Machiavelli begins the account of his day, he tells Vettori that he is staying at his country home and that he has not spent more than twenty days in the city since his imprisonment and torture earlier that year. He then describes the activity that he says kept him busy during the month of September (or, in some readings, November):

> Ho infino a qui uccellato a' tordi di mia mano. Levavomi innanzi dì, impaniavo, andavone oltre con un fascio di gabbie addosso, che parevo el Geta quando e' tornava dal porto con e libri d'Amphitrione; pigliavo el meno dua, el più sei tordi. Et così stetti tutto settembre; dipoi questo badalucco, ancora che dispettoso et strano, è mancato con mio dispiacere; et qual la vita mia vi dirò.

> Until now I have been snaring thrushes with my own hands. I used to get up before dawn, set the lime, and go out with a bundle of cages on me, so that I seemed like Geta when he returned from the port with the books of Amphitryon; I would catch at least two and at the most six thrushes. And this is how I

was occupied all of September; later this pastime, however spiteful and strange, ended, to my displeasure; and what my life is like I shall tell you.

Evidently, Machiavelli assumed that Vettori knew who Geta was. The various editors of Machiavelli's letters tell us that he was referring in this passage to the principal character of a fifteenth-century Tuscan verse novella, *Geta e Birria,* an adaptation of uncertain authorship of a twelfth-century Latin comedy, the *Geta* of Vitale de Blois, which was itself based on Plautus's *Amphitruo.* But they do not explain or even approach the problem of what the figure of Geta meant to Machiavelli, and how and why Geta carrying Amphitryon's books had anything to do, in Machiavelli's reading of the Geta story, with the snaring of thrushes. A closer look at the fifteenth-century text and the traditions that surrounded it can, I think, shed new light on Machiavelli's notion of himself as a "uomo litterato" in the letter of December 10, 1513.

Geta e Birria emerged from those popular literary currents of fourteenth- and early fifteenth-century Tuscany that delighted in taking satiric aim at the pretensions of learned and humanist culture.[17] Now thought to be the work of Ghigo d'Attaviano Brunelleschi and Domenico da Prato, and probably written some time between 1400 and the 1420s,[18] *Geta e Birria* enjoyed considerable popularity in Machiavelli's lifetime; there were at least four printed editions between 1476 and 1516.[19] As the story opens, the wealthy Amphitryon announces to his wife, Almena, that he intends to go to Athens and to remain there until he has "learned philosophy thoroughly" (5). He comforts Almena and asks for her patience and support, telling her that his "going away is honorable, for from it I shall acquire wisdom, which, as you know, surpasses every other thing" (9). Amphitryon takes Geta, one of his two servants, with him to Athens, leaving the other, Birria, at home with Almena. Geta is deformed, ugly, full of vices, sexually potent, and given to excesses of lust ("come porco era vinto di lussuria" [12–13]). But he is also loyal to and full of love for his master, "and this is why

17. On these literary and cultural trends, see Domenico Guerri, *La corrente popolare nel Rinascimento* (Florence, 1931); Antonio Lanza, *Polemiche e berte letterarie nella Firenze del primo Quattrocento,* 2d ed. (Rome, 1989); Achille Tartaro, *Il primo Quattrocento toscano,* Letteratura italiana Laterza no. 11 (Bari, 1981); and Marina Marietti, Danielle Boillet, José Guidi, and André Rochon, *Formes et significations de la "beffa" dans la littérature italienne de la Renaissance* (Paris, 1975).

18. See Gioachino Chiarini's introduction to his anthology, *Novelle italiane: Il Quattrocento* (Milan, 1982), xi–xiv. The edition of *Geta e Birria* used here is on 31–85; it will be cited by octave.

19. Joachim Rolland, *Les origines latines du théâtre comique en France (essai bibliographique)* (Geneva, 1972), 95–96.

Amphitryon tolerated his vices and his deformed condition" (15). Birria, by contrast, is lazy, slow, "the father of sleep, and keeper of the kitchen" (16), and he is delighted to learn that not he but Geta will shoulder the burden of Amphitryon's ambition. "Oh Fortune, sweet friend," he exclaims, "I now need undergo even less exertion" (19).

After seven years in Athens, where, "seeking true reason, he suffered much hardship in studying . . . and soon became a good philosopher," Amphitryon decides to return home and orders Geta to prepare their departure (31–32). But at this very moment Jupiter, infatuated with Almena's beauty, seizes the opportunity of the announced homecoming to assume the human form of Amphitryon and orders his son Archas (Mercury) to assume the form of Geta. Just as Amphitryon and Geta arrive at the port and Almena sends Birria to meet them, Jupiter and Archas appear at Almena's door. While Archas guards the house, letting no one enter, Jupiter receives the passionate welcome that the innocent Almena believes she is giving her husband (41–59).

Amphitryon sends Geta home from the port with some of his books—a "light load" ("piccol peso"), he assures him (69–72). As Birria and Geta approach one another on the road, Geta sees Birria but pretends not to; Birria, seeing Geta and wanting above all to avoid any part in the hauling of the books, hides in a cave off the road, hoping that Geta will pass by (72–74). This is the precise moment in the story that Machiavelli recalls in the letter to Vettori, and the first and most obvious connection to be made is that just as Geta attempts to persuade the reluctant Birria to take some of Amphitryon's books, so, too, did Machiavelli, as we know, want Vettori to accept his book. The subsequent "dialogue" between Geta (who knows that Birria knows what he wants of him) and Birria (who goes into hiding in order to avoid acknowledging what he knows Geta will ask) thus comically parallels the dilemma that Machiavelli faced concerning Vettori. Geta approaches Birria's cave, still pretending that he has not seen him, and wonders aloud how long he must go on living in such torment while Birria stays at home eating and sleeping. "I am worn down by this suffering; it is now seven years that I have had no rest." "Why doesn't Birria come to help me?" (75–77). He laments the hardships and deprivation he underwent in Greece (78); his master gave him no bread but instead "fed" ("pasceva") him something else whose taste was then bitter but that now makes him happy because of what he acquired through it: "ch'el nome mio per lo mondo fie sparto; / sommo loico son, onde si prova / che l'asino sia uom mostro per prova" (for my name will now spread throughout the world; I am a master of logic, by which it is proved, as I show with proof, that an ass is a man [79]). Geta continues: "So I will do with every animal, showing with syllogisms how they change form and name, each different from its original being [*mutar forma e nome, / ciascun del suo prim'esser diseguale*], and similarly with colors, with plants, and with fruits. And because he is lazy and worth little, I want Birria to become an ass so that I can load his back [with Amphitryon's books]" (80).

Already striking is the number of themes in Machiavelli's letter to Vettori that echo the details of Geta's lament. Like Geta, Machiavelli claims that he suffered hardships, and particularly poverty, in the process of gaining valuable knowledge during many (in his case, fifteen) years of study. Like Geta, he contrasts the meager fare of his actual meals—"Mi mangio di quelli cibi che questa povera villa et paululo patrimonio comporta" (I eat such foods as this poor farm and tiny patrimony allow)—with the metaphorical food of the wisdom of the ancients—"Mi pasco [precisely the verb Geta uses] di quel cibo che solum è mio, et che io nacqui per lui" (I feed on that food which alone is mine, and for which I was born). And just as Geta complains that while he has been suffering and learning Birria has been eating and sleeping, Machiavelli, making this comparison rather more obliquely, tells Vettori that he is happy to learn "with what order and tranquillity" ("quanto ordinatamente et quietamente") he was carrying out his duties in Rome and that the day would surely come when, with Fortune in a different mood, the ambassador would do well to "undergo greater exertion and keep a closer watch on things" ("durare più fatica, veghiare più le cose"); at any rate, he—Machiavelli—had certainly "not slept or played away" ("né dormiti né giuocati") the fifteen years that he had been studying the art of politics. Again, as with Geta, his "study" had given him no rest.

Then there are Geta's claims of having a sublime knowledge of the essences, forms, and names of things. Birria, still hiding in the cave and listening to these escalating pretensions to wisdom and philosophical certitude that he knows are designed to influence and persuade him to carry the books, remains skeptical and even contemptuous of Geta's silly and pompous pronouncements. For the moment, he mutters his objections to himself. When he hears Geta's plan to turn him into an ass, he grumbles: "But you won't take from me what nature gave me. I'll certainly answer directly what you plan to tell me, Geta, with your sophisms and false proofs: I am truly a man, as Jupiter likes me to be" (80–81). But Geta's rhetoric, instead of influencing Birria, is encouraging Geta himself to make even more exaggerated claims: "I' son esperto / di più cose sottili, e vie più nuove. / Apparato che s'è quel ch'una volta, / non può la scienza sua esser mai tolta" (I am an expert in many subtle things and in newer ways. Once one has learned something, that knowledge can never be taken away [81]). Machiavelli too, as we have already noted, refers to what he learned from the ancients as "scienza."

But Geta and Birria begin to misunderstand each other as Geta evidently now hears what Birria is saying. Birria protests that things will perhaps change in strange ways but that one cannot leave the world altogether—did Geta say that one could?—and that he, Birria, will always be Birria. Geta objects that Birria has forgotten that all things are mortal, including Socrates and Plato, and as he launches into claims that he has learned so much that his fame will live forever, Birria cuts him off, saying that Geta is the one who has apparently lost his memory, since he now insists that all things must die whereas he had just proved that nothing comes to an end (82–83). Frustrated over his inability to flush Birria out with words, Geta adopts a different tactic. Pretending to hear the noise of a rabbit from the cave and imagining out loud the meal it could provide the family, Geta picks up a stone and hurls it with all his might down into the cave, where it bounces around and comes rolling to a stop near Birria (84–87). Now frightened and fearing for his life, Birria yells to Geta: "Don't throw [any more stones]; I'm Birria, and I want to live by your mercy." Geta pretends not to believe that the voice he hears belongs to Birria until the latter emerges from the cave. He scolds Birria for hiding in a place where someone could easily have killed him. But Birria answers: "Where do you get the audacity, Geta, to stone whoever happens to be hiding? Your arrogance seems to me far too great." Their encounter ends when Geta orders Birria, not in fact to carry the books he had brought this far but to continue on to the port where an even heavier load awaits (87–91). Birria does so as slowly as possible and Geta proceeds home, now tingling in anticipation of the hero's welcome he will receive (93). "Almena and her son, and then the whole household, will give me a great welcome; and when the neighbors clearly understand how much knowledge sharpens my mind, they will all call me Master Geta [*quando chiar sapranno / quanta scienzia mia mente assottiglia, / Maestro Geta tutti chiameranno*]" (94).

It must have amused Machiavelli and Vettori to recall that Geta's new and revolutionary *scienza* took shape in Geta's mind, indeed in his imagination, in the course of the bumbling and ineffectual "dialogue" between a man in a cave and another outside. Apart from the parody of Plato, however, Machiavelli and Vettori both knew that *The Prince* was similarly born in the epistolary dialogue with Vettori during the spring and summer of 1513—a dialogue in which Machiavelli, needing Vettori's patronage and support, tried to persuade him to accept a whole series of bold ideas and conclusions, to which Vettori consistently expressed objections, qualifications, and outright skepticism. Trying to persuade Birria, Geta finally persuades himself and falls into the delusion that he is now a master of logic, the bearer of a new *scienza,* and soon to be an honored hero in the world to which he is happily returning after so many years in exile. Machiavelli too expected great things from his new *scienza:* a return to the world of politics, the grateful embrace of the Medici, and the support and agreement of Francesco Vettori. Just as the slave Geta daydreams about being called "Maestro Geta," so the ex-secretary Machiavelli thirsted for recognition of his new science by princes and ambassadors. For both, the new *scienza* held the promise of elevating former servants to a place of honor; of ending old relationships of subservience, dependence, and patronage; and of replacing them with new ones based on the equality and nobility of liberated "uomini litterati."

Of course, the joke is on Geta, and the episode in which he throws the stone into Birria's cave in frustration already alerts us that, although he may sound convincing to himself, he certainly is not fooling Birria and will not persuade those back home either. Could Machiavelli have written the celebrated line about wishing that the Medici would begin to make use of him, "even if they should have to begin by having me roll a stone [*voltolare un sasso*]," without thinking of Geta's stone throwing? Ezio Raimondi has illuminated the literary subtexts from Ovid, Terence, and Lucretius of Machiavelli's allusion in this passage to the myth of Sisyphus: the futility of politics, and yet the determination to persevere in the face of frustration.[20] In his own comical way, Geta belongs to the tradition; his rhetoric and his new science fail to move Birria, so he tries with stones. It is a moment of admission, even of confession, that despite all his self-assured claims to possessing a sublime knowledge, he really craves believers and has no choice but to begin with his skeptical fellow slave. Is the Machiavelli of the "voltolare un sasso" passage so very different? Is he not similarly acknowledging that he wants the attention of the Medici one way or another, even if those profound "cogitationi di questo subbietto" should fail to impress them?

But Geta is not finished with stones. An even more frustrating dialogue lies just ahead. In a sense it is only poetic justice: Geta has declared himself a master of the science of metamorphosis in order to trick Birria; and in the end he only tricks himself into believing that he, the former slave, really is a "maestro" of logic. But the gods, the true masters of metamorphosis, lie in wait to deceive and confuse Geta

20. "Il sasso del politico," in Ezio Raimondi, *Politica e commedia dal Beroaldo al Machiavelli* (Bologna, 1972), 165–72.

who, having arrived at his master's house, loudly proclaims that Geta is home and just as loudly wonders who it is that refuses to open the door and let him in. Frustrated, he picks up a stone and starts pounding the door (97–99). From inside, Archas speaks, with Geta's voice, claiming that he is Geta and that he is guarding the door to allow Amphitryon and Almena an undisturbed reunion: "But what fantasy [*fantasia*]," he asks, "sends you here to say that *you* are Geta?" (101). Geta's first, stupefied reaction is to exclaim that "this is the greatest miracle there ever was—that someone other than myself appears from his voice to be my spirit. Who can speak with the voice of Geta except Geta himself? How can this be?" Geta then has recourse to his logic: "I do know, however, that logic does not prevent two people from speaking with a similar voice. And it's also common enough for two people to have the same name" (102–3). But Geta still insists that *he* is Geta and wants the door opened. Geta's confusion deepens when Archas / Geta tells him the whole story of the encounter with Birria. Geta wonders how the mysterious stranger / self could have known all that (105–7). "However that may be, there's no one alive, except Geta, who speaks as I do. So have we become two who were one?" (108). But then he reminds himself of the basic principle of identity: "What's one is one; but"—now contradicting the principle—"I who speak am not one" (109). Geta wonders if he might be dead, and if so who killed him, when he suddenly gets the brilliant idea that this voice he hears must be that of the nymph Echo. Now, he predicts triumphantly, he can solve this tormenting problem by asking whoever it is whether he (or she) resembles Geta in ways other than the voice. "I'll find out if he is Geta in his acts and habits, or if he's only making fun of me; it's too awful to think that I might consume myself with doubt about being two, or none at all" (110–11). When Archas refuses even to let Geta see him, Geta loses his temper, tries to break the door down, threatens mayhem, and calls out to Almena (112–17). But when Archas threatens him in return, Geta, "more cowardly than a woman," backs off and asks only that his still hidden interlocutor describe himself (118–20). Archas gives such a perfect description of himself as Geta (121–23), and such an accurate account of Geta's adventures in Greece (124–33), that Geta finally surrenders: "Don't say any more: you are Geta, I am nothing. . . . You be me; I give myself to you, since nothing of me remains with me" (134). The stories that Archas tells about "his" time in Greece—stories that he presents as proof that he is Geta, and that Geta accepts as convincing evidence that he is no longer Geta—are, curiously, all about Geta's treachery and dishonesty with regard to Amphitryon. In the novella Geta had earlier been introduced as "loyal and full of love for his master." But now Archas recounts that Geta regularly stole money from Amphitryon, that he used the money to lavish favors on the women he seduced, and that, when Amphitryon asked why money was missing, Geta repeatedly lied, insisting that he had not stolen and could never do so, and asked indignantly how Amphitryon could think that Geta, or any man who believed in God, would swear by the Almighty and then break his promises (133). Geta, listening to Archas's story, acknowledges its accuracy and, precisely because he knows it is all true, concludes that whoever is speaking must be Geta, and that he is now "nulla." The truth about himself, spoken by another voice and in open contradiction of what the story first told us about Geta, finally provides Geta with the certainty that his essence has been denied him ("la essenzia mi si vieta") and transferred to the one speaking his truth (135). Addressing himself, he tries to assess his predicament logically:

> What will you do, Geta, seeing that you're alive and that Geta isn't with you? Has moral philosophy perhaps converted you into Plato or some other Greek? I'm a man and no other animal, and, if my understanding isn't blind, being a man I would be Geta, as I usually am; but then I'm nothing; and so I grieve. (136)

> If we have become two from one, the part should be less than the whole; I don't seem to be missing anything anywhere, and what's inside is all there, too. So how is it that, neither with two nor with one, am I able to straighten out the meaning of this? But nonetheless I'm still Geta; if this other part of me is outside, what do I conclude now? (137)

Geta wonders if the answer might be that his soul has left him and entered another; but how, comes his own rejoinder, could he be alive without "a spirit that understands, learns and remembers, hopes and fears, and expresses itself in actions or words?" (138). Geta is now in a labyrinth of hopeless nonsense and revolving contradiction in which he both is and is not. Finally, he blames logic for depriving him of his identity:

> Logic! May he be cursed who first told me that you were the flower of all learning; I thought it of great value to learn you, and to praise you I filled a thousand pages: Now you have so used your deceitful file [*lima*] that my name and my being take leave of me; where once I thought it useful to know you, now you harm me and oppress me as much as you can. (140)

Geta promises never again to speak of logic or its syllogisms, for its actions deceive, its proofs are false, and logicians will all meet the same unhappy fate (141–42). With these melancholy thoughts, he heads back down the road toward the port, presumably still carrying Amphitryon's books, when suddenly he sees Amphitryon coming in the opposite direction and wonders—again blaming logic—whether Amphitryon "is, or is not." But then he has a flash of hope: if Amphitryon greets him and calls him Geta, perhaps Geta will still be Geta after all (143–44). And so it happens (149–52), but not without more ridicule from Birria aimed at those who "go seeking new ways to learn wisdom in the lands of the Greeks" (156–57). When Geta tells Amphitryon that he found Geta guarding the door, and that this Geta told him that Amphitryon was in the bedroom with Almena (154–55), Amphitryon angrily denounces Geta's stupidity in words that begin to establish some link between birds and books and thus to make some sense of Machiavelli's comparison of himself going out to snare thrushes with Geta returning from the port with Amphitryon's books: "Un uccel sanza penne / ti fe' natura; in qual libro si trova / ch'un altro in te, o tu in altro ti muti?" (Nature made you a bird without feathers; in what book do you find that someone else can become you, or you someone else? [159]).

At one level, then, Geta was, for Machiavelli, the stock character of anti-humanist polemics, the silly pseudointellectual and pretentious self-styled man of letters who makes big claims to having unlocked the wisdom of the ancients and the secrets of philosophy, but who in reality is a fool, and a victim of his own foolishness, and in the end actually understands little or nothing of the books that he carries around. But why would Machiavelli compare himself to such a character? In part, he may have reflected on his own unhappy fate in 1513 in much the same terms with which *Geta e Birria* sums up the lesson of Geta's misadventures: "chi più sa, men vede / gl'inganni, quando più veder gli crede" (he who knows more sees the deceptions less when most he thinks he sees them [182]). But Geta may have meant other things as well to Machiavelli. Like Machiavelli, Geta is a servant who worked at another's bidding, got himself into trouble in the course of performing that service, and found himself, at least for a time, transformed by what he learned in the process. Geta, as both slave and self-made man of learning, embodies the double meaning of the Latin *litteratus* that may also be present in Machiavelli's "uomini litterati." A *litteratus* was, in one sense, a learned or liberally educated person, but could also be someone or something lettered in the sense of being marked with letters and thus branded, as, for example (and it appears in Plautus),[21] a *servus litteratus,* or branded slave. Geta, already a slave, is further marked by the letters—the learning, books, and philosophy—he encountered in Greece; they entrapped him, deceived him, and made him lose himself. The figure of Geta thus allows Machiavelli to ponder, and to tell Francesco Vettori that he is pondering, the multiple entrapments that so often snare "uomini litterati": beholden to patrons and political masters, deceived by their learning and books, victims of their own ambitions and naive pretensions, learned men, including poets, inevitably get themselves into trouble and meet unhappy fates. Machiavelli compares his own going out to snare birds with Geta's attempt to snare Birria through claims of possessing a new science as a way of referring to his own attempts during the summer of 1513 to snare Vettori, to convince him of the power of his new science, and to enlist his cooperation in the effort to carry it home in triumph. They both knew, of course, that Geta failed to persuade Birria; hence, the comparison to Geta is also Machiavelli's acknowledgement of his failure to persuade Vettori. It was in a sense, therefore, Machiavelli's confession of some worry that his fate might approximate Geta's. In having concocted the new "science" of *The Prince,* and in wanting too desperately to come home—with or without Vettori's help—as the hero of so great a conquest, would he, like Geta, find himself snared, deceived, alienated from himself, and more like the caged thrushes who sing for others than like their trapper?

The possibility that Machiavelli's description of himself snaring thrushes was meant to suggest, by way of the comparison to Geta, the risk of his own entrapment seems even more likely when we turn to the version of the Aesopic fable of "The Fowler and the Snake" that he was no doubt remembering as he wrote these lines. Given Machiavelli's fascination with animals and their allegorical potential,[22] Aesop would have been a favorite text of his in any case and at all times; but it seems quite likely that in, or before, the second half of 1513 Machiavelli was reading Ermolao Barbaro's fifteenth-century translation of the fables. The little allegory of the fox and the lion with which he began his letter to Vettori of August 26 of that year is taken directly from it.[23] A few pages further on in Barbaro's text he would have encountered the fable in which a fowler uses limed twigs to catch thrushes—precisely what Machiavelli describes himself doing. In his eagerness to snare a

---

21. *Casina,* act 2, sc. 6, line 401 in the Loeb Plautus, trans. Paul Nixon (Cambridge, Mass., 1965), 2:44–45. On slave characters in Plautus, see Erich Segal, *Roman Laughter: The Comedy of Plautus,* 2d ed. (New York, 1987), chaps. 4 and 5.

22. See Gian Mario Anselmi and Paolo Fazion, *Machiavelli, l'Asino e le bestie* (Bologna, 1984); and Ezio Raimondi, "Il politico e il centauro," in *Politica e commedia,* 265–86.

23. Machiavelli, *Tutte le opere,* ed. Martelli, 1154–55.

bird, the fowler fails to realize that he is stepping on a snake, which, angered, gives him a deadly bite. As the fowler is dying, he says: "Unhappy man that I am. I was trying to catch one thing with the wiles of hunting when I was myself deceived and caught by another."[24] Although Machiavelli does not make the connection explicitly, the figure of Geta alludes to the ironic outcome of the fowler's outing and fixes the allegorical transfer in the entrapment of self-styled men of learning. Like the fowler, Machiavelli might get himself trapped and, like Geta, he might do so with books. In the Aesopic fable, as he knew it from Barbaro, there is no mention of cages. That is a detail that Machiavelli added, perhaps because he actually used them but also because they make it possible to visualize the comparison between Geta the philosopher burdened by Amphitryon's books and Machiavelli the fowler carrying his bulky cages.

Another text whose echoes may be present in Machiavelli's letter is *Inferno*, canto 13, the canto of Pier della Vigna, Dante's version of the story of another poet, chancellor, and servant of the powerful who gave loyal service to his master and who also catastrophically lost that favor. Pier was punished with blindness and took his own life while in prison, for which Dante condemns him to the eternal punishment of the loss of his human form and the imprisonment of his soul in the form of a tree. Dante has Pier say of himself that he "held both the keys of [the Emperor] Frederick's heart," that he was the jealous keeper of his master's secrets ("dal secreto suo quasi ogn'uom tolsi"), and that he "bore loyalty to the glorious office [*fede portai al glorioso offizio*]," so much so that he "lost both sleep and the pulsing [of his blood]"—life itself. A bit later he insists again, despite all the accusations to the contrary, that "I never broke faith with my lord" ("già mai non ruppi fede / al mio segnor"). Machiavelli similarly protests to Vettori, and with a similar repetitive insistence, that "of my faith [*fede*] there should be no doubt, because, having always kept faith, I cannot now learn to break it; and he who has been faithful [*fedele*] and good for 43 years, as I have, must not be able to change his nature; and of my faith and goodness, my poverty is testimony." Machiavelli too underscores the quality and intensity of that service by claiming that he did not sleep away the years he dedicated to it.

Pier's tragic story has certain elements in common with Geta's comic fate; the most important is that both of these loyal servants and "let-

---

24. *Hermolai Barbari et Gregorii Corrarii Fabulae Aesopicae,* ed. Joseph R. Berrigan (Lawrence, Kans., 1977), 56–57: "Infelix ego, alium enim venationum astutiis depraehendere volens, ipse ego ab altero usque ad mortem aucupio deceptus sum." The tale of the fox and the lion is on 16–17.

tered men" made the mistake of overestimating their cleverness. They arrogantly assumed that their intelligence and conspicuous devotion to their masters would be rewarded with honor, privilege, and acclaim. Believing themselves to be cleverer than those they served, they indulged the fantasy of being able to manipulate them, of playing the fox to their masters' lion. Each reached too far: Geta imagined himself as the soon-to-be-celebrated master of logic who would receive a homecoming hero's welcome and then got testy with a stranger he failed to recognize for the god he was; Pier della Vigna, boasting of the skill with which he locked and unlocked Frederick's heart and fancying himself the keeper of his master's secrets, made his own pretensions and proximity to power too visible, thus provoking the envy that caused his downfall. Geta and Pier both forgot that "uomini litterati" who take political masters are and must remain slaves. Each imagined himself what he was not and could not be, and each was punished with a humbling and painful loss of self. The Pier della Vigna of *Inferno*, canto 13, is, as Virgil calls him, a "spirito incarcerato," a soul trapped in a tree in a "mesta selva" where "foul Harpies"—half bird and half human—make their nests and cause the trees pain by feeding on their leaves. Machiavelli's "day" in exile also begins in a grove and, as we have seen, has much to do with birds, entrapment, and loss of self. Did Machiavelli intend any allusion to the episode of Pier della Vigna? It may have been a far too painful version of the story he shared with Pier and with Geta for him to be able to acknowledge it in any direct way. But Dante, who also knew about the grim fate of "uomini litterati," was certainly much on Machiavelli's mind in the letter to Vettori, being mentioned twice. And in a letter that continually underscores the perilous vulnerability of "uomini litterati" who protest in anguish that they were, after all, faithful to their masters, the very mention of Dante's name may suffice to evoke the terrible story of Pier della Vigna.

All this literary entanglement—the mixing and filling of his own text with other texts, half acknowledged and half hidden and interwoven with each other, an intertextual commingling that leaves neither Aesop's fowler nor Geta nor the faithful, pleading ex-secretary nor the fowler / writer Machiavelli with an identity free of association with the others—becomes a parodic sub-version of the solemn story of discovery, redemption, and legitimation that, on first reading, the letter of December 10, 1513, wants to be. It subverts and even mocks conventional notions of control of the text, of the identity and secure possession of voice, and thus of the power to influence, in which letters had grounded their claim to partnership with politics. This complex of images and texts, once linked back to the parts of their stories that the letter does not explicitly refer to, releases the subtext of Machiavelli's fear of entrapment and loss of self in books, those of others and his own—as if (and this may be the heart of the matter) one could ever really make such a distinction. Later in the letter, as if to emphasize the purposeful nature of that first juxtaposition of birds, books, cages, and the fates of literary men around the figure of Geta, Machiavelli recreates the mix when he describes himself sitting in his aviary, presumably with the birds he had trapped, reading his poets (Dante, Petrarch, Tibullus, and Ovid) and remembering both their amorous passions and his own. One wonders to what extent Machiavelli was consciously invoking the two puns that link the name Geta to birds. The more obvious of the two is the mutual echoing of Geta and the "geti" with which, Machiavelli says (in the sonnet to Giuliano), his legs were shackled in prison. *Geti,* or jesses, are the straps, usually of leather, fastened to the feet of hawks or other birds of prey in order to control their movements; the term thus refers to birds, once hunters themselves, reduced to imprisonment and servitude. A second link between Geta and birds (and of both to the theme of metamorphosis) is the poetic usage of *geticus* (a proper adjective meaning Thracian) for the kind of swallow or nightingale (a thrush known for its nocturnal song) into which the gods transformed Procne, the Athenian wife of the Thracian prince Tereus, after the horrible revenge she inflicted on her husband for the rape of her sister Philomela; thus the "geticae volucres" that Statius compares in the *Thebaid* (12, 478) to suppliant and mournful women.[25] After all, Amphitryon did call Geta "un uccel sanza penne."

Geta very likely intrigued Machiavelli for still another reason: the textual migrations and transformations of name and character. The fifteenth-century *Geta e Birria* declares, in a sense quite plausibly, that Plautus "was the first inventor of this comedy" (182). And in another place the text claims to transmit the story "literally as Plautus sets it

25. In the *Aeneid*, bk. 3, lines 22–48, the "Getic fields" ruled over by "father Gradivus" (Mars) are similarly a place of broken faith, betrayal, and eternal entrapment in alien forms. Polydorus, the Trojan emissary treacherously murdered by the king of Thrace, is buried here, as Aeneas discovers when, to his horror and amazement, blood runs from the broken shafts of bushes growing on the burial mound. Aeneas and his band of exiles quickly decide that this is no place for them. It is, of course, this episode that Dante recreates in the canto of Pier della Vigna, which links betrayal (indeed, self-betrayal) and punitive metamorphosis as the paired fates of politically subservient men of letters and does so, as already suggested, in ways that offer certain parallels to the stories of Geta and Machiavelli. On the theme of metamorphosis from antiquity to the Renaissance, see Leonard Barkan, *The Gods Made Flesh: Metamorphosis and the Pursuit of Paganism* (New Haven, Conn., 1986). Barkan does not discuss Machiavelli, but see his important chapter on Dante with its reading of the Pier della Vigna episode, 137–70.

down" ("litteralmente come Plauto pone") (173). But Machiavelli certainly knew Plautus and must have realized that there is no Geta in the *Amphitruo;* the character is there (he is called Sosia), but not the name Geta. Machiavelli no doubt also noticed that in the *Amphitruo* Amphitryon is a general returning from a victorious war, not the amateur scholar who goes to Athens to study philosophy. Otherwise Plautus's story is recognizably similar: Jupiter's assumption of the human form of Amphitryon, Mercury's of that of Sosia, the innocent adultery of Alcumena, the confusion of identities, and a happy (if somewhat more dramatic) resolution. Machiavelli, of course, knew Terence even better than he did Plautus and hardly needed to be reminded, when reading *Geta e Birria,* that Geta is a character in Terence's *Phormio* and *Adelphoe* and is in both plays a slave. (Birria appears in *Andria,* the play that Machiavelli translated some years later.) Terence's Geta, unlike Plautus's bumbling and belligerent Sosia, is clever and witty. Trapped between the conflicting wishes of his master and the latter's son, the Geta of *Phormio* shows prudence, adaptability, and resourcefulness. He is loyal to his master, but this very "faithfulness to the old man," as he himself remarks, "cost me my shoulderblades." It is this same Geta who, signing on to Phormio's audacious plan and pretending not to worry about the consequences for himself, speaks a line that became famous and that must have particularly appealed to Machiavelli. When asked, "What will become of you?" Geta responds with mock heroism, "By Hercules, I don't know. The one thing I do know is this: Forever forebearant will I bear whatever Fortune bears [*fors feret feremus aequo animo*]."[26] Was Machiavelli echoing this Geta when he told Vettori that he would give vent to the malignity of his fate, "being content to let her drive me along this road"?

The character of Sosia and the name of Geta came together in the twelfth-century *Geta* of Vitale de Blois, who borrowed and abbreviated the plot of the Plautine *Amphitruo* and introduced into it the names of Terence's two slaves.[27] It was Vitale who transformed Amphitryon into a scholar, made books and learning a central theme of the story, turned Sosia into Geta and made him the principal character. In Vitale's little

26. *Phormio,* act 1, lines 76 and 137–38, in the Loeb Terence, trans. John Sargeaunt (Cambridge, Mass., 1979), 2:14–15, 18–19. The translation of Geta's line on Fortune is from Douglass Parker's version of the play in *The Complete Comedies of Terence,* ed. Palmer Bovie (New Brunswick, N.J., 1974), 243.

27. Text in *Three Latin Comedies,* ed. Keith Bate (Toronto, 1976), 15–34. Another good edition of *Geta,* with a French translation by Étienne Guilhou, is included in *La "Comédie" latine en France au xiie siècle,* with an introduction by Gustave Cohen, 2 vols. (Paris, 1931), 1:3–57. There is an older edition by Anatole de Montaiglon in the *Bibliothèque de l'école des chartes,* series 2, vol. 4 (1847–48): 474–505.

comedy (of just over 500 lines), Geta's two dialogues with Birria and Archas dominate the action. Chances are good that Machiavelli was aware of Vitale's part in Geta's textual migrations: over a hundred manuscripts of the *Geta* survive, and two of them, generally attributed to Boccaccio, are in the Laurentian Library in Florence.[28] Fifteenth-century interest in Vitale's *Geta* may have been stimulated by the rediscovery in the 1420s by Nicholas Cusanus of the dozen lost plays of Plautus, among them the *Amphitruo*. They became favorite texts of the humanists (so much so that Vespasiano da Bisticci mistakenly attributed Nicholas's find to Poggio Bracciolini).[29] In the 1480s Ermolao Barbaro filled in the missing 300 or so lines of the *Amphitruo*, and—just to bring us full circle—in 1487 Pandolfo Collenuccio did an Italian translation that was performed at Ferrara in that year and again in 1491.[30] In the meantime, of course, Vitale's *Geta* had inspired the Tuscan *Geta e Birria*, which, as already noted, went through at least four printed editions between 1476 and 1516.

With all this contemporary attention to Plautus, and given his own predilection for Terence,[31] his evident familiarity with *Geta e Birria*, and, I would guess, with Vitale's *Geta* as well, it seems quite certain that Machiavelli knew the "history" of Geta's literary transformations, of the ways he changed "form and name"—forced to do so (he was, after all, a slave) by texts that confused, decomposed and reconstructed his identity and thus made a mockery of any "science" of form, name, and identity. Geta's fate in the Tuscan *Geta e Birria* thus recapitulates and replays the dilemma of Sosia/Geta from Plautus to Terence to Vitale to Ghigo Brunelleschi and Domenico da Prato: how could any identity or unity, whether of a speaking subject or of a text, survive the inevitable encounters with other voices and texts? Terence called the deliberate mixing of elements from different comedies *contaminatio* and defended it, in the prologue to *Andria*, against those critics who "argue that plays should not be mixed together [*disputant contaminari non decere fabulas*]."[32] Vitale de Blois had done something similar in combining the plot of *Amphitruo* with characters (or names) from Terence.

28. Bate, *Three Latin Comedies*, 3; Rolland, *Les origines latines*, 77–97, and, for the Boccaccio manuscripts, 80–83.

29. Vespasiano da Bisticci, *Le vite*, ed. Aulo Greco (Florence, 1970), 1:543–44 n. 10.

30. Charles E. Passage and James H. Mantinband, eds. and trans., *Amphitryon: The Legend and Three Plays* (Chapel Hill, N.C., 1974), 113–15. The *Anfitrione, commedia di Plauto voltata in terza rima da Pandolfo Collenuccio* is published in *Biblioteca rara*, vol. 55 (Milan, 1864), 31–161.

31. Sergio Bertelli and Franco Gaeta, "Noterelle machiavelliane: un codice di Lucrezio e di Terenzio," *Rivista storica italiana* 73 (1961): 544–57.

32. See the foreword by Palmer Bovie to *The Complete Comedies of Terence*, xiv–xvii.

The fictional Geta can be said to exemplify, in his own "personal" and literary history, the process of literary *contaminatio*. Ghigo Brunelleschi and Domenico de Prato had transformed Vitale's *Geta* just as Vitale had mixed Terence and Plautus and Terence himself had combined parts of different Greek plays. So how could Geta have any certainty about his origins or about the kind of identity that comes from knowing from whom one is descended? Geta is continually remade and refashioned by texts, beyond his ability, despite all his science and logic, to do much about it.

Machiavelli's comparison of himself to Geta suggests that he had developed a more problematic understanding of the dialogue with Vettori, of the relationship of that dialogue to the writing of *The Prince* and to the expectations that he invested in it, and, ultimately, of his claims to be a "man of letters."[33] Geta makes all these matters more complex than they would otherwise seem. He transforms the dialogue between Machiavelli and Vettori into a confusion of voices in which easy distinctions between *meum* and *tuum* become blurred. Those voices themselves become intricate combinations of still other voices and texts, including Dante, Ovid, Petrarch, *Geta e Birria*, the woodcutters, the city friends who came to purchase wood, the butchers, millers, furnace-tenders, and, of course, the ancient men whose words Machiavelli transcribed into a book that was "his" only in the limited sense of being in his hand. In that Babel, could Machiavelli/Geta have had any assurance about secure possession of his own voice? The letter of December 10, 1513, is about the generation from multiple dialogues, migrations, and transformations of a new text—*The Prince*—and of a new Machiavelli "completely transferred" into the voices of the men of

---

33. For valuable treatments of the issues surrounding Machiavelli's sense of literature and literary vocation, see Carlo Dionisotti, "Machiavelli letterato," in his *Machiavellerie* (Turin, 1980), 227–66 (in English translation in the present volume); and Wayne A. Rebhorn, *Foxes and Lions: Machiavelli's Confidence Men* (Ithaca, N.Y., 1988). Much of Mario Martelli's work on Machiavelli is relevant to these themes. One can profitably begin with his "Preistoria (medicea) di Machiavelli," *Studi di filologia italiana* 29 (1971): 377–405, and continue with "Schede sulla cultura di Machiavelli," *Interpres* 6 (1985–86): 283–330, esp. 303–13. Two important studies of the literary and cultural traditions that shaped Renaissance notions of literature, originality, imitation, and intertextuality are Thomas M. Greene, *The Light in Troy: Imitation and Discovery in Renaissance Poetry* (New Haven, Conn., 1982); and David Quint, *Origin and Originality in Renaissance Literature: Versions of the Source* (New Haven, Conn., 1983). Neither work, however, deals with Machiavelli. The present essay emerged from a larger project on the Machiavelli-Vettori letters, in which the letter of December 10, 1513, is discussed from the perspective developed here as well as from those of other problems relating to the correspondence as a whole; see my book *Between Friends: Discourses of Power and Desire in the Machiavelli-Vettori Letters of 1513–1515* (Princeton, N.J., 1993). The letter of December 10, 1513, is treated in chapter 6.

antiquity. But whereas the traditional interpretation has fixed on that transference as the central moment of a story of discovery and of the affirmation of identity and calling, Geta alerts us to the letter's other story: its humorous and half-hidden other version of the same events, in which bumbling dialogue degenerates into mock conflict, books are at best a burden and at worst a trap, and those who lay claim to a "science" of forms and names are themselves continually transformed by the interlacing entrapments of language and letters. Machiavelli/Geta knows that the famous transference into the wise men of antiquity might be just another illusion in the endless play of textual metamorphosis.

The letter to Vettori is often read as a kind of preface or introduction to *The Prince*. In fact, of course, Machiavelli wrote it after he had completed a first draft of *The Prince* and it is, in a sense, the first interpretation of that work. Geta's role in the interpretation was to give Machiavelli some distance from himself, from the book he had just written, and from the solemn story, contained in the same letter, of how he had come to write it. The purpose of that distance was that it allowed him to see all three—self, book, and story—as inevitably implicated in those textual migrations and transformations, in the indeterminacy and mutability to which "uomini litterati" are especially vulnerable.

CHAPTER THREE

"TRANSFORMATION" AND "ADAPTATION" IN MACHIAVELLI'S *MANDRAGOLA*

Giulio Ferroni

THE prologue to *Mandragola* can be easily divided into two parts of equal length: the first part, consisting of the first four stanzas, introduces the mise-en-scène and the characters; the second part, consisting of the four subsequent stanzas, is a deeply felt presentation of the author's attitude to the play and to his public.[1] Such a division immediately risks suggesting a contrast between antithetical poles, the degraded and empty "matter" or subject (described in the first part) and the high-minded seriousness of the author (set in relief in the second part), with a deliberate structural separation between the comic status of the play's corrupt and foolish characters and our awareness of the author's personal heroism, which has been prevented by circumstances from finding expression in a sphere worthy of it. From this point of view, the second part of the prologue would be situated entirely beyond the horizon of the play, betraying the outsider's bitter gaze.

[Editors' note: The focus of Professor Ferroni's essay is on two frequently paired, thematically crucial terms from Machiavelli's critical vocabulary: *mutazione*, invariably translated here as "transformation," and *riscontro*, usually translated as "adaptation" (with exceptions noted in brackets). As throughout the works of Machiavelli, the accurate translation of key technical vocabulary is both indispensable and virtually impossible. *Riscontro* implies an encounter, a coming together or converging, sometimes literal but primarily metaphorical, between two opposite and even hostile beings or orders of reality. "Adaptation," though it does not convey the full range of significance of *riscontro*, does point to Professor Ferroni's typical use of the word, to imply change driven by a need to respond to intractable external circumstances. *Mutazione* might be translated with reasonable accuracy as meaning "mutation" were it not for the scientific connotations, factual and fictional, that now haunt that word for most anglophone readers.]

1. See Luigi Vanossi, "Situazione e sviluppo nel teatro machiavelliano," in *Lingua e strutture del teatro italiano del Rinascimento* (Padua, 1970), 1–108 (esp. 4–7).

It would thus signal either a will to nonparticipation in a world deprived of moral density and civic values (from this reading has developed the ethical-realistic interpretation of *Mandragola*), or the explicit documentation of an aspiration to the sublime of tragedy and a yearning for pure theory, disdainful at being forced into the degrading vulgarity of praxis and of comedy (from this position has developed the recent structuralist interpretation).[2]

Traversing divergent and inimical paths, the realistic and structuralist interpretations of *Mandragola* nevertheless converge in undertaking an "oppositional" reading of the prologue, which rests in both cases on a substantial undervaluation of the domain of comedy, considered necessarily inferior compared with the seriousness of politics or of theoretical and tragic abstraction, and therefore justifiable only as the indication of a forced absence from them. Thus Machiavelli's comic sensibility is seen either as woven through with bitterness because of the playwright's relegation to inaction, or as forced to confront an impossible but much sought-after tragic mode. In both cases we are facing obvious ideological distortions: the idealistic one, according to which authentic values should be definitively situated in what is serious, positive, and ethically decorous; and the structuralist one of an insoluble ontological opposition between tragedy and comedy, high and low, the sublime and the ridiculous.

The Machiavellian conception of man offers to comedy an autonomous and by no means subalternate role, however. Beginning with a fundamental ambivalence toward persisting humanist values like "*virtù*" and "reputation," and colliding with a reality that tends progressively to give the lie to those very values, it complicates itself in a paradoxical vision of human nature, which shatters the sublime and unitary humanist conception of the *dignitas hominis,* and resolves itself in a search for coexistence among contraries, for an alternation between extremes (and therefore also between the "high" and the "low," between the "serious" and the "comic"). For this purpose, the famous passage from the letter to Francesco Vettori of January 31, 1515, is exemplary:

2. The realistic interpretation derives from the classic essay of Luigi Russo, "Machiavelli uomo di teatro e narratore," in *Machiavelli*, 3d ed. (Bari, 1949), 89–165 (the essay dates from 1937). See also Franco Fido, "Machiavelli 1469–1969: Politica e teatro nel badalucco di messer Nicia," *Italica* 46 (1969): 359–75. The structuralist interpretation finds its extreme expression in Giorgio Bárberi Squarotti, "La struttura astratta delle commedie," in *La forma tragica del "Principe" e altri saggi sul Machiavelli* (Florence, 1966), 43–102.

Anybody who saw our letters, honored friend, and saw their diversity, would wonder greatly, because he would suppose now that we were grave men, wholly concerned with important matters, and that into our breast no thought could fall that did not have in itself honesty and greatness. But then, turning the page, he would judge that we, the very same persons, were lightminded, inconstant, lascivious, concerned with empty things. And this way of proceeding, if to some it may appear censurable, to me seems praiseworthy, because we are imitating Nature, who is variable; and he who imitates her cannot be blamed.[3]

The disposition to the comic is not defined here as a simple diversion marginal to a serious and composed humanism, like a provisional safety valve that refreshes energies, but is incapable of putting into question the norms of a world in which only "honesty" and "greatness" stand out. The passage from "great things" to "vain things" takes on instead the value of a vital movement, essential to taking full measure of humanity; it is the form of an adaptation to nature, of an attempt to meet and confront it, following the path of its variations. The affirmation of the equal dignity of the serious and the comic, of the validity of their coexistence in human behavior, thus refers to a central nexus of Machiavelli's thought: that is, to the discovery of the necessity for an accord or "adaptation" between the internal nature of the individual (which expresses itself in particular "modes of action") and the external nature (which is manifested to the individual through the continuous "variation" of Fortune).[4] The guarantee of happiness and success can be offered, in Machiavelli's anthropology, only by the individual's capacity for adapting his particular nature to the variations of Fortune, and thus of repeatedly "transforming" the manner of his actions, according to the direction of these variations. If Fortune moves continuously between extreme and opposite poles, we will be able to obtain an "agreement" (*riscontro*) with her only if we also know equally well how to shuttle between extremes, only if we are always ready to reverse our own "manner of acting" (if, in sum, we succeed in "trans-

---

3. See Niccolò Machiavelli, *Lettere,* ed. Franco Gaeta (Milan, 1961), 374. Translations of the letters are taken from *The Letters of Machiavelli,* trans. Allan Gilbert (Chicago, 1988, first published 1961), 184–85.

4. Cf. Letter no. 119 in Machiavelli, *Lettere,* ed. Gaeta, 228–31. For a detailed analysis of this letter, see Gennaro Sasso, *Niccolò Machiavelli: Storia del suo pensiero politico* (Naples, 1958), 185–94.

forming into the contrary [*mutare el contrario*]").⁵ The search for this perpetual and happy adaptation to Fortune and to nature, "which is various," sustains all the Machiavellian paradoxes regarding the necessity for the coexistence of contraries at the moral and behavioral levels, beginning with the famous paradoxes of *The Prince*, which can be summarized in the affirmation of the necessity of "knowing how well to use both the beast and the man" and in the consequent image of the centaur Chiron, symbol of the coexistence of different natures and of opposed behaviors, both necessary to whoever wishes to keep in step with the variety of situations and thus to resist the "variation" of Fortune (*The Prince*, chapter 18).

Thus the political problem of the means of acting on the contemporary scene is revealed as immediately contiguous with the anthropological problem of the search for "modes" that permit an adaptation to Fortune; *The Prince* is not only a political treatise but also the construction of a model of human behavior, in which the figure of the prince tends to be identified with that of the "sage" (*savio*) and "prudent" man.⁶ Chapter 25 of *The Prince*, however, which takes up with more theoretical rigor doubts that had already been expressed in the letter to Soderini, identifies an irresolvable contradiction in the Machiavellian idea of a human being capable of ranging between extremes. The conviction of the immutability of nature and of individual character, which for Machiavelli appears to be confirmed by contemporary experience, seems to destroy the very possibility of the existence of a bivalent person, capable of always adapting happily to Fortune. It is true that "if one changed [*mutassi*] one's nature with the times and with events, one's fortune would not change"; but here the edifice constructed in the preceding chapters is torn down, revealing that human beings remain "obstinate in their manners [*modi*]" and are incapable of effective transformations, and that success derives only from a provisional and random adaptation of their immutable internal nature to always variable, external nature.⁷

The anthropology of "transformation" and of the coexistence of contraries, despite this dry theoretical refutation late in *The Prince*, contin-

---

5. *The Prince*, chap. 18. [Editors' note: The translations from *The Prince* and *The Discourses*, as well as *Mandragola*, are those of Professor Ronald L. Martinez. Professor Ferroni cites from Niccolò Machiavelli, *Il Principe e Discorsi*, ed. Sergio Bertelli (Milan, 1960).]

6. On the prince as a model of perfect human behavior, see Felix Gilbert, "The Humanist Concept of the Prince and the *Prince* of Machiavelli," *Journal of Modern History* 11 (1939): 449–83.

7. For a precise analysis of chap. 25, see Gennaro Sasso, *Niccolò Machiavelli*, 262–78; and his commentary in Niccolò Machiavelli, *Il Principe* (Florence, 1964), 205–13.

ues to operate at several levels in the work of the Florentine secretary, who cannot easily accept a denial of the possibility of successful action. Though rejected at the speculative level, this anthropology is transformed into a genuine myth of the individual who knows he is both himself and his own contrary, thus guaranteeing valid adaptations to Fortune, which present themselves as the rewards for his paradoxical ambiguity, in opposition to the one-dimensional drabness of the contemporary world.[8] Beyond the "sublime" unity of the humanist personality, beyond an entirely positive conception of human nature, harmoniously grounded in the secure possession of a one-dimensional rationality, Machiavelli discovers the space of contradiction, the figure of humanity sheared by the ambiguous play of opposites, in which both the sublime of the "antique courts of ancient men" and the comic of the "thousand disputes and countless insults with offensive words" find their place.[9] And it is certainly not a matter of resolving this contradiction into a superior spiritual unity, of defining it as the capacity to subsume under the force of an exceptional personality the diverse components that constitute the eternal substance of humankind. The internal contradiction of the Machiavellian individual is born rather from striving toward a direct intervention in the contradictions of the real, through an "open" model of behavior, which may be summed up in a mythical model but always points toward direct action, however impossible, in the real world.

The myth of "transformation" coalesces through that of the *savio* or the prudent individual,[10] who knows how to employ contraries to a determinate end, in which wisdom and reason, as opposed to the folly of the vulgar, can shine forth. But the fact that the Machiavellian sage has need of contraries, that he discovers the equal validity of the inferior and the superior levels, of the high and the low, of "man" and of the

8. [Editors' note: Despite a preference for gender-neutral language, we have frequently retained the masculine singular pronoun, since it is clear, and never more so than in chap. 25 of *The Prince*, that Machiavelli's normatively "virtuous" individual is male. It is thus an especially significant moment in Professor Ferroni's argument when the attributes of the *savio* and the *virtuoso* are assumed, in Machiavelli's terms extraordinarily, by a woman, Lucrezia. See John Freccero's essay in this volume.]

9. These are the terms of the famous letter to Francesco Vettori of December 10, 1513 (letter no. 140 in Machiavelli, *Lettere*, ed. Gaeta, 303). Cf. Giorgio Bárberi Squarotti, "Il Machiavelli fra il 'sublime' della contemplazione intellettuale e il 'comico' della prassi," in *Lettere italiane* 11 (1969): 129–54.

10. From this point of view, the ideal of the "prudent" Machiavelli shows its partial relation to that of Pontano in *De prudentia* (1508); cf. Mario Santoro, *Fortuna, ragione, e prudenzia nella civiltà letteraria del Cinquecento* (Naples, 1967), 23–65 and 179–231; as well as Brian Richardson, "Pontano's *De prudentia* and Machiavelli's *Discorsi*," *Bibliothèque d'Humanisme et Renaissance* 33 (1971): 353–57.

"beast," constitutes in any case an effective disruption of the integrity of the humanist, Christian ideal. It introduces a revolutionary element into anthropological reflection, a paradoxical slant that will find successors only in marginal sectors of Italian culture and that will be completely abandoned by an official culture committed to contesting and condemning the entire political oeuvre of the Florentine secretary.[11]

I have sketched this argument so as to suggest the close nexus between the idea of the comic and the central nuclei of Machiavelli's thought, and to trace the lines of an anthropological myth that operates in all his literary constructions, not to mention in his personal behavior. (One thinks of Guicciardini's comment that Machiavelli had a reputation for being "extravagant in opinions outside the normal and the inventor of new and unusual things."[12]) The myth of "transformation" and of "adaptation" to Fortune does not only furnish a first and wholly Machiavellian authorization for the writing of a comic work, in the interval between the writing of serious political treatises, but in fact can be located in the structure of the *Mandragola*, whose theatrical operations and conflicts can be measured precisely according to this perspective of a transformation in the nature of the protagonist, and of the search for an adaptation to antagonistic forces. Even from this point of view, the comic production of Machiavelli certainly does not appear to be a minor and peripheral moment in an otherwise engaged and far more problematic career. Rather it should be seen as a comic site in which a conception of humanity is fully debated. Theater and politics meet via anthropology.[13] They find a point of convergence, not in an abstract opposition of sublime tragic theorizing and "low" comic praxis, or the opposition between a serious tendency toward the real and the silliness of odd recreational "doodling" (*badalucco*), but rather in the central contradiction inherent in Machiavelli's conception of humanity, located between extreme and reversible poles and searching for models of transformation and of adaptation. The most general and apparent form of this contradiction is precisely that of a transformation from gravity and seriousness to levity and vanity, a transformation that in fact defines the comic genre. Comedy is thus configured as a form of adaptation to an external reality that can no longer be measured and shaped through the use of the serious schemata of political meditation.

11. See Franco Fido, *Machiavelli, storia della critica* (Palermo, 1965).

12. In Machiavelli, *Lettere*, ed. Gaeta, 408 (translation by Ronald L. Martinez).

13. I take up here the terminology of Fido's essay, "Machiavelli 1469–1969," which tends to link theater and politics as the "evidence of a disproportion" between the political energies used in writing *Mandragola* and the theatrical entertainment that results.

The terms of this argument will be more clear from a direct reading of the play. We should first return to the prologue of *Mandragola* and identify its several levels, keeping in mind what I have said thus far regarding the paradoxical and nonhierarchical meaning of the Machiavellian opposition of the serious and the comic.[14] For purposes of analysis, the opening four stanzas can be divided into two parts, the first part consisting of the first two stanzas and perhaps the first three verses of the third, and the second part consisting of the third and fourth stanzas. In addition to the formulas of ingratiation (the *captatio benevolentiae*) and the request to the spectators for silence, the first part presents with an unusual richness of detail the mise-en-scène by situating the dwellings of the principal characters. The third and fourth stanzas emphasize elements that we will call "anthropological": the characters pass in review and are placed within a typology of human categories divided according to level of value and interest.

The prologue places the protagonists of the love interest, to whom the third stanza is dedicated, in sharp relief to the other characters. It emphasizes the nobility of Callimaco and Lucrezia, their tendency to maintain a level of quality that seems to exceed that of all the others. But the text also suggests that Callimaco bears his distinctive traits in a merely external and factitious way: that of social appearance, of a courtier's seeming that hides his real nature, of a kind of worth unsupported by superior inner sagacity. ("This one, among all his companions, to judge by his marks and traits, bears the honors of nobility and worth.")[15] Lucrezia is described, in more lapidary fashion, with an attribute that might appear generic and even equivocal—"una giovane accorta" (a shrewd young woman)—but that in fact anticipates the considerable sagacity (*saviezza*) and prudence attributed to her in the

14. For the text of the comedy I cite the edition of Roberto Ridolfi, *La Mandragola* (Florence, 1965), which makes use of the edition of 1518 found in the Laurenziano Rediano codex 129. Regarding this edition, see Fredi Chiappelli, "Sulla composizione della *Mandragola*," *L'approdo letterario* 11 (1965): 79–84; and Chiappelli, "Considerazioni di linguaggio e di stile sul testo della *Mandragola*," *Giornale storico della letteratura italiana* 86 (1969): 252–59. See also the reviews by Vincenzo Romano in *Belfagor* 21 (1966): 614–23; and Roberto Tissoni, "Per una nuova edizione della *Mandragola* del Machiavelli," *Giornale storico della letteratura italiana* 83 (1966): 241–58. For the reply by Ridolfi, see "Ritorno al testo della *Mandragola*," *Studi sulle commedie del Machiavelli* (Pisa, 1968), 103–34. Only when this essay was already set in proof was I able to consult the new text of *Mandragola* edited by Mario Martelli in Niccolò Machiavelli, *Tutte le opere di Machiavelli* (Florence, 1971); for textual problems relating to *Mandragola*, see li–lvii.

15. The distinction between an authentic knowledge intrinsic to the individual and the exteriority of power and worth derived by accident and unsupported by a superior awareness is constant in Machiavelli's works, especially in his last phase; see, for example, the dedication of *The Discourses* to Zanobi Buondelmonte and Cosimo Rucellai.

course of the play. The reference to the deception to be practiced on her ("A shrewd young woman / was much beloved of him, / and by him was deceived, / as now you'll hear") is no gratuitous game of contradictory terms (that is, "shrewd" and "deceived"), but rather an affirmation of the positive value of that deception, which is explained and justified precisely by the initial "shrewdness." We will, in fact, see that Lucrezia's sagacity consists precisely in the full acceptance of this deceit, which will offer her a felicitous form of adaptation to Fortune. Thus the sly remark to the audience—"I'd like you to be deceived as she is"—is not just a conventional knowing wink, but a salute to the possible shrewdness of members of the audience and to their consequent accessory deceitfulness, an attempt to direct toward the spectators the lesson of that central model of human behavior represented by Lucrezia in *Mandragola*.

In this anthropological presentation of the characters developed in the prologue, at least four levels of value are definitely traced,[16] which we will find arrayed as diverse theatrical functions in the construction of the play. The first, positive but ambiguous level is represented by Lucrezia. (The opposition of "shrewd" and "deceived" already announces the paradoxical terminology for this character.) A second level, also ambiguous, but without positive valence, is represented by Callimaco. (His external position as a protagonist dedicated to success, endowed with formally noble attributes, alternates with a real but subaltern and uncertain substance as a "slavish lover.") A third, neutral level is represented by the "economic" deviousness (though not without the lucidity of reason) of friar Timoteo and Ligurio (who continuously produce offers and propositions for the characters situated at different levels, interfering with them on numerous occasions). And a fourth, inferior level, one absolutely without rational calculation, in which "folly" triumphs, is represented by Nicia.

Such a direct presentation of the material reveals the absence in Machiavelli of any intention of distancing it from himself. His motive, rather, is to make that material grate violently against his own commitment as a man of theoretical and political responsibilities. And the discourse that develops in the next four stanzas of the prologue resolves itself not in a declaration of the "unworthiness" of the subject matter, but instead in a broader definition of the realm of the comic, of the relation between that "material" and the present "times," of the nexus that the author playfully establishes with his public through the

---

16. This "anthropological" prologue, Machiavellian in its entirety, cannot be derived from traditional Terentian examples (for which see Marvin T. Herrick, *Comic Theory in the Sixteenth Century* [Urbana, Ill., 1950], 147–75).

text.[17] The most famous and most frequently cited passage in defense of the author's putative disdain for his subject matter is the one in which he, on the contrary, offers the most essential evidence to support the thesis I have been arguing:

> E, se questa materia non è degna,
> per esser pur leggieri,
> d'un uom, che voglia parer saggio e grave,
> scusatelo con questo, che s'ingegna
> con questi van' pensieri
> fare el suo tempo più suave,
> perché altrove non have
> dove voltare el viso,
> ché gli è stato interciso
> mostrare con altre imprese altra virtúe,
> non sendo premio alle fatiche sue.

> And if this matter is unworthy
> —as it is but light—
> of a man who wishes to appear sage and sober
> excuse it with this, that he attempts
> with these vain thoughts
> to make his sad time sweeter,
> because he has nowhere else
> to turn his face;
> for he has been forbidden
> in other enterprise to show his worth,
> no reward being offered for his work.

The opposition between light matters or "vain thoughts" and "a man who wishes to appear sage and sober," reveals perfectly the paradox of the passage already cited from the letter of January 31, 1515. Just as reference was made there to the amazement that good common sense would display at the rapid shifts between "greatness" and vanity in the Machiavelli-Vettori correspondence, so here the opening hypothesis refers to the amazement the audience might feel at the disparity between the "unworthy" subject matter and the "sage and sober" author. In the letter the contradictoriness of attitudes was justified and exalted

---

17. The militant tone of the prologue to *Mandragola* and the active direction of its poetics have been cogently remarked upon by Nino Borsellino, "Per una storia delle commedie di Machiavelli," *Cultura e scuola* 33–34 (1970): 229–41 (see, in particular, 233–36).

insofar as it looked toward an imitation of nature, to an agreement with external reality. Similarly, here the substitution of "vain thoughts" for virtuous "enterprise" is offered as the guarantee of an accord with the present "sorry times" and as the last paradoxical possibility of acting on them to make them in some way more bearable. And this attempt to "make his sad time sweeter" is valid not only in the sense of a *vitae difficilioris recreatio*,[18] of a provisional compensation sufficient to forget, for a brief moment, the wounds inflicted by bad luck; it is instead the only possible manner of keeping a bold face when encountering Fortune in the present circumstances, to stare her down. The locution "because he has nowhere else to turn his face" directly recalls the expression "turn one's face to luck" (or "to Fortune") used frequently by Machiavelli to signify precisely the individual's adaptation to the unforeseeable variations of *Fortuna*.[19]

A necessary sign of a happy adaptation to the times will be given by a "reward for effort"; and if a reward has been lacking for the political work of Machiavelli, there will be no lack of a paradoxical reward for this his comic work. The sixth stanza develops the argument regarding the reward that the author will obtain by making "sweeter" the sad present. At the same time, by calling into the question both the spectators and the Florentine milieu, the stanza reveals the polemical turn that the Machiavellian idea of the comic implies. The reward that the present times will offer consists simply in the smirks and slanders of the public ("the reward he expects is that each / will stand aside and smirk / speaking ill [*dicendo mal*] of what he sees or hears"). This, then, is further proof of the disappearance of "ancient virtue," and of the malignant situation that renders pointless any effort directed at great enterprises, because of the slander inevitably directed at them. It seems almost as if Machiavelli, in recognizing this deplorable contemporary situation, prepares himself passively to accept it, to submit to the offer of "slander" as the sole "reward for effort."[20] And it might appear that

18. According to the terms of Pontano in his *De sermone*, as noted by Ezio Raimondi in "Il teatro del Machiavelli," *Studi storici* 10 (1969): 769.

19. The same expression is found not only in *Mandragola*, act 4, sc. 1, but, as Chiappelli suggests ("Considerazioni," 256), in *Asino* 3.86–87 ("to the blows of one's fortune one must / turn one's face free of tears"). See Machiavelli, *Il teatro e tutti gli scritti letterari*, ed. Franco Gaeta (Milan, 1965), 280. See also Machiavelli, *Lettere*, ed. Gaeta, 234 ("turn my face . . . to Fortune") and 323 ("show your face to Fortune"); cf. Raimondi, "Il teatro del Machiavelli," 757.

20. Cf. Borsellino, "Per una storia delle commedie," 235. The same relation between "effort," "rewards," and the threat of "slander" may be found in the proem to the first book of the *Discourses*.

in this manner, the already remarked attempt to "make his sad time sweeter" condemns itself to defeat, recognizes itself as pointless.

To be sure, in comparison with the model of "ancient virtue," to which "other enterprises" and other "rewards" would be appropriate, the comic domain appears to be almost forced on the author, an "adaptation" imposed more by the weight of public disdain and "speaking ill" (*maldicenza*) than by a completely free decision. But it is not a question of an adaptation that is purely passive and without its own recourses. Machiavelli does not limit himself to registering moralistically his consciousness of the speaking ill that attacks any serious enterprise, or that seems in fact to be the cause of contemporary decadence, but takes on his own shoulders the same capacity for speaking ill, accepts it in its entirety as a polemical weapon, turns it back against the smirks and slanders of the public, makes of it a personal means of responding to the slings and arrows inflicted by the outrageous present:

> Pur, se credessi alcun, dicendo male
> tenerlo pe'capegli,
> e sbigottirlo o ritrarlo in parte,
> io l'ammonisco, e dico a questo tale
> che sa dir male anch'egli
> e come questa fu la sua prim'arte,
> e come in ogni parte
> del mondo, ove el "sí" sona,
> non istima persona,
> ancor che facci sergieri a colui,
> che può portar miglior mantel che lui.

> But if some believe that by speaking ill
> they'll hold him back by his hair
> or intimidate or much dissuade him,
> I would warn them: and say to them
> that he too knows full well how to speak ill,
> and how this art was the first he learned;
> and how, wherever he's found
> in the world where the "sì" sounds,
> he is no respecter of persons,
> though he might be a servant to some
> allowed to wear better cloaks than he.

The appropriation to himself of "speaking ill" further emphasizes the validity of the comic sphere. To it Machiavelli attributes the role of "first art" in his own cultural baggage, equal in privileges with the political "art."[21]

In this light, the "speaking ill" of the prologue to *Mandragola* reveals even more clearly its own ambiguity. It is a positive element of polemic and confrontation with the present, when it is deployed by the "sage" capable of orienting with clarity his choices and judgments. The sage (with whom the author identifies) can rationally direct the same "speaking ill" against those who are not endowed with rational intelligence, who exercise perhaps a power unsupported by an adequate "wisdom."[22]

> Ma lasciam pur dir male a chiunque vuole.
> Torniamo al caso nostro,
> acciò che non trapassi troppo l'ora.
> Far conto non si de' delle parole,
> né stimar qualche mostro,
> che non sa forse s'e s'è vivo ancora.

> But let us allow whoever wishes to speak ill,
> and return to our affair,
> lest the hour grow too late.
> We should place no stock in words,
> nor much respect some brute
> who scarcely realizes he's alive.

Naturally, from the spectator's point of view, these words also wink at the audience. They do not postulate a sheer distance between themselves and the author, but seem rather to request the complicity of the audience so as to isolate "some brute who scarcely realizes he's alive." The necessity of the theatrical convention (occurring during a festival, a social divertissement) precludes an exclusively polemical relation to the public, requiring also a level of complicity between the public and the author, a form of consensus—shielded though it may be—between the motives of the staged fiction and the interests of the spectator. If the contrast between a public that "stays aside and smirks / speaking ill of what it sees or hears" and an author who "also knows

21. On the possibility of establishing links between the Machiavellian anthropology and the "carnivalesque" strain of European culture as reconstructed by Mikhail Bakhtin in his fundamental study *Rabelais and His World*, trans. Helene Iswolsky (Cambridge, Mass., 1968), see Raimondi, "Il teatro del Machiavelli."

22. On this distinction between his own "knowledge" and the senseless power of those who wear, though only superficially, "better cloaks," see, again, the dedication to *The Discourses*.

how to speak ill" and is "no respecter of persons" were enacted in a radical and definitive register, no theatrical space would remain available. Rather, numerous suggestions throughout the prologue elicit the participation, even ideological, of the spectators in the events that will be presented. In any case, the "speaking ill" of the last three stanzas contrasts precisely with the "benignity" and the "being gracious" invoked at the beginning of the prologue, and offers itself almost as a paradoxical inversion of those more conventional and sociable motives. The high point of this offer of complicity with the public is in the already noted wish, directed at the female spectators, that they should suffer the same deceit practiced on Lucrezia, and thus participate in her "shrewdness" and "prudence."

Without question, the prologue sheds light on the ambiguity of the play's theatricality. Its theatricality is viewed, on the one hand, as a form of pitiless aggression toward a distanced public, immersed in the foolish game of "speaking ill," and on the other hand, as the benign occasion of "laughter" and of "doodling" for a public that is perfectly complicit with and close to the author. The typical spectator is seen both as a gifted and knowing observer of the qualities of the characters and the meaning of the story, and as a "brute / who scarcely realizes he's still alive," blinded by a vain and blowhard foolishness. Thus two distinct groups wait, in front of the stage, for the spectacle to begin. For the first group the *fabula* will have one meaning, because its members will be able to seize the rhythm of the "transformations" and understand how the "vain thoughts" might not be inappropriate to a "man who wishes to appear sage and sober"; for the second group there will be only the possibility of a paralyzed shuttling back and forth in the narrow space of a negative, unilateral "speaking ill," quite opposed to the positive version that the author claims for himself and incapable of reaching self-consciousness or of achieving an effective "adaptation" to the real. The first group will be able to find its own image in Lucrezia, will be able to expect from the play a "deception" to be accepted with eyes open; the second group will probably be able to recognize itself (but will perhaps not even be capable of that) in Nicia, irrationally content in his own idiocy, in his own immobile blindness.

In the first scene of *Mandragola* we find a condition of almost complete theatrical immobility. This condition is not justified by a presumed Machiavellian disposition to eliminate the possibility of an event or to define a static universe a priori; it is justified, rather, because of the particular role that Callimaco assumes in it, a role that will necessarily be undercut by successive developments. According to the normal comic-erotic scheme, the position of Callimaco in the comedy should be absolutely central. To the young and gallant lover destined for success should naturally pertain the task of presenting himself as a positive model; he should offer himself to the spectators' sympathy and to their preference for identifying themselves with the most prestigious figures presented on the stage. The lady beloved by this gallant should, conversely, remain largely in the condition of a passive object, receiving the burnish of exemplarity only as a reflection of the victorious lover.[23]

The first scene displays Callimaco precisely in this central and static position. He is shown as a hero who wishes to offer himself to the public as defined, from the outset, by prestigious habits and attributes that inscribe him in a pattern of courtliness whose familiar forms will guarantee an unproblematic assent from the viewing public. This presentation of Callimaco as the protagonist at all levels is sustained by a passive and subaltern reference point—the servant Siro, whose role is to confirm as given and systematized the behavior of the central character, adding to it naught but a monotonous nod of assent. Siro thus exists to create for Callimaco the condition of a facile "adaptation," acting like an object on which Callimaco can mirror with excessive security the essence of his own prestigious behavior.[24]

Initially, Callimaco appears to be a perfect model of the courtly lover, like a hero of a novella who, with the support of a widely recognized literary tradition,[25] can acquire the ideological consent of the public. The witticism with which Callimaco cuts off Siro's halfhearted criticism of the impetuous force of his desire shows again that in Callimaco, the noble courtly demeanor is associated with a clear distinction from inferior social levels, and is figured as the attribute of a certain material and social power:

> *Siro:* If you had spoke to me of it in Paris, I'd have known how to advise you; but now I don't know what to tell you.

23. Speaking of this "normality" of the comic-erotic scheme, I do not wish to refer to an essential structure of comedy, but to a schematic form that projects itself through a *longue durée* of the Western tradition: a wholly ideological form and, as such, one that generally resolves itself in support of the "normality" of the constituted and conservative cultural organization.

24. Siro is denied the most traditional task of the servant in classical comedy, that of the astute assistant to the realization of his master's plots. Such tasks in *Mandragola* are placed entirely in the hands of the "parasite" Ligurio. For his part, Ligurio redefines Callimaco by undermining the role (that of protagonist) that his conversations with Siro initially seemed to assign to him.

25. For the motif of falling in love by report and for the sequence "desire-ideé fixe-journey-real beauty," the immediate reference is to *Decameron*, 7.7. On this and other allusions to Boccaccian models in *Mandragola*, see Raimondi, "Il teatro del Machiavelli," 757 (also Vanossi, "Situazione e sviluppo," 8–14).

Callimaco: I haven't told you this because I want your advice, but so as to somewhat relieve my mind, and so that you will dispose yourself to help me, as the need arises.[26]

But by positioning the story of Callimaco against the background of the "wars" and the "ruin" of Italy,[27] Machiavelli introduces into his courtly profile a note of discord that raises contradictions, complicates with uncertainties and hesitations the consensus built around the exemplary character. In addition, as a result of the experience of falling in love, Fortune has already entered the scene to upset the happy "adaptation" of the French sojourn ("but as it seemed to Fortune that I had too good a time of it, she arranged that one Cammillo Calfucci should arrive in Paris"). This new circumstance forces Callimaco to search for a new kind of adaptation that will resolve itself in an erotic union with the beautiful Lucrezia.

A displacement of the positive courtly veneer from the "noble" protagonist swiftly follows. Precisely in the quest for an "understanding" (*riscontro*) with Lucrezia, Callimaco, despite the successful outcome of his seduction, loses the gloss of exemplarity with which he first appeared to the public. He is bogged down in a series of partial adaptations to other characters, who make him lose the initiative in guiding the action, and thus leave him prey to hesitations, uncertainties, gropings.

In reality, the social concept of the positively marked protagonist is demystified and disallowed; the very complicity, social and obvious, between stage and spectator is put into question and refuted. From the point of view of the Machiavellian sage, the "honor and worth of nobility" are nothing but pure appearance, a mask that conceals an insignificant "slavish lover." To Lucrezia accrues the consensus that belongs to the authentic sage (and it matters little that she is a female character); to her belongs the *virtù* capable of joining battle with Fortune, to the point of undergoing decisive transformations in the nature of the self. Nothing could be further, in short, from a facile, static image of bourgeois felicity.

The central importance of Callimaco begins to wane in the very first scene, when he is forced to pose the problem of the means of approaching Lucrezia and to become aware of her "nature," which seems to render such an approach impossible:

26. Cf. Raimondi's reference ("Il teatro del Machiavelli," 757) to the letter to Vettori of June 10, 1514 (Machiavelli, *Lettere*, ed. Gaeta, 343).

27. Another reference to the disastrous Italian political situation is found in the passage in which Callimaco narrates his "determination" to depart for Florence ("nor thinking any more about war or peace in Italy" [act 1, sc. 1]).

> In the first place her nature makes war against me, for she is
> wholly chaste and in every way alien to the ways of love; she has
> a supremely rich husband, who allows himself to be ruled in all
> things by her, and, though not young, he appears not wholly old;
> she has no relative or neighbors that meet with her at vigils and
> feasts, or at other pleasant events wont to delight young people;
> no rude mechanicals wait on her at home; all the servants and
> footmen tremble before her; so that there is no opportunity for
> corruption to enter.

It is not the courtly love of Callimaco that becomes the reference
point around which the comedy turns, but the "nature" of Lucrezia.
The other characters (and Callimaco with them) must limit themselves
to acting to create the conditions for a "corruption" that will "make her
be of a different nature," and overturn her moral attributes.[28] In comparison with Lucrezia, Callimaco plays not the part of the "virtuoso"
capable of making himself ready for a rational adaptation to the forces
of the real, but rather that of an external "occasion" that Fortune offers
to Lucrezia so that she will be disposed to undergo a transformation of
nature that will lead her to fuller happiness. Paradoxically, Callimaco
himself takes on the role of object, revealing himself as one of the
components (and perhaps not the most essential one) of a mechanism
of Fortune. Callimaco cannot take aim directly at Lucrezia; he must lose
himself in a play of relationships offered him, at several levels, by
Ligurio and Nicia. Already the third scene of act 1 defines a relationship, between Callimaco and Ligurio, which is the perfect inversion of
that between Callimaco and Siro in the first scene. Ligurio is preeminent, determining every judgment on personalities and events.[29] Ligurio not only gives precise orders to Callimaco (of whom he is only
the adviser) but goes so far as to leave him in the dark regarding the
substance of the new plan, and imposes on him, for the subsequent
scenes, a passive role, completely secondary to Ligurio's initiatives and
without any knowledge of them.[30]

Callimaco finds himself obeying an order to participate in a fiction
he has had no part in devising, and being commanded to move with-

28. Cf. act 1, sc. 1: "That place could make her become of another nature."

29. Vanossi has insisted on a complementary sharing of functions between Callimaco
and Ligurio ("Situazione e sviluppo," 14–30); the subaltern position of Callimaco has,
however, been underlined by Luigi Blasucci in the introduction to Niccolò Machiavelli,
Opere letterarie (Milan, 1964), xvi–xvii; and by Franco Fido, "Machiavelli, 1469–1969,"
366–67.

30. Cf. act 1, sc. 3: *Callimaco.* You revive me. This is too great a promise, and you feed
me on hopes too great. *Ligurio:* You'll know about it when it's time; it's not necessary that

out knowing the immediate outcome of his own movement. What is more, his reflections on Ligurio's *fede,* in the first scene and then again in the third scene, show him in a state of uncertainty concerning the very choices of those characters to whom he must adapt himself—an uncertainty that precludes him from governing events, and finally from even distinguishing their trajectories:

> I believe it, though I realize your sort lives by deceiving men. Nevertheless, I do not think I will be likewise deceived, because, on your doing so and my becoming aware of same, I would see that I took action, and you would from that moment lose the use of my house, and all hopes of having what I have promised you for the future. (Act 1, scene 3)[31]

In his confrontation with Nicia, before whom he must play the role of the illustrious doctor who has come from France, Callimaco is wholly subordinate to Ligurio's maneuver; he must recite the comedy of his own "presence."[32] Thus, the dominating figure of Ligurio devalues the noble displays of Callimaco, reveals the slavishness of his behavior; what would have made him an ideal protagonist is debased through an inessential adaptation to his foolish antagonist, Nicia. The "parasite" directly opposes the game of social prestige that Callimaco embarks on with Nicia, making the two of them participants in a useless whirl of exterior formalities that are extraneous to Ligurio's pronounced and rational confidence, which scarcely requires cultural adornments.

After the two scenes (the second and sixth) that Callimaco plays before Nicia, after the confirmation of his inability to act, which is linked to his vanity about his "honor and worth of nobility," Ligurio can jettison him as a dead weight, an object that might indeed prove

---

I tell you now, because we'll scarcely have time to act, much less to talk. You go off home and wait for me there; and I'll go and find the doctor; if I should bring him to you, follow what I say and adapt yourself to it. Also in act 1, sc. 3, note Ligurio's brusque order to Callimaco: "I want you to do things my way."

31. Cf. act 1, sc. 1, where Callimaco's justificatory response to Siro's doubts about the parasite's "faith" indicates a hesitant insecurity: "When something is in someone's best interest, you can trust that when you tell him about it, he will serve you faithfully. I have promised him, if he succeeds, to give him a good deal of money; if he fails he garners a lunch and a dinner, and in any case I won't dine alone."

32. Ligurio offers for the approval of Nicia the exterior and wholly formal attributes of Callimaco: "And if you, having spoken to him, don't think that he, because of his bearing, his learning, his skill in speaking, is a man to gather to your bosom, say that I myself am not such" (act 2, sc. 1).

damaging to the central action of the play—the third act, which stages the first effective phase of the "corruption" of Lucrezia. Thus the second act concludes with the pitiless elimination of Callimaco, who is sent on a casual stroll through the streets of Florence, ridiculed because of his fear of being left alone, an inessential figure:

> *Callimaco:* Say! don't leave me by myself.
> *Ligurio:* You seem besotted.
> *Callimaco:* Where do you want me to go now?
> *Ligurio:* Here and there, up this street, down that. It's a big place, is Florence.
> *Callimaco:* I am a dead man.

The third act unfolds without him, has no need for a character who provides no possibility of movement, who can only reemphasize, behind the appearance of a prestigious reputation, his own nature as a slavish and maddened lover.[33]

Simpler and more immediately recognizable is the definition of Nicia, he who in the external comic structure represents a priori the opposed negative pole, which Northrop Frye would call the *alazon*.[34] In reality, the negativity of Nicia is recognized not so much in his position as obstacle to Callimaco's success, in his relation to the journey of the protagonist toward his *felicitas*, as in his static condition as a "fool," in his passive irrationality inscribed in bourgeois norms and conventions. To these norms, as we have seen, Callimaco does not know how to oppose the aristocratic distance of the Machiavellian sage; he tends instead to make them the object of an adaptation that is not only tactical but essentially a revelation of the dose of "madness" and the slavishness that afflicts Callimaco himself.[35]

Certain anthropological details pertaining to Nicia, which remain constant throughout the play, are immediately put in relief. His stupidity and his foolishness are underlined by Callimaco. And Ligurio will subsequently inscribe this stupidity in a larger context, to the point of making it an exemplary model of "madness" and revealing its nexus

33. The servant Siro defines Callimaco as "maddened" (act 2, sc. 4).

34. Northrop Frye, *Anatomy of Criticism* (Princeton, N. J., 1957), 39–40, 172.

35. Certain very subtle similarities of behavior linking Callimaco and Nicia can be noted: both need to reaffirm their "faith" in Ligurio (already noted of Callimaco; for Nicia, see act 2, sc. 3: "I think that your advice is good"; and act 2, sc. 1: "On this score I want to rely on you"); and both must play additional roles (Callimaco that of a physician, Nicia that of a deaf man, in act 3).

with the irrational and topsy-turvy condition of Fortune, by identifying the absurd adaptation that the matrimonial bond has imposed upon the foolish Nicia and the wise Lucrezia.

> I do not think that there is in the world a bigger fool than he; and how Fortune has favored him! He is rich; she is a beautiful woman, well-behaved and capable of ruling a kingdom. And it seems to me that rarely do marriages bear out the proverb that says: God makes men, and they pair off!—because frequently one sees a well-qualified man end up with a dog [*bestia*], and on the other hand a prudent lady turns up with a fool.

Drawing on topoi from popular meditations on marriage, Ligurio links the theme of adaptation with that of "madness."[36] In Machiavelli the ideal of the sage and the prudent individual, capable of interpreting the movements of reality and of adapting his own nature to its varying directions, is developed in a constant relation to its own perfect contrary, that is, to madness, the absence of rational dominion and control. The clash with a political and social universe dominated by insecurity and unwilling to submit itself to a fixed, anthropocentric order has produced a revolutionary deepening and inversion of that humanistic ideal. Wisdom has discovered that it can affirm itself only in relation to its own contrary, in perpetual allusion to the world of ignorance, in persistent and ambiguous polemic against irrationality and folly.

But in this detached contemplation of its own overthrow, wisdom obtains the fruit of a decisive lesson: the "sage" becomes aware that he can become truly wise only if he also makes use of madness, only if he immerses himself in the conflicts of the real, opening himself to all of its contradictory developments, while maintaining his own control and his own rational enlightenment (he must know how to be at once "in earnest" and "gamesome," must know how to "act the fool", as sug-

---

36. This opposition should be seen in relation to the general question of Renaissance concepts of madness. See Michel Foucault, *Madness and Civilization,* trans. Richard Howard (New York, 1965), esp. chap. 1, "Stultifera navis," for a reconstruction of the meaning of images of folly and animality in northern Europe during the fifteenth century and for the reappropriation of the theme of folly in a humanistic model (e.g., by Erasmus and, I would add, by Ariosto). From the Italian side, which Foucault does not treat, one should begin at least with Alberti. Cf. Robert Klein, "Un aspect de l'herméneutique à l'âge de l'humanisme classique: Le thème du fou e l'ironie humaniste," in *L'umanismo e ermeneutica,* ed. Ernesto Castelli (Padua, 1963), 11–25; and the collection of essays also edited by Castelli, *L'umanesimo e la follia* (Rome, 1971).

gested in *The Discourses*).[37] "Virtue" is recognized precisely in the capacity for change (*mutamento*), in the refusal to remain fixated upon the one-sided obsessions to which the vulgar herd of fools clings.[38]

The fool, however, is he who does not know how to live with the continual tension between day and night, between seriousness and levity, between man and beast. He remains blindly anchored to his fixed mania, from which he cannot imagine displacing himself; he refuses to perceive the reverse side of things; he revels in his own fixation by devaluing whatever is contrary to it.[39] In *Mandragola* the folly and the "simplicity" of Nicia are precisely linked to his own fixed and one-sided obsession, which forces him to follow to its end the path of his ignorance, leading straight to his final status as a cuckold. This obsession is the "desire to have offspring" (explicitly declared by him in the second scene of act 1, and recalled often thereafter),[40] which makes of Nicia the blind and satisfied victim of a trick he never realizes has taken place.

> Quanto felice sia ciascun sel vede
> chi nasce sciocco ed ogni cosa crede!
> Ambizione nol preme,
> non lo muove il timore,
> che sogliono esser seme

37. "It is necessary then to play the fool, as did Brutus; and you play the fool often, praising, speaking, seeing, doing things against your own inclination, to please the prince" (*The Discourses*, bk. 3, chap. 2).

38. In this connection, see the letter to Vettori of January 5, 1514 (in Machiavelli, *Lettere*, ed. Gaeta, 315), which takes its cue from the various sexual manias of Giuliano Brancacci and Filippo Casavecchia to signal the contrast between the "dialectical unity" of the consciousness and behavior of the sage and the incidental variety of the manias of the fools: "Magnificent ambassador, there are none here except crazy men, and few there are who know this world, and who [also] know that he who tries to act in the ways of others never does anything, because men never have the same opinions. These do not know that he who is thought wise by day will never be held crazy by night; and that he who is thought a man of substance, and effective, whatever he does to refresh his spirit and live happily will bring him honor and not blame; and instead of being called a bugger or a whoremaster, it will be said that he is tolerant, ready, and a good companion." The same motif recurs in "La vita di Castruccio Castracani," collected in *Istorie fiorentine*, ed. Franco Gaeta (Milan, 1962), 38.

39. On the connections between the theme of madness and the imagery of an "animalesque world," see again the letter to Vettori of January 5, 1514 (Machiavelli, *Lettere*, ed. Gaeta, 315–16).

40. In act 2, sc. 2 ("I do not have sons, and I want them"); in the comic anticipations of act 3, sc. 8 (*Nicia:* You revive me entirely. Will he be a boy? *Ligurio:* A boy. *Nicia:* I am moved to tears) and in act 5, sc. 2 (Then we talked of the baby, and I already seem to have the little squirt in my arms!).

di noia e di dolore,
bramando aver figlioli
crederia ch'un asin voli
e qualunque altro ben posto ha in oblio,
e solo in questo ha posto il suo disío. (Act 2, song)

How happy is each can well be seen,
who's born a fool and everything believes!
Ambition does not spur him,
fear leaves him unmoved
(these are customarily the germs
of discomfiture and pain).
This your doctor
so desires to breed
he'd believe that asses fly.
Every other advantage he's forgotten
And of this one alone he's besotten.

The immutability of "nature" in the fool is made evident not only by his inability to understand the direction of the events of the play but by his own physical immobility, the confining spaces of his narrow existence. Act 1, scene 2 hinges entirely on Nicia's obsessive practice of never leaving his house, of "not letting the [cathedral] dome out of his sight." These passages also count as a satire on the limited and provincial horizons of a certain Florentine bourgeoisie. It is at this point that the thematics of "madness" and of "foolishness" are joined to the polemic with the public (or at least that sector of the public compromised by the negative traits Machiavelli recognizes in the Florentine middle class). The figure of Nicia is situated directly at the center of that play of "speaking ill" of which the prologue has shown the meaning; like "some brute / who scarcely knows if he's alive," he personally makes use of a chatty form of "speaking ill." But the speaking ill by Nicia is notable above all when it refers precisely to the Florentine situation, to the context contemporary with *Mandragola*. It assumes the aspect of a moral and political critique, an exposé of the Florentines' hostility to authentic *virtù* and genuine cultural values, of the otiose and workaday habits of Nicia's fellow citizens, of their ambiguous complicity with state power:

Nicia: This master of yours is a worthy.
Siro: More than that, even.
Nicia: He must be valuable to the French king.
Siro: Very.

Nicia: And for this reason he must willingly remain in France.

Siro: So I believe.

Nicia: He does well. There are nothing but diddlyshitters in this city; no virtue is esteemed here. If he were here, no-one would give him a second look. I know what I'm talking about, because I've shit my pants learning a few *abc*'s; and if I had to earn my living from it, I tell you I'd be up shit creek!

Siro: Do you earn a hundred ducats a year?

Nicia: Go on, not a hundred lire, not a hundred pence! And this is because anyone of our kind who is without status in this city, can't get a dog to bark at him, and we're good for nothing but going to wakes, or to weddings, or to hang out down at the Proconsul's bench all day leering at the girls. But I give them all a wide berth, I don't need anyone at all; let him who's worse off than me do the same! (Act 2, scene 3)[41]

Speaking ill of his own city, and expressing awed and absolute appreciation for everything that comes from France, derives from the same narrow attitude that he would seem to be holding up to ridicule. Nicia is in effect completely enclosed in the horizon that he pretends to criticize. His florentinity is perfectly contiguous with his "madness." Through him Machiavelli polemically reproduces the characteristics of the foolish public that maliciously gossips about his comedy; through Nicia he guarantees the possibility of revenging himself, just as maliciously, against that same public, but also offers to the public of the "sages" an occasion for detached laughter.[42]

On this level of the theatrically mediated polemic against the "madness" of the Florentine bourgeoisie can be located the political mainspring of *Mandragola*.[43] It is not a definition of precise programs and

41. Raimondi ("Il teatro del Machiavelli," 779) has rightly called attention to this "negative image" of Florence furnished by Nicia.

42. For the identification, in *Mandragola,* of this polemic against the Francophilia of the bourgeoisie under Piero Soderini, the suggestions of Giorgio Padoan ("*La Mandragola* del Machiavelli nella Venezia cinquecentesca," *Lettere italiane* 22 (1970): 161–86 [esp. 169 and 177]) are fundamental.

43. I would not wish my repeated references to a Machiavellian antibourgeois polemic to be misunderstood. The "bourgeoisie" to which I refer is simply the social and political class that supported the Florence of Soderini. The fact that Machiavelli polemicizes, throughout his works, against the ideological confusion and political incompetence of this class does not exclude the possibility of a subsequent association of the Florentine secretary with a "bourgeois" ideology more broadly defined.

precise homologies with the contemporary situation,[44] nor a bitter realization of the absence of a political universe, but rather the revelation
of anthropological dimensions that continually raise the possibility of
the identification or exclusion of a public, an audience, with which the
(author's) relationship is always necessarily political. This is a natural
conclusion if one notes that the comic genre and its accompanying
spectacle are not purely pleasure-giving forms but are the vehicles of
an "adaptation" to the conditions of a "miserable time" when Fortune
appears to favor fools. In *Mandragola* the accidental initial adaptation
between Nicia and Lucrezia (constituted by their marriage bond),
caused simply by malignant Fortune and certainly not by rational direction, is necessarily stripped away by a new and exceptional event.
After that event, every adaptation to Fortune will await the decision of
the "sage," Lucrezia, who is capable of distinguishing the interior
structure of things, of refusing every one-sided expression of herself, of
changing her own nature, if necessary. The centrality of the sage is
illuminated by means of contrast with the comic presence of the "fool,"
who is incapable of moving himself, of distinguishing between day
and night, between waking and sleeping, or of understanding the
meaning of what others are doing around him. Nicia asks:

> Is it day, or night? Am I awake, do I sleep? Am I drunk, and I
> haven't yet had a drink today—that I am going along with this
> blarney? We'd agreed to say one thing to the priest, and he says
> something else; then he wanted me to play deaf, and I would
> have had to cram pitch in my ear like the Danes in order not to
> hear the nonsense he has spoken, God knows to what end! I'm
> out twenty five ducats, and we've not yet spoken of my business,
> and they've planted me here like a ladder-rung in its slot. (Act 2,
> scene 7)

Compared with Callimaco and Nicia, Ligurio appears to be wholly
deprived of environmental and sociological implications; he exists only
as a function of his own role in the comedy, which never sinks to the
level of the merely supporting one that, in the classic scheme, falls to
the "parasite."[45] Instead he serves both as the governor and artificer of

---

44. As has been argued by Theodore A. Sumberg in *"La Mandragola:* An Interpretation," *Journal of Politics* 23 (1961): 320–40; and Antonio Parronchi in "La prima rappresentazione della *Mandragola," La bibliofila* 64 (1962): 37–86.

45. The blindness of Francesco De Sanctis, who took Ligurio to be the traditional type
of the "parasite," and then complained about the lack of space devoted to appropriate

the stage action, and as the pitiless critic of the actions of other characters, of their preoccupation with unnecessary complications that delay the unfolding of the action. Both as the "director" and as the commentator who "makes it strange,"[46] he moves wholly in terms of the structure and development of the play. His purely structural function and his independence from sociological attributes guarantee him the freedom to serve as a critic of the residues of the common and incongruous reality present in Callimaco and Nicia. We are thus aware of a singular form of "estrangement"; it is not the reference to reality that demystifies the pretenses of invention, but rather the demands of invention and construction that unmask the too narrow limits of a reality mired in compromised and fictitious social forms. This means that the structural essence of Ligurio does not tend toward abstraction or toward the devaluation of reality in general, but toward the demystifying critique of a partial and irrational reality. Whether commenting on the incongruity of the behavior of the characters or orchestrating a specific event, Ligurio does nothing else but prepare a condition of Fortune to which the wise Lucrezia, in a wholly autonomous decision, adapts her "nature."

Thus it is not a question of giving to Ligurio the weight due an authentic protagonist of the play or even an image of the Machiavellian prince. His own economic interest in the deception that he weaves is scarcely mentioned; his interest is above all directorial, aimed at the gratuitous construction of spectacle.[47] Nor does it seem appropriate for us to speak of Ligurio as possessing an embittered ethical nature,[48] even in an inverted sense, resting on an awareness of his own "malice" and on his contemplation of a world dominated by a corrupt confusion of values and interests. Detachment from the world of the other charac-

---

comic details, is well known; see his *Storia della letteratura italiana,* ed. Niccolò Gallo (Turin, 1966), 2:559.

46. According to the definition of Raimondi, "Il teatro del Machiavelli," 780.

47. For the "gratuitousness" of Ligurio's motivations, see his remarks to Callimaco in act 1, sc. 3 ("and were the utility that I feel and hope for not there, there's the fact that your blood is joined in sympathy to mine, and I want you to fulfill your desire, almost as much as you do") and act 5, sc. 4 ("I take great pleasure in your every good, and precisely what I told you has taken place"). As for Ligurio's role as theatrical director, in the first two acts alone he can be seen giving important "stage directions": at the end of act 1, sc. 2; at the end of act 2, sc. 2 and sc. 6. Note also that the only precise indication of locations on stage in the first two acts comes from Ligurio, when he points out Callimaco's house to Nicia (act 2, sc. 1), and that Ligurio designs and regulates the movements in and out of the houses of Nicia and Callimaco (e.g., act 2, sc. 2).

48. Blasucci (in the introduction to Machiavelli, *Opere letterarie,* xxi) insists on the "ethical nature" of Ligurio.

ters is always internal to the structural function of Ligurio; it does not arise from moral dimensions.

In the first two acts, it is the anthropological and sociological definition of Callimaco and Nicia through their reciprocal adaptation, rather than the rhythm of theatrical invention, that prevails. In the third act, the directorial capacity of Ligurio opens the way to a succession of adaptations, of fictions, of displacements. His efforts culminate in the powerful scene of the encounter and clash between Lucrezia and friar Timoteo—characters that appear before the spectators for the first time in this act, and that escape the control of Ligurio. Unlike Callimaco and Nicia, they operate in relative autonomy, free from the manipulations of the "parasite."[49]

Friar Timoteo is placed in a singular sphere, whose horizon is untouched by the initiatives of Ligurio. In effect the figure of the friar occupies a complex position in the comedy. Like Ligurio, Timoteo evades any precise anthropological definition, but unlike the parasite, this character cannot be reduced to the linearity of a structural function without sociological and environmental connotations. He maintains the rigorous consistency of a structural character, essential to the movement of the play and fully conscious of it, yet he refers us to a precise world, extraneous to the theater, and describes with realistic coherence his own universe of habits, manners, and friaresque language.[50] His actions, as it is easy to recognize, are guided by purely economic motives, which do not result so much from the externalization of a personal "nature" as from his social placement as the exponent of a religion perceived precisely as an economic and utilitarian institution. In the play the profit motive and "wickedness" (*tristizia*) are the natural basis of the universe, of reality—a situation that for Machiavelli does not constitute a problem but, if anything, is merely the objective residue of observation and judgment. To introduce moral turns, even if inverted, into such a universe reduces the Florentine

49. In the last part of act 3, at the central moment of his encounter with Lucrezia, it is Timoteo himself who assumes to some extent the role of the director, and with respect to Ligurio: "You go off to church, I'll wait here for the women. Stay aside so that you're not seen; and once they've gone, I'll tell you what they've said" (sc. 8); "O Ligurio, come out here!" (sc. 12). Nevertheless, the directorial role of Ligurio remains preeminent through most of the act and functions even with respect to friar Timoteo in the fourth scene, which is an example of framing a new and fictitious supplemental intrigue within the central one, with the false story of the niece of Nicia, pregnant "in a convent"—a story that serves to test the pliability of the friar.

50. Vanossi, in "Situazione e sviluppo," 44, has thus been able to speak of "an intermediate position" for Timoteo, who for him "represents the point of highest tension between the scrutiny of reality and the demands of structure."

secretary to the role of forerunner (however masked) of an idealistic and petit bourgeois morality, perhaps with the intention of relieving him of the burden of infamy placed on him by Catholic tradition.[51] In Machiavellian terms, a distinction between positive and negative behaviors can take place only on the plane of rationality and in the capacity for adapting oneself to the diverse movements of the real.

In *Mandragola* the "economic" base of reality is presented as the external dimension of Fortune, with which the "prudent" Lucrezia must clash and to which she must adapt, impressing on the real her own seal of sagacity. To understand why friar Timoteo should be the character in whom the economic and utilitarian attributions appear most concentrated, we must first ascertain why the task of introducing Lucrezia (in the only real dialogue in which she participates on the stage) to the mass of Fortune's forces that she will need to confront in giving supreme proof of herself, should be assigned precisely to him.

I have several times noted that this, the highest "anthropological" value, belongs to the character of Lucrezia, to whom—as the figure of the beloved lady and the logical object of deception—the external schema of the erotic intrigue conventionally assign a wholly passive and receptive role in comparison with that, traditionally more significant, of the male lover. Machiavelli, however, breaks the external schema and the expectations of a public quick to recur to a well-authorized ideology. He inverts the meaning of the relation between Callimaco and Lucrezia, completely devaluing the former and giving the latter exceptional and isolated relief. This relief is all the more clear in that it is sustained by the almost total absence of Lucrezia from the stage. The tenth and eleventh scenes of the third act and the final scene of the comedy aside, Lucrezia is always remote, frequently named and exalted in terms that sharply delineate her isolation and her distance from the horizon of the other characters and the movements of the play. Even the crucial moment that defines her "transformation" and her "adaptation" to Fortune does not unfold on the stage but is only related from afar, by the complacent Callimaco (act 5, scene 4).

Furthermore, her distance from the stage underpins the possibility of offering her as a positive model and as a possible substitute for the

---

51. The most fastidious, most extreme statement of this "moralistic" interpretation of the character of the friar (and of *Mandragola* in general) is found in the writings of Riccardo Bacchelli, "'Istorico, comico e tragico,' ovvero Machiavelli artista," *Nuova antologia* 90 (1960): 3–20. As to Machiavelli's position on religion, discussion of which would be out of place here, it will suffice to consult the essay of Alberto Tenenti, "La religione di Machiavelli," *Studi storici* 10 (1969): 709–48.

members of the audience (especially the female spectators ["and I would wish / that you should be deceived as she was"]). This model and this substitution suggest themselves to us precisely because Lucrezia too finds herself, in part, outside the stage scene, observing it, as do the spectators themselves. For this reason her only conversation takes place with friar Timoteo, the character who is most aloof from the scene, who most observes others and is most nearly joined to the spectators.

The isolation of Lucrezia is due to the exceptional attribute of "sagacity," which is assigned to her by the other characters (recall Ligurio in act 1, scene 3: "a beautiful woman, sage, well-mannered and capable of ruling a kingdom"). Her sagacity is situated at the outset in a particular personal "nature," composed of piety and goodness, firm in its total acceptance of the rules of moral comportment. She is "most honest, and wholly alien to the business of love" (act 1, scene 1), "sage and good" (act 3, scene 9); her "prudence and rigor" (act 4, scene 1) are situated consciously in the same coherent morality, but with a coherence that is a sign of superior "gravity," the buttress of an exemplary "reputation."

But in order to overcome the absurd matrimonial adaptation that Fortune has imposed on her by joining her to Nicia, in order to reach a degree of success and of happiness, the "sage" lady must "adapt herself to" (*porsi a riscontro con*) a situation that does not accord at all with that goodness and that "grave" moral universe. The action carried forward by the comedy arrays before her a complex of circumstances that exclude the practicability of these values of chastity and goodness.

Chapter 18 of *The Prince* shows that it is a supreme and useful thing to "appear pious, faithful, humane, whole, religious and to be such," but that it is equally necessary "to be so constructed in your will, that, when it is necessary not to be such, you are able and know how to change into the contrary" (*mutare el contrario*); chapter 25 affirms with clarity the "happy" condition of whoever "suits his way of proceeding to the quality of the times." We know that the ambition of the Machiavellian sage was to always know how to adapt his own "way of proceeding" to the "variations" of Fortune, changing with a heroic effort his own "nature," despite the theoretical premise of the impossibility of this "transformation." Faced with a situation in which her natural goodness finds no vital space, Lucrezia realizes this ambition of the sage to be transformed, disposing herself to "become of another nature" in yielding to the corruption of her own goodness,[52] passing from

---

52. These are the terms used by Callimaco in act 1, sc. 1, in passages already cited.

one who is "perfectly good" to one who is "honorably wicked,"[53] thus achieving a happy adaptation to Fortune.

Act 3, scenes 10–11 present the direct collision between Lucrezia and the situation to which her grave and honest "way of proceeding" no longer adapts itself. Hence, the dryness and hardness of the language of the sage woman before a universe that appears hostile and incomprehensible to her earlier nature, or rather "strange," beyond any possibility of measure and valuation ("But of all the things discussed, this seems to me the strangest" [scene 10]; "but this seems to me the strangest thing that was ever heard" [scene 11]). Her brief remarks in response to the elaborate discourse of friar Timoteo mark her critical detachment when faced with this unheard-of "strangeness." She refuses to acknowledge the precise terms mentioned by her captious interlocutor ("Do you speak seriously, or are you merely joking?"; "May God will it!"; "To what do you persuade me?"; "Where are you leading me, father?").

The presence of notable hints of ritual significance betrays even more directly the heroic and almost mythical meaning of this expected transformation, and includes the comedy within the circle of an authentic rite of rebirth and fecundation, as Raimondi has perspicaciously suggested.[54] Lucrezia's reference to a mythical occasion of resurrection of a destroyed humanity ("for I'd scarcely believe it, were I the only woman left in the world, and human nature were to rise again from me, that such a role would be given to me" [act 3, scene 10]); the allusion of friar Timoteo to the biblical episode of Lot's daughters ("the Bible says that Lot's daughters, thinking themselves alone in the world, had congress with their father" [act 3, scene 11]); the final recommendation given by the friar, with the promise to recite the fecundating prayer of the angel Raphael ("I will entreat God for you, I will say the prayer of the angel Raphael, so that he may accompany you" [scene

53. This is the well-known language of *The Discourses*, bk. 1, chap. 18, the contemporaneity of which makes clear the paradox that rules Machiavelli's anthropology and whose terms were noted by Russo in "Machiavelli," 108–11, in his passionate reevaluation of the character of Lucrezia; see also Eugenio Levi, "La *Mandragola* di Machiavelli," in *Il comico di carattere da Teofrasto a Pirandello* (Turin, 1959), 48–62. More recently, Blasucci has insisted on the central importance of Lucrezia; see the introduction to Machiavelli, *Opere letterarie*, xvii–xix, and the very useful notes. All these critics have, however, emphasized the "moral" value of the character, without revealing its more far-reaching meaning as a model of political behavior.

54. Raimondi, "Il teatro del Machiavelli," 774–75, 783. Raimondi, making use of Frye and Bakhtin, has associated with the ritual ordering of *Mandragola* the countertendency of a "parodic thrust" and of "the comic ambivalence, flavored with a tendency toward desecration, of the carnival farce."

11]);[55] and Lucrezia's final invocation ("God and our lady help me" [scene 11])—all are hints of a ritualizing religiosity that underline in an exemplary manner the significance of the conflict between Timoteo and Lucrezia, the tendentially mythical and sacral rhythm in which external Fortune offers occasion to the "sage" woman who must gird herself to control and dominate it.

But the comedy can take on these mythical and ritual values only by overturning them, by giving the lie to every "grave" sacrality with that subtle aroma of blasphemy that rules the circumstances and discourse of Timoteo. Fortune can reveal her own divinity only through the screen of the comic. Moreover, the inverted terms that characterize the theatrical unfolding of the supreme Machiavellian anthropological myth should not be forgotten; nor should we forget that in *Mandragola* the sage must be drawn within the comic zone of "vain thoughts." For this reason the sage is encircled by a sphere of blasphemous malice, and for this reason above all, "he" [editors' note: Italian "savio"] is represented by a female character, relegated by tradition and by definition to the lower stratum, to the levity of the fields of love and pleasure. In the world of the comedy, the sage has reversed (him/her)self, incarnated in a woman, contemplating struggle with Fortune not in the terms of political jousting, but in those of erotic relationships.

The traditional erotic motif offers to the sage the image of a happy relation to Fortune, one that can be easily incorporated, as it is in *Mandragola*, by a plot that includes both erotic deception and the affirmation of a female figure. In the toils of this "levity," the hard struggle of the sage with the external world can become an easier, and a victorious, one. The indulgence of love thus becomes for Machiavelli almost an occasion of recuperation, allowing the discovery of an easy adaptation to Fortune in contrast with the far more difficult and problematic conditions in the political arena.[56] Descending to the comic, the "serious" individual finds there a paradoxical guarantee of success through the symbolic figure of a lady "sage and good," through her capacity for accepting her own "corruption" and "transformation." The fulfillment of this success is necessarily accompanied by a blasphemous contamination of serious themes.

The sage woman, for her part, must establish a close relation with a universe that is "low," must allow herself to the assisted by the "beast"

---

55. For the biblical reference (to the first book of Tobit), see Raimondi, "Il teatro del Machiavelli," 774.

56. Cf. Machiavelli's comments on love in a series of letters to Vettori beginning in 1514 (Machiavelli, *Lettere*, ed. Gaeta, 322–23, 343, 347).

precisely during the salient moments of her joust with Fortune. In fact, the companionable baggage, Sostrata, defined explicitly as "a beast" by friar Timoteo (act 3, scene 10), accompanies Lucrezia in her encounter with the friar, and will be close to her in the culminating moments of the nocturnal deception (Sostrata announces it already in act 3, scene 11: "I myself want to put her to bed tonight"); Lucrezia therefore has need of the "beast," and she reminds us again of the Machiavellian prince, who must "know how to make good use of both the man and the beast."[57]

The colloquy with Timoteo, even though not resolved in the much-awaited transformation of nature, puts into evidence the conditions for it and prepares its realization. From then on, Lucrezia, though absent from the stage, is definitively established as the effective mistress (*dominatrice*) of the drama, its total center. The gestures and movements of the various other characters in the last two acts are ordered in ever more mobile and farcical directions, and offer pretexts for masking and for a whirling, gratuitous play. No longer do they serve for the rigorous construction of lots. They avoid the earlier concern with defining "natures" and setting forth anthropological data. The rule of Ligurio is henceforth relegated to the mise-en-scène of the masquerade in act 4, which receives its meaning more by virtue of the gratuitousness of its enactment that as a result of its functional role in the plot. All the characters have become objects with respect to Lucrezia, who has reversed the position she apparently occupied at the outset, which, it then seemed, should have made her the passive object of the desires and initiatives of Callimaco.

Callimaco, for his part, attempts at the beginning of act 4 to present himself once again in a positive way, as an aspirant to the role of protagonist of the play. The monologue in the first scene is his meditation on the contradictoriness of the real and on the power of Fortune:

57. It would be extremely interesting to link this "centauresque" dimension of the play's protagonist to the image that adorns the frontispiece of its first edition (reproduced in Ridolfi, ed., *La Mandragola*, 15, and in his *Studi sulle commedie*, 30), that of a centaur playing the lyre. (Nino Pirrotta, in Pirrotta and Elena Polvoledo, *Music and Theater from Poliziano to Monteverdi*, 120–21 [Cambridge, 1982, first published in Italian, 1969], first called attention to the image.) This is probably the figuration of that Chiron who, in chap. 18 of *The Prince*, is presented as a pedagogical model, perfect in being "half beast and half man," of the necessary bivalence of the Machiavellian "sage." The image on the frontispiece might allude, symbolically, to the inner meaning of *Mandragola*, to its role as a model for the affirmation of a *virtù* capable of shuttling between the different "natures." The identification of such an allusion can be confirmed, however, only by a scrutiny of the iconographic tradition and of the contacts that Machiavelli could have had with that tradition.

And is it true that Fortune and nature hold the scales in balance: she does not do you a good turn, but a bad one rises up to meet it. As hope has grown, so fear has grown as well. Woe is me! Is it possible that I can live in such affliction, perturbed by these fears and hopes? I am a ship vexed by two different winds, which fears the more the closer it is to port.

Having displayed this awareness of his own condition, Callimaco seems to take on the image of a superior wisdom that permits him to stare in the face of luck as both a "man" and a "sage" without indulging in sterile and unproductive emotional hesitations:

What are you doing? are you mad? When you get her, what will happen? Will you recognize your error, will you regret your efforts and the thoughts you've had? Don't you know what little good is found in the things a man desires, with respect to those that man supposes he will find? On the other hand, the worst that can come about is that you'll die and burn in hell; yet so many others have died! and so many men of good parts are in hell! Should you be ashamed of going there? Turn your face to luck, flee mischance, or, not being able to flee from it, bear it like a man; do not prostrate yourself, do not cheapen yourself like a woman.

The reference to the force of the "man" and the weakness of the "woman" acquires an equivocal sense, if we note that it is precisely to a woman that *Mandragola* attributes the role of self-sufficient wisdom. But despite the richly authentic Machiavellian detail ("and so many men of good parts are in hell!") and despite his attempt to emerge from his condition of crazed lover, Callimaco remains mired in his comic "slavishness"—because of the indeterminateness of his laments, because of his insufficient awareness of the ambiguities of the erotic universe.

With any possibility of reintroducing Callimaco in a positive light as protagonist discarded, it is Ligurio who assumes the task of organizing the nocturnal masquerade, which partly deprives him of his usual attitude of detachment and nonparticipation in direct intrigue, and immerses him, together with the other characters, in a gratuitously theatrical activity. From this point on, I reiterate, the drama and its action are entrusted completely to the initiative of the present-absent Lucrezia. In orbit around her, the theatrical action can freely accelerate and articulate itself in a play of pure gestures and figurative suggestions, approaching ballet as a representational limit.

The prevalence on the stage of these diversions cannot signify, in my opinion, the enactment of a "corruption of the drama," of an explosion of the "negativity" of the material.[58] Rather, it constitutes a theatrical manner of confirming the definitive affirmation of the "sage" Lucrezia, of emphasizing that from this point on, the other characters will exhaust their tasks as builders of a mechanism of Fortune and can be reduced to objects of gratuitous doodling. (A "doodle" or "bauble" ["badalucco"] is not necessarily a negative term for Machiavelli, since it functions as a necessary comic foil to the central emphasis on the "sage.") The drama of Lucrezia would be one-sided and conventional if it did not have as its mirror this antithetical opening to an arbitrary and unbridled comic thrust. The game of disguises becomes most intense at the entrance of Nicia on the stage in scene 8,[59] the figurative contours of which were announced by Ligurio's sally in the preceding scene. He there underlined precisely the ridiculous nature of this appearance of the old "doctor":

Who wouldn't laugh? He has an old doublet on, that doesn't cover his ass. What in the devil does he have in mind? He seems one of these canonical owls, with a little sword worn beneath: Hah hah! he's blubbering I know not what. (Act 4, scene 7)

Around Nicia also unfolds the facile Calandrinesque trick of the hepatic aloe nuts (which has its source precisely in Boccaccio's novella of Calandrino and the stolen pig, *Decameron,* bk. 8, chap. 6) and the jocose mimesis of a military maneuver, in the masked squad that Ligurio trains for the "assault" on the "young lummox" (*garzonaccio*)—"I want to be captain, and draw up my army for the day. On the right attacking horn let Callimaco be placed, I'll come up on the left; between the two horns stands the doctor, here; Siro will be the rear guard, to relieve whatever troops begin to waver. We fight under the name of Saint Cuckoo" (act 4, scene 9). The gratuitousness of this make-believe is emphasized to such an extent that one even suspects its indefinite repeatability and thus the possibility of a reduplication of the whole scene. (The same concern strikes Nicia: "I wouldn't want us to bob for a crab, who'd be old or sickly; so that we'd have to repeat this little game tomorrow evening".)

To the free comic play of these scenes (including act 5, scene 2 as

---

58. This is the thesis of Vanossi, "Situazione e sviluppo," 54, who also furnishes useful suggestions concerning this scene. Regarding the insertion of these scenes into an "'unworthy' context," see also Bárberi Squarotti, "La struttura astratta," 72.

59. Ezio Raimondi has noted the emphasis on masquerades and disguises in *Mandragola* ("Il teatro del Machiavelli," 782–83), referring as well to the definition of the "carnivalesque world" furnished by Bakhtin in *Rabelais and His World*.

well) corresponds the absolute concentration of Lucrezia's speech, which defines the fulfillment of her change of nature and her impassive and complete acceptance of the new conditions with which fortune has presented her. This speech is assigned to Callimaco in the fourth scene of the last act; conveying the message in the words of the young and lucky lover emphasizes the difference in level between Callimaco and Lucrezia, making clear that every decision and every solution derives definitively from the will of Lucrezia, and that Callimaco, in this final moment, is consigned to an auxiliary role.

The reasons Callimaco believes have convinced Lucrezia to take him on as a lover appear, in this light, rather generic: the promise of eventual matrimony upon the death of Nicia, and his own undeniable superiority, as a male, to the old doctor:

> After I had made myself known to her, and I had given her to understand the love I bore her, and how easily, given the simplemindedness of her husband, we could live happily without risk of discovery, and promising her that, upon such time as God saw fit to do away with him, I would take her as a wife; and she, over and beyond my sound arguments, had tasted the difference between Nicia's performance in bed and my own, and between the kisses of a young lover and those of an aged husband.

To the obviousness of these reasons, Lucrezia does not even answer; she does not even take them into consideration. She prefers instead to reaffirm, in a closely and rigorously calibrated speech, the circumstances and meaning of her own "corruption":

> Now that your cleverness, the idiocy of my husband, the stupidity of my mother and the wickedness of my confessor have led me to do what I should never have done on my own account, I want [*voglio*] to judge that this comes to pass because of a heavenly decree that has so willed it, and I am not sufficient to refuse what heaven bids me to accept.

The four grammatical subjects listed in the initial clauses summarize the forces of Fortune that have worked on Lucrezia. The four characters named find here the recognition of their condition as authors of the situation offered by Fortune, with which the sage woman has clashed and to which she has had to adapt. When she is confronted with this situation, the active and judging subject (not by chance is the governing verb "I want") remains preeminent; the acceptance of Fortune is entirely conscious and counts as an acceptance of responsibility, as a taking possession of the circumstances. Thus Lucrezia now gives orders to Callimaco and formulates precise plans for the future:

> Therefore I take you as my lord, my master, my guide; I want you to be my father, you my defender, and you my entire good; and, what my husband has wished for a single night, I want him to have always. You will then become his godparent, and you will come this morning to church, and thence you will come to dine with us; and the coming and going will be up to you, and we will be able to be together, at any time, without suspicion.

If we were dealing with the conventional solution to an amorous intrigue, we would find a profusion of sentiment and traditional heroic motifs in this speech. Instead, Lucrezia delineates a genuinely political relationship with Callimaco (note the terms "lord," "master," "guide," "father," "defender," which have also been interpreted as supporting the definition of Lucrezia as a symbol of the "body" politic and of her lover as a symbol of the "prince"[60]). Everything in this relationship derives from the personal decision of the sage woman (note the repetition of "I want" and the succession of future tenses by which Lucrezia imposes on her interlocutor a temporal dimension that she alone establishes).

Callimaco's reaction to this rigorous choice by Lucrezia remains conventional and unfocused, suspended between the inability to respond adequately and the rehearsal of traditional erotic and eudaemonistic motifs:

> Hearing these words, I was about to die of the sweetness. I was unable to answer to even a fraction of the extent that I would have wished. So much so that I find myself to be the happiest and most satisfied man who ever lived; and if this joy were not to fail because of death or age, I'd be more beatified than the blessed, holier than the saints.

In order to accept in a strictly autonomous way a new fortune, the wise Lucrezia has had to know how to "change natures," how to attain the perfect antithesis of her former goodness. Her appearance on the stage, at the conclusion of the play, yields physical and gestural evidence of this accomplished transformation, revealing in her an entirely new and different manner of proceeding, one that seems to Nicia *alla pazzeresca,*

---

60. See the previously cited articles by Sumberg, "*La Mandragola:* An Interpretation"; and Parronchi, "La prima rappresentazione della *Mandragola.*"

drawing from him repeated marveling exclamations ("Look how she answers! You'd think her a cock! . . . You're very bold this morning!" [act 5, scene 5]). Sostrata explains: "she's a bit changed" ("alterata"—made other"); Nicia confirms the meaning of this "alteration" by placing it within the rhythm of a rebirth and resurrection ("for it's just as if, this morning, you had been reborn" [scene 5]); and friar Timoteo reiterates the sense of youthfulness regained that is implicit in the transformation of Lucrezia from one who is "perfectly good" to one who is "honorably wicked" ("And you, Madam Sostrata, you have, in my opinion, set a shoot on the old stump" [act 5, scene 6]).

This affirmation of youthfulness finds a precise place in the Machiavellian ideological universe, as a corollary to the affirmation of the ability to effect an active "adaptation" to Fortune, as a mythic image of political vigor and success. It is this willingness to "change natures" that is the guarantee of youthfulness. If, as has been argued, "youthfulness" constitutes the "myth" of *Mandragola*,[61] it does not do so in an archetypical or metahistorical sense. Rather, youthfulness makes possible a resolution of the contradictions of Machiavellian ideology in an image of power, of energetic virtù, of success. The youth of Lucrezia can make real that transformation of nature that appeared impossible from the perspective of the theoretical travails of *The Prince*. The myth of youthfulness is also present in chapter 25 of *The Prince*, in the advice to "be impetuous" and the affirmation that Fortune is "the friend of the young," which offer a symbolic and passionate escape route from the theoretical discovery of the impossibility of a constant "adaptation" to Fortune. "Youthfulness" is, in the last analysis, an essential myth for Machiavelli's anthropology as a whole; we will be able to establish its active presence in the *Clizia* as well, which will provide an opportunity to outline some of its fundamental characteristics, especially in relation to the negative myth of "old age."[62]

In its invocation of the theme of youthfulness as the foundation for those of "transformation" and "adaptation," *Mandragola* confirms itself as the comedy of the "sage's" success, affirms its existence within the comic orbit where it may only "make [Machiavelli's] sad time sweeter." More than a degradation of the self in "unworthy" material and by means of a female character, the Machiavellian sage here finds a literary and symbolic rescue from the evil of the times, a realization within

61. See Raimondi, "Il teatro del Machiavelli," esp. 783–84; following the suggestions of Frye's "archetypal criticism," he identifies the myth of *Mandragola* as that, precisely, of youthfulness (*giovinezza*).

62. [Editors' note: The original Italian essay continues the discussion of the "mutazione" and "riscontro" theme in *Clizia*. See also the essay by Ronald L. Martinez in this volume.]

the theatrical space of something that appears to be unavailable to him in the real world.

But *Mandragola* escapes the conditions of pure literary sublimation; the symbolic route to the rediscovery of the energies that lead the "sage" to success is inverted and ambiguous. Crossing the terrain of "vain thoughts," the play also knows how to mock both itself and the outside world maliciously, to laugh at every sacred and ritual deployment of the myth that it proposes. Laughing (thanks to the means of "speaking ill") at the social, moral, and religious values of the Florentine bourgeois class, descending as far as possible into the "lowlife" of the comic world, the sage finds a more than merely literary accord with external "nature" and with the "times," rediscovering the active value of laughter, of comic invention, of the mocking smirk, of that aspect of humanity which tradition was wont to keep hidden and almost to condemn.[63] Thus, concluding at the moment when the characters enter church to celebrate a religious rite ("let us all go to church, and there we will say the usual prayer" [act 5, scene 6]), *Mandragola* offers a final happy inversion of the world of established values, a final comic and mocking glance at material which by tradition would be presumed "worthy"—which, indeed, in a universe both "honest" and "grave," would be presumed to be virtually sacred.[64]

Translated by Ronald L. Martinez

63. On this "comic" strain in Western culture, consult, again, Bakhtin, *Rabelais and His World,* for confirmation that it is something more than a tradition of intellectual satire. The "laughter" of *Mandragola* does not have a satiric intention; its aim is rather to reveal a fundamentally "bivalent" dimension.

64. Only when my essay was already in proof was I able to read the essay by Giovanni Aquilecchia, "La favola *Mandragola* si chiama," in *Collected Essays on Italian Language and Literature, Presented to Kathleen Speight,* ed. Aquilecchia, Stephen N. Cristea, and Sheila Ralphs (Manchester, 1971), 73–100. This essay proposes with remarkable rigor a mythic-symbolic interpretation of *Mandragola,* departing from a precise justification of the title and going back to the most ancient sources of the superstitions relating to the extraction of the herb mandragora. Machiavelli's comedy reveals itself, in this reading, as the parodic mimesis of these superstitions and of the Christian-symbolic interpretations that were given of them, especially in biblical exegesis. The meanings identified by Aquilecchia, although not immediately congruent with my perspective concerning the play, nevertheless illuminate many of its details (e.g., in the description of ritual spaces and of the relative extent of jocular deconsecration). [Editors' note: For a more recent discussion, see Ronald L. Martinez, "The Pharmacy of Machiavelli: Roman Lucretia in *Mandragola,*" *Renaissance Drama* 14 (1983): 1–43.]

CHAPTER FOUR

BENEFIT OF ABSENCE: MACHIAVELLIAN VALEDICTION IN *CLIZIA*

Ronald L. Martinez

STUDENTS of *Clizia* have recognized that the play's plot, in which the aged Nicomaco attempts the seduction of a foundling girl he has raised, fictionalizes the self-reprobation of Machiavelli's passion, late in his life, for the singer Barbera Salutati. So read, the spectacle of Nicomaco's decay in *Clizia* literally stages the failure of Machiavelli as lover and man of action. The autobiographical datum, however, is the point of departure for a meditation within *Clizia* on larger questions of temporal decline and renewal, and on the place of the humanist within his tradition.

In a sense Machiavelli's last work, *Clizia*, has never fared exceptionally well with readers, who have seen it as evidence of Machiavelli's failing powers and growing discouragement; the play's effects have been judged both excessively farcical and disconcertingly somber.[1] But it is precisely the atypicality of *Clizia* as a Machiavellian product that is of interest. After the audacity of *Mandragola*, the orthodox exercise of imitation that is *Clizia* raises questions about Machiavelli's relation to classical antiquity at a late stage of his life. Despite the farcical and

Except where otherwise noted, English translations of Machiavelli's works are from *The Comedies of Machiavelli*, ed. and trans. David Sices and James B. Atkinson (Hanover, N.H., 1985); *The Discourses of Niccolò Machiavelli*, ed. and trans. Leslie J. Walker, S.J., 2 vols. (London, 1975); *Florentine Histories*, trans. Laura F. Banfield and Harvey C. Mansfield (Princeton, N.J., 1988); *The Letters of Machiavelli*, ed. and trans. Allan H. Gilbert (Chicago, 1961).

1. See Giorgio Padoan, "Il tramonto di Machiavelli," *Lettere italiane* 33 (1981): 457–81; Niccolò Machiavelli, *The Comedies of Machiavelli*, ed. and trans. David Sices and James B. Atkinson (Hanover, N.H., 1985); and Giulio Ferroni, *Mutazione e riscontro nel teatro di Machiavelli e altri saggi sulla commedia del '500* (Rome, 1972), 19–137.

obscene elements that abound in the play, the humiliation of the protagonist tests the generic limits of comedy. The presence of a biographical motive for writing the play puts into the foreground problems of the relation between the author, his play, and circumstantial historical and biographical contexts. As a valedictory work, in which Machiavelli projects a difficult existential situation, the play appears to be a sober meditation on male ambition and power—*virtù*—and their limits, suggesting a kind of retraction of key tenets of Machiavelli's mature thought. Indeed, the play is in many respects Machiavelli's testament as a playwright, humanist, political thinker, and citizen.

Clizia after Mandragola

Insofar as *Clizia* represents Machiavelli's comic legacy, he must reckon with his own previous masterpiece, *Mandragola.* I have argued elsewhere that an oblique but searching allegorism is fundamental to that play. In the context of the account given in the *The Discourses* of the political and military successes under the Roman constitution, the description of the subversion of Monna Lucrezia represents a parody of the heroism of Roman Lucretia, the story of whose rape and suicide constitutes an etiological fable of the Roman *virtù* lacking in Machiavelli's Florence. Written during Machiavelli's forced exile from politics, the play bids a sardonic farewell to republican virtue that salves with amoral carnival license the frustration of the playwright's political ambitions and ideals.[2] Though *Mandragola* has usually been sharply distinguished from *Clizia* with respect to quality and mood, recent critics have come to see that Machiavelli's two original plays in fact have much in common beyond the conspicuous reference, in *Clizia,* to the engaging and corrupt friar Timoteo of *Mandragola.*[3] Drawing on the metaphor of military campaigns against female chastity (the virginity of Clizia, the married chastity of Lucrezia), both plays develop Machiavelli's stated views on rivalry over women as a catalyst for political

---

2. See Ronald L. Martinez, "The Pharmacy of Machiavelli: Roman Lucretia in *Mandragola,*" *Renaissance Drama* 14 (1983): 1–43. Hanna Fenichel Pitkin, in *Fortune Is a Woman: Gender and Politics in the Thought of Niccolò Machiavelli* (Berkeley, Calif., 1984), gives a similar reading; the two accounts are independent.

3. For parallels, see especially Padoan, "Il tramonto di Machiavelli," 477–81; Niccolò Machiavelli, *Mandragola, Clizia* (with an introduction by Ezio Raimondi) (Milan, 1984), 55–56; Luigi Vanossi, "Situazione e sviluppo nel teatro machiavelliano," in Vanossi et al., *Lingua e strutture del teatro italiano del Rinascimento* (Padua, 1970), 76–77; Ferroni, *Mutazione e riscontro,* 123–25, 128–30. The commission for writing *Clizia* was developed in conversations at Fornaciari's villa after a performance there of *Mandragola.* See Roberto Ridolfi, *The Life of Niccolò Machiavelli,* trans. Cecil Grayson (Chicago, 1963), 208–9.

conflict.[4] Whereas in the *Mandragola* a tragic background is provided by the heroic example of Roman Lucretia—a background that subtly undercuts the triumphant amorality of Lucrezia's corruption—in *Clizia* the comic action, culminating in the humiliation of Nicomaco, touches on the tragic archetype of punished pride or hubris. (In Plautus's *Casina*, Machiavelli's source play, the old man, the *senex*, is symbolically castrated.)[5]

The tragic resonances in both plays, and their stake in liturgies of cathartic violence, are closely related to their underlying patterns of carnival festivity: both plays are explicitly set during carnival, which in Renaissance Florence lasted from Epiphany until Shrove Tuesday.[6] The adulterous economy merrily established in *Mandragola* is echoed, but also castigated, in the drubbing and humiliation of Nicomaco, whose senescent priapism is a form of misrule, the excess of a patriarch whose pretense at rejuvenescence brings chaos to his household. In this connection, the plot (and the plotting) in both plays thematizes the danger of public humiliation for the middle-class family: in *Mandragola* because of scandals that might arise from Timoteo's stratagems ("the entire house of Calfucci will be disgraced" [act 3, scene 4]) and in *Clizia* because of the designs of the paterfamilias on the child raised by his wife.[7] Implicit in both plays are Machiavelli's recurring anxieties about the possibility of regenerating the Florentine polity, obscurely symbolized in *Mandragola* by the desire of Nicia Calfucci to have a child (act 1,

4. On siege imagery in *Mandragola* and its debt to Livy, see Martinez, "The Pharmacy of Machiavelli," 12–13. Machiavelli discusses women as political catalysts in *The Discourses*, bk. 3, chap. 26. For discussion, see Martinez, "The Pharmacy of Machiavelli," 9–10; and Pitkin, *Fortune Is a Woman*, 115–31. The idea can be traced back to Livy (cf. Helen North, *Sophrosyne: Self-Knowledge and Self-Restraint in Greek Literature* [Ithaca, N.Y., 1966], 287–90); and to Aristotle (cf. Pitkin, *Fortune Is a Woman*, 115).

5. On the symbolic castration of the senex, see Giorgio Chiarini, "In margine a un'edizione commentata della Casina: questioni filologiche e letterarie," *Studi italiani di filologia classica* 49 (1977): 226. On the tragic aspects of Nicomaco, see Luigi Russo, *Machiavelli*, 3d ed. (Bari, 1949), 130–33; Vanossi, "Situazione e sviluppo," 75–76, 104–7; and Ferroni, *Mutazione e riscontro*, 132.

6. In Renaissance Italy, carnival was the preferred season for theatrical performances. *Clizia* refers to carnival as being in progress (act 2, sc. 3); see also act 3, sc. 1 and act 2, sc. 3. On carnival patterns in *Mandragola*, see Martinez, "The Pharmacy of Machiavelli," 21–23.

7. In *Clizia*, Cleandro introduces this topic in act 1, sc. 1: "è una tresca el fatto nostro" (our affairs are a scandal [my translation]); in *Mandragola*, Nicia fears that his extralegal attempts to produce offspring will come to the attention of the authorities: "che non si sappia per amore degli Otto" (it better not be found out, for love of the High Court [act 2, sc. 6]).

scene 2) and in *Clizia* by Sofronia's fierce protectiveness of the foundling placed in her charge—as if Clizia, a survivor of the reduction
of Naples by Charles VIII, were herself the fragile symbol of Italian
liberty.

The resemblances linking the two plays are formal as well as structural. The success in the early Cinquecento of Plautus's *Menaechmi* and
of Bibbiena's *La calandra*, which imitates features of the Latin play, may
well account for the reliance of Machiavelli's plots on foundlings,
changelings, and bed tricks as plot devices—what might be called,
after Ariosto's version of these techniques, "supposition."[8] In *Mandragola*, Callimaco is substituted for Lucrezia's husband, Nicia, in order
to absorb the supposed virulence of the mandrake root; in *Clizia*
Nicomaco's idea is to take the place of his own servant in the bridal
bed. Of these plot devices, the prominent pharmacopoeia of *Mandragola* returns, attenuated, in *Clizia*; instead of using a lethal (if imaginary) fertility drug, Nicomaco relies on sexual stimulants (e.g., *satyrion*) and adopts a metaphorics of perfumes drawn from Plautus's
Casina.

But the genial remedy of the bed trick devised, in *Mandragola*, by
friar Timoteo is, in retrospect, undermined by the plot of *Clizia*. For in
Clizia it is the wife, Sofronia, who devises therapeutic remedies
("rimedi"); and her remedies are designed not to satisfy, but rather to
refuse and chastise, male desire and *virtù*. To appreciate the difference
of the two texts in this respect, we have merely to compare the splendid rejuvenation of Lucrezia with the grotesque, failed rejuvenation of
Nicomaco. This contrast notwithstanding, the underlying principle
governing the outcomes of the two plays is similar: the dangerous
vitality of the female, whose adversarial relationship to male *virtù* is
ambiguous in the older play, becomes fully explicit in *Clizia*. The surprisingly cooperative, indeed dangerously vigorous Lucrezia in *Mandragola* is replaced in *Clizia* by the efficient Sofronia and the invisible,
irresistible Clizia. In act 3, scene 7, Sofronia, citing Clizia's prepubes-
cence, opposes Nicomaco's furious insistence that the marriage of
Clizia to his servant Pirro be celebrated on the same evening:

> *Sofronia:* Io dubito che la non abbia *l'ordinario* delle donne.
> *Nicomaco:* Adoperi *lo straordinario* degli uomini! Io voglio che la
> meni stasera. [Emphases added]

8. In *Casina* there is an emphasis on replacement or "supposition" in the acrostic
argument, for Casina is a foundling, a *puella expositicia*. With regard to reliance on this
kind of plot device (and its parallel origins in the tales of Boccaccio) in Ariosto, Bibbiena,
and Machiavelli, see Padoan, "Il tramonto di Machiavelli," 458–66. Cf. Giorgio Chiarini,
"Casina o della metamorfosi," *Latomus* 37 (1978): 119–20.

Sofronia: I doubt she has women's ordinary monthlies.
Nicomaco: Let her use what's extraordinary in men! I want you
to bring her to me this evening. (My translation)

With this reappearance of the terms Machiavelli uses elsewhere to
discuss the establishment and maintenance of political orders, the conflict of male and female is distilled to one that is archetypal and biolog-
ical, literally between the menses (*l'ordinario*) and deflowering violence
(*lo straordinario*).[9] The time- and nature-bound (and thus orderly) cyclicality of the female body is also opposed to the aggressive, disrup-
tive *virtù* of the male (a version of Greco-Roman *andreia*, "maleness").
The terms in act 3, scene 7 suggest that Nicomaco's autumnal infatua-
tion is an act of violence not only against the peace of his household
and his city ("you turned Florence upside-down" [act 5, scene 3]), but
against nature and time as well: against a sage temperance represented
by Sofronia, which reflects the temporal embeddedness of human existence. The play raises a recurring question in Machiavelli's political
meditation: the choice and timing of action, the problem of harmonizing human desire with Fortune and Necessity.[10]

Thus *Clizia*, both in general and in detail, continues Machiavelli's
principal concerns as a man and a thinker and marks important developments that are not merely retreats or evidence of discouragement.
Readers note the closeness of the fictional temporal setting of the two
plays, one taking place in 1504 and one in 1506, though they were
written some seven years apart at distinct moments in Machiavelli's
career. Both plays take as their historical point of reference Charles
VIII's invasion of Italy, an event widely recognized by Machiavelli and
his contemporaries as being decisive in determining the misfortunes of
Italy in the Cinquecento.[11] The chronological coupling suggests that

9. On *l'ordinario* and *lo straordinario* in the political writings, see J. H. Whitfield, "On
Machiavelli's Use of Ordini," *Italian Studies* 10 (1955): 19–39; John Najemy, "Arti e Ordini
in Machiavelli's *Istorie fiorentine*," in *Essays Presented to Myron P. Gilmore* (Villa I Tatti
series 5, no. 2) (Florence, 1978), 161–91; and John Najemy, "Machiavelli and the Medici:
The Lessons of Florentine History," *Renaissance Quarterly* 35 (1982): 560–61, 568–76.

10. The loci classici are *The Prince*, chap. 25; *The Discourses*, bk. 3, chap. 9; Machiavelli,
Letters, ed. Gilbert, 119; "Capitolo on Fortune," 100–115 (Niccolò Machiavelli, *Il teatro e
tutti gli scritti letterari*, ed. Franco Gaeta [Milan, 1965], 314).

11. The early chapters of Francesco Guicciardini's *The History of Italy* (trans. and ed.
Sidney Alexander [New York, 1969]) (especially chaps. 1–2) are the locus classicus; but
see Machiavelli's *The Art of War*, bk. 7 (Niccolò Machiavelli, *L'arte della guerra*, in *Tutte le
opere di Niccolò Machiavelli*, 2 vols., ed. Francesco Flora and Carlo Cordié [Milan, 1949–
50], 1:618–19), and the last words of Machiavelli's *Florentine Histories* (bk. 8, chap. 36):
"ruined, and are still ruining, Italy." On this attitude, see Felix Gilbert, *Machiavelli and
Guicciardini: Politics and History in Sixteenth-Century Florence* (Princeton, N.J., 1965), 256–

the two plays might form a diptych, for they deploy diverse responses to a deteriorating political climate and community.[12] If *Mandragola* is coyly ambivalent, rejoicing in the audacious and disenchanted inventiveness of the author of *The Prince* while showing traces of the persistent republican idealism of the author of *The Discourses, Clizia* appears to be a product of the author of the revisionist *Florentine Histories*—a Machiavelli disillusioned about the capacity for effective human action in general and for the regeneration of Florentine republican *virtù* in particular but also more meditative regarding collective institutions and the historical cycles that transcend individuals.[13] Implicit in this meditation is Machiavelli's consciousness of his own role as a senex whose relation to the community is put into question by approaching death—a relation that may be characterized in terms of both absence and monumentalization, the vanishing of the historical self and the fashioning of a fictional, textual self suitable for inclusion in the tradition. In this context the action of *Clizia*—the struggle between Sofronia and Nicomaco over a highly reputed, but invisible object of desire—becomes a dialogue between competing visions of the place of *virtù* in history and in the natural order—not only *virtù* generally but the *virtù* of Niccolò Machiavelli in particular, since it is his senescence that is mirrored in the play. In another sense, *Clizia* is a valedictory work that enacts Machiavelli's metamorphosis from erotic and political agent to author and cultural monument.

Titles: Plautus's *Casina* and *Clizia*

Plautus's *Casina* is exceptional among Roman comedies for a number of reasons that I suggest influenced Machiavelli: (1) with a title handed down by tradition (it was not Plautus's original title of *Sortientes*), it is the only surviving Latin play to be named after a character who never appears (Chiarini, "In margine," 221); (2) it is the only comedy of

---

70; Ricardo J. Quinones, *The Renaissance Discovery of Time* (Cambridge, Mass., 1972), 175–86; Padoan, "Il tramonto di Machiavelli," 478–79.

12. Cf. Tambara in Roberto Ridolfi, *Studi sulle commedie del Machiavelli* (Pisa, 1968), 208, 316.

13. *Clizia* was composed late in 1524 or early in 1525 and was performed for the first time in January 1525. See Beatrice Corrigan, "An Unrecorded Manuscript of Machiavelli's La Clizia," *Bibliofilia* 63 (1961): 78–79; and Roberto Ridolfi, *The Life of Niccolò Machiavelli,* 208–9. The composition of the play thus coincides with the final revision and correction of the *Florentine Histories* preparatory to their consignment to Pope Clement VII (May–June 1525). The valedictory speech of the old condottiere Fabrizio Colonna (Machiavelli, *The Art of War,* 7:619–20) has also been suggested as a reflection of Machiavelli's exhaustion in the 1520s. See Ferroni, *Mutazione e riscontro,* 114; Padoan, "Il tramonto di Machiavelli," 490.

Plautus or Terence whose prologue includes material from the play's revival a generation after the author's death—in other words, the only play that has an explicitly posthumous prologue; (3) it is the most nearly tragic of Plautus's comedies in its imposition of a figurative castration on the offending senex; (4) it is also one of the most obscene (Padoan, "Il tramonto," 469). The last two of these reasons I have already acknowledged; the second I will return to later; the first requires additional comment here.

Aelius Donatus recommends in his commentary on Terence that the names of comic characters should have *ratio et etymologia* (etymology and explanation). The critic is thinking, and comic practice bears him out, of conventional names for the personae of Latin New Comedy: the old man or senex (e.g., Chremes), the wife and mother or *matrona* (Cleustrata), the unmarried girl or *virgo* (Philocomasium), and the whore or *meretrix* (Bacchis), and so on.[14] That Machiavelli was sharply aware of the implications of his comic names cannot be doubted; the numerous associations (for a Florentine) attaching to the name of Lucrezia in *Mandragola* should suffice as an indication. In *Clizia*, Machiavelli's naming is also conspicuously motivated, beginning with the *bricolage* implicit in the name Nicomaco, which is a stitching together of portions of the author's first and last names. The question of naming is peculiarly important in the case of the eponymous *Clizia* because she never appears. This too is a convention of comic form. Donatus notes that free-born Athenian maidens were not as a rule represented on stage; the unmarried women who do appear in *fabulae palliatae* (so called because characters appear in Greek dress, the *pallium*, and not in the Roman toga) are usually slaves or courtesans.[15] But in *Clizia* Machiavelli goes beyond observing Donatus's canons; he makes the absence of the eponymous character central to the play's meaning and structure. Clizia's importance is inversely proportional to her absence. For clues to the meaning of this absent heroine and her name, we can learn much from Machiavelli's model, Plautus's *Casina*.

14. The commentary of Donatus on Terence was widely reprinted with Renaissance editions of that playwright, including those published at Treviso in 1477 and Venice in 1491. For a discussion of the etymological principle, which goes back to Aristotle, Pliny, and Horace, see Marvin T. Herrick, *Comic Theory in the Sixteenth Century* (Urbana, Ill., 1950), 63; J. C. Austin, "Significant Names in Terence," *University of Illinois Studies on Language and Literature* 7 (Urbana, Ill., 1922): 9–23; and Antonio Staüble, *La commedia umanistica del Quattrocento* (Florence, 1968), 171–75. The principle is attested to by Plautus himself ("nomen omen," Persa 625), and Saracenus begins his commentary on Plautus (1499) with an onomastic analysis of the dramatis personae.

15. See Aelius Donatus, *Commentum terenti,* ed. Paulus Weissner (Leipzig, 1908), in his comments on *Andria,* line 413, and *Adelphoe,* line 487.

W. T. MacCary and Giorgio Chiarini have argued that the name Casina can probably be associated with *casia* or cassia, the bark from which cinnamon, and cinnamon oil or unguent, are elaborated.[16] The functions, in Plautus's play, of naming a character after a sweet-scented spice are multiple; it is one of the onomastic conventions, for attractive girls or prostitutes were often named after sweet-smelling or sweet-tasting substances (e.g., Glycerium in *Andria*, from *glukús*, "sweet"). But, Chiarini argues, there is more to Plautus's naming. The allusion to a sweet-smelling Casina emphasizes the disruption of social codes by the anonymous Plautine *senex amans*, who perfumes himself (as might a younger man, properly a lover) and engages in licentious activities unsuitable to his age and station (as pointed out by his wife, Cleustrata; cf. Chiarini, "Per la storia," 151). Myrrh and cassia were, in Roman custom, frequently paired as ingredients in perfumes, and they were both used as spices in funeral ceremonies, consistent with the moribund state of a senex whom his wife refers to as *pabulum Acherontis* ("a meal for Acheron" or, more idiomatically, "worm's meat") (Chiarini, "Per la storia," 152). Chiarini (150–51) adds his own suggestive coda to his list of meanings for Casina's perfumed name: although she is absent, her importance in driving the plot means that she is perceived throughout the play only in the form of her "perfumed" name—in sharp distinction to the foul-smelling senex. In this sense, she is linked to the topic of reputation, even to the play itself as one renamed by its reputation—which is, like the sweet odor of Casina, a good one.

My thesis rests not on the assumption that Machiavelli knew the full range of implications of the name Casina, but rather on the way he orders the range of implications of the name Clizia in his own play. Machiavelli does in fact pick up Plautus's olfactory vocabulary in *Casina*. It is applied to Eustachio, whose cosmetic improvements make him look like a scrubbed cesspool, perfumed in night soil ("cesso ripulito," "profumato nel litame," act 2, scene 5), and above all to Nicomaco, both to his bad breath and stinking body ("fetida bocca," "puzzolente membra," act 4, scene 1) and to his ridiculous affectation of perfume ("odorifero," act 4, scene 4). The use of this vocabulary in *Clizia* is most evident in act 3, scene 4. Sofronia simultaneously sees, smells, and perceives the perfumed Nicomaco. Implicitly, she tells him she *knows* his folly, his depravity, his malodorous shame: "ti guato e odoroti

16. See T. Maccius Plautus, *Casina*, ed. W. T. McCary and M. M. Willcock (Cambridge, 1976), 96, 126, 187; Giorgio Chiarini, "In margine a un'edizione commentata," 220–22; Chiarini, "Casina o della metamorfosi," 115–16; Chiarini, "Per la storia dell'esegesi Plautina: i versi didascalichi della Casina: Prologo 29–34," *Studi classici e orientali* 31 (1982): 144–53; Claudio Questa, *Parerga plautina (struttura e tradizione manoscritta delle commedie)* (Urbino, 1985), 66n.

anche: tu sai di buono; bembè, tu mi riesci" (I am looking at you, and I can smell you, too. What an aroma! You are certainly making an impression on me!). Here his "odor" and his "infamy" coincide. But how is Clizia linked to these aromatic topics?

Clizia is herself curiously named. As I suggested earlier, the problem of her naming reflects emphases derivable from the Latin play. The Greek name *Klytie*, from the Greek *klytos*, meaning "famous, renowned," attests to Clizia's existence in the play exclusively through the spoken evidence of others, through *fama* (reputation) and *rumore* (hearsay). This dimension of Clizia's role in the play may derive from Plautus's use of Casina as an unseen presence and sweet fragrance in contrast to the putrefaction and disordered self-perfuming of the senex, although in Machiavelli's play the antithesis of the good name and reputation—the fame—of Clizia (cf. the Latin *inclita*, "renowned") is the shame and infamy that Nicomaco brings upon himself. The effects of hearsay, rumor, and scandal are constant in the play: the scandal over the outrage to Clizia will destroy the reputation of Nicomaco's household. ("You have nothing to lose but house and home," remarks Palamedes [act 1, scene 1] on hearing of the old man's passion; "our affairs are all in a turmoil," rejoins Cleandro, conceding wide knowledge of the scandal.) In an oft-cited passage (act 2, scene 4), Sofronia laments Nicomaco's loss of respectability. Sofronia's principal card in the contest with her husband for the safety of the girl is her repeated threat to cause a scandal, which, in Nicomaco's burlesque etymology, earns her the name of *Soffiona*; but the venom of the appellation returns to Nicomaco, for the infamy she would blow to the four winds is his.

Clizia's fame—her beauty, her irresistibility—and Nicomaco's infamy are plausibly Machiavelli's specific adaptations of Casina's fragrance and its converse, the malodorousness—and ill repute, bad odor—of the Plautine senex. As we will see, the question of Nicomaco's infamy is tied to some of the play's ultimate implications as Machiavelli's ironic self-mockery.

Name and Cynosure

The "absent" Casina and Clizia also function to anchor other important metaphoric series in the two plays. The topic of sexual pursuit as a military expedition, requiring the virile virtues (or parodies of them) is, of course, frequent not only in Plautus but throughout Roman literature, especially the amatory works of Ovid, which have influenced medieval and Renaissance European literature in this respect. The topic is a recurring one for Machiavelli, who draws on it for the notorious chapter 25 of *The Prince*, where Fortune is said to favor the young because they can more strongly master her—a passage recalled by Cleandro in *Clizia* (act 4, scene 1), and in *Mandragola*, where the assault on Lucrezia's virtue is compared to the siege of a city. In *Clizia*, the rivalry for the girl is presented as a combat ("la fanciulla che si combatte," prologue); the two proxies are compared to generals laying siege to a town ("ognuno le ha posto il campo intorno" [act 2, scene 3]); the various expedients and schemes are compared to ambushes ("aguato") and the honing of weapons ("ognuno aguzzi e sua ferruzzi" [act 2, scene 5]). Most elaborately, the comparison of sexual apparatus to weapons introduces an asymmetrical gender difference between the two "armies": "You watch out, yourselves. You have the weapons, and we don't," Sofronia reminds her male antagonists before the final tussle of Nicomaco and Clizia/Siro (act 4, scene 12).[17]

In *Clizia*, then, as in *Casina*, an unseen girl is the cynosure or focus of the four men who desire her. The same inference can be drawn in Machiavelli's prologue, which concludes that "this story is called Clizia" because Clizia is "the girl that is being fought over." In this sense, Clizia is a combining form, almost an en*clitic* object, as the repeated use of her name in the play suggests. In Plautus's play, the name Casina appears twenty-nine times, which is as many as all the other characters together (cf. Chiarini, "Per la storia," 152); in the Italian play, the name Clizia appears thirty-seven times. Not only is Clizia's name used frequently (another proof of her "fame"), it is joined as an object to a gamut of verbs for acts men can do with, and to, women. The absent girl is thus a categorical female object, grammatical and physical.

My pun leads us to another possible etymology of the title character in Machiavelli's play. Clizia is the normal translation into Italian of Clytie, the daughter of Ocean who—in Ovid's narrative of the myth—having once fallen in love with the sun and lost his love, was changed into a heliotrope flower and so turns always to face the sun.[18] With respect to the function of Clizia as the focus of attention, Machiavelli might have understood the name of Clizia (as the lexicographer Niccolò Tommaseo would a few centuries later) as reflecting the Latin *inclinare* because Ovid's Clytie always turns or inclines (*vertitur*) to the sun (which, in its own right, inclines toward sunset). In Machiavelli's

---

17. The military terminology in *Casina* and its influence on *Clizia* are discussed by many readers: cf. Plautus, *Casina*, 28–29 (on *Casina* alone); Ferroni, *Mutazione e riscontro*, 113–14; Vanossi, "Situazione e sviluppo," 64–75; Chiarini, "Casina o della metamorfosi," 110–13 (on *Casina* alone); Padoan, "Il tramonto di Machiavelli," 479–80; Machiavelli, *Mandragola, Clizia*, ed. Raimondi, 48–52.

18. Ovid, *Metamorphoses* bk. 3, lines 256–70.

play, the "inclinations" are reversed and it is the male characters Nicomaco, Eustachio, Pirro, and Cleandro who incline toward Clizia, who cleave to her famous beauty. Clizia's name in this sense fixes her not merely as a haunting absence but also—as we have just seen—as the cynosure toward which all desire inclines. Her action in the play thus reflects one of Machiavelli's often reiterated beliefs regarding the immutability of innate nature.[19]

Clizia's name is also important because it is all that has ever been known of her: her "fame" and her "name" literally coincide. When she was entrusted to Sofronia and Nicomaco by her rescuer, Beltramo di Guascogna, who had seized her at the sack of Naples, he gave only her name ("solo significò che si chiamava Clizia" [act 1, scene 1]). The onomastic emphasis is balanced by her absence in the play; from the outset, the audience is warned to think of Clizia as invisible and unattainable. The prologue announces: "Don't expect to see her, though, for Sofronia, who has brought her up, does not wish her to come out, for modesty's sake. And so, if anyone is sighing for her, he had better resign himself" ("arà pazienza," literally, "he'll have to be patient").

After this unpromising introduction, Clizia's absence is frequently repeated and tied to her allusive name. This can be seen in the drawing of lots, which Machiavelli shifts to the third and central act of the play (lines 295–419 of 1018 in Plautus). Machiavelli also alters the form of the lottery as he found it in his source. In Machiavelli's play, the drawing has two parts. First the name of a contestant (Pirro or Eustachio) is drawn; then another drawing is made, which indicates whether the winner of the first drawing wins or loses the second drawing. There are two lots: one has Clizia's name on it, and one is left blank ("una polizza bianca")—it *lacks* her name. Eustachio, whose name is drawn on the first drawing, giving him a chance to draw to win, draws, on the second drawing, the blank—making him a loser. The double draw skews the game: Pirro does not *win* Clizia; Eustachio *loses* her. Clizia's name, so often on everyone's lips, cannot appear, cannot be *sorted,* not even on a lot (the writing of the lots itself, as if technically obscene, is done offstage, in the house); she cannot appear as *written.* The blank lot is more than the alternative to Clizia: it is itself the sign of Clizia as a nonappearance. Indeed, the terms in the lottery regarding "winning" Clizia—"and whoever gets Clizia can have her, and the other will have

19. *Inclinare, declinare* are Machiavelli's terms for the inclinations of nature that make it difficult for even the man of *virtù* to meet the changing circumstances of fortune; cf. *The Prince,* chap. 25: "Nor is there found any man so prudent that he can accommodate himself to this [change in fortune]; one reason is that he cannot deviate from the way nature inclines him" (my translation); and *The Discourses,* bk. 3, chap. 9: "It is impossible to go against what nature inclines us to."

to have patience" (translation modified)—echo the terms of the prologue, recommending the *pazienza* of whoever desires to see her. Suitors and spectators alike must be content to possess Patience, and her
alone.

Clizia's removal from the action is emphasized with an additional
detail. In her first appearance in the play, Sofronia informs us that she
has locked Casina and Doria, the maidservant, *in camera*. Machiavelli
draws here on the commonplace of New Comedy sociology, which
gives to the matrona the keys to the female quarters (the *conclavis* or
gynaecium) where the virgo is kept from the sight of men.[20] This is the
first, conventional removal of Clizia. Late in the play, however,
Sofronia informs Cleandro that Clizia had been sent, on the eve of her
supposed marriage, to a convent, disguised as a manservant, so that
during the nocturnal castigation of Nicomaco she was not merely non-
existent (in a nonspeaking, nonappearing role) but also fictionally distant, spirited away (*trafugata*), precisely as Nicomaco had feared. At
play's end it is announced that there is to be a wedding between Clizia
and Cleandro; but these nuptials are not shown—they are to be conducted entirely indoors, in the space dominated by Sofronia ("we shall
not leave this house again until we have arranged this new wedding").
Thus despite its generic conventionality, the removal of Clizia from the
scene of dramatic representation progressively undercuts the desire of
both Nicomaco and Cleandro, his son, who for their part become more
ardent as they imagine approaching the object ("for the closer a man is
to his desire, the more he desires it; and since he cannot have it, he feels
greater torment").[21] As her suitors approach, Clizia recedes, always
moving away. She is a kind of vanishing point, a theoretical infinity
like the *punto di fuga* (literally, "point of flight") of a Renaissance perspective stage set.

Clizia only acts by means of Doria's invented account of her madness, and when impersonated by Siro—that is, when she is presented
as a rumor or a false representation. When Clizia does presumably
"appear," it is under a disguise that negates her sex: as a transvestite
male servant with his face covered. Even this appearance exists for the
playgoer only in Nicomaco's report of the fatal night, and it is the
central fact of that report that this "Clizia" is not a she, but, with
strident obviousness, a he. As Nicomaco describes it, Siro his manservant stands erect—surely in both senses—on the nuptial bed, grimac-

20. Cf. Terence, *Phormio*, 86; *Eunuchus*, 583.
21. Again, a Machiavellian topic; cf. *The Discourses*, bk. 1, chap. 37: "Nature has so
constituted men that, though all things are objects of desire, not all things are attainable;
so that desire always exceeds the power of attainment, with the result that men are ill
content with what they possess and their present state brings them little satisfaction."

ing and offering the ithyphallic gesture. This moment is Nicomaco's nadir; he has been mocked by his own servants, deceived by his wife's stratagem, and deprived of Clizia. Although, structurally, it is a moment of recognition and reversal, of *cognitio* and *conversio*, comic expectations here are not fulfilled; the negation of Clizia's sex in her "metamorphosis" into Siro is neither a triumph of male force nor a felicitous reunion with a lost parent. On the contrary. As we saw, Clizia's removal from the scene is an effect of Sofronia's foresight, and the substitution of Siro for the girl is the culmination of Sofronia's plan. Thus Nicomaco's sight of Siro is perhaps the most focused image in the play of the blockage of desire, of the defeat of Nicomaco's attempt to prevail with *virtù*. Beneath the "recognition" of Clizia as Siro is Nicomaco's painful awareness of his defeat and impotence; behind the reversal of Nicomaco's hopes is the powerful apotropaic figure of Siro, driving Nicomaco from the bridal chamber. Siro is a kind of terminal herm marking the limit not only of the old man's hubris in attempting to rape his foster child, but of his pretenses at rejuvenation, his hopes for a paradise of irresponsible pleasure.

Time and Temperance

In *Clizia* as in Plautus, the frustration of the senex by the stratagems of his wife is the principal action. One of Machiavelli's principal modifications of *Casina*—in which the name of Cleustrata's son is omitted from the dramatis personae—is the introduction of Cleandro, the son-as-rival, as a character. But, as Padoan ("Il tramonto," 475) notes, Cleandro is a feckless, passive figure in contrast both to his father, who is fired by passion for Clizia, and to his mother, who engineers Nicomaco's defeat. In no sense the patrilineal successor to Nicomaco, Cleandro fails in the Oedipal contest and requires assistance first from his mother and subsequently from the deus ex machina of Ramondo's appearance. Sofronia, however, is in no sense a procuress for her son; she shields Clizia from father, son, and servants alike. At the end of the play, she pointedly denies Cleandro the certainty of access to Clizia with phrasing that emphasizes her control of the girl's movements ("Maybe she will come home, and maybe she won't, as I see fit" [act 5, scene 5]). Sofronia's prohibition would appear to be merely the result of the apparent difference in the social status of the nubile children, were it not for Cleandro's complaint that his suit, seemingly victorious at Nicomaco's exit, is now blocked by his mother ("First I had to contend with my father's passion, now I have to contend with my mother's ambition" [act 5, scene 5]). The rivalry of father and son— itself filtered through Pirro and Eustachio—veils the central rivalry between Sofronia (an *uxor dotata* [endowed wife] in more than the legal sense) and both male figures. As Sofronia reports, the defeated Nicomaco has given her power of attorney ("He has given me carte blanche [*foglio bianco*]; and he wants me to manage [*ch 'io governi*] everything my way [*a mio senno*] from now on"); this carte blanche recalls the blank slip ("polizza bianca") negatively signifying Clizia in the central lottery scene (act 3, scene 7). By linking the two moments, Machiavelli makes of Clizia's invisibility an expression of Sofronia's power. And though it might seem that the arrival of Ramondo, Clizia's father, countermands Sofronia's hegemony and restores patriarchal prerogatives, a close reading of the final scene of the play reveals several ambiguities.

After his humiliation Nicomaco is mewed up at home ("chiuso in casa"), precisely the space Sofronia dominates. It falls to Damone, Nicomaco's friend and ally, to arrange the marriage alliance with Ramondo that Nicomaco cannot but accept. But like Nicomaco's supposed reform following his drubbing, Ramondo's intervention seems merely structural. Sofronia speaks the play's last, ambiguous words: "Sanza uscire più fuora si ordineranno le nozze, le quali fieno femmine e non maschie, come quelle di Nicomaco!" (We shall not leave the house again until we have arranged this new wedding. And this time it will be man and wife, not man and man, like Nicomaco's!). Connubial moments in the play have thus far been pointedly all male: Siro, the false Clizia, mocks his master by poking his "dagger" ("something hard, solid, and sharp" [my translation]) into Nicomaco's hindparts.[22] But exactly what Sofronia might mean by "nozze femmine" (female nuptials) is unclear; if symmetry with the "nozze maschie" (male nuptials) were to be preserved, Cleandro would have to suffer castration. So rigorous a deduction may be excessive; nevertheless, in the context of Nicomaco's pasting, Sofronia's farewell to the spectators completes the frustration of the expectations already discouraged in the prologue, where the audience is told to give up hope of seeing Clizia. As in *Casina*, where the nuptials are conducted off stage, the union of Cleandro and Clizia is relegated to the *dentro*, "inside" the stage buildings. By reiterating the division of "dentro" (inside) and "fuori" ("outside"), Sofronia again blocks male desire to see Clizia (echoed by Cleandro in act 5, scene 4: "let her come back home, so I won't be deprived of the

---

22. On the transvestite, homoerotic theme in the source play *Casina*, see Jane M. Cody, "The 'Senex Amator' in Plautus's *Casina*," *Hermes* 104 (1976): 453–76; and Chiarini's contestation in "In margine a un'edizione commentata," 227–28.

sight of her"), the icon of male desire.[23] The continual absence of Clizia thus ratifies the interdiction of male succession, authority, and *skopophilia;* the phallus itself is co-opted into Sofronia's stratagem in the form of Siro's ithyphallic ban.

In fact, Sofronia's domination of events and control of the space of the stage set can be traced to the failure of her proxy, Eustachio, to win the lottery in act 3, that is, to the central scenes of the play; a Pyrrhic victory leads to Sofronia's ultimate triumph. Despite the temporary success of Nicomaco and Pirro, acts 4 and 5 are entirely in the control of women (with some help from Cleandro, who overhears key elements of Nicomaco's plan). The scene (act 4, scene 10), closely adapated from Plautus, in which Sofronia, by refusing to call Sostrata (wife of Damone) away from her house, prevents its being rigged up for the violation of Clizia, is symbolic of the shift of initiative. This hegemony over the stage buildings ("case") is then confirmed by the madness of Clizia, narrated by the maid Doria, which effectively denies Nicomaco access to his own house and forces him to depart without his dinner. The gynocracy Machiavelli establishes at play's end extends to the formal elements of the text itself: the final act opens, and Nicomaco's humiliation is narrated, by the female servant Doria; its last words are spoken by Sofronia. Thus women define the limits of the play's articulation and of the sexual career of author and protagonist alike. With Clizia as the invisible but constant focal point, and with Sofronia and Doria as principal agents, it is women who *contain* the play's action just as it is the *gynaeceum,* the suite of female chambers, that contains the effective off-scene plotting that undoes Nicomaco. And it is Sofronia and Doria who manipulate the unseen cynosure, the phantom Clizia who organizes male desire. Of course, the frustration of Nicomaco's lust by Sofronia is only one of several interdictions of male desire by powerful, allegorized women in the Machiavellian oeuvre. As in *Mandragola,* where Lucrezia's increase in power after sexual knowledge makes her a figure of Nature and Fortune, Sofronia's increase in power with the humiliation of Nicomaco—and her mysterious (because never visible) relationship to Clizia—confirm their status as an allegorical pair, the elderly, controlling female (*Natura/Fortuna*) and the younger,

23. Machiavelli's audience for *Clizia* at Fornaciari's villa, probably mixed—women certainly attended (and often sponsored) theatrical performances in Renaissance Italy—was, to judge from the report of Donato Giannotti, predominantly composed of well-to-do male Florentines, not excepting some of the younger Medici; cf. Corrigan, "An Unrecorded Manuscript," 79. As in Roman comedy, female roles usually would have been played by men; the invisible Clizia's "real" femininity is thus a kind of metatheatrical conundrum.

attractive and dangerous female (*Occasio*), according to established Machiavellian typology, as Hanna Fenichel Pitkin has shown.[24]

The head-to-head antagonism of Sofronia and Nicomaco, modeled on that between the senex and Cleustrata in *Casina* (that is, between *uxor dotata* and *paterfamilias*), is a rarity in Latin New Comedy plots.[25] Despite Machiavelli's tendency to envision the matrona as a controlling, antagonistic figure representing Nature or Fortune, in *Clizia* the figure of Sofronia also represents a *vivere civile*, the urbane style of civic life.[26] Sofronia embodies, both etymologically and behaviorally, the Hellenic (and traditionally female) virtue of *sophrosyne* (self-restraint), normally rendered in Latin as *temperantia* but also as *moderatio, pudicitia* (chastity), *sobrietas*, even *sapientia*.[27] Conversely, Nicomaco's name suggests (as does Nicia's in *Mandragola*) a general victorious in battle. The antagonism is thus fundamental; the virtues that a deviant Nicomaco is attempting, unsuccessfully, to exercise are parodies of male *virtù*, of *andreia*—virtues that, from the time of the Greek tragedians and Plato, have been conceived as potentially in tension with the socially circumscribed virtues of restraint and moderation, that is to say, sophrosyne. The lack of measure, the *dismisura*, of Nicomaco (his unseasonable eroticism, frequenting of taverns and gambling dens, use of cosmetics, willingness to flaunt decorum in order to have his way—contextually, his hubris) are comic forms of the furious *arete* (excellence, *virtù*) of the hero, which can lead to tragic destruction.[28] This behavior emerges in the play as tragic parody. The scene (act 3, scene 1) in which Nicomaco,

24. On Machiavelli's typology of old and young women as "versions of a generalized female power," see Pitkin, *Fortune Is a Woman*, 135 and 169.

25. See Cody, "The 'Senex Amator,'" 453; the conflict in *Casina* is unique among Plautus's plays. For a view that the antagonism of Sofronia and Nicomaco is central to *Clizia*, see Machiavelli, *Mandragola, Clizia*, ed. Raimondi, 53–54.

26. Pitkin's typology is too rigid here, for it excludes the female from representing a *vivere civile*. In making Nicomaco's chief antagonist a strongly nurturing and civil, indeed civilizing, figure, Machiavelli deftly scrambles his own typical oppositions.

27. Despite the obvious meaning of Sofronia's name, few scholars have pursued its implications; but see Machiavelli, *The Comedies of Machiavelli*, ed. Sices and Atkinson, 30–31. With regard to the iconography and language of sophrosyne in antiquity and the Renaissance, see Helen North, *Sophrosyne*; and North, *From Myth to Icon: Reflections on Greek Ethical Doctrine in Literature and Art* (Ithaca, N.Y., 1979). For a discussion of sophrosyne as a markedly feminine virtue in Hellenic and Roman thought, see North, *Sophrosyne*, 252–53, 307–8; and North, *From Myth to Icon*, 47–54. The accommodation in Latin of the complex Greek term is discussed in North, *Sophrosyne*, 261–68, and in North, *From Myth to Icon*, 45–46.

28. On this tension, see North, *Sophrosyne*, 170–73, 189–90; and North, *From Myth to Icon*, 107–8. On the antagonism between hubris and sophrosyne, see North, *Sophrosyne*, 178–79; and North, *From Myth to Icon*, 26–33. For most recent critics, the triumph of a (so-called) bourgeois moderation over Machiavelli's previous celebration of astuteness and

like some demented Heracles or Ajax, threatens to destroy his own
household if he is not obeyed, is the best example:

> Voglio che questa sera queste nozze si facciano; o io, quando non
> arò altro rimedio, caccerò fuoco in questa casa.

> I want the marriage to take place this evening; or else, if I have no
> other remedy, I will set fire to this house.

Nicomaco's excesses violate the sophrosyne or temperantia (including
sobriety, modesty, chastity, and self-control in general), in the general
Latin sense of the term, that Sofronia embodies.[29] Nicomaco's chastise-
ment is thus much more than Machiavelli's fictional account of erotic
resignation or his narrow escape from association with the Corpus
Christi plot, as claimed by G. D. Bonino (*Il teatro*, lvii–lx). Rather,
Machiavelli's treatment of Nicomaco is a full critique of the aggressive
virtù—often expressed as compelling masculine sexual desire—whose
analysis had dominated his mature thought. The plot of *Clizia* expresses the timely acknowledgment of both natural cycles and social
forces that are more comprehensive than the military and dynastic
history created by the ambitions of *patres patriae* and political strate-
gists, and parallels the subtle critique in the *Florentine Histories* of the
straordinario as a Medici technique, as John Najemy ("Machiavelli and
the Medici") has argued. How Machiavelli defines what replaces the
masculine *straordinario* I will consider in a moment.

There is one dimension of sophrosyne or temperantia that is particularly striking and that I propose both organizes Sofronia's allegorical
function in the play and has a metadramatic implication, since it immediately concerns the ordering of a dramatic plot. I am referring to the
measure and regulation of time. The inclusion, in the iconography of
temperance (*sophrosyne*), of first the sandglass and then the clock, are
closely associated with the elevation of bourgeois time management as
a virtue in early modern Europe.[30] Sofronia practices and decrees the

---

occasionally effective violence leaves a decidedly bad (or sad) taste. See especially Nino
Borsellino, *Rozzi e intronati: Esperienze e forme di teatro dal 'Decameron' al 'Candelaio'* (Rome,
1974), 137–41; Padoan, "Il tramonto di Machiavelli," 479–81; Niccolò Machiavelli, *Teatro*,
ed. G. D. Bonino (Turin, 1979), lix–lx.

29. Sofronia's speech in act 3, sc. 4, in which she reproaches Nicomaco for consorting
with "giovanetti" and frequenting the taverns, gambling dens ("dove si giuoca"), and
brothels ("ripariti in casa femine"), enumerates violations of self-restraint. For a discussion of chastity, sobriety, modesty, and prudence as aspects of sophrosyne (and temperantia), see North, *Sophrosyne*, 249; and North, *From Myth to Icon*, 183–89.

30. The emphasis among the Italian merchant and commercial classes on the proper
husbanding and use of time is well known; a locus classicus is Leone Battista Alberti, *I*

rational and moderate use of time. This principle dominates her oft-cited speech (act 2, scene 4), for which there is no Plautine source, praising Nicomaco's former daily regimen, which, readers have noted, recalls Machiavelli's letter to Francesco Vettori (1513) detailing his own habits while in exile at the Albergaccio.[31] *Tempus* and *modus*—time, measure, restraint—as the productive and powerful habits of a class and society, are the secret of Sofronia's personal power and symbolic import. But Sofronia's husbanding of time is also a principle of the plot. Nicomaco's unruly and precipitate desire to marry off Clizia the same evening is in conflict with Sofronia's caution and temporizing (her *festinare lente*); she responds by manipulating the action, which unfolds in time for her to discover the truth of Nicomaco's undignified passion.[32]

Machiavelli cites, in *The Discourses*, book 1, chapter 3, the motto of Aulus Gellius, *veritas filia temporis* (time gives birth to truth): "That their evil dispositions often do not show themselves for a time is due to a hidden cause which those fail to perceive who had had not experience of such contrariness; but in time—which is said to be the father of all truth—it reveals itself." The motto describes how the plot of *Clizia* functions. The secret and shameful passion of Nicomaco, concealed throughout much of the play in his proxy, is nosed out and brought to light by Sofronia. The whole play unfolds with the spread of this domestic scandal, from Cleandro's first confession of it to Palamede, to the publication, within the household, of Nicomaco's shame at play's

---

libri della famiglia (On the Family), ed. Girolamo Mancini (Florence, 1908), 3.1, in which time is listed along with the soul and body as a precious property of the self. On this topic, see also Jacques Le Goff, "Merchant's Time and Church's Time in the Middle Ages" and "Labor Time in the 'Crisis' of the Fourteenth Century: From Medieval Time to Modern Time," in *Time, Work, and Culture in the Middle Ages,* trans. Arthur Goldhammer (Chicago, 1980). The "rational" use of time became a refrain of humanist educators; see Quinones, *The Renaissance Discovery of Time,* 189–93. On the medieval and early Renaissance figure of temperantia, see Rosemond Tuve, "Notes on the Virtues and Vices," *Journal of the Warburg and Courtauld Institutes* 26 (1963): 289; Lynn White, Jr., "The Iconography of Temperantia and the Virtuousness of Technology," in *Action and Conviction in Early Modern Europe,* ed. Theodore K. Rabb and Jerrold Seigel (Princeton, N.J., 1969); and North, *From Myth to Icon,* 226–38.

31. Machiavelli, *Lettere,* ed. Franco Gaeta (Milan, 1961), 301–6. For the parallel, see Machiavelli, *Mandragola, Clizia,* ed. Raimondi, 47; Vanossi, "Situazione e sviluppo," 74; and Ferroni, *Mutazione e riscontro,* 111.

32. Palamede concludes the first scene of the play by recommending to his friend Cleandro that he "temporeggiati el meglio puoi" (temporize as best he can [my translation]). On the relation between the notorious Renaissance motto *festina lente* and the virtue of temperance, see North, *Sophrosyne,* 385. On the popularity of this motto in the Renaissance, see Edgar Wind, *Pagan Mysteries of the Renaissance* (New York, 1968), 97–112.

end. The play is replete with language relating to concealment—words and expressions such as "occulto" (hidden), "scoprire" (discover), "secreto," "apalesare" (reveal), "rinchiuso" (enclosed), "inviluppato" (wrapped up), "nascondere" (hide). Nicomaco's correction administered through temperantia is thus in one sense an effect of time itself. This aspect of the play may be linked to a confessional purpose; according to Machiavelli's biographer Roberto Ridolfi, the play was taken by its first audience to be an acknowledgment of the author's affair with Barbera Salutati.

Machiavelli carefully frames the play in temporal terms. The *kairos* or critical moment of Nicomaco's attempt hastily to marry off Clizia—which determines the action of the play—is carefully placed in the carnival season (thus early in the year, probably January) and set against the previous year (during which Nicomaco had strayed from his former good habits), against the previous twelve years (since 1494, when Clizia was left with Nicomaco and Sofronia), and, finally, as in the first lines of the prologue, against the sweep of historical time ("Athens . . . in ruins"). Nicomaco's night with Clizia/Siro is measured off by Doria ("We spent the night counting the minutes as they went by" [act 5, scene 1]) in terms of the reported stages of his humiliation ("now he is mounting his attack, now they are wrestling together"). And Sofronia conceives the old man's reform as a return to the right mark ("ritornare al segno"), which is the behavior of one year ago ("da uno anno indietro" [act 5, scene 3]). Nicomaco complains: "I should think it might be better for you not to make a complete fool of me. Isn't it enough for you to have done it all this past year, and yesterday, and last night more than ever?" (act 5, scene 3)—a remark that identifies Sofronia as the controlling figure of the play's temporal range, as well as of its inner spaces. The play dramatizes a contest between Nicomaco's violent disturbance of the orderly progress of time (including an attempt to evade decrepitude) and Sofronia's defense of that order, which includes the economy of the household, the social world, and the *vivere civile*. The contest is expressed most strikingly, as we have seen, in Nicomaco's insistence that Clizia submit to *lo straordinario degli uomini* before she has begun her "monthlies"— *l'ordinario delle donne*. But Nicomaco's violence against the natural order of time is itself ironic, since his age (seventy, the biblical life span) argues for his own emblematic representation of time.

In the play's action, Nicomaco imitates many of the gestures of the Plautine senex; he takes satyrion and consumes undercooked pigeon flesh ("verdemezzo") in an attempt to restore his sexual force. Reference is made to Nicomaco's lack of teeth ("sanza denti"), to his foul breath and drooling mouth ("fetida bocca"). In a chilling passage,

Nicomaco speaks complacently of his steel-trap jaws—between which, as Pirro realizes to his dismay, Clizia is to be seized and masticated: "I expect I'll find the poor girl chopped to pieces" (act 4, scene 2; my translation). Like the allegorization of Sofronia as mistress of rationalized time, Nicomaco becomes the embodiment of hoary and despairing age, like a Saturn devouring his children.[33]

The elapsed time represented in the play, from the daily round to the dozen years since the invasion of Charles VIII, works, for Nicomaco, as so many strokes of the clock—*battiture*, or castigations, in the terms Machiavelli uses elsewhere for the severe but purgative violence that sometimes restores states. Nino Borsellino (*Rozzi e intronati*, 138–39) first noted the close relationship between the phrase "ritornare al segno" (return to the mark), referring to the return of Nicomaco to his previous exemplary moral and social responsibility, and the phrase "tornare al segno" in the proem to the third book of *The Discourses*, where Machiavelli refers to the frequent necessity of bringing republics back to their origins in order to restore them to health. Unlike collectivities, however, Nicomaco cannot return to a previous point; as a numerical individual, he cannot be restored or reborn. Sofronia's embodied allusion to clock time has, therefore, a sharply negative aspect as far as Nicomaco is concerned. Time leads Nicomaco to the other embrace, the embrace adumbrated by his desire for an unattainable Clizia: the embrace of the tomb. The phrase "dormire con Clizia" (sleep with Clizia), echoing the death-wishing senex in *Casina* ("If luck fails me, I'll make a pillow of my sword / and lie on it" [verses 307–8]), is the final inclination to which Nature will bend him. The other senex in the play, Clizia's natural father, Ramondo, also speaks of the chance to see his daughter as being coordinated with his death ("And I thank God for granting that, before I die, I may see my daughter again," act 5, scene 6; my translation). Ramondo's mood is valedictory; like Nicomaco, he wishes to see Clizia and die. Thus Clizia, in representing the fantasized terminus of sexual pleasure ("O sweet night, will I ever get there?" [act 4, scene 2]), is associated with the final decline leading to death. The play's conclusion ratifies Machiavelli's view that Nature imposes absolute limits on the flexibility of *virtù*: even those who dominate Fortune must eventually fall before the absolute limit of Nature, which decrees the senescence of all mixed bodies, from individuals to city-states and republics.[34]

33. On the iconography of Chronos and Saturn in relation to time, see Erwin Panofsky, *Studies in Iconology: Humanistic Themes in the Art of the Renaissance* (New York, 1972), 97–112.

34. For Machiavelli's use of the topics of birth and rebirth, disease and senescence to describe the rise and fall of states, see *The Discourses*, bk. 1, chap. 2; bk. 3, chaps. 1 and 9.

Valediction in Clizia

Sed absentes prosunt pro praesentibus

That the allegorical configuration is so sharply delineated in the story of the play and in the functions of Clizia suggests the extent to which Machiavelli had brought to awareness his own habit of allegorizing powerful female figures. *Clizia* also marks a shift, in that Nature and Fortune, once treated as the antagonists of *virtù*, are now envisioned as tied to a fundamental modus of human existence that must, of necessity, be accepted. Because they are embodied in the temperate Sofronia, the feminized powers of Fortune and Nature are, in Machiavelli's last synthesis, themselves tempered; this modification of the allegorical antagonists seems to reflect the ethical tempering of the author himself.

Nicomaco's senescence in *Clizia* is an instance of personal extinction framed by larger patterns of historical and institutional repetitions. In one sense, the decline of the individual, whether Nicomaco or Niccolò Machiavelli, is also a microcosm of the decline of empires, of "Athens . . . in ruins."[35] The fact of historical extinctions is a recurring topic in Machiavelli's work, especially his meditations on the consequences for Italy of the French invasions (as found in *Mandragola* as well as *Clizia*).[36] That Clizia's status should derive from the epochal 1494 invasion suggests that a historical event is the cause of the play's action, that history is the macrocosmic frame for Nicomaco's lesson. As we have seen, much is suggested by the use of terms like "battitura" and "inclinare" in references to both states and the aged Nicomaco. Other terms used in *Clizia* also echo the language Machiavelli uses elsewhere to refer to the historical process: "caso" and "sorte" (chance, lot) are used in the discussion of Fortune's lottery and the jousting for Clizia; "guastare" and "acconciare" (spoil, fix) describe Sofronia's action on Nicomaco's plots (act 1, scene 1; act 5, scene 3), but also Fortune's effects on the world; "guastare" and "racconciare" are the effects of Fortune's agents "ozio" (idleness) and "necessità" in the tercets on Fortune. "Riscontro," used by Sofronia ironically to refer to Nicomaco's

---

35. This is the topic of Lucretian pessimism—already rendered sufficiently classical by Virgil's use of it in *Georgics* 2.497: "res Romanae perituraque regna" (the Roman empire and realms doomed to perish [my translation]). See the *Capitolo* on Fortune, 142–50 (*Il teatro*, ed. Franco Gaeta [Milan, 1965], 316), where the ancient empires are listed as the prey of Fortune.

36. For example, *The Discourses*, bk. 1, chap. 37 ("that city will soon be brought to ruin"); proem to bk. 2 ("after ruin had overtaken the Romans"); bk. 1, chap. 1. See also *Florentine Histories*, bk. 2, chap. 1, referring to Italy: "Thus, provinces come by these means to ruin"; and bk. 8, chap. 36: "ruined, and are still ruining, Italy"; as well as *Mandragola*, act 1, sc. 1: "the wars in Italy, which ruined our country" (my translations).

approaching "male nuptials" with Siro, echoes Machiavelli's formulaic use of "riscontro" in the political works to mean not only an encounter but a match or an adaptation to time or circumstance.[37] "Riconoscere," employed in the political works to describe the self-examination incumbent on social beings (*The Discourses*, book 3, chapter 1), is adapted in *Clizia* to identify the conventional purpose of comic art ("It is useful . . . for young ones, to learn about the avarice [*cognoscere l'avarizia*] of an old man"). I suggest that it is also Machiavelli's self-invitation to Delphic wisdom, his recognition of the limits to heroic autonomy, and his prescience of the fatal *riscontro* of *virtù* with decline and death. There is, however, more than merely defeat in store here. In comparing Machiavelli's prologue with the prologue of his classical model *Casina*, we find indications of how Machiavelli conceived of his legacy to posterity.

As I have suggested, key elements in *Casina* subsequently exploited in *Clizia* are foreshadowed in the prologue to Plautus's play: the significance of the title (prologue, 30–32); the import of the "absent" Casina in the play's workings (note the conspicuous return to a discussion of the *puella* ["revortar ad illam puellam"], prologue, 79); and the strategic absence of key characters due to the demiurgic will of the playwright ("Plautus noluit"—referring to the son, who does not appear [prologue, 65]), who can add or delete characters at will (cf. Ronconi, "Interpretazione," 238–39). Most striking of all is the postulation of two moments—that of the author and that of a posterity that celebrates his contribution and his reputation after he has become one of the *absentes* (20). The two moments in the Latin prologue are replaced in *Clizia* by the temporal abyss separating the Athenian from the current Florentine instance of the *favola* in question:

> For Athens is in ruins: its streets, its squares and its buildings can
> no longer be recognized. Furthermore, its citizens spoke Greek,
> and you would not understand that language. Consider, therefore,
> the events which occurred in Florence.

In the space of a generation, between the first performances of *Casina* (or rather *Sortientes*) and its revivals, Machiavelli finds the opening he needs to introduce what is both a central project of Renaissance humanism and a recurring concern of Machiavelli as a student of Roman history: the revival and the *translatio* of antiquity into an intelligible

---

37. Cf. *The Discourses*, bk. 3, chap. 9; Machiavelli, *Letters*, ed. Gilbert, 119; *The Prince*, chap. 25; *Capitolo* on Fortune 100–105 (*Il teatro*, ed. F. Gaeta [Milan, 1965], 315).

(and useful) contemporary form. The project is closely related to the act, and the ethos, of the *translator* himself.

All three sections of the prologue touch on some dimension of *recognition* and *knowledge* that the author will both facilitate and obstruct. In the first, the unrecognizability of Athenian buildings and the unintelligibility of Greek—the deletions of history—are to be remedied by the author's translations; he will, however, suppress historical names. In the second, the audience will be helped to recognize the personae ("in order that you may better recognize them") but is told to give up hope of seeing Clizia. In the third, the author will furnish knowledge of vice and virtue to the new generation ("It is useful . . . for young ones, to learn about the avarice of an old man") and will also restrain his range of expression ("and he refrains from speaking ill").

In presenting this complex ethos of the author, the prologue anticipates some of the serious themes dramatized in the defeat of Nicomaco—the destructiveness of time, the importance of reputation, the social contract between old and young, the function of tradition. Although the author's mediation of the Athenian "caso" (case) to a Florentine audience might seem to express *in nuce* Machiavelli's project as a humanist and historian, the emphases of the prologue differ from those of Machiavelli's well-known proposals for a Florentine militia or for an effective prince. The prologue to *Clizia* presents the author as a veteran cultural mediator, balanced between reporting a gossipy tale (novella) and enunciating a story, a *fabula* with didactic value; between arousing male appetite for a beautiful foundling and chastening it with an exemplum of domestic rape interdicted by a protofeminist community; between contemplating a ruined and unintelligible antiquity and restoring it in the idiomatic forms of the present. He tempers new and old, the tragic and the farcical, self and community, pleasure and instruction, ruin and reconstruction. Most of all, the author's care to present himself as a *uomo costumato*—that is, discreet, restrained, and didactic (mixing, in Horace's terms, usefulness and pleasure) mark him as temperate (*sophron*), and this distinguishes him sharply from the headstrong and distempered Nicomaco.

It is not that we must choose here between the author of the prologue and Nicomaco as expressions of the "real" Machiavelli. The role of *uomo costumato* serves as both antithesis and balance to Nicomaco and brings the *autore* into Sofronia's camp—joins her in defense of the claims of a *costume* and *ordine* that is not one of the heroic *straordinario* but rather one of the domestic *ordinario*. Indeed, just such an averaging of the two "authorial" figures in the play exemplifies the principle of balancing force and restraint that characterizes ancient Greek speculation on virtue.[38] There is thus in *Clizia* a systematic "tempering" of Machiavelli's literary ethos and project. I have suggested that it is a consciously valedictory gesture, in which the author prepares for death and monumentalization. This preparation is rather grandiosely framed by the invocation—it begins the prologue—of the historiographical topos of *anakyklosis*, the cyclical return of the same events over historical time.

In contrasting Nicomaco's decline and the Polybian theory of recurring historical types, the prologue juxtaposes the renewability of collectivities with the inevitable extinction of individuals. With this juxtaposition, Machiavelli's use of the Latin preface of his model, in which *Casina* is treated as an old play worthy of revival because of its value for contemporary audiences, appears thematically central to *Clizia*, indeed is a figure for the predicament of the author himself. That the apparently slight *Clizia* should furnish the basis for one of Machiavelli's principal enunciations of the Polybian topic in the late work has occasioned little comment or surprise.[39] In Machiavelli's adaptation of the topos in *Clizia*, time brings back the same situations and events ("casi") but not the same individuals:

> If men reappeared in the world in the same way as do events, not a hundred years would go by before we would find ourselves together once again, doing the same things as now.

The exclusion of individuals from the cycle is due, of course, to their mortality. Implicit in Machiavelli's reliance on the Polybian topic is the idea of a natural cycle, a *physeos oikonomia* of growth and decline caused by the heavens that overwhelms even the best-conceived constitutions; such a cycle affects individuals catastrophically, since it annihilates them.[40] This is, as we have seen, the predicament of

38. On Plato's persistent coupling of the spirited and the restrained, of andreia and sophrosyne as, respectively, the motor and bridle of civilization, see North, *Sophrosyne*, 170–73.

39. The other principal adaptations of Polybius VI in Machiavelli's political texts are in *The Discourses* (bk. 2, chaps. 39 and 43; bk. 2, proem; bk. 3, chap. 1); and in *Florentine Histories* (bk. 3, chap. 1; bk. 5, chap. 1).

40. With regard to the Polybian account in which he foresees the necessary decline of all institutions, even those established under the mixed constitution of the Romans, see Gennaro Sasso, *Niccolò Machiavelli: Storia del suo pensiero politico* (Naples, 1958). Sasso denies that Machiavelli embraces the impersonal, fatalistic aspect of Polybius's thought. But it is difficult to assent to Sasso's strictures in view of a passage like *The Discourses*, bk. 3, chap. 1, in which the state is described as a "mixed body" susceptible to disease and decline. Sasso appears to claim that Machiavelli never wavered from his affirmation of human autonomy and effectiveness in history (see esp. 368–69); in a sense, this is precise-

Nicomaco-Machiavelli, which is foreshadowed in the first lines of the play.

What is less often noted is that the Polybian theory of cycles is adapted, in the prologue to *Clizia*, to the demands and traditions of the comic genre and its transmission over time. Given its situation in the prologue, Machiavelli's allusion to the Polybian cycles is inescapably also a citation of the Terentian topos—commonly repeated in Renaissance comic prologues—that nothing has been said that has not been said before ("nullum est iam dictum, quod non dictum sit prius," *Eunuchus* 41 [Ronconi, "Interpretazione," 228–29]). In fusing the roles of historian and *commediografo*, Machiavelli has the Polybian topos of recurring events function as the basis for the *translatio* of comic artistry from Greece to Rome and thus to Italy.[41] From this perspective, Sofronia's restraint of Nicomaco illustrates the same principles that guide the literary imitation of the author, eager to be thought *costumato*; the existential crisis of the protagonist and the poetics of the comedy share the same logic. With his specifically dramaturgical version of the Polybian topos, the dramatist-humanist stakes out his own specifically literary sphere of influence, poised between the ruins of previous civilizations and his own certain ruin, but anchored in a community that he hopes to inform and that will be preserved thanks to his mediation.

A crucial detail for Machiavelli's conception of his authorial status in *Clizia* appears in the first twenty lines of Plautus's prologue, where the contrast is established between "antiquae comediae" and "novae comediae" (old comedies and new comedies), between "veteres fabulas," "antiqua opera" (old works, old stories) and current, less qualified coin ("novi nummi"). The current revival is presented as being beneficial to the younger generation ("so that they will be informed [*ut cognoscant*] we zealously offer this work"); and the author is described as already a classic—a past winner in dramatic competition, a flower of poets, a beneficial ancestor:

---

ly the attitude that *Clizia* questions and castigates. For more balanced analyses of Machiavelli's view of the rise and decline of states and constitutions, especially the more pessimistic views of the period coinciding with the *Florentine Histories* and *Clizia*, see Felix Gilbert, "Machiavelli's *Istorie fiorentine*: An Essay in Interpretation," in *Studies on Machiavelli*, ed. Myron P. Gilmore (Florence, 1972), 92–97; and Najemy, "Machiavelli and the Medici," 574–76. Pitkin (*Fortune Is a Woman*, 273–84) examines the corporeal metaphors of *The Discourses*, bk. 3, chap. 1, in terms of gender-determined limitations on Machiavelli's understanding of how institutions are "reborn."

41. On the problem of conceding borrowing while claiming innovation in the comic prologue, see Alessandro Ronconi, "Interpretazioni Plautine e Terenziane nei prologhi alle commedie del '500," in *Interpretazioni letterarie nei classici* (Florence, 1972), 226–32, esp. 231. Machiavelli's appeal to the topic of *imitatio* is noted by Raimondi in his edition of Machiavelli, *Mandragola, Clizia*, 41.

Haec cum primum acta est, vicit omnis fabulas. Ea tempestate flos poetarum fuit, qui nunc abierunt in communem locum. Sed tamen absentes prosunt [pro] praesentibus. (17–20)

When first acted, this play vanquished all the others. It was the best effort of the poets who then lived, they who have departed to the common resting place. Yet, although absent, they benefit those still here.

It is a description that Machiavelli, the earnest purveyor of antiquity to the corrupt present, might have envied, and did imitate. The prologue of *Clizia* anticipates, in fact, the author's hoped-for transformation into a man of good reputation (a "uomo costumato") and ultimately into a benefactor, an educator of the *giovani*, that we have just traced. Thus the concern in *Clizia* with reputation and fame, both in the form of Nicomaco's shame and in the form of Clizia (she who is known only by report), resonates with the Renaissance cult of personal fame as something that is intrinsically valuable, as a vote of confidence in the continued life of the community, and as itself the social reward owing to *virtù* and its accomplishments. The drubbing of Nicomaco staged in *Clizia* consequently goes beyond mere self-chastening; it finally helps the author make his bid for fame as a playwright, humanist, and civilizer—in Machiavelli's typology, for elevation to the rank of a co-founder, an *ordinatore*—one who joins in the continuous struggle to reestablish a *vivere civile*, now understood in a new, more comprehensive way.

Punto di fuga

Thus *Clizia* prepares for the passage of its author into the *communem locum* (with a double meaning: both the "place of all the dead" and the "collective memory") referred to in Plautus's prologue. To put it another way, it prepares for his disappearance. We have seen how persistent is the focus on the absent character both in Plautus and in Machiavelli; though absent, Clizia determines the stratagems of the play and her name permeates it throughout. The only other absence in the play of equivalent importance is that of the historical author, concealed behind both the author of the prologue and Nicomaco. This author, though distinct from the work, is yet "present" in it as its efficient cause; once dead, he is absent altogether, though the play, his effect, remains in some sense a vestige of him. In this context, the use of the invisible Clizia as the focus of the play's struggle of wills makes her the most nearly adequate mirror image or echo of authorial presence. Machiavelli, the veiled or absent demiurgic author, is paired with the female cynosure, in a curious coincidence of opposites (the feminine as object and the male as subject), both having (in Tennyson's phrase) "become a name." The coincidence is poignant because the girl's invisibility in the play acts as a hidden metaphor projecting the author's future disappearance, his death—a final link between the author, Clizia, and death in the infinity behind the *punto di fuga,* the vanishing point of the Renaissance perspective stage set.

The programmatic absence of Clizia and the "absence" of Niccolò Machiavelli—who appears only by onomastic sleight of hand, a verbal equivalent of Clizia's name—may explain the elusive relation of the play to Machiavelli's passion for Barbera Salutati, the biographical occasion for the composition of *Clizia* mentioned at the beginning of this essay. As one of the singers of the canzones between acts, Barbera had, at the play's first performance, an ambiguous relation to the play's action, both framing it and marginal to it.[42] Machiavelli's representation of his senescent passion in the play *Clizia* is similarly ambiguous: Barbera's presence inside the play (represented as Clizia) and outside the play (as the flesh-and-blood singer of the songs) is both continuous and discontinuous, as is Machiavelli's presence inside the play (represented as Nicomaco) and outside the play (as its author). This ambiguous "contamination" of formal and biographical elements also characterizes the play as artifact: *Clizia* is both a regular comedy, imitating a play written in Rome in the second century B.C. about a case ("caso") that took place in Athens, and the projection of a subjective state and a *fait divers,* a "caso" that took place, just the other day, in Florence. The figure of Machiavelli, both dramatic author and aging lover, mediates the objective and subjective modalities of the play, as well as its status as a *translatio* of the antique and a representation of the modern.

The importance of Barbera's role recalls the origin of the play's action in Nicomaco's diseased fantasy (*fantasia*), his foolish dream of a sexual rebirth in old age—a male fantasy that, in the Mediterranean world at least, may be fairly termed archetypal. It is precisely such a fantasy that the play destroys; in its place is the author's equally subjective but tempered vision of the play as a step in his transformation into a *uomo costumato* and social benefactor. From this viewpoint we may speculate, along with Giulio Ferroni, that the enigmatic Clizia shifts her focal point in Machiavelli's imagination. If in the play *Clizia* represents Nicomaco's fantasy of recovering his virility, even a kind of figure of elusive *giovinezza* (youthfulness), from the point of view of the author, the idea of the desired female object Clizia becomes the play

42. Nino Pirrotta, *Li due Orfei: Da Poliziano a Monteverdi* (Turin, 1975), 152–56.

Clizia itself, now offered not as a sexual enticement to male spectators but as a therapeutic spectacle beneficial to the community. The author's insistence that he, and his play, are characterized by *onestà* is the basis of Sofronia's solicitude for the foundling daughter. Rather than finding in the work a substitute for an unattainable gratification, the author makes the play the monument to his bettered (because battered) reputation: his *fama*, as adumbrated in Clizia's name.[43] At the same time, Machiavelli's ironic and exaggerated self-flagellation for being a decrepit and foolish old man seems a final gambit of the old fox, a countermove to the inexorability of time, a stake of his skill in making *virtù* of necessity.[44] As *Mandragola* attempts to assuage the bitterness of exile with deviltry and laughter, *Clizia*, by appealing to the humanist ideal of the literary work as testament to and embodiment of the author's reputation, works as an emollient for inevitable physical decline.

43. Machiavelli's fame in the generation after his death was in fact based on his comedies; *Clizia* especially was widely imitated. See Russo, *Machiavelli*, 149–50; and Beatrice Corrigan, "*Il Capriccio:* An Unpublished Italian Renaissance Comedy and Its Analogues," *Studies in the Renaissance* 5 (1958): 74–86.

44. Machiavelli, in a late letter to Guicciardini (Ridolfi, in *The Life of Niccolò Machiavelli*, 320, argues for a date after October 20, 1525, just a few months before the composition of *Clizia*), signs himself *istorico, comico et tragico*. He wrote, of course, no tragedy of which we have knowledge. He was, however, both a practicing historian and a successful commediografo. For Ridolfi, the tragedy in question is Italian history, and for Giorgio Bárberi Squarotti ("L'arte della guerra o l'azione impossibile," *Lettere italiane* 20 [1968]: 287–306), the "tragedy" is *The Prince*; but the letter to Guicciardini (which mentions Barbera) may also suggest the psychological background of Machiavelli's last literary work, in which both comic and tragic elements, *tempus flendi* ("a time to weep") and *tempus ridendi* ("a time to laugh"), are combined in a complex text referring both to historical events and to biographical fact.

CHAPTER FIVE

THE POLITICIAN
AND THE CENTAUR
Ezio Raimondi

THE zoomorphic images in chapter 18 of Machiavelli's *Prince* make an indelible impression on the reader. They epitomize a thought process whose strands are entwined in the search for concreteness through a deep binary movement, branching out to the sentence surface through geometric figures. Nietzsche, a perceptive decoder of antitheses and paradoxes, ascribed this movement to Machiavelli's skillful juxtaposition of a grave, hard, dangerous thought and the galloping, capricious tempo of an unrestrained *allegrissimo*. But although Machiavelli's critics subscribe almost unanimously to this reading, they do not substantiate it with an analysis of his mechanisms of composition, particularly his surprise superimpositions and the thematic force they generate. His technique deserves attention, in order to better isolate certain structures of Machiavelli's reasoning in his going "after the real truth of the matter" rather than "what people have imagined" (*The Prince*, chapter 15).

If the section on the qualities of a man of government is treated as a unit, then chapters 15, 16, 17, and 19 all begin with and develop the same pattern, typical of a formal treatise:

Chapter 15: It remains now to be seen.
Chapter 16: Let me begin, then, with the first of the qualities
  mentioned above.
Chapter 17: Continuing now with our list of qualities, let me say.
Chapter 19: Now that I have talked in detail about the most

important of the qualities mentioned above, I'd like to discuss the others briefly under this general heading.[1]

Chapter 18, by contrast, dispenses with these didactic links. On the premise that conflict sustains political life, this chapter takes direct aim at a burning conflict. The world of ideal virtue is universally celebrated: "How praiseworthy it is for a prince to keep his word and live with integrity rather than by craftiness, everyone understands." But the sphere of experience teaches the opposite: "Yet we see from recent experience that those princes have accomplished most who paid little heed to keeping their promises, but who knew how craftily to manipulate the minds of men."

Machiavelli establishes the conflict between keeping one's word and craftiness from the outset, in part through syntactic division. The first paragraph ends with the victory of those who manipulate over "those who tried to act honestly." "Everyone knows" that integrity does not provide a strong foundation for power (a statement that conceals the paradox that, according to the raw logic of the real, craftiness affords a much more solid base). The writer remains outside the proposition, hidden beneath the chiasmus of "everyone knows" and "we see," until he suddenly emerges, at the next beat, opposite the plural "you" (*voi*) of a collective interlocutor. In a usage more common to another genre, the dialogue, this "you" is introduced as an audience for the speaker's reflections.

The speaker goes to the roots of the phenomena with a formula taken from Cicero's *De officiis*: the "two ways of settling a dispute."[2] However, the quotation lacks an internal signal, thus placing it in a very different context from that of the Ciceronian model and raising the suspicion that Machiavelli's calculated adaptation of his source material might disguise a deformity or a forced interpretation. In *De officiis*, Cicero says that we must turn to force in the extreme case that diplomatic confrontation proves to be in vain ("si uti non licet superiore" [1.11.34]), and he syntactically emphasizes the exceptional nature of armed conflict by comparison with the peaceful *modus* of reason. When Machiavelli transcribes this sentence, he replaces a conditional

---

1. [Editors' note: Translations of *Il Principe* are from Niccolò Machiavelli, *The Prince*, trans. and ed. Robert M. Adams (New York, 1977); translations of *Discorsi* are from *The Discourses of Niccolò Machiavelli*, ed. and trans. Leslie J. Walker, S.J., 2 vols. (London, 1975); emendations are marked by brackets. All other translations from primary Italian texts are by Michael Moore. Translations from Latin texts, except where otherwise noted, are by Robert Ultimo.]

2. Cicero, *De officiis*, trans. Walter Miller, in the Loeb Classical Library (Cambridge, Mass., 1961), 1.11.34. All translations are from this edition.

with a causative ("But as the first method does not always suffice, you sometimes have to turn to the second"), and thereby radically modifies the statement's deeper meaning. The transition from law to force, from that which is peculiar to man to that which defines the beast, does not imply a principle of deviation or degradation. It is a fact of "experience," an equal player that is coldly inscribed within the more general law of cause and effect. Thus his conclusion that "a good prince must know how to make good use of both the beast and the man" stands in open contrast to the *De officiis*, just as does the existence of "badly or well used cruelty" (*The Prince*, chapter 18). Cicero's Monophysitic theses, instead, describe a sublime "hominis figura" ("figure of man" [3.20.82]), uncompromised by the "immanitas beluae" ("ferocity of the beast" [82]), or by abandonment to the irrational "appetitus" that would turn him into a wild animal.

This divergence grows wider, submerging into a cunning web of deceptions and denials that destroy the Ciceronian text without ever mentioning it. Machiavelli achieves this in two ways: through the unexpected intervention of the centaur, as proof that the prince has a dual nature, and "one without the other has no lasting effect"; and by returning to the examples of the fox and the lion, according to the model of Ciceronian thought.[3] But the moralist of *De officiis* invokes a censorship of rejection: "wrong may be done, then, in either of two ways, that is, by force or by fraud, both are bestial: fraud seems to belong to the cunning fox, force to the lion; both are wholly unworthy of man, but fraud is more contemptible."[4] By contrast, the politician in *The Prince* reverses the situation to favor a reality based on facts, in a wholly positive value judgment.

The relationship between the texts is also epitomized by comparison of Machiavelli's "great liar and hypocrite" (*gran simulatore e dissimulatore* [chapter 18]) with Cicero's original precept that "pretence and concealment [*simulatio dissimulatioque*] should be done away with in all departments of our life" (3.15.61). So decisive and insistent is his commutative operation that the critical reader might easily think that Machiavelli distorts and estranges Cicero in order to strike at the very

3. Compare with the discussion of the indissoluble nexus of the soul and the body in Lucretius, *De rerum natura*, trans. W. H. D. Rouse, in the Loeb Classical Library (Cambridge, Mass., 1937): "nec sine corpore enim vitalis edere motus / sola potest animi per se natura, nec autem / cassum anima corpus durare et sensibus uti" (for neither can the nature of the mind show vital motions alone by itself without the body, nor again deprived of mind can the body endure and use the senses [3.560–62]).

4. Cicero *De officiis* 1.13.41: "cum autem modis, id est aut vi aut fraude, fiat iniuria, fraus quasi vulpeculae, vis leonis videtur; utrumque homine alienissimum, sed fraus odio digna maiore."

heart of the humanist ethic of ideal virtues and "imagined things." The truth of "how you live" can only be the reversal, the bitter caricature, of "how you should live" (cf. *The Prince*, chapter 15).

The ideological opposition of fraud and force is reinforced through style. Style represents a way of seeing and of constructing the scenes of a mental space, "une manière absolue de voir les choses," according to Flaubert. And Gianfranco Contini has claimed that style denotes a gnoseological position. The function of Cicero's equation *vis-fraus* = *leo-vulpecula* falls somewhere between the didactic and the illustrative, and thus occupies a minor register, Machiavelli expands this equation into a dynamic series of metonymic syntheses and restores it both to the matrix of its original genre, the fable, and to the evidence of a familiar, domestic, animal world.

Machiavelli's penchant for the short apologue (animal proverb), for reducing qualities to animate images, reflects the influence of Luigi Pulci and the burlesque writers, from Domenico Burchiello to Bernardo Bellincioni.[5] In his own narrative experiments in the first *Decennale*, he constantly transfigures historical events into dramatic fables of animals fighting with each other. Despite the often rough and summary quality of the tales, they have a pleasant inventiveness, almost a kindling of fantastic humors.[6] In these fables the "beast" truly incarnates the physical obsession of violence and the aggressive appetites that lurk and flare up in the impassive body of nature.

Machiavelli's interest in the language of fable and apologue extends beyond his youthful poetry; it is also insinuated into the expressive experience of the period when he wrote *The Prince*. The satirical natu-

5. Their stylistic devices include: "disse la volpe, maliziosa e vecchia"; "e cadde come il tordo sbalordito"; "e noti ognun la favola d'Isopo / che il lione ebbe bisogno d'un topo"; "quattro cornacchie con tutte lor posse / a quattro nibbi vollon far gran guerra"; "i' ti ricordo della rana e il ratto"; "meglio è fringuello in man, che in frasca tordo"; and, in a political work by Bellincioni that is fairly close to Machiavelli's text, "el Moro ha della volpe e del leone / e non tende alle mosche mai la rete."

6. Notice the following sequences from the poem: "volsono e' Galli di Romagna el becco / verso Milano" (*Decennale* 1.256–57); "Ascanio, suo fratel, di bocca a'cani / sendo scampato" (1.265–66); "al Cavallo sfrenato ruppe 'l freno" (1.334); "dove l'Orso lasciò piú d'una zampa, / e al Vitel fu l'altro corno mozzo" (1.401–2); "sentí Perugia e Siena ancor la vampa / de l'idra" (1.403–4); "Ascanio Sforza, quella volpe astuta, / con parole suavi, ornate e belle" (1.449–50); "va tendendo a' vicin laccioli e rete" (1.533). Of these, the most memorable is the emblematic scene of Valentinus lying in ambush: "e rivolti fra lor, questi serpenti / di velen pien cominciar a ghermirsi, / e con gli unghioni a stracciarsi e co' denti / ... / ... / ... / e per pigliar e' suoi nemici al vischio, / fischiò suavemente, e per ridurli / ne la sua tana, questo bavalischio" (1.388–90, 394–96). In this scene, Machiavelli deliberately fuses reminiscences of Pulci's *Morgante* with echoes of the Malebolgia in Dante's *Inferno*.

ralism of *Asino* testifies to it, as do his many letters written between 1513 and 1514, which vividly capture the speech of a free, brilliant conversation with a sharp comic accent, and with all the outbursts, eccentricities, vexations, and mystifications of a character interpreting himself.[7] His anecdotal and grotesque vein as a burlesque animal fabulist becomes clear, whether he is describing a widower who ended up "three or four days like a dumbbell," or representing the "parable" of a hunter of young boys chasing after "a plumb little thrush, whom he stopped with a stick, a candle and a bell, and skillfully led to the bottom of the ravine, below the cave where Panzano dwelled."[8] In another story, his jesting leads to a realistic and pungent episode from Aesop's fables: "Our Philip is like a buzzard, who when there are no dead bodies in the country, flies a hundred miles to find one; and after he has gorged himself, he sits on a pine tree and laughs at the eagles, hawks, falcons and the like, who die of starvation for half the year in order to feed on delicate foods."[9]

The fable genre echoes throughout these examples, especially in what his benefactor, Francesco Vettori, called the "story of the lion and the fox." Machiavelli improvised this tale and placed it in the preamble of a political letter illustrating his own state of momentary embarrassment. This fable comes straight out of the manual, executed with quick, firm brush strokes, within a framework of essential objects and gestures: "In doing this I was like the fox when he saw the lion. The first time he was almost scared to death, the second time he stopped to look at him from behind a bush, and the third time he spoke to him."[10] This passage immediately recalls the fox and lion in *The Prince*, where the two animals are also placed in opposition to each other, but with the addition of "traps" or "wolves." This correlation between the two texts does not define a thematic or stylistic area, but rather a working method in which the fable functions as a learning device, a paradigm of typical situations.

Critics have pointed out that animal fables always contain a repertory of power relationships, a catalog of roles that each of us plays in human society. However, Machiavelli's commentators have failed to

7. "Il mio parlar mai non verrebbe meno, / s'io volessi mostrar come infelici / voi [uomini] siete più ch'ogni animal terreno. / Noi [bestie] a natura siam maggiori amici" (I would never finish talking if I wished to show how much more unhappy you [humans] are than any other terrestrial animal. We [beasts] are better friends of Nature [*Asino* 8.103–6]).

8. See letters nos. 126 and 147, in Niccolò Machiavelli, *Lettere*, ed. Franco Gaeta (Milan, 1961), 243, 327–28.

9. Letter no. 143, in Machiavelli, *Lettere*, ed. Gaeta, 315.

10. Letter no. 138, in Machiavelli, *Lettere*, ed. Gaeta, 292.

realize that the parallel sequences, "the lion cannot protect himself from traps" / "the fox cannot protect himself from wolves," elliptically conflate two Aesopian *fabulae* taken from Lorenzo Astemio's humanistic anthology (*Fabulae ex graeco in latinum* [Greek Fables in Latin], 1495). The first, "The Lion Who Was Taught by a Fox to Escape from His Chains," is the story of a fox coming to help a lion who had fallen into a trap:

A lion caught in a snare was trying with all his might to break the chains, but the greater the effort he made to draw the snare apart, the tighter he was held. A fox was passing by the spot, when he saw what was happening: "You won't escape by might [*viribus*], my king," he said, "but you will by intelligence [*ingenio*]. For that trap must be loosened and untied, not pulled apart." And this the lion did, and as soon as the snare that held him tight had been loosened, the lion ran free. This fable shows that the intellect [*ingenium*] is far more important than brute strength.

In the second, "The Lion Who Sought a Part of the Wolf's Prey," both the wolf and the fox confront the lion. The wolf becomes easy game because of his stubborn violence. The fox is ready to give up immediately. The correspondence between this fable and chapter 18 of *The Prince* may seem merely generic, on the order of a hint to be acted upon, perhaps in tandem with an Apuleian echo: "vulpinaris amasio . . . sic inermem vix a lupulis conservo" (sly fox. . . . I can scarcely keep you safe from the . . . [she-wolves] [*Metamorphoses* 3.23]).[11] It is, however, all that Machiavelli needs to paint his canvas portraying a conflict between the fox and the wolf. The lion settles the conflict in favor of the weaker animal, in perfect symmetry with the fable of the traps—except that the protagonists' roles have been reversed. On the one hand, there is the triad lion-trap-fox; on the other, the triad fox-wolves-lion. The unexpected multiplication of "wolves" creates a morphological contrast between the singular of the subject / object and the plural of the obstacle / opponent.

Machiavelli's style relies on the syntactic force of concision and reductive antitheses. The lower strata of his semantic fields gather cultural refractions and hidden quotations; he invests these strata with the strategy of the subsidiary idea in such a way that the idea only starts to glimmer after a process of intertextual conjecture. His epigrammatic

11. Apuleius, *Metamorphoses*, ed. and trans. J. Arthur Hanson, in the Loeb Classical Library (Cambridge, Mass., 1989), 1:166–67.

schema appear to be submerged and hidden beneath the uniform density of the linguistic fabric. Within the extremely brief device of the sentence, Machiavelli transcribes the geometric points of a fable's dynamic in what André Jolles calls its "simple form."[12] The tension created by this grafting is sharpest where the tone of the enunciation is most normal, in the same way that a joke is often funnier when a comedian tells it deadpan, without letting on that he is joking.

As a rule, the animal fable requires a detached observer, whose only care is the pure sequence of gestures and roles. The only gaiety this allows is the gray hilarity of a disenchanted intellectual who organizes his experience of an obscure world into a theater of images, almost always with the backing of a hierarchy of power. Thus, in chapter 18 of *The Prince* the emblems of the fox and the lion are restored to the fable's original movement. They are not created out of language torn from their living context. On the contrary, they are functions of a relationship, units of force captured in the act of opposition, at the most dramatic moment of a story that can be repeated ad infinitum.

Machiavelli bases his inferences on the concreteness of objects and individuals ("you have to be a fox in order to be wary of traps, and a lion to overawe the wolves"). Any attempt at abstract conceptualization would destroy the most unique component of his ideological style. His style translates reasoning into gesture, an ordinary perception of common sense, and assimilates the idea with the individual, the body that constitutes its vital sign. This process results from a minute and refined classifying logic, reminiscent of what Claude Lévi-Strauss calls savage thought.[13]

The animal world in its most direct, perceivable reality emphasizes ideas and relationships that are later elaborated through reflection, on the basis of empirical facts. Analysis and synthesis, the extreme opposites, coincide in a single binary science of the concrete. The symbolism of equivalencies and differences between man and nature creates a system of calculation, of comparison and ordering, which can be applied to the universe of animate and inanimate things. The humanization of natural laws, according to Lévi-Strauss, is thus accompanied by a naturalization of human actions, which is prone to an emblematic transcription intensifying the gestural and dynamic aspect of behavior and the energy flow that it carries. Thought and sensibility are not disassociated, because thought becomes the perception of a visible

---

12. [Editors' note: See André Jolles, *Einfache Formen* (Tübingen, 1965).]

13. [Editors' note: See Claude Lévi-Strauss, *The Savage Mind* (Chicago, 1966; first published in French, 1962), esp. chap. 2.]

force, the experience of a process spatialized in distinct and opposite figures. In his studies of Plato, Eric A. Havelock describes a similar process as "tribal" memory.[14]

The tendency to place in the foreground and dramatize the concept and its intellectual connections can also be found in the syntactic relations that codify and refract this tendency into a combinatory series of semantic alternations. The beginning of the paragraph deals with quality and modes of being, along the traditional order of "keep his word," "live with integrity," and "craftily manipulate." But at the end of the paragraph, the syntagm "based on loyalty" (*fondati in sulla lealtà*), with its combination of an abstract determinant and a concrete verb (a combination that Machiavelli almost always uses to imply a hierarchical, oppositional relationship), signals a shift in perspective toward the pole of physical evidence. This pairing prepares us for the homogeneous metonymy of the new verbal group "make good use of the beast and the man," which then generates the realistically condensed segment "pick the fox or the lion."

From a semantic perspective, the nominal group "fox-lion" is an example of the concrete replacing the abstract ("craftiness / fraud-force"), but with many dimensions; it transfers the term of quality to a typical individual who manifests the quality in its purest degree, and implies the determination of the "person of the fox and of the lion." Chapter 19 explicitly clarifies this ("what good use he made of the person of the fox and the lion"), in oblique consonance with the Ciceronian doctrine of "two characters" (*De officiis* 1.30.107). Each of us is "invested by nature" (*a natura inductus*) with one "persona"; as for the other character, related to society and to our place within it, it is assumed that "what role we ourselves may choose to sustain is decided by our own free [will]" (1.32.115).

But in both cases, whether we are dealing with "nature" or with "character," the deep structure of the enunciation is still the objectification of an inner attitude that becomes a possibility to grasp. This is the dynamic moment of a multiple personality, unified by an intelligence that coincides with the body at the same time as it transcends, supports, and controls it. The instrumental intensification of the relationship and its correlative image of a contact between a juxtaposed subject and object (the Latin originator, "uti aliquo," also means "to have experience, a relationship with someone") radicalizes the action's impulsiveness in its transition from one state to another according to the

14. [Editors' note: See Eric A. Havelock, *Preface to Plato* (Cambridge, Mass., 1963), esp. chap. 3, "Poetry as Preserved Communication."]

dialectic inherent to a precarious balance, never safe from sliding into the void and the "ruins" of a crisis. Like "being based on the lion," the verb "to use" is absorbed by the semiotic, inchoative, and dynamic nucleus of "to pick," whereas "to be" is in fact equal to "to become." Even the apparently definitive appearance of "a most ferocious lion and a very clever fox" in chapter 19 disguises a tension between forces similar to the tension that agitates the universe, since "all our actions imitate nature," and "worldly things" cannot "stop."

All of these factors lead us back to the myth of the centaur, to the center of the analysis of the double image of the prince, with his fantastic and almost visionary naturalism, associated with the erudite taste for exegesis and symbolic language. Though the writer may proceed by sudden connections and dispense with intermediate links, he must show his cards from the inside by openly imitating the allegorical method of "covered" or "figural" teaching. He had already done so in chapter 13 of *The Prince* with a "figure from the Old Testament," from the story of David. He would later do the same in *The Discourses* (book 2, chapter 12), with the "poetic fable" of Anteus, king of Lybia who "when attacked by Hercules . . . was insuperable as long as he awaited him within the confines of his own kingdom, but . . . when induced by the craft of Hercules to leave it, he lost both his throne and his life."

However, in contrast with the Platonic-Christian approach of the humanist hermeneutic, Machiavelli's hermeneutic knows only one key of political decoding. This proves especially surprising when he applies it to a biblical text, as when he describes Moses as "simply an agent sent by God to do certain things" (chapter 6). Comparison of this passage with chapter 18 uncovers a curious analogy between the pairing of the prophet and his "mighty teacher" (*gran precettore*), and the pairing of Achilles and Chiron, who was also a "teacher" but "half beast and half man." Even more remarkable is the political equivalence between God and the centaur, in a halo of mystery that might even be somewhat mocking. The reductive univocality of Machiavelli's reading of Chiron is so sculpted and so urgent that it obscures the "ancient authors" to whom he supposedly refers.

Machiavelli was not educated in a true humanistic school, but to his culture the centaur generally symbolized the violence and brutality of a man who denied the law of reason and turned into a tyrant, the enemy of justice. In the *Genealogie deorum gentilium libri* (Genealogy of the Gentile Gods), Giovanni Boccaccio declares: "The centaurs were warriors indeed, men of exalted courage, unbridled [in their passions] and inclined to every evil deed; we know them as accomplices and as mercenaries, as agents of crime, to whose strength and loyalty a tyrant runs at once" (9.27.98c).[15] And he reaffirms his position in his exposition of Dante's *Commedia*. In the fifteenth century, Cristoforo Landino wrote a commentary on Dante in the light of Neoplatonic teaching and concluded: "Just as the upper limbs of the centaur are human and the lower limbs are bestial, so tyrannical desires initially have some rational parts, but later the more they push forward in their progress the more bestial they become [from which we can deduce that] sin is the boundary between the horse and man."

The figure of Chiron attenuates the negative connotations of the centaur's intrinsically evil bestiality. Since Chiron was the mythical teacher of heroes, he cannot be only a beast. Boccaccio specifies that he "fed" Achilles: "Not in the form that others are usually fed. Instead he made him prepare his food only with the bone marrow taken from animals he had captured. He did this so that through regular exercise Achilles would become strong and ready to withstand the labors."[16] Landino in his turn recollects that the centaur "was said to be half-horse because he was a bellicose man, since the horse is an animal fit for war; whence Achilles, a bellicose man, is said to be his disciple." He proposes to make the centaur an intermediate allegory of "the man who despite his brutal ambitiousness and his lust for power, is nevertheless not without some learning and reason and some sense of justice."

Coluccio Salutati follows this line more resolutely and positively in *De laboribus Herculis*, in which he treats Chiron as a symbol of the active life peculiar to politicians: "Because he was the teacher of Hercules, Achilles, and Aesculapius, he sees that the more we exert ourselves in this life that we call active, the more we begin to learn that the exercise itself, namely the working life, should in some way be a teacher to us" (3.11.15).[17] However, Salutati still assigns a servile function to the animal part and reiterates the primacy of reason, of humanity overcoming the animal appetites of nature.[18]

---

15. Giovanni Boccaccio, *Genealogie deorum gentilium libri*, ed. Vincenzo Romano, 2 vols. (Bari, 1951), 2:470. Cf. Boccaccio, *Esposizioni sopra la Comedia di Dante*, in *Tutte le opere di Giovanni Boccaccio*, ed. Giorgio Padoan, 6:600 (canto 12, allegory 28).

16. Boccaccio, *Esposizioni sopra la Comedia*, 6:308 (canto 5, letter no. 117).

17. Coluccio Salutati, *De laboribus Herculis*, ed. B. L. Ullman, 2 vols. (Zurich, 1951), 1:212.

18. "Chiron's upper body is in the image of a man, that is, of the rational soul; the lower is in the form of a horse, through which, we might say, the active life is represented. For when reason, which we have in common with the angels, commands the natural appetite we share with the wild beasts, we pursue an active life full of virtue, and this is the truly human life. But if instead our natural appetite is in command of our reason, a thoroughly bestial, not human, life will result. If natural appetite is overcome by the swift command of reason, and without any resistance to that reason, the life that

Even in Salutati's "political" exegesis, the insurmountable limit remains an ethic of interiority and of self-control in conformity with a Platonic spiritualism that predates Marsilio Ficino's Christianized Platonism. According to Ficino's formulation "unicus in nobis est homo, bestiae vero sunt multae" (the man in us is one; but the beasts are many [*Letters* 4.27]), and human dignity consists in the repression of the *affectus bestiarum* (bestial passions).[19] This immediately brings to mind Giovanni Pico della Mirandola's *Oratio de dignitate hominus* (Oration on the Dignity of Man), with its thesis of man as "chameleon," who enfolds microcosmically the many orders of being: "It is a trite saying in the schools that man is a lesser world [*minorem mundum*] in whom there is seen to be a body mixed with the elements and a celestial spirit and the vegetable soul of plants and the sense of brutes and reason and the angelic intelligence and the likeness of God" (*Heptaplus*, 2d proem).[20]

But this line of thought does not lead us to *The Prince*. To truly approach Machiavelli and his worldly religion of the "fortress of the body," of the "brutal and bold" practice, it is necessary to go back even further, before Salutati, to a culture that still conserved the myth of the warrior, or of the variant myth of the hunter. Xenophon, one of the authors most present in the pages of *The Prince*, transmits a non-moralistic image of the centaur in two works: *De venatione* (1.3–4), when he praises Chiron's virtuous work; and *Ciropedia* (4.3.17–22), in Chrysantha's speech to the Persians to persuade them to fight on horseback.[21] In the latter, the orator's decisive argument is an example

---

results will be above the human condition, and should be called angelic, not human. But natural appetite or sensuality was not inappropriately represented by the figure of a horse; for there is no animal more obedient to man than the horse, who rides on steadily if a human holds the bridle; but should the horse be left to go ahead on his own, without bridle or human rider, he will often fail to reach his intended goal" (Salutati, *De laboribus Herculis*, ed. Ullman, 1:217).

19. Marsilio Ficino, *The Letters of Marsilio Ficino* (London, 1981), 60–62.

20. [Editors' note: See Giovanni Pico della Mirandola, *Oratio de dignitate hominis, Heptaplus, De ente et uno, e scritti vari*, ed. and trans. Eugenio Garin (Florence, 1942), 192. The translation is by Charles Trinkaus, from his *"In Our Image and Likeness": Humanity and Divinity in Italian Humanist Thought*, 2 vols. (London, 1970), 2:508, 794–95 n. 17. Compare the related passage from Pico della Mirandola, "Oration on the Dignity of Man," trans. Elizabeth Forbes, in *The Renaissance Philosophy of Man*, ed. Ernst Cassirer, Paul Oskar Kristeller, and John Herman Randall (Chicago, 1948), 225: "Whatever seeds each man cultivates will grow to maturity and bear in him their own fruit. If they be vegetative, he will be like a plant, if sensitive, he will become brutish. If rational, he will grow into a heavenly being. If intellectual, he will be an angel and the son of god. . . . Who would not admire this our chameleon?"]

21. Machiavelli read Filelfo's translation of the *De venatione* into Latin [here translated by the editors into English]: "I recall that the ancients studied hunting with Chiron from

from the fable of the Hippocentaur, whose physical and intellectual excellence can be equaled only by a soldier who becomes a horseman.[22]

Of the texts available to Machiavelli, none prefigures the centaur of *The Prince* so closely, to such an extent that it seems like an iconological precedent, as this one. The connection is reinforced by the taste for the primitive and the "savage," of a broadly Lucretian inspiration. We can see this in a Florentine painter such as Piero di Cosimo (1462–1521), who was intent on exploring a distant landscape of monsters and primitive forces through the neurotic subtleties of his imaginative naturalism.[23] However, even more prominent than Machiavelli's integration of Chiron into a homogeneous milieu of attitudes and ideas is his mysterious ability to extract the vital essence of myth from anecdote, and to reduce an archetypal figure to a sign. His centaur becomes a symbol of power, reflecting the logic of an ancient anthropology, a vision of the world predating and opposed to the Christian view.

Georges Dumézil has shown how, in the Indo-European system, two antithetical forms of sovereignty alternate, embodied by the figures of Mitra and Varuna in the Hindu Veda.[24] Mitra is the image of creative, violent, magic power; Varuna is a just and peaceful sovereign, both sage and priest. When these royal myths were assimilated by Roman culture, they were secularized and translated into events from a national pseudohistory. However, the opposition between the two power figures was not lost. It was reproduced in the dialectical relationship between the first Sabine kings, Romulus and Numa Pompilius, in terms of the polarity between the charisma of *celeritas* ("swiftness")

---

a very young age and learned many noble things, from which they derived great virtue, a virtue which makes them even now worthy of our admiration." It is no accident that Machiavelli, in his turn, talks about "always being on the hunt."

22. The humanistic translation reads: "Of all the animals, I love especially the Hippocentaurs, assuming they existed, since they used human prudence, taking counsel before things happen, and the craft of human hands, while at the same time they also possessed the speed and strength of the horse. For this reason, they both seized what fled from them, and put to flight whatever they desired. And so even I too, when I become a horseman, will conduct myself in a similarly sound manner. For I will be able to foresee things with a human mind, and I shall take up arms with my hands, and, carried by my horse, I will turn away my opponent by its strength, nor, just like the Hippocentaurs, will I be conquered by nature."

23. [Editors' note: See Erwin Panofsky, "The Early History of Man in Two Cycles of Paintings by Piero di Cosimo," in *Studies in Iconology: Humanistic Themes in the Art of the Renaissance* (New York, 1972, first published 1939), 39–68.]

24. [Editors' note: See Georges Dumézil, *Mitra-Varuna: An Essay on Two Indo-European Representations of Sovereignty*, trans. Derek Coltman (New York, 1988, first published in French, 1948).]

and the ethic of *gravitas* ("weightiness"), and between *terrible* and *benevolent* rulers.[25]

Livy portrays Romulus as a warrior, an aggressive and merciless young hero, full of an energy that generates life even in the impetus of destruction. He is associated with exuberant and adventurous youth, the idea of a purifying violence, the myth of an unexpected creation, and the instinct for speed and improvisation. The centaur is one of the fabled creatures by his side, because, as Dumézil points out, it is analogous to the warrior's *celeritas*.[26]

Machiavelli follows Xenophon by elevating the centaur to a symbol of the prince and the statesman. In this way he intuitively restores the mythic category of sovereignty, which he identifies primarily with Romulus. In chapter 17 of *The Prince*, Machiavelli defends Valentinus from the accusation of cruelty: "People thought Caesar Borgia was cruel, but his cruelty [patched up (*racconcia*)] the Romagna, united it, and established it in peace and loyalty." Here he invokes the same principle of "mending" (*racconciare*) used in *The Discourses* to justify the violence of the founders of Rome: "It is a sound maxim that reprehensible actions may be justified by their effects, and that when the effect is good, as it was in the case of Romulus, it always justifies the action. For it is the man who uses violence to spoil things, not the man who uses it to mend them [*per racconciare*], that is blameworthy" (Book 1, chapter 9). This concordance is symptomatic; moreover, it has a synecdocal, "part for whole," value. If the problem of violence is solved in the same way for Valentinus and Romulus, then a prince skilled in "war and orders and its discipline" is modeled on the ideology of power represented by Romulus: the extreme life force, the moment of creative élan.

Numa Pompilius represents gravitas in the form of a peaceful and contained regality, whose main function is to guarantee the stability and continuity of government. In *The Prince,* such a rule is overshadowed by the triumphal archetype, the centaur. At the end of chapter 19, after the long excursus on the Roman emperors (so unlike the monarchs of the heroic age), Machiavelli distinguishes between the virtues necessary to "found a state" and those that are "useful and creditable in preserving a state already stabilized and secure." Even in this case, his primary concern is the prince's character, "half beast and half man," and the multiplicity of his actions, depending on whether the fox or the lion prevails in him, and his "mind [is] ready to shift as the winds of Fortune and the varying circumstances of life may dictate" (chapter 18). The dialectic of force and cunning (although the fox

25. [Editors' note: See Dumézil, *Mitra-Varuna*, 45–55.]
26. [Editors' note: See Dumézil, *Mitra-Varuna*, 38, 40.]

also designates another type of force) remains inside the same individual, and it does not give rise to an alternative of complementary figures until the introduction of the concept of *Fortuna* in chapter 25.

This dramatic chapter postulates a prince "who adjusts his behavior to the temper of the times," and man's impossibility of "going against the inclination of nature." Chapter 25 introduces the opposition between cautious and rash politicians, which cannot be conciliated in a single subject. This opposition is attenuated by the final corollary, "it is better to be rash than cautious." Once again, Machiavelli opts for the myth of Romulus, as if the image of power were inseparable from the image of youth, nature, and the peak of his creative cycle. *Fortuna* is "a friend of the young" since the young are less "cautious" and more "brutal." The continuous image of an erotic relationship implies that youth has the characteristics of a fox, capable of converting audacity into calculation, and vitality into a strategy to dominate a woman and her "traps." This is another component of Romulus's nature.

The image of the cautious old prince (as embodied in the person of Numa) will not acquire a thematic consistency equivalent to that of its antagonist until the *Discourses*. In this later work, Machiavelli rereads Livy, and possibly Plutarch, no longer in terms of individual political action, and in extraordinary times, but in terms of the state and its continuity. In other words, he focuses on the structure that emerges through the work of the generations and of the statesmen as an exemplary form of "civic life." Machiavelli engages in a systematic colloquy with Livy's text. Through the history of the seven kings, combined with the legends of the new indigenous line, common to the entire Indo-European world, he seizes on the profound logic of the generative paradigms of the historical process. Like a humanistic anthropologist who anticipates not only Giambattista Vico's "perpetual historic myth" but Dumézil's, Machiavelli must base his historical reading on the "variety of happenings" and on individuals in their constant functions as parts of the whole.

This is the moment of Numa, the priest-king who succeeded Romulus and brought a "ferocious" people to "civil obedience by means of the arts of peace." He proved that religion is "the instrument necessary above all others for the maintenance of a civilized state" founded on the "good institutions" that can make a state durable (*The Discourses*, book 1, chapter 11). In the intense, essential style of *The Discourses*, Machiavelli reconstitutes the symbolic dyad of warrior and wise man. If Romulus appears to be the hero of "extraordinary action," determined, violent audacity and brutality at the service of the common good, then Numa is the "maker of laws" who governs through religion and bases his power not on arms but on the mystery of an imagined relationship with God. As a contrast to "furor," he offers the "caution" of a "grave man." He is superior to Romulus because "where there is religion it is easy to teach men to use arms," but "where there are arms, but no religion, it is with difficulty that it can be introduced" (book 1, chapter 11).

However, the relationship between their natures, the development of the Roman state, and the problem of alternating "successors" carries a different message. By Rome's great "fortune," the first triad of rulers consisted of a "fierce and warlike" king, a "peaceful and religious" king, and a king who was "a lover of war rather than peace" (book, 1 chapter 19). The attributes of these three figures correspond to the broad categories of political behavior. Machiavelli's overriding preference is still for Romulus, and for whoever resembles him. Since Romulus relies "on prudence and on arms," he can face any situation, except the most desperate. Unlike Numa, he does not depend on outside forces "according to the times or the fortune that befalls him." In a certain sense, it is as if the choice between "rash" and "cautious" were reborn with regard to the duration of the state. Although Machiavelli acknowledges the religious prince's irreplaceable role, his fundamental paradigm is still the warrior-politician, the only one capable of acting in a "ruined" world and in the evil times of decadence. Romulus teaches this by taking "a corrupt city, not, with Caesar, to complete its spoliation, but . . . to reform it" (book 1, chapter 10).

Machiavelli interprets Romulus in an anti-Ciceronian spirit as the "builder" and "physician" who can create (*racconcia*) a new order even in violent times. He is also a cautious and skillful (*virtuoso*) man of war, who does not hesitate to institute the Senate, more interested in a free and "self-governing state than . . . absolutism or tyranny" (book 1, chapter 9). Alongside Machiavelli's growing awareness of corruption, and of the involutional dangers that threaten every political body, he consolidates the myth of youthfulness and vitality that can reinvigorate an aging organism when its processes, its "humors," slacken or change to its "detriment," and not to its "health." Thus one of the merits of the Roman republic, so exemplary in the "order of history," was that it gave its citizens the Consulate, "without respect to age or to birth," and that it took advantage of its youths, even in positions that required the "prudence of an older man," because they alone possess "expeditious-ness" and are "vigorous of mind" (book 1, chapter 60).

This notion of vitality is rooted in the dialectic of birth and death, almost in the deep cycle of sexuality, and derives from a single governing idea beneath the universe of concepts. Machiavelli never abandons this dialectic but ends up almost obsessing over it, in the alternating flux of hopes and mortifications, of fantasies, renunciations, and adjustments, that make him both a dramatic character and a comic actor who separates wisdom from moderation. According to Francesco Guicciardini, who knew him quite well, his was an extravagant and paradoxical mind.

In a March 1526 letter to Guicciardini, Machiavelli said he sensed that he was living in times that "require audacious, uncommon, and strange resolution." Once again he gave vent to the ancient preference for "crazy things," for "fearless plans," to the point of appearing "ridiculous." The letter outlines a picture of an imminent war, on top of which he stands with his "banner of fortune," Giovanni de' Medici, a lord who is "audacious, impetuous, of great ideas, who chooses great struggles."[27] This image of Giovanni's youthfulness, similar to that of the Prince who must beat and bend *Fortuna,* provides one last glimpse of the centaur symbol. The complementary figure of Chiron can also be noted in the margins of Machiavelli's own statement, except that rather than Achilles, his interlocutor is a phantasm of the mind or of desire, a book with a missing addressee, the writer's projected *double.* Ultimately myth does not exclude the bourgeois mask. A modern Chiron amid the firearms, standing beside the uncorrupted force of the warrior, perhaps Machiavelli uses the fantastic ambivalence of the centaur to conceal his solitude as a writer, his destiny as an intellectual and a scholar.

Translated by Michael Moore

27. Letter no. 212, in Machiavelli, *Lettere,* ed. Gaeta, 457–58.

CHAPTER SIX

MEDUSA AND THE MADONNA OF FORLÌ: POLITICAL SEXUALITY IN MACHIAVELLI

John Freccero

O NE usually thinks of Machiavelli as the political theorist who un-
masked the political myths of his predecessors by treating politics as an
autonomous realm, not subject to ethical or moral considerations. *The
Prince* is concerned with what he called "effective truth"; that is, truth
that is operative in the real world, in spite of the efforts of those in
power to mask it from their subjects. By openly acknowledging the
usefulness of force and fraud and by dispelling the myths and cant
surrounding issues of power and legitimacy, Machiavelli stated what
had always been obvious to successful tyrants, but rarely to their victims. His candor earned for him not only the opprobrium of moralists,
but the gratitude of patriots as well.

Nevertheless, there is a trace of "political theology" that shows remarkable persistence even in the work of so great a demythologizer:
the myth of the state as a political body. It is true that the corporate
metaphor pervades our languages, however vestigial the concept of
the "body politic" may be. We are scarcely conscious of the original
physical sense of the word "member," just as the words "head" or
"chief" in the context of social organization no longer seem figurative.
In political rhetoric, the dormant figure is revived when necessary to
persuade individual "members" to act against their self-interest for the
good of the "head."[1] What interests us here, however, is Machiavelli's
speculative use of the figure to lend a certain vitality to the political
entities to which he applies it. The "state" described by such a corporate metaphor can no longer be thought of as a passive object—the

---

1. On the history and importance of the image, see Ernst H. Kantorowicz, *The King's
Two Bodies: A Study in Medieval Political Theology* (Princeton, N.J., 1957), esp. chap. 5.

Prince's *estate*—but assumes by implication a separate identity.[2] More-over, the body is gendered: the state or the realm is like a spouse to the ruler who possesses her. Commentators are sometimes embarrassed by Machiavelli's sexual aggressivity and dismiss it as though it were irrelevant to his politics. We shall see, however, that because of the metaphor of the state as female, there is in his work a certain homology between sexual politics and political sexuality. His apparently "sexist" remarks about *Fortuna,* for example, have political implications that cannot be dismissed as simply as the distasteful allegory by which they are conveyed.

The corporate fiction appears throughout Machiavelli's work, not always with mythic force, but often with more than merely etymologi-cal resonance. Class distinctions are regularly referred to as "humors" and disorders are described as wounds, sores, or disease.[3] In *The Dis-courses,* the metaphoric body of Rome is said to have been a healthy organism, with a life of its own; its heart and vital organs were armed, even when its extremities were not.[4] In *The Prince,* however, contempo-rary Italy seemed to have strength in its members but not in its head.[5] It was a body beaten, enslaved, and, very nearly, dead:

> Italy [has been] reduced to her present state; . . . she [is] more
> enslaved than the Hebrews, more abject than the
> Persians . . . headless, orderless, beaten, stripped, scarred, overrun,
> and plagued by every sort of disaster. . . . Left almost lifeless,
> [she] waits for a leader who will heal her wounds . . . and
> minister to those sores of hers that have been festering so long.
> Behold how she prays God to send someone to free her from the
> cruel insolence of the barbarians; see how ready and eager she is
> to follow a banner joyously, if only someone will raise it up.[6]

This impassioned appeal is addressed to a prince who, like a new Moses, is called upon to deliver from bondage an Italy that is clearly a woman.

Traditional rhetoric had established the figure of the "body politic" regally clothed, chaste, and, of course, female. Without a legitimate Caesar, however, she was not a lady but a whore: "non donna di

---

2. See J. H. Hexter, "*Il Principe* and *lo Stato,*" *Studies in the Renaissance* 4 (1957): 113–38.

3. On "humors," see *The Discourses,* bk. 1, chap. 4. On "mixed bodies," see bk. 3, chap. 1. On "disease," see *The Prince,* chap. 3.

4. *The Discourses,* bk. 3, chap. 30.

5. *The Prince,* chap. 26.

6. Translations are by Robert M. Adams from Machiavelli, *The Prince* (New York, 1977)—occasional emendations are marked by brackets.

provincie, ma bordello!" Machiavelli's enslaved Italy was a direct descendant of Dante's *serva Italia*, but unlike Dante, the Florentine secretary would not be content merely to pray for an imperial savior to marry her with God's blessings. Italy, like Lady Fortune, was there for the taking. It was up to the would-be prince to seize and possess her.

There is a considerable difference between coming to the rescue of Italy and assaulting Lady Fortune, because Fortune is not a *woman*, in spite of recent assertions to the contrary, but has traditionally been a courtly *lady*:[7]

> But I do feel this: that it is better to be rash than timid, for Fortune is a [lady (*donna*)] and the man who wishes to hold her down must beat and bully her. We see that she yields more often to men of this stripe than to those who come coldly toward her. Like a [lady] too, she is always a friend of the young, because they are less timid, more brutal, and take charge of her more recklessly.

Italy is a Cinderella whom the prince is urged to make into a lady. Where there is no king, one can become a prince by seizing someone else's lady.

Sexuality is for Machiavelli the emblem of the insatiability of human appetite, which is by nature able to desire all things and by fortune limited to the acquisition of very few.[8] This thoroughly Augustinian contradiction is the source of all discontent and envy. We may perhaps discern a hint of Machiavelli's private experience in the bitter remark about the lady's preference for younger men—one is reminded of the painful and hollow laughter in *Clizia*—but the fantasy rape of Lady Fortune is more than just the expression of sexual aggressivity. It is also the metaphorical assault of a political arriviste on the established social order. In the absence of traditional structures of legitimacy, the prince establishes his authority by taking what he wants.

In chapter 26 of book 3 of *The Discourses*, entitled "How Women [*femine*] Can Be the Cause of the Ruin of the State," Machiavelli surveys occasions on which the catalyst for social revolution was the possession or loss of a woman. It is important to point out that "cause" in this context means *proximate* cause; that is, the *occasion* for the ruin of

---

7. *The Prince*, chap. 25. See Hanna Fenichel Pitkin, *Fortune Is a Woman: Gender and Politics in the Thought of Niccolò Machiavelli* (Berkeley, Calif., 1984). Pitkin fails to note the distinction in Renaissance Italian between *femina* ("woman") and *donna* ("lady"). The important sociological point is amusingly recalled in a Frank Loesser song in the musical *Guys and Dolls* (1953), when a gambler prays, before shooting his dice, "Luck, be a Lady Tonight!"
    8. See the introduction to *The Discourses*, bk. 2.

the state. The women he discusses are clearly pawns rather than instigators of violent struggle. The first occasion was a struggle between patricians and plebeians in the city of Ardea over whether an orphaned noblewoman should be given in marriage to a noble or to a plebeian, after she had been offered to both. The second was the rape of Lucretia, which led to the downfall of the Tarquins, and the last was the rape of Virginia, which caused the overthrow of the decemvirate. The rhetoric of Machiavelli's invitation to take Lady Fortune by force must be read against the background of these myths of violation.

By placing these three stories together, Machiavelli makes it clear that rape (including forced marriage) is both the subjugation of another human being and a violation of the prerogatives of the males to whom she belongs in the class structure. Revolution breaks out in the instance of the orphaned noblewoman, but not as it does in the case of Lucretia and Virginia; that is, not because a family or a class is dishonored, but rather because it is not clear to whom she belongs. She is the occasion for a struggle between social classes in a city at war with itself, a pretext for social transgression. In these examples, sexual violence is a social crime, a seizure of property rather than an exchange.

If one carries this analysis further, the allegorical rape of Lady Fortune would also appear to be an attack on class structure. She is a *lady* because medieval tradition granted her that station as a sign of her inviolability. The proper response to a lady was to long for her from afar; yearning valorized the social barrier and distance preserved it. In this context, sexual violence against a metaphoric "donna" stands for a defiance of the social structure within which erotic etiquette is inscribed. It is a brutal figure for the refusal of Christian resignation.

In a text that Machiavelli knew well, Dante struck the analogy between erotic distance and resignation to the social status quo. In *Inferno*, canto 7 (94), he portrays Lady Fortune as a courtly lady oblivious to the vulgarity of her suitors: "Ella *si* è beata e ciò non ode" (She is blessed unto herself and doesn't hear these things). Here Dante uses the same untranslatable reflexive verb that he had used to describe the passage of Beatrice in his earlier love poetry: "Ella *si* va, sentendosi laudare" (She goes off by herself, hearing herself praised [my emphasis]). The presence of the reflexive of separation—*si*—in both verses underscores the analogy between erotic yearning and social aspiration: Fortune is as unmoved by the attention of her suitors as Beatrice was unmoved by Dante's youthful sighs. Machiavelli's violent rhetoric accepts the analogy but rejects the resignation dictated by courtly convention. The force of the argument is directed against the notion that one's place is fixed by birth rather than by ambition. It presses a Dantesque line of reasoning to a radical conclusion. If, as Dante had argued in *Convivio,* book 4, nobility is not a function of aristocratic birth, then neither is the power that nobility wields; anyone can dare to be prince. From a modern perspective, we may say that the offensive courtly code that transforms a woman into a prize is made more offensive by urging that the prize is there to be seized.

The coarseness of this imagery is deliberately meant to contrast with Dante's political rhetoric, to which *The Prince's* rhetoric, has a close, if ambivalent, relationship. The Latin title and subtitles of *The Prince* might have led Machiavelli's first readers to expect a treatise written in conformance with conventional decorum and that shocking or obscene details would thus be passed over in silence. Such *reticentia* had the effect of addressing, or indeed creating, a community of the like-minded, like a wink or a nudge in the ribs. To speak the horror or the obscenity is to refuse membership in such a community and to address those who are outside it. Often these are its victims. This is the substance of Antonio Gramsci's reading of *The Prince:* a work about political power addressed to those "who do not know" because they have never had it.[9] For Gramsci, Machiavelli's rhetoric serves to create a new, demystified audience in which he places his hopes for the liberation of Italy.

Although it contrasts with traditional political rhetoric, Machiavelli's use of obscenity and horror for shock value is not without precedent. A famous episode in *The Prince* is startlingly reminiscent of Dante's *Inferno,* although the execution of Remirro de Orco is meant to illustrate Borgia's political technique, rather than the Divine Will. Cesare had apparently ordered his lieutenant to repress the people of Cesena. He soon became so good at his task that he earned the enmity of the people:

> And because [the duke] knew that the recent harshness had generated some hatred [against him], in order to clear the minds of the people and gain them over to his cause completely, he determined to make plain that whatever cruelty had occurred had come, not from him, but from the brutal character of the minister. Taking proper occasion, therefore, he had him placed on the public square of Cesena one morning, in two pieces, with a piece of wood beside him and a bloody knife. The ferocity of this scene left the people at once stunned and satisfied. (*The Prince,* chapter 7)

9. Antonio Gramsci, "Note sul Machiavelli," in *Quaderni del carcere,* ed. Valentino Gerratana, 4 vols. (Turin, 1975), vol. 3, esp. 1598–1601.

The sundered body of Borgia's minister recalls the cloven bodies of Dante's sowers of discord or the crucified body of Caiaphas, who was guilty of precisely the kind of conspiracy Machiavelli espouses. Caiaphas told the Pharisees that it would be fitting to put one man to death to save an entire people (*Inferno*, canto 23, 117), a principle echoed approvingly in *The Discourses* when the subject is the rape of Lucretia. So too, Mosca incited his cohorts to murder with a lapidary phrase that rivals Machiavelli's terrible candor: "capo ha cosa fatta" (canto 28, 107), memorably rendered in the words of Macbeth: "If it were done when 'tis done, then 'twere well it were done quickly." Texts such as these give voice to what are supposed to be unspeakable secrets of political power.

The horror that Machiavelli dares to speak is the horror of politics in the real world. If we are no longer shocked by it, it is largely thanks to his exposé. His cynicism sometimes seems a mask for outraged idealism, a cry of pain rather than a dispassionate analysis. By his own logic, the maxims Machiavelli offers must always have seemed self-evident to those who have held power. It is unlikely, for example, that any successful ruler would need to be told that "the injury done to a man should be of such a nature as to make vengeance impossible," any more than a businessman would have to be reminded of Saint Augustine's ironic advice: "Buy cheap, sell dear."[10] However valid strategically, such principles are of limited tactical value. They are shocking, however, because they are offered without fear or embarrassment, as though they were infernal confidences, uttered out of the world's earshot.

Long before Machiavelli, Dante sought in *Inferno* to break the conspiracy of silence concerning the acquisition of political power. In canto 27 of *Inferno*, Guido da Montefeltro is portrayed as willing to reveal the secrets of his subversive art because he no longer fears public exposure. Guido's remarks constitute Dante's demystification of political authority in general and papal authority in particular. At the same time, they provide an example of the irony of *Inferno*, where all is as in real life, except that shameful secrets are revealed and injustice is punished. It was perhaps to evoke the tradition of infernal revelation that T. S. Eliot used these versus to introduce "The Love Song of J. Alfred Prufrock":

> S'i' credesse che mia risposta fosse
> a persona che mai tornasse al mondo,
> questa fiamma staria senze più scosse;

10. Augustine *De Trinitate* 13.3.

Ma però che già mai di questo fondo
non tornò vivo alcun, s'i'odo il vero,
sanza tema d'infamia ti rispondo.

If I thought my reply were to one who might ever return to the
world, this flame would be still; but since no one has ever
returned alive from this depth, if what I hear is true, I shall
answer you without fear of infamy. (*Inferno*, canto 27, 61–66)

Coaxed by a power-drunk pope into telling him how to overthrow the
city of Palestrina, the condottiere replied, "Promise much, deliver little." This single phrase synthesizes endless intrigue and pronounces a
moral judgment that is clear, although silent. Machiavelli's aphorisms
are written in the same tradition, except that they are not framed in the
context of an infernal journey. Unlike *Inferno*, Renaissance Italy provides no place to stand from which a moral standard might be applied
to such advice. It is as if we were all in hell.

There are several other details in canto 27 that seem to be evoked
by *The Prince*. For one thing, Machiavelli's celebrated reference to
the lion and the fox is usually ascribed to his reading of Cicero, but
it also occurs in Guido's definition of his own political guile. The
advice he gives is referred to as "fraudulent counsel," not because
it does not work—on the contrary, it is completely efficacious—
but because it advocates the commission of fraud, as does *The Prince*.
Guido's slyness extends to God's judgment, which he tried to evade by
his last-minute conversion. "It might have worked [*giovato sarebbe*],"
he says, had he not been outsmarted by the Pope, whom he calls a
prince (*principe*) of the new Pharisees. We may observe in passing
that Machiavelli's last example in *The Prince* of a leader with *virtù* is
also a Pope: Julius II. Reading the canto of Guido with Machiavelli in
mind produces the anachronistic and uncanny impression that Dante
is seeking to refute Machiavelli's concern for "what works"—"la verità
effettuale."

In this most ironic of cantos, the prescriptive value of infernal secrets
is undercut by infernal condemnation; this is, after all, hell. The sur-
roundings call into question every assertion of the damned. Without
such a framework, the conversation between Guido and the Pope
would be indistinguishable from what we could imagine to have been
the dialogue between Machiavelli and the aspiring leader whom he
may have been addressing. Guido's story is clearly ironized by the
infernal framework. By further ironizing it, *removing* the infernal
framework and giving the advice "straight," Machiavelli doubles the

negation and yields a deceptively positive portrait. In hell, Machiavelli's advice makes perfect sense.[11]

A further parallel between the two texts brings us back to the political body. In Guido's infernal monologue, he tells us that Pope Boniface came to seek his advice as physician:

> Ma come Costantin chiese Silvestro
> d'entro Siratti a guerir de la lebbre,
> così mi chiese questi per maestro
> a guerir de la sua superba febbre.

But as Constantine sought out Sylvester within Soracte to cure his leprosy, so this one sought me out as the doctor to cure the fever of his pride. (*Inferno,* canto 27, 94–97)

This moment marks for Dante the beginning of the infection that had always afflicted Italy: the donation of the empire by Constantine to the Church. It is the disease from which Italy still suffered in Machiavelli's day, with a complication that could prove fatal: the invasion of foreign bodies. So too, it is as physician to the *stato* that Machiavelli offers his advice:

You have to keep an eye, not only on present troubles, but on those of the future, and make every effort to avoid them. When you see the trouble in advance, it is easily remedied, but when you wait till it is on top of you, the antidote is useless, the disease has become incurable. What the doctors say about consumption applies here: in the early stages it is hard to recognize and easy to cure, but in the later stages, if you have done nothing about it, it becomes easy to recognize and hard to cure. (*The Prince,* chapter 3)

Politics is thus the art of medicine, rather than ethics, as it was in the Quattrocento.[12] It is a praxis requiring interventions that are sometimes cruel and violent, but always dispassionate. In *The Discourses,* the subject is "health maintenance" in ancient Rome. In *The Prince,* however, it is emergency medicine for contemporary Italy.

The distinction between the two kinds of medicine is at the heart of

11. Sebastiano De Grazia's title, *Machiavelli in Hell* (Princeton, N.J., 1989), suggests this connection, although the point is not made explicitly.

12. For debates on the relative dignity of law and medicine in the Quattrocento, see Eugenio Garin, ed., *La disputa delle arti nel Quattrocento* (Florence, 1947).

the difference between Machiavelli's two great works. In the early 1950s, Jacques Maritain observed that there was no trace of duration in *The Prince*, no distinction between the temporality of the individual and the temporality of the state. Neither posterity, which is extension in time, nor the human community, which is extension in space, seemed to enter into the calculations of the prince.[13] J. G. A. Pocock, in *The Machiavellian Moment*, describes the political emergency for which *The Prince* was written.[14] His title points to its timeless "punctuality." To turn from *The Prince* to *The Discourses*, however, is to turn from a political moment to historical time, from a no-man's-land to the Roman republic, where the emphasis is on the continuity between the past and the future. The commentary focuses on Machiavellian *duration* in republican Rome. The character of the prince, his *virtù*, is decisive, surgical, and timely. Given the etymology of the word, from *virtus* and *vir*, it inevitably carries with it masculine or even phallic associations. In contrast, *The Discourses* are less concerned with phallic *virtù* than with survival and posterity.

A passage in the third book of *The Discourses* is notorious for its grotesque quality and for its questionable verisimilitude. After the myth of the prince himself it constitutes, according to Gramsci, the most important of Machiavelli's political myths.[15] In the dialectic of concealment and revelation of political secrets, it represents an extreme case. The anecdote serves as an emblem of the widowed state without a prince—no longer enslaved and abject, as was Dante's Rome, but rather possessed with a potential energy enabling her to survive.

Caterina Sforza is mentioned in chapter 20 of *The Prince* as the Lady of Forlì. The context is a discussion of the relative usefulness of fortresses to rulers under siege. Machiavelli's conclusion, which he reaches from an analysis of Caterina's fate on two separate occasions when she sought refuge in her fortress, once successfully and once not, is that "the best fortress that there is is not to be hated by the people." This passage identifies Caterina as an emblem of the people, in spite of her aristocratic birth. It is as such that she reappears in *The Discourses*, book 3, chapter 6:

> Ammazzarono, alcuni congiurati Forlivesi, il conte Girolamo loro signore, presono la moglie e i suoi figliuoli che erano piccoli, e

13. Jacques Maritain, *The Range of Reason* (New York, 1952), esp. chap. 11, "The End of Machiavellianism."

14. J. G. A. Pocock, *The Machiavellian Moment: Florentine Political Thought and the Atlantic Republican Tradition* (Princeton, N.J., 1975).

15. Antonio Gramsci, "La matrice," in *Sotto la mole, 1916–1920* (Turin, 1960), 181.

non parendo loro potere vivere sicuri se non si insignorivano della
fortezza e non volendo il castellano darla loro, Madonna Caterina
(che così si chiamava la contessa) promise ai congiurati che, se la
lasciavano entrare in quella, di farla consegnare loro, e che
ritenessero a presso di loro i suoi figliuoli per istatichi. Costoro
sotto questa fede ve la lasciarono entrare; la quale, come fu
dentro, dalle mura rimproverò loro la morte del marito e
minacciogli d'ogni qualità di vendetta. E per mostrare che de' suoi
figliuoli non si curava, mostrò loro le membra genitali, dicendo
che aveva ancora il modo a rifarne. Così costoro, scarsi di
consiglio e tardi avvedutisi del loro errore, con un perpetuo esilio
patirono pene della poca prudenza loro.

Some conspirators who were citizens of Forlì, killed Count
Girolamo, their Lord, and took prisoner his wife and his children,
who were little ones. It seemed to them, however, that their lives
would scarce be safe unless they could get hold of the citadel,
which its governor declined to hand over. So [Lady (*Madonna*)]
Caterina, as the countess was called, promised the conspirators
that, if they would let her go to the citadel, she would arrange for
it to be handed over to them. Meanwhile they were to keep her
children as hostages. On this understanding, the conspirators let
her go to the citadel, from the walls of which, when she got
inside, she reproached them with killing her husband and
threatened them with vengeance in every shape and form. And to
convince them that she did not mind about her children she
exposed her [genital members] and said that she was still capable
of bearing more. The conspirators, dumbfounded, realized their
mistake too late, and paid the penalty for their lack of prudence
by suffering perpetual banishment.[16]

The scene calls to mind, if only by contrast, a familiar literary theme
associating a woman's body with the walls of a castle or city. In the
Chanson de Roland, the assault of a castle or city is figured as rape
(Charlemagne is said to have ravaged Spain: "The castles taken, the
cities violated");[17] in the *Roman de la Rose,* sexual assault is allegorized
as the storming of a fortress. It would be difficult to imagine a more
radical departure from such literary conventions than Caterina's ges-

16. Translation from Machiavelli, *The Discourses of Niccolò Machiavelli,* ed. and trans.
Leslie J. Walker, S.J., 2 vols. (London, 1975).
17. Jacques Le Goff, *The Medieval Imagination* (Chicago, 1988), 161.

ture. Rather than submit to her captors, the Lady of Forlì first beguiles and then terrifies them with her reproductive power.

Caterina's gesture is analogous to the phallic taunt of an ancient warrior, but her vengeance is prophetic rather than immediate. She in fact remarried and gave birth to Giovanni delle Bande Nere, the romantic soldier of fortune who was to replace Cesare Borgia in the hopes and the esteem of Machiavelli after the duke's death. For Gramsci, however, her power was not so much historic as it was mythic. The image of Caterina was to him an emblem of the *matrix* from which future generations would proceed in sufficient numbers to overwhelm their oppressors.

The passage in *The Prince* just quoted associated the historical Caterina with both fortresses and the people. By extending that association, Gramsci transformed her into an inexorable force, an allegory, rather than a person. Whatever human grief she might have felt was, like Medea's, insufficient to deter her from her purpose, which Gramsci identified, in his most impassioned moment, with history itself. It did not seem to matter to him that she was by no means a woman of the people; he was able to transform her historic identity into political myth by interpreting her reproductive power as a social force. Two mythic figures loomed up from Machiavelli's text: the prince, emblem of the revolutionary party, and Madonna Caterina, which is to say, history itself. For Gramsci, she was a more appropriate emblem of the struggle of the Italian people than either the brutalized female slave figure in the last chapter of *The Prince* or the ridiculous nineteenth-century personification dressed in a peplum, and carrying a scepter.[18]

There are folkloric elements in this narrative that are thoroughly consistent with such a mythic interpretation, yet they derive from a cultural context so far removed from Machiavelli as to suggest that Gramsci may have had parody in mind. The characterization of Caterina as the archetypal mother evokes the more traditional version of that image: the Virgin Mary as *Mater Omnium*. Caterina may be thought of as a fierce caricature of those images of divine maternity found on medieval walls and city gates, welcoming outsiders and offering sanctuary to those within.[19] Perhaps the most familiar of such

18. For further discussion of Gramsci's reading of Machiavelli, see Federico Sanguineti, *Gramsci e Machiavelli* (Bari, 1982), esp. 3–7.

19. See Nilda Guglielmi, "L'image de la porte et des enceintes d'après les chroniques du moyen âge," in *Fortifications, portes de villes, places publiques dans le monde méditerranéen*, ed. Jacques Heers (Paris, 1985), 106. The French word *enceinte* ("enclosure") seems to carry with it the analogy between the gate and the body.

representations is *La Madonna della Misericordia,* opening wide her mantle to expose the spiritual progeny clustered around her [see illustration 1]. Caterina seems in Gramsci's reading to be a secular version of that liminal icon, fierce rather than comforting, displaying her reproductive power not proleptically, in terms of the children she would one day produce, but with brutal directness. In accordance with literary convention, her body stands metonymically for the fortress, but its power is apotropaic; she is more like a Medusa than a mother.

In at least one instance, popular piety could depict the Virgin proudly exhibiting her reproductive power rather than simply nurturing her Son. The pose captured by Piero della Francesca in *La Madonna del Parto,* of a pregnant woman about to open her gown with her right hand, her left hand placed somewhat aggressively on her hip, strikes an obvious, almost anatomical analogy between Mary's garment and her body [see illustration 2]. It is a decorous and metaphoric version of Caterina's gesture.

Both of these gestures are *revelations* (*re-velatio,* "un-veiling") in the sense given to the word by Saint Paul, when he refers to the coming of Christ as an "unveiling" of the radiant face of Moses.[20] The parting of the Virgin's gown is a figure for the interpretation of Christianity's central mystery, a stripping away of successive veils of significance, from the tent, with its anatomically symmetrical angels, to her body, the last veil covering the unborn child at the center of the painting ("tent" is from the Latin *tabernaculum,* that is, *tabernaculum Dei,* the "Virgin's body").[21] Similarly, Caterina's "unveiling" of herself reveals an as yet nameless power, not unlike the messianic Moses so fervently entreated in the last chapter of *The Prince,* in whom Machiavelli placed his hope for Italy's deliverance.

To speak of unveiling and of the apotropaic obstacle at the gates is, for the student of Italian literature, inevitably to recall the moment in canto 9 of Dante's *Inferno* when the pilgrim and his guide try to enter the city of Dis and are repulsed by demons who threaten from the ramparts to summon the Gorgon. The threat of the Medusa in the action of the narrative seems to trigger a pause in the story and what is perhaps the most famous of Dante's addresses to his readers:

> O Voi ch'avete li intelletti sani,
> mirate la dottrina che s'asconde
> sotto 'l velame de li versi strani.

20. 2 Cor. 3:12–16.

21. See the discussion of Bruce Cole in *Piero della Francesca: Tradition and Innovation in Renaissance Art* (New York, 1991), esp. 77, for the etymology of "tent." For a survey of analogous images, see Gregor Lechner, *Maria Gravida* (Munich, 1981).

1. Piero della Francesca, *La Madonna della Misericordia*. Sansepolcro, Pinacoteca Comunale. Alinari / Art Resource, N.Y.

2. Piero della Francesca, *La Madonna fra due Angeli, detta del Parto*. Monterchi, Cappella del Cimitero. Alinari / Art Resource, N.Y.

O you who have sound understanding, mark the doctrine that
is hidden under the veil of the strange verses! (*Inferno*, Canto 9,
61–63)

The significance of the passage for Dante's poetics arises from the
importance of vision in erotic poetry. The Medusa represents the
glance that once enamored and now stuns the observer, a demystification of poetic seduction as it was represented, for instance, in the
Roman de la Rose or in Dante's own earlier love poetry. We shall see that
what makes this episode particularly relevant to Machiavelli's anecdote is that a subsequent passage in the poem, relating the dream of the
Siren, indirectly associates the Medusa with the sight of the female sex.

The Medusa figures a rejection of the themes that Dante celebrated
in his youth. The poet of *Inferno* seems to regard the eros that once
beguiled him as now constituting an obstacle to his spiritual progress:
"Se 'l Gorgon si mostra e tu 'l vedessi, / nulla sarebbe di tornar mai
suso" (If the Gorgon shows herself and you should see her, never
would you return to the world above [56–57]). The same threat is
repeatedly recalled in the poem—indeed, one could characterize the
love poetry of the *Commedia* as erotic revisionism[22]—but most pointly
in a dream in Purgatory, where it is represented not by the Medusa but
rather by the Siren's womb (*Purgatorio*, canto 19, 1–33). The pilgrim
dreams of her song and is bewitched until Virgil strips away her
clothing, revealing her horrible sex: "mostravimi il ventre." The dramatic and verbal echoes suggest that the Medusa and the Siren are
both images of a male terror of the female sex, but the implied misogy-
ny is not peculiar to Dante or to the Middle Ages. It is in fact rooted in
the most ancient of mythological traditions. A. A. Barb, bemused by
the scandal provoked by Freud's reading of the Medusa, demonstrated
that the Medusa and the Siren were related in antiquity precisely as
alternate representations of the primordial womb, the *Diva Matrix*.[23]

If the connection to the episode of the Siren suggests an indirect
allusion to female sexuality in Dante's Medusa, there is conversely
something of the Medusa in Caterina's sex, discernible perhaps in a
few anomalies in the text of *The Discourses*. First, the phrase *le membra
genitali* is odd as a description of the female sex. Not only is the word
"member" unexpected but the plural number is perplexing. The equivalent Latin phrase usually describes only the male sex. In written Ital-

22. John Freccero, "Medusa: The Letter and the Spirit," in *Dante: The Poetics of Conversion*, ed. Rachel Jacoff (Cambridge, Mass., 1985), 119–35.
23. A. A. Barb, "Diva Matrix," *Journal of the Warburg and Courtauld Institutes* 16 (1953):
esp. 208–12.

ian before Machiavelli, there seems to have been only one recorded usage that applied to females, in a medical treatise of the fourteenth century, but modern dictionaries usually cite Machiavelli as the earliest example. Second, there is an almost obsessive use of alliteration in the last lines. It is true that prose stylists of the Cinquecento were especially fond of this device, but in the description of Caterina's gesture, there are no fewer than eight external alliterations in *m* and two internal: "dalle mura . . . rimproverò . . . la morte del marito . . . minacciogli . . . mostrare . . . mostrò le membra genitali . . . modo." The horrified reaction of the conspirators to this gesture is also described with obsessive alliteration: "perpetuo . . . patirono . . . pene . . . poca prudenza." The key word in the alliterative description of Caterina's gesture seems to be *mostrò,* the word that recurs in Dante's similar "revelations," as we have seen; the word that is highlighted in the second group of alliterations is *pene.* Whether intentionally or not, these words are indistinguishable from the words for "monster" and for the male organ.

Caterina's appearance at the castle wall is meant to ward off would-be assailants precisely as the head of the Medusa was meant to ward off potential attackers from ancient cities and fortifications. An attempt to evoke that emblem with its fearsome snakes could account for the bizarre plural "members," as well as for the alliterations that are, at some level, iconic. We recognize in the insistent return of these primal sounds, *m* and *p,* the phonic image of the mother and the father, as Roman Jakobson has suggested, phonic images that would also serve to identify Medusa, the mother's usually terrifying counterpart, and Perseus, her less-than-formidable enemy.[24]

The association of mother and Medusa is by now a commonplace of psychoanalytic literature, since it was first suggested by Freud, for whom it represented the terror of castration, caused by the boy's first sight of his mother's genitals:

> The terror of Medusa is thus a terror of castration that is linked to the sight . . . of the female genitals . . . surrounded by hair. . . .
> The hair upon Medusa's head is frequently represented in works of art in the form of snakes, and these are once again derived from the castration complex. It is a remarkable fact that, however frightening they may be in themselves, they nevertheless serve actually as the mitigation of the horror, for they replace the penis, the absence of which is the cause of the horror. This is a

24. Roman Jakobson, "Why 'Mama' and 'Papa'?" *Selected Writings* (The Hague, 1962), 1:538.

confirmation of the technical rule according to which a multiplication of penis symbols signifies castration.[25]

Freud here interprets the myth of the Medusa as though it corresponded to a specific event in the life of any male child, a primal sight inspiring a terror of castration. The sight of Caterina's genitals also inspires fear, but for very different reasons. Her sex is the proleptic representation of her vengeance, an emblem of political survival through reproductive power.

For Machiavelli, the Medusa's face is not the horror that it would appear to be in the traditional male imagination or to Freud himself, who under the circumstances finds even a nest of snakes reassuring.[26] The multiplicity of heads or members that provides the basis for Freud's sexual interpretation of the Medusa gives the myth a possible applicability in the political realm. The importance of the use of the Italian feminine plural for a neuter Latin noun, *membrum*, is that it signifies a collectivity: specifically, the unity of a body with a plurality of members. The neuter pronoun *unum* in the motto of the United States, "E pluribus unum," points unmistakably to the neuter noun *corpus*, and thus to the persistence of the rhetorical commonplace with which I began this essay, the "body politic." The body's gender is crucial, however, for the *membra* of a woman's body include the future as well as the past. Caterina stands for such a collectivity. She is without a husband, but is far from being the disconsolate widow that Dante had used to portray Rome.[27] On the contrary, her autonomy is her strength, sufficient to discourage her would-be possessors.

In the Renaissance, rulers had a political reason to fear the Medusa, apart from the usual psychosexual anxieties. About five years after the

25. Sigmund Freud, "Medusa's Head," in *Sexuality and the Psychology of Love*, ed. Philip Rieff (New York, 1963), 212–13.

26. See Neil Hertz, "Medusa's Head: Male Hysteria under Political Pressure," *Representations* 4 (1983): 27–54. With characteristic brilliance, Hertz concentrates on the Freudian reading of the Medusa as representing castration. In the subsequent discussion of his paper, Catherine Gallagher points out that the threat of Medusa/mother is also the threat of *generativity* (Gallagher, Joel Fineman, and Hertz, "More about Medusa's Head," 55–57). This is Machiavelli's Medusa, although the threat is perceived to be directed against the conspirators.

27. On several occasions, to describe Jerusalem, Rome, or Florence, Dante quotes the opening versus of the Lamentations of Jeremiah: "How solitary lies the city, once so full of people! / Once great among nations, now become a widow." See in particular the excursus of *Purgatorio*, canto 6. See also Nancy Vickers, "Widowed Words: Dante, Petrarch, and Metaphors of Mourning," in *Discourses of Authority in Medieval and Renaissance Literature*, ed. Kevin Brownlee and Walter Stephens (Hanover, N.H., 1985), 97–108, 270.

death of Machiavelli, Benvenuto Cellini cast the masterpiece of his lifetime, the bronze Perseus that was to be erected in the Loggia dei Lanzi in Florence. Several pages of his autobiography are devoted to recounting how he cast the statue at the insistence of Cosimo I, the grand duke of Tuscany. Mythographers traditionally identified the Medusa as *Discordia*, but according to one of Cellini's editors in the nineteenth century, the duke meant the statue to have a political significance: he imagined himself to be a Perseus, putting down the Medusa of republicanism. The statue was therefore meant as a warning against any attempt to usurp his power. *Discordia* in the political order seems close to what Machiavelli would have called "tumult," a form of civic strife that is sometimes of benefit to the state, no matter how tyrants feel about it.[28] In any case, Machiavelli was spared any knowledge of the statue or of the fact that the grand duke who commissioned it was the son of Giovanni delle Bande Nere and the grandson of Caterina Sforza.

To see the Medusa's face in the body of Caterina is to read historical significance into the reproductive force of nature. It is also to see in the body of a woman no longer the passive sign of political power, an object to be possessed, but rather an autonomous force waiting for a husband to minister to her. We cannot attribute to Machiavelli an anachronistically enlightened view of women in society any more than we can credit him with a democratic spirit; yet it is undeniable that he saw in Caterina Italy's only hope, in the absence of a prince.

28. *Vita di Benvenuto Cellini* (Milan, 1811). The editor is Giovanni Palamede Carpani. His conjecture is repeated by Mary McCarthy in *The Stones of Florence* (New York, 1959). For an exhaustive discussion of the statue, its pedestal, and iconography, see Kathleen Weil-Garris, "On Pedestals: Michelangelo's *David*, Bandinello's *Hercules and Cacus*, and the Sculpture of the Piazza della Signoria," *Römische Jahrbuch für Kunstgeschicte* 20 (1983): 377–415 (esp. 408ff., where the iconographic tradition is surveyed). On the "tumult" in Machiavelli, see *The Discourses*, bk. 1, chap. 4, line 17. I should like to acknowledge the generous help of my friend Nancy Vickers with the iconographic problem.

CHAPTER SEVEN

POLITICS ON THE WARPATH: MACHIAVELLI'S *ART OF WAR*

Barbara Spackman

FROM classical rhetorical manuals to poststructuralist treatises on neorhetoric and semiotics, analogies between military and textual strategies have bound together the arts of rhetoric and war. In *A Rhetoric of Motives*, Kenneth Burke reminds us that Cicero likened his list of rhetorical devices to weapons that may be used to threaten or attack, or "can be brandished purely for show," suggesting that the deliberative, forensic, and epideictic functions of rhetoric find their counterparts— or perhaps even models—in acts of war.[1] Burke himself places war under the rubric of rhetoric (as opposed to "grammar" or "symbolic"), not only because military strategy, like rhetoric, is designed to produce an effect upon an audience but also because, as a "disease of coopera-tion," war is a "perversion" of the rhetorical principle of identifica-tion.[2] More specifically, it is precisely in his essay on Machiavelli and "administrative rhetoric" that Burke notes the semiotic force of the nonverbal acts of both the politician and the warrior in *The Prince*: "military force can persuade by its sheer 'meaning' as well as by its use in actual combat."[3] Burke's notion of rhetoric spills over into the terri-tory claimed by semioticians; if language may be considered symbolic action, nonverbal acts may have rhetorical force. It is not surprising, then, that Umberto Eco, too, takes up the analogy to military strategies in his analysis of textual strategies and their relation to the "model reader" in *Lector in fabula* (The Role of the Reader). Just as textual strategies construct a "model reader," so do military strategies create a

1. Kenneth Burke, *A Rhetoric of Motives* (Berkeley, Calif., 1969), 68.
2. Burke, *A Rhetoric of Motives*, 22.
3. Burke, *A Rhetoric of Motives*, 161.

"model adversary" whose every move might be foreseen.[4] Eco's definition of a "text" suggests that what at first seemed an analogy may in fact be a homology: "a text is a product whose interpretive fate must be part of its own generative mechanism; to generate a text means to activate a strategy made up of previsions of the other's moves."[5] According to this definition, military strategies are every bit as textual as literary ones. Such analogies do not occlude the violence and violation of war—on the contrary, by insisting upon the discursive character of war, they make visible the potential violence of any text; the difference between "texts" would be one not of kind but of the degree of violence imposed. Indeed, whereas the literary text plays upon the polysemy of verbal language and allows the reader various interpretive choices in order to create suspense, *le plaisir du texte*, and so on, the principal aim of military strategy is the creation of a univocal discourse that excludes alternatives in order to elicit that one interpretive choice necessary to win. Military strategy *as* discourse is ideological discourse par excellence, for it aims to cause the adversary to consent to his own defeat, to do willingly what you would have him do, willy-nilly. A literary text may, in Eco's terms, be more or less "open" or "closed"; military discourse, however, must present itself as open and unpredictable and yet be the most closed and predictable discourse possible. To put it in Econian terms, the "inferential walks" of the enemy must end up in the pass where ambush awaits; in Burkean terms, we might say that if verbal rhetoric aims both to persuade and *convincere*, military "rhetoric" aims both to *con-vincere* and to *vincere*.

To analyze a military manual such as Machiavelli's *Art of War* as a fighting cousin of rhetorical manuals, then, cannot be taken as a "textualist" attempt to diminish the violence of war. Indeed, as Machiavelli describes it, warfare has little to do with brute force and much to do with brute semiosis; it aims not so much to destroy the enemy's physical resources as to construct a seemingly invincible discourse of power. War for Machiavelli is an extension of politics, or, to put it in Foucauldian terms, "war" and "politics" are but two ways in which a multiplicity of force relations may be coded, two different strategies (or texts) that may be adopted to integrate those relations.[6] Were we to seek a modern parallel to the strategies Machiavelli recommends, we would find it not in guerrilla warfare, but rather in the symbolic cold wars that concentrate on the accumulation of nuclear arms. The strate-

---

4. See Umberto Eco, *Lector in fabula: La cooperazione interpretativa nei testi narrativi* (Milan, 1979), 54–55.

5. Eco, *Lector in fabula*, 54 (my translation).

6. Michel Foucault, *The History of Sexuality*, trans. Robert Hurley (New York, 1980), 93.

gies that Machiavelli recommends are of greater interest to those who threaten war than to those who "make war" with chemical weapons or terrorist attacks. That this is true of *The Art of War* will come as no surprise to readers of Machiavelli's other works; Foucault has named Machiavelli as among the few to have "conceived the power of *The Prince* in terms of force relationships," and Michael McCanles has argued that *The Prince* is itself a guide to the politics and paradoxes of deterrence.[7] An examination of *The Art of War,* a text long considered behind its own times, now takes on a peculiar relevance; in the age of nuclear war, of war *as* threat, and hence *as* rhetoric, Machiavelli's understanding of the "circular validation of text by force and of force by text"[8] hits the mark.

And yet, as Felix Gilbert has aptly written, "for today's student of Machiavelli, *The Art of War* is not his most exciting work."[9] Much of the text is taken up with detailed technical information regarding the drawing up of the army in, for example, "snail-shaped marching formations" ("formazioni a chiocciola") or formations "with a horned front" ("con la fronte cornuta"), details that occasioned Matteo Bandello's ridicule and seem, to some readers, to be the sign of a delirious and deluded obsession with technical rationalism.[10] The interest of the text for a modern reader, however, lies not in calculations of how many thousands of pikemen or velites are necessary, but rather in the rhetorical nature of the strategies advised, and in the "textual" war that is produced. Our analysis can begin, then, with what must be excluded

7. Foucault, *The History of Sexuality,* 97; Michael McCanles, "Machiavelli and the Paradoxes of Deterrence," *Diacritics* 14 (1984): 12–19. See also, in this "nuclear criticism" issue of *Diacritics,* Jacques Derrida's remarks on the essential rhetoricity of nuclear politics, in "No Apocalypse, Not Now (Full Speed Ahead, Seven Missiles, Seven Missives)," 20–31.

8. Michael McCanles, "Machiavelli and the Paradoxes of Deterrence," 139.

9. Felix Gilbert, "Machiavelli: The Renaissance of the Art of War," in *Makers of Modern Strategy: From Machiavelli to the Nuclear Age,* ed. Peter Paret (Princeton, N.J., 1986), 23. Recent studies of Machiavelli, in fact, devote little more than the obligatory few pages to *The Art of War.* See, for example, J. G. A. Pocock, *The Machiavellian Moment: Florentine Political Thought and the Atlantic Republican Tradition* (Princeton, N.J., 1975), 199–203; Hanna Fenichel Pitkin, *Fortune is a Woman: Gender and Politics in the Thought of Niccolò Machiavelli* (Berkeley, Calif., 1984); and Wayne A. Rebhorn, *Foxes and Lions: Machiavelli's Confidence Men* (Ithaca, N.Y., 1988).

10. Hanna Fenichel Pitkin, for example, writes: "The details seem to go far beyond the functionally efficient, as if by getting the technical details right, one could control the bloody and unpredictable realities of war. It is as if Machiavelli felt: 'if only our generals made the streets in their encampments of precisely the right width and at right angles to each other, we Italians would no longer be pillaged and raped and killed by the invaders from northern Europe'" (Pitkin, *Fortune Is a Woman,* 71–72). Matteo Bandello's ridicule of Machiavelli appears in the dedication to Giovanni de' Medici that prefaces Novella 40 in vol. 2 of Bandello's *Novelle.*

from Machiavelli's art of "textual" war: the seemingly most "modern" element of all, firearms.

It is, of course, a commonplace that Machiavelli erred in underestimating the potential of artillery, and remained a man of his time in failing to understand or foresee the usefulness and importance of firearms.[11] It is true that Machiavelli remained unconvinced of the efficiency of artillery, in spite of the rather dramatic example of 1494, and that he considered it cumbersome and unreliable.[12] Fabrizio Colonna, Machiavelli's mouthpiece in the dialogue, offers a number of reasons for the exclusion of artillery from his ideal battle, but it is the last, "laughable" reason that is of greatest interest:

Yet another reason led me to act without firing my artillery; you may perhaps laugh at it, and yet I do not think that it is to be scorned. There is nothing that occasions greater confusion in an army than having its sight obstructed; this is a circumstance that has been the ruin of many gallant armies whose sight was obstructed either by dust or by the sun. And nothing more than the smoke that artillery makes when fired impedes sight. It would be more prudent, therefore, to let the enemy blind himself than for you to go seeking him, blinded [*però io crederrei che fusse più prudenza lasciare accecarsi il nimico da se stesso, che volere tu, cieco, andarlo a trovare*].[13]

Machiavelli's underestimation is due neither to Ariostean nostalgia nor entirely to distrust of technological developments and their accuracy, but rather to semiotic considerations. For Machiavelli, war is a form of politics in which semiotic activity and communicative needs are of

---

11. See Gilbert, "Machiavelli: The Renaissance of the Art of War," 28–29. For discussions of reactions to gunpowder during the Renaissance, see J. R. Hale, "Gunpowder and the Renaissance: An Essay in the History of Ideas," in J. R. Hale, *Renaissance War Studies* (London, 1983), 289–420; and Ullrich Langer, "Gunpowder as Transgressive Invention in Ronsard," in *Literary Theory/Renaissance Texts*, ed. Patricia Parker and David Quint (Baltimore, 1986), 96–114.

12. On the military significance of the year 1494, see J. R. Hale, "War and Public Opinion in Renaissance Italy," in J. R. Hale, *Renaissance War Studies*, 359–87; and Piero Pieri, *Il Rinascimento e la crisi militare italiana* (Turin, 1952).

13. Niccolò Machiavelli, *The Art of War*, a revised edition of the Ellis Farneworth translation, ed. Neal Wood (New York, 1965), bk. 2, 96. I have in all cases modified the Wood/Farneworth translation in order to make it more literal. References to the Italian text (Niccolò Machiavelli, *Dell'arte della guerra*, in *Arte della guerra e scritti politici minori*, ed. Sergio Bertelli [Milan, 1961]) appear in brackets following the English-text references; e.g., (bk. 2, 96 [413]). This argument against the use of artillery does not appear in *The Discourses*.

great importance. The use of artillery would disturb these processes and contaminate the essential semiotic univocity. The last reason, then, is anything but laughable: the smoke caused by artillery fire would block the visibility necessary for communication and thereby introduce "noise" into the channels of communication, both within one's own army and between one's own army and that of the enemy. Fabrizio points out that the same smoke and confusion might become useful if one wished to impair the enemy's vision, or to block those channels of communication. But the usefulness of artillery is judged not from the point of view of destructive force, but rather from the point of view of messages that can or cannot be transmitted, of the "text" that can or cannot be constructed. To be forced to "andare cieco a trovarlo" would have disastrous results, primarily because discipline, the very back-bone of the army, would come undone. Discipline itself depends upon channels of communication; the general's voice, the colored banners, the roll of drums, the order of the troops according to the arms they carry, and so on, would be obscured by the smoke and literal noise of artillery:

> But let us return to our organization [*ma torniamo all'ordine nostro*], and resuming the subject of drills, I say that to make a good army it is not enough that the soldiers be inured to hardships and fatigue, strong, swift, and expert in the use of their weapons; they must also learn to keep their ranks, to obey words of command and signals and sounds, and to observe good order, whether they halt, advance, retreat, march, or engage the enemy; for without discipline, with every strict diligence observed and practiced, an army will never be good for anything. And without doubt ferocious and disorderly men are much weaker than timid and orderly ones, because order chases timidity from men, and disorder diminishes ferocity. (*The Art of War*, book 2, 61 [374–75])[14]

By introducing noise—both literal and figurative—into the channels of communication, artillery destroys both sight and the "order" upon which the army's effectiveness depends. The strategic moves and various kinds of semiotic behavior that Machiavelli advises are literally invisible, inaudible, unreadable, if the channels of communication are not clear.

14. Wood/Farneworth elides "ma torniamo all'ordine nostro" and translates simply "But let us resume our subject." One of the difficulties in translating *The Art of War* lies precisely in the polyvalence of the term *ordine*, used by Machiavelli to mean "order," "rank," "organization," "formation," and "state."

The importance of sight cannot be underestimated, for it is upon the ability to see that is founded the ability to foresee, to predict and anticipate the enemy's moves (and thereby to construct the military "text"). In this dramatization of the state and its power, the most important strategies are those that create the illusion of force and that aim to conquer through the use of appearance, rather than through the use of brute force. Even in the thick of battle, in the moment in which one might expect recourse to physical force, brute force may be used to transmit a message, and to lie:

> I have observed from the conduct of many great generals among the ancients that when they knew where the enemy placed the main strength of their army, instead of employing the strongest of their own forces, they appointed the weakest of their troops to oppose them in that quarter and appointed the strongest of their troops to oppose the weakest of the enemy; afterward when the battle had begun, they ordered their choicest troops not to press the enemy, but only to sustain the charge; they ordered the weakest to allow themselves to be beaten and to retire gradually into the rear of the army. This generates two great disorders for the enemy: first, the best part of the enemy's army is surrounded, and second, while they consider themselves sure of an immediate victory, only rarely do they not fall out of rank and out of order, whence follows their immediate defeat. (Book 4, 113 [427–28])

The strategy of opposing one's own weak points to the enemy's strong points, and vice versa, aims to cause the enemy to underestimate one's strength and therefore to act upon a strategy based upon false premises, a strategy willed and foreseen by one's own general. The loss of "weak" soldiers counts for little; they are but the extremities of the body politic, not essential organs. In another example, Fabrizio describes a general who, having lost the battle in terms of the number of soldiers killed, had all the dead buried during the night so that in the morning, the "victorious" army believed that it was instead the defeated army, and withdrew. It is not a question of "life and death," but rather of the projection of the appearance of power, the production and interpretation of signs. The primary target of Fabrizio's strategies is not the destruction by whatever means and at whatever cost, of life and property, but rather the disturbance of the other army's strategic predictions. The most effective strategy is therefore one that creates confusion and disorder in the enemy camp, without damaging either the order or the predictions of one's own camp.

To these ends, the study—and extensive quotation—of classical treatises on the art of war provides not only a guide to the most successful strategies but also a guide to military commonplaces, frames of behavior that we might call the military *doxa*.[15] It is precisely this doxa that one should violate in order to take the enemy by surprise or, as Machiavelli writes, to "cause some strange incident to happen whose novelty may cause him to marvel and thus stand indecisive and without acting [*stare dubbio e fermo*]. This is what Hannibal did when he was surrounded by Fabius Maximus; he fastened lighted torches to the horns of many oxen at night so that Fabius, suspended by this novelty [*sospeso da questa novità*], did not think to block his passage in any way" (book 6, 172–73 [484–85]). Machiavelli's strategies are above all paradoxical, that is, in the rhetorical sense, counter to the doxa: the sight of oxen crowned with torches had presumably not yet entered military doxa. The network of expectations and conventions that constitute the military doxa is interrupted, just as conversational conventions might be disrupted by an "offensive" comment that leaves the interlocutor momentarily speechless, "sospeso da questa novità."[16] Machiavelli's strategy aims to exploit that moment of "speechlessness" as the adversary attempts to interpret the offensive move and find an appropriate response. But in order to minimize the space left to *Fortuna* in such a tactic, Machiavelli recommends the reinforcement of old commonplaces and, if necessary, the creation of new ones. By instilling certain expectations as to one's own habits, one creates new doxa that will lull the enemy into complacency: "Domitius Calvinus laid siege to a town and used to march around it every day with a good part of his army. Hence the besieged, imagining he did it only as a drill, began to grow remiss in the guards; when Domitius perceived this, he made an

15. For a semiotic analysis of "frames," see Eco, *Lector in fabula,* in particular, 78–85; on Machiavelli's use of classical sources, see L. Arthur Bird, "Le fonti letterarie di Machiavelli nell'Arte della guerra," *Atti della Reale Accademia dei Lincei* 5 (1896): 187–261.

16. The example is drawn from Frontinus, as are many of Machiavelli's examples. Another Frontinian example illustrates this principle in a more humorous fashion: "When the army of the consul Quintus Minucius had marched down into a defile of Liguria, and the memory of the disaster of the Caudine Forks occurred to the minds of all, Minucius ordered the Numidian auxiliaries, who seemed of small account because of their own wild appearance and the ungainliness of their steeds, to ride up to the mouth of the defile which the enemy held. The enemy were at first on the alert against attack, and threw out patrols. But when the Numidians, in order to inspire still more contempt for themselves, purposely affected to fall from their horses and to engage in ridiculous antics, the barbarians, breaking ranks at the novel sight, gave themselves up completely to the enjoyment of the show" (Frontinus, *The Stratagems,* trans. Charles E. Bennett [Cambridge, Mass., 1950], bk. 1, 16). On the theorization of conversational conventions in semiotics, see H. P. Grice, "Logic and Conversation," in *Syntax and Semantics: Speech Acts* (New York, 1975).

assault on the town and conquered it" (book 7, 194 [505]). Either there are already commonplaces to exploit or one creates them, always in order to violate their rules; it is a sort of sadistic Pavlovianism in which the enemy is trained to respond to certain signals, only to be punished for his aptitude. The often repeated analogy between military strategy and the game of chess begins to come apart at its seams precisely because the conventions of chess never change, whereas in the art of war only those who change the rules can win. War is the continuous creation and violation of the rules of the game.

One does not, however, begin with a tabula rasa, and the sedimentation of frames and interpretive reflexes that constitutes the doxa can be as harmful as it is useful. If it is always possible to take the enemy by surprise on the days sacred to his religion, it is also true that religion, superstitions, and the ideologies of daily life represent ossified interpretive reactions that can hinder the creation of new commonplaces, new frames. Faced with a similar obstacle, one must adopt a different strategy: the forceful reinterpretation of conventional signs. In the context of *The Art of War,* it is often necessary to use this strategy in order to reinforce the morale of one's army:

> The commanders of armies in former times had one difficulty to struggle with from which our generals at present are in a great measure exempt; that was interpreting bad omens so that instead of seeming adverse, they might appear to be favorable and propitious. For if a thunder and lightning storm descended upon the camp, if the sun or moon were eclipsed, if there were an earthquake, or if the general happened to fall while mounting or dismounting his horse, the soldiers interpreted it as an unhappy presage and were so frightened that they gave only faint resistance to any enemy that attacked them. As soon as such an accident occurred, therefore, they endeavored to account for it by natural causes, or to interpret it for their own purpose and advantage. When Julius Caesar landed in Africa, he happened to fall as soon as he set foot on shore; he immediately cried out, "Africa, I take possession of thee." (Book 6, 176 [487])

If it is not possible to conceal an accident or evil omen (always the preferable alternative), one must adjust the interpretive mechanism in order to attribute all that happens to one's own designs, to one's own *virtù* rather than to misfortune. Should an unforeseen incident occur, one must present it as already foreseen, part of a complicated and preestablished program. One must never trip on the stage of power without immediately regaining the appearance of strength. The unforeseen must be reinterpreted as that which has already been foreseen; a "natural" sign cannot exist without the consent or direct intervention of power. One must combat not only the strategic activity of the enemy but also the reservoir of commonplaces and interpretive habits to be found in both camps. Machiavelli offers yet another example:

> If you are aware of any accident happening during the action which you think may alarm your men, it is best either to conceal it, if you can, or to pervert it to the good [*è cosa prudentissima il saperlo dissimulare e pervertirlo in bene*]. This is what Tullus Hostilius and, later, Lucious Sulla did. The latter saw a body of his forces go over to the enemy he was fighting; seeing that the defection had greatly alarmed his own men, he immediately spread a report through his army that it was done by his own order [*per ordine suo*]; this not only agitated the army, but raised their spirits to such an extent that he emerged victorious. (Book 4, 118 [142])

Machiavelli seems here to be aware of a certain violation of "nature" in this move: a justified fear is "perverted" in a more desirable direction; an unforeseen event is "perversely" reinterpreted as one willed and foreseen, "per ordine suo." One can exploit interpretive reflexes only when their beneficial presence is certain; one may, for example, quite confidently exploit the fear of God in an army of believers (and Machiavelli laments the absence of such faith in contemporary armies precisely for this reason). Otherwise, interpretive mechanisms must remain in the hands of power. A general must not only order his troops on the battlefield, he must also order the signifieds in the semantic field.

Machiavelli's reduction of the role of *fortuna* by means of interpretive violence (a move familiar to readers of *The Prince*) has led critics to suggest that his art of war is purely and paralytically theoretical.[17] Giorgio Bárberi Squarotti, for example, argues that Machiavelli's emphasis on foresight renders action impossible; the formation of a perfect model of action, in which all is foreseen, precludes the possibility of action, and hence of history itself.[18] One might argue, in agreement

---

17. For a discussion of the reduction of *fortuna*, see Barbara Spackman, "Machiavelli and Maxims," in *Reading the Archive: On Texts and Institutions*, ed. E. S. Burt and Janie Vanpee, *Yale French Studies* 77 (1990): 137–55.

18. See Giorgio Bárberi Squarotti, "L'arte della guerra o l'azione impossible," in *Machiavelli, o la scelta della letteratura* (Rome, 1987), 231–62; originally published in *Lettere italiane* 20 (1968): 281–306. Bárberi Squarotti grounds his argument on Fabrizio Colonna's "total lack of faith in the possibility of transforming anything" (235), and in particular, on

with Bárberi Squarotti, that any rigorously *theoretical* model of action (that is to say, etymologically, a model that *sees* all) precludes the possibility of action, in which case only a "faulty" theoretical model would allow for the "openness" that Bárberi Squarotti seems to desire. Yet his critique seems to posit the possibility of a theory of war that would instead open itself to the unforeseen, to "the infinite inventiveness of things" ("l'infinita inventività delle cose"), and thereby escape the realm of "pure theoresis" ("pura teoresi"). What such a theory might be is not stated, but what Bárberi Squarotti mistakes for a claim that total foresight is possible is, I would argue, Machiavelli's claim that the *appearance* of total foresight is possible. It is precisely because total foresight is not possible that interpretive violence must be done. The unforeseeable (whether in the guise of *occasione* or of *fortuna*) *is* the enemy of the strategist and tactician, and the Machiavellian art of war is about nothing other than the unforeseeable, and the actions to be taken in order to *reinterpret* that unforeseeable as always foreseen, always predicted. His text aims to create a certain semiotic sensibility, to enrich intertextual competence, and to teach a language of power.

Put into action, this sensibility is concretized in three fundamental rules: (1) never trust appearances, but always project the appearance of being in total control; (2) do not rely upon any habitual "frames" but create them yourself with the goal of violating their parameters and taking the enemy by surprise; and, above all, (3) anticipate and upset the enemy's predictions. In an extreme example, the latter ruse is accomplished by claiming the enemy's predictions and strategies as one's own: "Let me recommend a general rule to you: the greatest remedy that you can use against the enemy's designs, is to do of your own volition what he endeavors to force you to do, for by doing it of your own volition you may proceed with order and to your own advantage and his disadvantage; but if you are compelled to do it, it will be your ruin" (book 4, 121–22 [435]). In what seems a perversely suicidal attempt to maintain discipline and order, one is to make the enemy's designs one's own designs. It is clear that a continual adjustment of strategies and orders so as to predict the enemy's moves implies the impossibility of programming *al tavolino*. The discipline advised by Machiavelli is necessary not only to carry out preestablished orders but

---

his harsh judgment of the nature of "man" at the end of bk. 7 of *The Art of War*. Fabrizio's peroration, however, deals with a particular category of "man" and his lack of faith is a quite specific one: a distrust and condemnation of mercenaries, of "foreign armies" and "men obligated to others and not to me" (bk. 7, 208, 516). A possibility of "transformation" does exist for "raw, honest men who are their own subjects" ("uomini semplici, rozzi e proprii") (210, 518). Pitkin also laments the bloodless, eminently rational and nondialogic nature of Machiavelli's text (69–72).

to change orders *with* order. As Machiavelli puts it: "Change the plan [*muta partito*], when you are aware that the enemy has foreseen it" (book 7, 203 [512]). It is as though the army were an extremely skillful commedia dell'arte in which the actors change roles or even the entire plot according to the reactions of the audience. In the case of the literary text, textual strategies are established once and for all and the reader can cooperate or opt out (that is, can choose to be a model reader, or not). In the case of politics on the warpath, however, strategies must adapt themselves, from moment to moment, to the strategies of the enemy in order that he can become the model enemy—that is to say, defeated. But it is impossible to cooperate with or react to the audience that is the enemy without the greatest possible visibility and audibility, even during the battle itself. One must see what is happening in order to foresee what will happen. To "do of your own volition what he endeavors to force you to do," it is essential to be able to distinguish the adversary's moves and, to react to those moves, it is equally necessary to communicate new tactics and strategies to one's own troops by means of "sounds" or "calls" that are "clear and distinct." Once again Machiavelli's concern is with univocity; indeed, Fabrizio lists the most univocal words to be used in giving orders: not "back" ("a dietro") but "retreat" ("ritiratevi"); not "turn" ("voltatevi") but "left face! right face!" ("a sinistra! a destra!") (book 5, 138 [453]). There can be no room for the detours caused by "inferential walks"; with regard to "a dietro", Machiavelli refers his reader to an episode cited in *The Discourses* (book 3, chapter 14) in which the order "fall back" ("fatevi indietro") (given so that one of the soldiers might have sufficient room in which to break the chain that was the last obstacle to entering the city square) was, as it passed from rank to rank, distorted to "retreat" ("addietro") with the result that the soldiers not only withdrew, but fled.

The barking of orders is not the only verbal activity required of the general; he must be a master not only of military "rhetoric" but of verbal rhetoric as well. Whereas the rhetorical and semiotic manuals with which we began this discussion seemed to call for an identification of the arts of rhetoric and war, Machiavelli's military manual seems to cast rhetoric as little more than a gentle prod:

> It is an easy matter to persuade or dissuade a few people of a thing, for if words are not sufficient, you may use force and authority; but the great difficulty lies in removing from a multitude an opinion that augurs ill and is contrary either to the commonweal or to your own opinion; in that case, you can avail yourself of nothing but words [*non si può usare se non le parole*],

189

which must be heard by everyone, if you would persuade
everyone. For this reason, it was necessary that great generals be
orators. (Book 4, 127–28 [440])

If the nonverbal rhetoric of war is a matter of producing appearances
and of violently imposing the desired interpretation of those appearances, verbal rhetoric in this art of war seems, at first, a perplexingly
mild-mannered operation. Whereas he who speaks to the few may
always have recourse to authority or force, the general must use verbal
rhetoric to "remove" opinions that augur ill and can, it seems, have no
recourse to violence, "non si può usare se non le parole" in dealing
with multitudes—and one's own troops. The general must aim to inspire confidence in his troops, promise rewards, uncover deceit, ignite
and extinguish passions. As Ezio Raimondi has written, the warrior's
rhetoric "cannot lie" but rather "brings forth hidden energy."[19] Yet the
art of using "only words" has, in the recent past, had disastrous results;
later in the text Fabrizio rails against a different group of rhetoricians:

Before our Italian princes had tasted the blows of wars from
beyond the Alps, they thought it sufficient for princes to think up
sharp retorts in their studies, to write beautiful letters, to excel in
drollery and repartee, to know how to spin a fraud, to decorate
themselves with jewels and gold, to eat and sleep in greater
magnificence and luxury than their neighbors, to surround
themselves with lascivious pleasures, to treat their subjects
haughtily and avariciously, to rot in indolence, to give away
military honors and preferments, to scorn those who endeavored
to point out anything that was salutary or praiseworthy, and to
will that their words be the responses of oracles [*responsi di
oraculi*]. They did not foresee (weak as they were) that by such

---

19. Ezio Raimondi ("Machiavelli and the Rhetoric of the Warrior," *MLN* Italian issue
92 [1977]: 1–16) sees in Machiavelli's representation of the rhetoric of the warrior "an
intensely political interpretation of rhetoric [that] involves an extremely positive view of
the role of the audience as an active role, and [that] has a direct, profound relation with
the democratic or, we may say, republican ideology that informs all of the *Discourses*" (9).
Though at this point in his article Raimondi is dealing with the figure of the general in
chap. 33 of bk. 3 of *The Discourses*, rather than with the passage of *The Art of War* that is
here at issue, his interpretation would apply equally well to the initial presentation of the
task of the warrior as rhetorician in *The Art of War*. Yet even in *The Discourses* it is not only
or primarily the general's verbal rhetoric that inspires confidence: "Le cose che lo fanno
confidente sono: che sia armato ed ordinato bene, conoschinsi l'uno l'altro." (To give an
army such confidence they must be well armed and disciplined, and the men must know
each other.) Niccolò Machiavelli, *Il Principe e Discorsi*, ed. Sergio Bertelli [Milan, 1960],
475).

conduct they were preparing themselves to be the prey of whoever might attack them. All this resulted in the great terror, the rapid flights, and the astonishing losses [*i grandi spaventi, le súbite fughe e le miracolose perdite*] of 1494; hence it happened that three of the most powerful states in Italy were ravaged and laid waste more than once. (Book 7, 210–11 [518])

Rotting in the jeweled splendor of epideictic rhetoric, these princes paved the way for the French invasion of Italy. In *The Prince,* Machiavelli had blamed mercenaries for the conditions that allowed the French to "take Italy with chalk" ("pigliare la Italia col gesso"); here instead it is rhetoric, and the humanist culture in which the Italian princes were schooled, that are presented as the source of "le súbite fughe e le miracolose perdite."[20] The general's rhetoric, then, must be of a different kind, yet the examples that Machiavelli offers only serve to strengthen the resemblance between princely sitting ducks and the warrior:

Ancient generals also had several other religious ceremonies that had a very good effect on all their enterprises, and would have still in any place where religion is held in due reverence. Sertorious knew this well; he used to have consultations with a hind that he said was sent by the gods to assure him of victory. Sulla pretended to converse with an image he had taken out of the temple of Apollo, and several generals have given out that God appeared to them in dreams and commanded them to fight the enemy. In the days of our ancestors, when Charles VII of France was at war with the English, he pretended to be advised in everything by a virgin sent from heaven, commonly called the Virgin of France. (Book 4, 128–29 [441])

The resemblance is disturbing for, like the princes, these generals would have their words be "responsi di oraculi." The examples contradict the opening claim that authority cannot be used by the general, for here religion, in the guise of a talking deer or Joan of Arc, is invoked as *auctoritas.* The text cannot *tell* the difference between the two rhetoricians. Indeed, what distinguishes the general's rhetoric from that of the princes is precisely what Machiavelli says must be excluded from it, for the confidence the general must inspire comes not merely from words, but also from the "rhetorization" of military force. At the end of book 4,

20. For a discussion of Machiavelli as "continuator and critic" of humanism, see Raimondi, "Machiavelli and the Rhetoric."

Machiavelli writes: "Arms cause confidence" ("la confidenza la causa l'armi") (book 4, 129 [442]).[21] Whose arms are these that cause confidence? The crucial difference between the rhetoric of the princes and that of the warrior appears to be that behind the general's verbal rhetoric stands military "rhetoric," the threat of death: "The necessities may be many, but the strongest is that which forces you to win or die" ("che ti costringe o vincere o morire") (book 4, 129 [442]). The "necessities" at stake are the rhetorical strategies available to the general; arms rather than rhetoric cause confidence, but arms are effective precisely as threat, that is, as rhetoric. The arms that cause confidence are presumably one's own, but the arms that enforce the threat "do or die" are presumably those of the enemy camp, wielded now as rhetoric against one's own troops. What Machiavelli's text seems to want to occlude is that verbal rhetoric used in the art of war turns even one's own troops into an enemy to be threatened. In the opening statement, that the general can use only words and can have no recourse to force, Machiavelli's *own* rhetoric acts as a cover-up of the violence that, inevitably, resurfaces at the end of the passage. Indeed, in book 2 we find what may be a gloss on the relation between impotent princes and Machiavelli's general: "Nor did the ancients consider anything more beneficial in a republic than to have many men well trained in arms, because it is not the splendor of jewels and gold that causes the enemy to submit to you, but only the fear of arms" (book 2, 58 [372]). The principle can be applied equally well to the enemy and to one's own troops. It is now clear why Machiavelli can, in *The Prince*, blame the French invasion on the use of mercenaries and, in *The Art of War*, lay the blame on rhetoric: rhetoric and force are interdependent. The impotence of the princes' rhetoric (backed only by jewels and gold) is due to their lack of arms of their own, the lack of a force that would validate their rhetoric; and that impotence is made visible by the arms of the enemy troops, by a force that arrives unexpectedly, and hence unrhetorically—not as part of the "text" produced by one's own strategies. There is—at least in war—no

21. The immediate context in which the phrase *la confidenza la causa l'armi* appears encourages one to read it as a syllepsis, in which a singular verb is governed by a plural subject. In that context, a series of causal relations is presented: "La quale ostinazione è accresciuta dalla confidenza e dall'amore del capitano o della patria. La confidenza la causa l'armi; l'ordine, le vittorie fresche e l'opinione del capitano. L'amore della patria è causata dalla natura; quello del capitano, dalla virtù più che da niuno altro beneficio" (442). The Ellis Farneworth translation elides the syllepsis: "This resolution is commonly heightened either by the confidence they put in themselves, their arms, armor, discipline, good order, and lately-won victories, or by the esteem they have for their general. Such esteem is a result of the opinion they have of his *virtù*, rather than of any particular favor they have received from him; or it is a result of the love of their country, which is natural to all men" (129).

room for violence that cannot be rhetoricized (and hence no room for firearms), or for rhetoric that is not validated by force. Today this formulation should be alarmingly familiar; it is what Michael McCanles has called the first paradox of nuclear deterrence: "we have discourse that has meaning only insofar as it refers to arms, while arms in turn have meaning only insofar as they are articulated in discourse."[22] If, as McCanles argues, this was one of Machiavelli's fundamental insights, it is, now, our own global military and rhetorical predicament.

22. McCanles, "Machiavelli and the Paradoxes of Deterrence," 14.

CHAPTER EIGHT

VIRTÙ AND THE EXAMPLE OF AGATHOCLES IN MACHIAVELLI'S *PRINCE*

Victoria Kahn

> Only at a remove from life can the mental life exist, and truly engage the empirical. While thought relates to facts and moves by criticizing them, its movement depends no less on the maintenance of distance. It expresses exactly what is, precisely because what is is never quite as thought expresses it. Essential to it is an element of exaggeration, of over-shooting the object, of self-detachment from the weight of the factual, so that instead of merely reproducing being it can, at once rigorous and free, determine it.
> —*Theodor Adorno*

> What gods will be able to save us from all these ironies?
> —*Friedrich Schlegel*

MACHIAVELLI'S innovation in the history of political thought, it is often argued, lies in his revision not only of Scholastic but also of humanist notions of imitation and representation, a revision that is reflected in his own representation of the realm of politics. When humanism and Scholasticism alike are seen as proposing an idealist or an a priori notion of truth, this case is easily made. As many critics of *The Prince* have remarked, Machiavelli scandalizes his readers not because he advises the prince to act in ways previously unheard of, but because he refuses to cloak his advice in the pieties of Scholastic or Christian humanist idealism. Instead, he insists that the prince acts in a world in

I am grateful to Charles Trinkaus for his helpful criticism of an earlier draft of this essay. The epigraphs are from Theodor Adorno, *Minima moralia*, trans. E. F. N. Jephcott (London, 1978), 126–27; and from Friedrich Schlegel, "Uber die Unverständlichkeit," *Kritische Schriften* (Munich, 1964), 538 (my translation).

which there are "no prefigured meanings, no implicit teleology,"[1] in which order and legibility are the products of human action rather than the a priori objects of human cognition. To recognize this, he argues, is to acknowledge the reality or truth of power, over against an idealist notion of truth conceived in terms of representation, as correspondence to some a priori standard of judgment or, more specifically, to some a priori moral ideal. Machiavelli accordingly declares his divergence from the idealist tradition of reflection on political affairs in the famous opening to chapter 15:

> Since I intend to write something useful [*utile*] to an understanding reader, it seemed better to go after the real truth [*la verità effettuale*] of the matter than to repeat what people have imagined. A great many men have imagined states and princedoms such as nobody ever saw or knew in the real world, for there's such a difference between the way we really live and the way we ought to live that the man who neglects the real to study the ideal will learn how to accomplish his ruin, not his preservation.[2]

It is important to see, however, that although Machiavelli criticizes the Stoic and idealist moral philosophy of some humanists, he borrows from the more flexible pragmatism of others, according to whom truth is governed by an intrinsically ethical standard of decorum and consensus. Only when we recognize Machiavelli's imitation of and final divergence from this humanist tradition of pragmatism (and it is in this sense that the term *humanist* will most often be used in the following pages), will we be able to chart his innovation in political thought with any precision. I will argue that Machiavelli moves beyond the constraints of previous humanist reflection on the pragmatic nature of truth—which from his perspective offers yet another version of a mimetic, correspondence, or idealist theory—to a conception of truth as power, in which the pragmatic humanist version of truth itself becomes one weapon among others in the prince's strategic arsenal.

Imitation and Representation

From the very beginning of *The Prince* it is clear that Machiavelli is drawing on the resources of humanism, in particular its notion of

---

1. Sheldon Wolin, *Politics and Vision* (Boston, 1960), 224.
2. Niccolò Machiavelli, *The Prince*, trans. and ed. Robert M. Adams (New York, 1977), 44. Throughout, I have substituted *virtù* for the various English translations Adams

imitation.[3] Like the humanists, he wants to educate his reader's practical judgment, the faculty of deliberation that allows for effective action within the contingent realm of fortune, and like them he recognizes that such education must therefore focus on particular examples rather than on the general precepts appropriate to theoretical reason. Furthermore, Machiavelli is concerned, as the humanists were, with criticizing an unreflective relation to past examples that would take the form of slavish imitation, simple re-presentation, or a one-to-one correspondence. In fact, it is precisely in the absence of correspondence, of a mirror reflection of the exemplar, that the humanist prince or poet finds both the room to exercise his own will and the measure of his own achievement. Correct imitation accordingly involves imitating and realizing a flexible principle of prudential judgment or decorum. And this in turn gives rise to texts designed to dramatize and inculcate such judgment, whose rhetoric is, therefore, not ornamental but strategic.

Thus, in the prefatory letter to *The Prince*, Machiavelli justifies his gift of a text to Lorenzo de' Medici by suggesting that the latter will be a more effective ruler if he learns to imitate the double perspective, the reflective distance, offered in *The Prince*: "To know the people well one must be a prince, and to know princes well one must be, oneself, of the people" (3 [14]). And in chapter 14, "Military Duties of the Prince," Machiavelli makes the humanist claim for textual imitation even more forcefully by comparing skill in government to skill in reading, by making the ruler's landscape into a text and the text into a realm of

---

provides. References to the Italian text are taken from Machiavelli, *Il Principe e Discorsi*, ed. Sergio Bertelli (Milan, 1960), and are given in the text in brackets following English-text references; e.g., (44 [65]).

3. Recent interpretations of *The Prince* in the context of the humanist notion of imitation include Mark Hulliung, *Citizen Machiavelli* (Princeton, N.J., 1983), esp. 130–67; Hanna Fenichel Pitkin, *Fortune Is a Woman: Gender and Politics in the Thought of Niccolò Machiavelli* (Berkeley, Calif., 1983), 268ff.; and Thomas M. Greene, "The End of Discourse in Machiavelli's *Prince*," in *Literary Theory/Renaissance Texts*, ed. Patricia Parker and David Quint (Baltimore, 1986), 63–77. Gennaro Sasso also discusses Machiavelli's notion of imitation in *Niccolò Machiavelli: Storia del suo pensiero politico* (Naples, 1958), 381–89. For earlier treatments of Machiavelli in the context of humanism, see Felix Gilbert, *Machiavelli and Guicciardini: Politics and History in Sixteenth-Century Florence* (Princeton, N.J., 1965); and his "The Humanist Concept of the Prince and the *Prince* of Machiavelli," *The Journal of Modern History* 11 (1939): 449–83; as well as Allan H. Gilbert, *Machiavelli's Prince and Its Forerunners: The Prince as a Typical Book De Regimine Principum* (Durham, N.C., 1938). In considering Machiavelli's rhetoric, I have also benefited from Eugene Garver, "Machiavelli's *The Prince*: A Neglected Rhetorical Classic," *Philosophy and Rhetoric* 13 (1980): 99–120; from his *Machiavelli and the History of Prudence* (Madison, Wis., 1987); and from Nancy Struever's chapter on Machiavelli in her *Theory as Practice: Ethical Inquiry in the Renaissance* (Chicago, 1992).

forces. The prince is advised to learn to read the terrain ("imparare la natura de' siti") and to "read history and reflect on the actions of great men." Here, to imitate great men means to imitate imitation, that is, to "take as a model of [one's] conduct some great historical figure who achieved the highest praise and glory by constantly holding before himself the deeds and achievements of a predecessor" (43 [64]).

Machiavelli's defining truth pragmatically (*la verità effettuale*), rather than ontologically or epistemologically as correspondence to a fixed or absolute origin, would also seem to be consonant with humanism. And yet, if Machiavelli's notion of imitation appears to be essentially humanist, his own pragmatic definition of truth is not; for Machiavelli preserves the humanists' strategic sense of rhetoric only to separate it from its presumed origin in (the author's) and goal of (the reader's) intrinsically ethical practices of imitation. In rejecting the Ciceronian and humanist equation between *honestas* and *utilitas*, the faith that practical reason or prudence is inseparable from moral virtue, Machiavalli thus turns prudence into what the humanists (and their detractors) always feared it would become—the amoral skill of *versutia* or mere cleverness, which in turn implies the ethically unrestrained use of force—in short, *virtù*. He thus opens up a gap between the political agent and the political actor—or rather he makes the agent an actor who is capable of (mis)representation: the prince must appear to be good, virtuous, and so on in order to satisfy his people and thus to maintain his power (chapter 15).[4]

This redefinition of representation as ruse and thus of mimesis as power is the aim of *The Prince* as a whole,[5] but it finds a particularly forceful articulation in chapter 18. Machiavelli begins this chapter by distinguishing between human law and bestial force, but he then abandons the first pole of his binary opposition and proceeds to locate the range of political invention within the single second term of bestiality. Imitation may be a specifically human quality requiring the exercise of judgment, but the objects of imitation are bestial craft and force. Furthermore, the imitation of (bestial) nature has as its goal not correspondence to some fixed, determinate reality but the appearance of (what is conventionally accepted as) truth.

---

4. Machiavelli's separation of the political agent from the political actor anticipates Hobbes in chap. 16 of *Leviathan*. On the distinction between cleverness or versutia and prudence, see Aristotle, *Nicomachean Ethics*, trans. Martin Ostwald (New York, 1962), 1144a.25–1144b (hereafter cited as *NE*).

5. See the discussion by Pierre Manent, *Naissances de la politique moderne: Machiavel, Hobbes, Rousseau* (Paris, 1977), 19: "If ruse is, in Machiavelli's eyes, the principal resource of political action, that is because ruse responds to the essence of the political situation" (my translation).

Here illusion is being turned against itself in order to present a truth to the people that will at the same time be effective for the prince. If, in the age-old debate between rhetoric and philosophy, the humanists want a rhetoric that is grounded in the truth and also effective, Machiavelli takes the further radical step not of subordinating or compromising truth in the interests of power, as he has sometimes been charged with doing, but of mutually implicating representation and force. Representation no longer involves even the correspondence to a practical standard of truth but has instead become theatrical. Correct or successful imitation no longer demands the exercise of self-knowledge and moral discretion but has itself become a rhetorical topic of invention to be manipulated in the interests of power.[6] Conversely, power becomes in part, if not entirely, an effect of the representational illusion of truth.

Machiavelli thus borrows—or imitates—the humanists' rhetorical strategies in order to educate his reader to an antihumanist conception of imitation and practice. My aim in the following pages is to clarify Machiavelli's similarity with and divergence from the humanists by taking a close look at what we might call, for heuristic purposes, the repertoire of figures in Machiavelli's strategic rhetoric. These heuristic figures should also help us to discover how Machiavelli's revision of the humanist notion of practical reason is at one and the same time the condition of *virtù* and the potential obstacle to its realization. As we will see, although Machiavelli's realistic analysis of the realm of politics avoids the ethical domestication of *virtù*, it threatens to allegorize, reify, or demonize *virtù*, thus finally undermining the flexible political skill that the strategic rhetoric of *The Prince* was designed to encourage.

Irony and Hyperbole

For hyperbole is a virtue [*virtus*], when the magnitude of the facts passes all words, and in such circumstances our language will be more effective if it goes beyond the truth than if it falls short of it.
—*Quintilian*

Machiavelli's criticism of the humanist version of pragmatism follows from his recognition of the intrinsic irony of politics, or of action within the contingent realm of human affairs: "If you look at matters carefully, you will see that something resembling virtue, if you follow it, may be your ruin, while something resembling vice will lead, if you

6. Thomas M. Greene, *The Light in Troy: Imitation and Discovery in Renaissance Poetry* (New Haven, Conn., 1982), 142, 172, 184.

follow it, to your security and well-being" (45 [66]).[7] But this formulation also allows us to see that Machiavelli wants to control this irony, or
rather that he conceives of the man of *virtù* as someone who can *use* the
ironies of political action to achieve political stability. (The refusal to *act*
in the face of such ironies Machiavelli called literature; see *Florentine
Histories*, book 5, chapter 1.)[8] This recognition of the irony of politics
leads in turn to a revision of humanist argument in *utramque partem* (on
both sides of a question). The humanists, following Aristotle, believed
that it is necessary to be able to argue on both sides of a question, not so
that one might actually defend a false position but so that one can
anticipate and thereby more effectively rebut an opponent's arguments.[9] Machiavelli, however, argues that the prince will actually have
to oppose what may appear to be good at a given moment. In fact, in
Machiavelli's view, it is the humanists who are guilty of trying to
accommodate at a single moment contrary qualities or arguments (e.g.,
in chapters 16 and 17) when they claim that the good and the useful are
always compatible. Knowledge *in utramque partem* is necessary according to Machiavelli because "the conditions of human life simply do not
allow" one "to have and exercise" only morally good qualities (45 [65];
cf. chapter 18, 50 [73]).

It is precisely this intrinsic irony of politics—the gap or lack of a
mimetic relation between intention and result—that both allows for
and requires solutions that seem extreme from the perspective of the
humanist ideal of *mediocritas* (the "middle way").[10] Hence the place of
hyperbole and exaggeration in Machiavelli's rhetoric. On the one hand,
the examples of great men will always seem hyperbolic or excessive
to—beyond the reach of—the imitator. On the other hand, Machiavelli
argues, this hyperbole has a rhetorical and pedagogical function.

> Men almost always prefer to walk in paths marked out by others
> and pattern their actions through imitation. Even if he cannot
> follow other people's paths in every respect, or attain to the *virtù*
> of his originals, a prudent man should always follow the footsteps
> of the great and imitate those who have been supreme. His own
> *virtù* may not come up to theirs, but at least it will have a sniff of
> it. Thus he will resemble skilled archers who, seeing how far away

7. Wolin discusses Machiavelli's view of the intrinsic irony of politics in *Politics and
Vision*, 227.

8. Cited by Hulliung, *Citizen Machiavelli*, 137.

9. Aristotle *Rhetoric* 1355a.20–1355b.5.

10. As Hulliung (*Citizen Machiavelli*, 158–59) and Sydney Anglo (*Machiavelli* [New
York, 1969], 244–49) have remarked, Machiavelli's rejection of mediocritas is also reflected in his antithetical, either/or style of arguing.

the target lies, and knowing the *virtù* of their bow, aim much higher than the real target, not because they expect the arrow to fly that far, but to accomplish their real end by aiming beyond it. (16 [30])

In this view, hyperbolic examples do not correspond to things as they are but to what they might be; they are figures of action rather than perception, of desire rather than cognition or representation. Hyperbole as a mode of speech or behavior is thus the proper response to the irony of politics: it is predicated on a recognition of one's distance both from the situation as it stands and from the situation one would like to create, but it also involves the recognition that such distance—as in the epigraph from Adorno—is itself a precondition of considered action. Finally, hyperbolic action is often ironic according to the classical definition of irony (Quintilian *Institutio oratoria* 8.6.54; 9.2.44–47) because it involves saying or doing one thing in order to arrive at its opposite. In short, the world of Machiavellian politics is intrinsically ironic, and the most effective mode of behavior in such a world is theatrical and hyperbolic. An analysis of the example of Agathocles in chapter 8 will serve to illustrate this point. At the same time, it should also help us to see how Machiavelli's strategic practice as a writer imitates that of his ideal prince.

Strategic Style: The Example of Agathocles

In a world where a flexible faculty of judgment is constitutive of *virtù*, it is not surprising that Machiavelli should offer us no substantive definition of his terms. This is not simply a failing of analytical skill, as Sydney Anglo has complained,[11] but a sophisticated rhetorical strategy, the aim of which is to destabilize or dehypostatize our conception of political virtue, for only a destabilized *virtù* can be effective in the destabilized world of political reality.[12] In this context, the most effective critique of an idealist or mimetic notion of truth and of representation will be one that stages or dramatizes this lack of conceptual stability, rather than simply stating it as a fact. This rhetorical indirection would not in itself differentiate Machiavelli from the humanists. What is important to see, however, is that Machiavelli uses humanist rhetoric theatrically for antihumanist purposes. Chapter 8 on Agathocles the Sicilian is an exemplary instance of how the Machiavellian

---

11. Anglo, *Machiavelli,* 209.

12. Nancy Struever has an interesting discussion of the dereification of *virtù* in *Theory as Practice,* 157.

critique of representation implicates the humanists' ethical pragmatism as well.

In chapter 8, Machiavelli presents Agathocles as an example of someone who rises to power not by *virtù* or fortune but by crime. Readers of *The Prince* have tended to interpret this example in one of two ways. In this narrative, some argue, Machiavelli registers his own discomfort with the notion of *virtù* that he has been elaborating: it does violence to his sense of morality as well as to that of the reader. J. H. Whitfield speaks of Machiavelli's condemnation of Agathocles, and Claude Lefort remarks on the "réserve troublante" that qualifies Machiavelli's admiration of this figure.[13] Others see the story as an illustration of a cruel but effective use of violence. The interpreters who fall into this camp then differ as to whether this use of violence is immoral or amoral.[14] But in neither case is Machiavelli's own interpretation of Agathocles as one who rose to power by means of crime subject to scrutiny.[15] Thus, although the proponents of the first interpretation make note of Machiavelli's qualifications of Agathocles' actions ("Non si può ancora chiamare virtù ammazzare li sua cittadini"; 42), they read this qualification as a simple pun ("It certainly cannot be called 'virtue' to murder his fellow citizens"; 26) and so save Machiavelli from the charge of failing to make moral distinctions. The second group of interpreters, in accepting the story of Agathocles as an illustration of the uses of crime rather than of *virtù*, make an analogous moral distinction between the excessive cruelty of Agathocles and the politic restraint of the man of *virtù*. In both cases one would argue that this making of distinctions was precisely Machiavelli's intention. Following from the story of Cesare Borgia in chapter 7, the next chapter would serve, in these readings, to correct the reader who had begun to think *virtù* identical with crime. In chapter 8 Machiavelli would then reassure

13. J. H. Whitfield, *Machiavelli* (Oxford, 1947), 80 and 108; Claude Lefort, *Le travail de l'oeuvre Machiavel* (Paris, 1972), 376. See later in this essay for further discussion of Lefort's position. Another representative of Whitfield's position is Jerrold Seigel, *"Virtù* in and since the Renaissance," in *Dictionary of the History of Ideas* (New York, 1968), 4:476–86.

14. For the first position, see Gennaro Sasso, *Niccolò Machiavelli*, 296ff.; Gabriele Pepe, *La politica dei Borgia* (Naples, 1945), 281–82; and Ugo Dotti, *Niccolò Machiavelli: La fenomenologia del potere* (Milan, 1979), 179ff.; for the second, see J. G. A. Pocock, *The Machiavellian Moment: Florentine Political Thought and The Atlantic Republican Tradition* (Princeton, N.J., 1975), 152 and 167.

15. Greene, in "The End of Discourse," notes the tenuousness of the distinction between Borgia and Agathocles (70), but sees this as evidence of a breakdown in the concept of *virtù* rather than a deliberate strategy on the part of Machiavelli. Manent, *Naissances* (16), however, sees the distinction as deliberately false.

the reader by acknowledging that there is a difference between the two.

In fact, however, there is hardly a less reassuring experience of reading in *The Prince* than that of chapter 8. And it is a chapter whose disturbing quality increases as we read further in the work: in chapter 6 Machiavelli describes the relation of *virtù* and *fortuna* as a dialectical one, but he goes further in chapter 25 when he claims that *fortuna* and *virtù* divide the world of events between them. How then, we wonder, could crime be a third term in Machiavelli's analysis of the way princes rise to power?

In spite of the title and the first paragraph of chapter 8, Machiavelli's introductory remarks about Agathocles seem to confirm the polar opposition of chapter 25. He tells us that Agathocles "joined to his villainies such *virtù* of mind and body that after enlisting in the army he rose through the ranks to become military governor of Syracuse" (25 [41]). And a little further on he reiterates that Agathocles' success was due to *virtù*: "Considering the deeds and *virtù* of this man, one finds little or nothing that can be attributed to fortune" (26 [41]). But, then, anticipating his reader's objections, he quickly adds:

> Yet it certainly cannot be called *virtù* to murder his fellow citizens, betray his friends, to be devoid of truth, pity, or religion; a man may get power by means like these, but not glory. If we consider simply the *virtù* of Agathocles in facing and escaping from dangers, and the greatness of his soul in sustaining and overcoming adversity, it is hard to see why he should be considered inferior to the greatest of captains. Nonetheless, his fearful cruelty and inhumanity, along with his innumerable crimes, prevent us from placing him among the really excellent men. For we can scarcely attribute to either fortune or *virtù* a conquest which he owed to neither. (26 [42])

How are we to make sense of the vertiginous distinctions in this paragraph? Russell Price has suggested that Machiavelli is differentiating in this passage between the military *virtù* and glory ["gloria"] that apply to captains and the political *virtù* and glory that apply to "the really excellent men."[16] Of the former he writes: "It seems that [Agathocles] . . . deserves credit for his martial spirit and deeds (that is, as a *capitano*) after he became ruler; what blackens his reputation is how he became ruler, because he treacherously slaughtered his friends

16. Russell Price, "The Theme of *Gloria* in Machiavelli," *Renaissance Quarterly* 30 (1977): 588–631.

and fellow citizens. Trickery and violence are to be condemned in a ruler or an aspiring ruler. . . . The stain he incurred by the way he seized power is indelible like original sin (611)." Apart from the dubious appropriateness of an analogy with original sin for a writer of such rabid anti-Christian sentiment, this analysis fails to take account of the fact that Borgia also used trickery and violence to secure his power but is nevertheless not being offered as an example of one who rose to power by crime. Furthermore, although Borgia is not condemned by Machiavelli, neither is he called one of the really excellent men, a phrase that, as J. G. A. Pocock reminds us, refers to legislators rather than new princes.[17]

A more sophisticated version of Price's analysis is presented by Claude Lefort, who argues that the introduction of the theme of *gloria* in chapter 8 signals a turning point in the argument of *The Prince*. Whereas the earlier chapters were concerned with the necessary exercise of violence in the acquisition of power, the example of Agathocles introduces the necessity of *representing* oneself to the people in a certain way in order to hold on to the power one has acquired. Machiavelli had previously emphasized the self-sufficiency of the prince; he now places the action of the prince in a social context in which it acquires its real significance (380–81). In this way, *virtù* itself is neither identical with nor exclusive of crime, but it does require glory, and it is this concern for glory that will induce the prince to moderate his violent behavior and take greater interest in the welfare of his people. According to this reading, in the sentence that begins "Yet it certainly cannot be called *virtù* to murder his fellow citizens," it is *called* that should be stressed: *virtù* is not equal to crime, though even a "virtuous" man (Borgia, for example) may find it necessary on occasion to act criminally. Yet if Lefort is not as reassuring as those readers who claim that Machiavelli is asserting a clear-cut distinction between military and political (moral) *virtù*, he nevertheless claims that there is a distinction between Borgia and Agathocles, one that does not lie in the nature of their deeds, since both were guilty of criminal behavior, but rather in the fact that the deeds of the latter "were committed without justification, or without a pretext [*sans masque*], by a man whom nothing, except his ambition, destined to reign . . . a man—Machiavelli took the trouble to make clear—*di infima e abjetta fortuna*, the simple son of a potter" (380; my translation).

It is not so much the crimes of Agathocles that constitute his original sin, according to Lefort, as his lowly birth. But this interpretation trivializes both the notion of representation and that of fortune in *The*

---

17. Pocock, *The Machiavellian Moment*, 168.

Prince, neither of which, as Lefort elsewhere recognizes, is a static   X
concept involving a one-to-one correspondence, according to which
the bad fortune of lowly birth would forever restrict Agathocles' possibilities for representing himself in a favorable light. In fact, by the end
of the chapter Agathocles is offered as an example of someone who
used cruelty well rather than badly, and who was consequently "able
to reassure people, and win them over to his side with benefits" (28
[44]). It would seem, then, that far from excluding Agathocles from the
category of "representative men," Machiavelli goes out of his way to
stress his inclusion.

As we have seen, most readings of chapter 8 respond to the pressure
to make distinctions that is implicit in the apparently contradictory
reiteration of *virtù.* But it is important to see that clear-cut or permanent
distinctions are finally what cannot be made. Throughout *The Prince*
Machiavelli sets concepts in polar opposition to each other and then
shows how the opposition is contained within each term so that the
whole notion of opposition must be redefined.[18] Thus he begins chapter 25 by telling the reader that "fortune governs one half of our actions, but that even so she leaves the other half more or less in our
power to control." Fortune is then presented as a natural force, a torrential stream against which men can take countermeasures "while the
weather is still fine." But this opposition is a generalization that under-
goes startling revision when we come to "the particulars." For a man's
ability to take countermeasures—his *virtù*—turns out to be a fact of
(his) nature and thus a potential natural disaster over which he has no
control:

> If a prince conducts himself with patience and caution, and the
> times and circumstances are favorable to those qualities, he will
> flourish; but if times and circumstances change, he will come to
> ruin unless he changes his method of proceeding. No man,
> however prudent, can adjust to such radical changes, not only
> because we cannot go against the inclination of nature, but also
> because when one has always prospered by following a particular
> course, he cannot be persuaded to leave it. (71 [100])

In this more particular view, human nature is itself a torrential stream
that cannot redirect its course with dikes and restraining dams; the
favorable constraints are instead introduced by fortune. The purely
formal *virtù* that is the ability to "adjust one's behavior to the temper of

18. See *The Prince,* chap. 12, on the pseudodistinction between laws and arms, as well
as chap. 19 on arms and friends.

the times"—and that is precisely *not* constancy of character—is not a quality that can be attributed once and for all; it is rather a generalization that designates only the fortunate coincidence of "nature's livery and fortune's star." Or, as Machiavelli writes of men of *virtù* in chapter 6: "Without the opportunity their *virtù* of mind would have been in vain, and without that *virtù* the opportunity would have been lost" (17 [31]).

If we now return to chapter 8, we can begin to see why Machiavelli cannot call Agathocles' crimes virtuous. In the light of chapter 25, it seems that we should place an even stronger emphasis on *called:* in the case of neither Borgia nor Agathocles can crime be called *virtù*, because *virtù* cannot be *called* any one thing. In short, once the temporal dimension of circumstance is introduced, the fact that crime cannot necessarily be called *virtù* means also that it can be called *virtù*. The danger of chapter 7 is not only that we might identify Borgia's murder and treachery with *virtù* but also that we would identify *virtù* with any particular act—criminal or not. The aim of the passage, in short, is to dehypostatize *virtù*, to empty it of any specific meaning. For *virtù* is not a general rule of behavior that can be applied to a specific situation but is rather, like prudence, a faculty of deliberation about particulars.

On one level, then, the conclusion of the paragraph concerning Agathocles' *virtù* ("for we can scarcely attribute to either fortune or *virtù* a conquest which he owed to neither") seems to reinforce the distinctions between *virtù*, fortune, and crime with which the chapter began—perhaps as an ironic concession to the reader's moral sensibility. On another level, it simply points up the incommensurability between the generalizations of *fortuna* and *virtù* and the specific instances that cannot be usefully subordinated to any (conceptual) generalization. How else is it possible to explain the end of chapter 8, where Machiavelli makes a distinction between two sorts of cruelty—cruelty used well and used badly—thereby placing the distinction between *fortuna* and *virtù* within cruelty itself: "Cruelty can be described as well used (if it's permissible to speak well about something that is evil in itself) when it is performed all at once, for reasons of self-preservation" (27–28 [44]). Once again the emphasis is on *chiamare* ("Bene usate si possono chiamare quelle [se del male è licito dire bene]"), but here the temporal dimension is explicit, as is the consequent and necessary making of distinctions within "cruelty." And once again, in the parenthetical remark, Machiavelli speaks to the reader's moral sensibility—but he has answered the implied question even before it has been posed. Cruelty *can* be called "well used" because Machiavelli has just done so in the preceding clause. The adverbial *bene* then takes on some of the paronomastic color of the earlier paragraph on *virtù*. The reader wonders if it is permissible to speak *good (bene)* words about evil, whereas Machiavelli replies by speaking *well (bene)*.[19]

These lines are important because they contain in little Machiavelli's critique of humanism. The humanist's assumption that *honestas* is compatible with *utilitas*, reflected in the maxim that the good orator is necessarily a good man, is politically useless to Machiavelli, however it is interpreted. When the goodness of the orator is interpreted to mean in conformity with ethical goodness (*honestas;* see Cicero *De officiis* 3.3.11, 3.11.49), then the maxim is a stoic tautology and the question of the orator's effectiveness (*utilitas*) need not enter in. When the orator's goodness is interpreted to mean persuasiveness as well as moral rectitude, then the claim that the orator is a good man is a synthetic judgment that is also idealistic and unfounded. One has only to look to experience to recall that many morally good men have been politically ineffective. Here the criterion of correct action is not moral goodness or the intrinsically moral judgment of prudence but the functional excellence or effectiveness of *virtù:* a *virtù* we might say, parodying Aristotle, that demonstrates its own excellence by being effective.[20] In speaking well rather than speaking good words, Machiavelli both dramatizes and thematizes this functional virtuosity. He shows that *virtù* is not a substance but a mode of action (not a noun, but an adverb) by speaking well about acting well.

The linguistic play of this paragraph and the earlier one on *virtù* are thus part of a rhetorical strategy to engage the reader in a critical activity that will allow him to discover not the content of "what should be" but the formality of what in any particular situation "can be."[21] Here, if the reader's "natural" disposition to make moral distinctions ("everyone agrees") may be compared to the natural force of the river in chapter 25, which serves as a metaphor for Fortune, Machiavelli's prose is the countermeasure that attempts to channel or redirect this course by introducing the element of reflection. In the rewriting of a metaphor from Quintilian (*Institutio oratoria* 9.4.7). Machiavelli pro-

19. Struever also discusses the general conflation of the ethical good and the amoral well in *The Prince* in *Theory as Practice,* 157.

20. Aristotle writes: "It is this kind of deliberation which is good deliberation, a correctness that attains what is good" (*NE,* 1141b.20). My definition of *virtù* as functional excellence is taken from Hulliung's discussion of the similarity between *virtù* and *aretē:* "Since the Latin word *virtus* meant almost exactly what *aretē* had meant in popular Greek usage, simply to use the Latin language as it had always been used had the effect, whether intended or unintended, of undoing the Platonic and Aristotelian effort of reworking and philosophizing pagan values. Once again, 'excellence' was synonymous with all that is heroic, noble, warlike, great"; *Citizen Machiavelli,* 136–37. See also 194–98, 212–17 and 253 on Machiavelli's critique of stoicism.

21. This phrase is taken from Whitfield, *Machiavelli,* 117.

poses a style that is powerful precisely because it is rough and broken. He thus duplicates on the poetic level the practical problem of judgment that the prince will have to face—that of applying the rule of *virtù* to the particular situation at hand. Or, as Roland Barthes has written of Machiavelli's work, "The structure of the discourse attempts to reproduce the structure of the dilemmas actually faced by the protagonists. In this case reasoned argument predominates and the history [or discourse] is of a reflexive—one might say strategic—style."[22]

Theatricality

The suggestion that Machiavelli's style is strategic means not only that the prince may learn something about strategy by reflecting on Machiavelli's prose (the structure and vocabulary of his examples) but also that the actual strategies he recounts may tell us something about Machiavelli's strategy as a writer. And this reciprocity in turn allows us to read the example of Agathocles in the light of Machiavelli's earlier remarks on Borgia. As a number of critics have remarked, Machiavelli's position as counselor is in some ways analogous to that of the new prince. Both are "student[s] of delegitimized politics,"[23] and for both the problem is how to impose a new form not only on matter but on already informed matter. But Machiavelli's *virtù* as a writer is not simply, as some readers have suggested, to dramatize in the writing of *The Prince* the resourcefulness and inventiveness of the effective ruler but also to manipulate his audience in much the same way that the prince must manipulate his subjects. In the first case, imitation involves the cultivation of a purely formal flexibility of judgment or *disponibilità;* in the second, that judgment is tested by the appearances of the text itself. Thus in chapter 7 Machiavelli proposes Borgia's behavior in the Romagna as an example worthy of imitation, and in chapter 8 he imitates it in order to test whether the reader has learned the lessons of

---

22. Roland Barthes, "Le discours de l'histoire," *Social Science Information* 6 (1967): 72. Michael McCanles, in a book that came to my attention after the completion of this essay (*The Discourse of "Il Principe,"* vol. 8 of *Humana Civilitas,* Studies and Sources Relating to the Middle Ages and Renaissance [Malibu, Calif., 1983]), proposes a reading of chap. 8 similar to the one I am offering here. He tends, however, to maintain a strict opposition between Christian virtue and *virtù,* even as he denies any substantive definition of the latter. That is, although he argues throughout his book for the dialectical understanding of *virtù* as necessarily including its opposite, he suggests here that what is evil from a Christian point of view will necessarily be good from a political point of view and vice versa (see 63). He also does not discuss Agathocles' conversion to representation at the end of chap. 8 (see 59–65).
23. Pocock, *The Machiavellian Moment,* 163.

chapter 7. In short, there are striking analogies not only between the careers of Borgia and Agathocles but also between the effect of Borgia's behavior on his subjects in the Romagna and Machiavelli's effect on the reader in chapter 8.

When Borgia took over the Romagna, he discovered that "the whole province was full of robbers, feuds, and lawlessness of every description" (22 [37]). His way of "establish[ing] peace and reduc[ing] the land to obedience" was to counter lawlessness with lawlessness: "He named Messer Remirro de Orco, a cruel and vigorous man, to whom he gave absolute powers. In short order this man pacified and unified the whole district, winning great renown" (22 [37]). But like Agathocles, Borgia knew that excessive authority can become odious,

> so he set up a civil court in the middle of the province, with an excellent judge and a representative from each city. And because he knew that the recent harshness had generated some hatred, in order to clear the minds of the people and gain them over to his cause completely, he determined to make plain that whatever cruelty had occurred had come, not from him, but from the brutal character of the minister. Taking a proper occasion, therefore, he had him placed on the public square of Cesena one morning, in two pieces, with a piece of wood beside him and a bloody knife. The ferocity of this scene left the people at once stunned and satisfied. (22 [37])

This story provides us with two examples of cruelty well used. The first is de Orco's, the second Borgia's. The function of the first is primarily destructive and repressive: to pacify his subjects. The function of the second is theatrical and cathartic; this too pacifies the subjects but by the theatrical display of violence rather than its direct application to the audience. The first example reestablishes justice from the perspective of the ruler; the second stages this reestablishment from the perspective of and for the ruled. As this theatrical display suggests, the story also provides us with two examples of representation well used. In the first, there is an element of representation insofar as Borgia delegates his power, but this delegation is ultimately a way of concealing the fact of representation (i.e., representation has become ruse) so that he can deny responsibility for de Orco's cruelty—as he does so effectively by means of (and this is the second example) his theatrical representation in the public square of Cesena.

The example of Agathocles in chapter 8 is just such a theatrical display on the part of Machiavelli. Like Borgia, Machiavelli is concerned with making a distinction between *virtù* and crime—not because they are mutually exclusive but because they are not identical. And like Borgia, he sets up a court with the reader as judge. "He determined to make plain that whatever cruelty had occurred [in the example of Agathocles] had come, not from him, but from the brutal character of the minister" (i.e., of his example). The reader is morally satisfied or reassured by Machiavelli's supposed condemnation of Agathocles, just as the people of the Romagna were by the dramatic and brutal disavowal of Remirro's brutality. But the reader who is taken in by this excuse is in the position of a subject rather than of a prince—for Machiavelli has not presented the example of Agathocles in order to pacify his readers but rather to try them. In short, Agathocles is proposed as an example for the prince who might have need to follow him, and the ability to determine that necessity is also the *virtuous* ability to make discriminations about what constitutes *virtù* with respect to any given situation. The example of Agathocles is a test of *virtù*.

The Avoidance of Tautology

When we turn from the examples of Borgia and Agathocles to the rest of *The Prince*, we see that this work is filled with examples of such extreme, ironic, or hyperbolic situations and actions. The most extreme example is perhaps Machiavelli's advice that the best way to keep a city is to destroy it (see chapter 5, 14 [28]; see also *The Discourses*, book 2, chapter 23; book 3, chapter 40). Many readers have thought that Machiavelli here and elsewhere could not possibly mean what he says, that he is ironic in the sense of unserious.[24] But the example of Agathocles has shown that what is mere exaggeration from the perspective of the conventional virtues may be simple pragmatic advice for the student of *virtù*. This advice will seem hyperbolic because it is beyond good and evil, because it involves the transgression of the conventional philosophical constraints on knowledge (knowledge as cognition of the truth) in the direction of knowledge defined as power.[25] But here precisely lies the problem. Although Machiavelli argues in chapter 15 that *virtù* involves knowledge that is useful or effective, he does not want to claim that *virtù* guarantees success. To make this claim would be to fall into a version of the tautology of *honestas* and *utilitas* that he condemns in the same chapter. If there were such a skill as a *virtù* that

24. See Adams's remarks on this example in his edition of *The Prince*, 14. See also Leo Strauss, *Thoughts on Machiavelli* (Chicago, 1958), 82; and Felix Gilbert, *Machiavelli and Guicciardini*, 165–66.

25. On Machiavelli's anticipation of Nietzsche, see Hulliung, *Citizen Machiavelli*, 30.

always yields success, then there would be no fortune or contingency; but contingency is precisely what makes room for *virtù*—indeed, what makes *virtù* necessary in Machiavelli's eyes. Still, a *virtù* that never resulted in success would be patently absurd. Thus Machiavelli claims early in *The Prince* that if we follow the examples of *virtù* that he presents, success will *usually* or most often result (11 [12]).

These ambiguities concerning the relation of *virtù* to success are reflected in Machiavelli's claim to be guided by the *verità effettuale della cosa*. On the one hand, he means that he will approach politics realistically, rather than idealistically, by beginning with things as they are. In this view, as Felix Gilbert has argued, "the measure of worth of a political figure [is] . . . formed by his capacity to use the possibilities inherent in the political situations; politics [has] its own criteria to be derived from existing political opportunities."[26] On the other hand, implicit in the claim to be guided by the *verità effettuale* is the assumption that such an approach will prove to be *effective*: in short, that one does not simply imitate necessity but that one can manipulate it— effect it—to one's own advantage.

Machiavelli's vacillation is apparent throughout *The Prince*. Sometimes he equates *virtù* with successful political action; at other times he insists on distinguishing between the two.[27] In the first case, *virtù* becomes the goal of technical deliberation, and Machiavelli sounds like a dispassionate political analyst, subordinating means to ends. (The danger here, of course, is to assume that anyone who succeeds demonstrates *virtù*, when in fact success might be due to chance rather than to the activity of the individual.) In the second case, *virtù* is a practical skill that may be an end in itself, and thus structurally (although not ethically) similar to the classical notion of prudence.[28] In this way

26. Felix Gilbert, *Machiavelli and Guicciardini*, 120.

27. *Virtù* is equated with success in chap. 8 (28 [44]), 19 (59 [84]), and perhaps chap. 25 (71 [100]), where Machiavelli equates the good with what is effective; cf. the end of chap. 25, where failure is equated with inaction. *Virtù* is differentiated from success in chap. 4 (14 [28]), chap. 6 (16 [30]), and chap. 7 (20 [34–35]). In *The Discourses* (bk. 3, chap. 35), Machiavelli remarks on the superficiality of judging by the result, as he does in the *Florentine Histories*, bk. 4, chap. 7; and bk. 8, chap. 22. On this problem of the relation of *virtù* to success, see Alkis Kontos, "Success and Knowledge in Machiavelli," in *The Political Calculus: Essays on Machiavelli's Philosophy*, ed. Anthony Parel (Toronto, 1972), 83–100.

28. I borrow the distinction between technical and prudential from Aristotle (*NE*), who argues that *technē* is concerned with production (the end results), whereas prudential deliberation is a process, and an end in itself. The many critics who argue that *virtù* is technical skill are right if they mean that the prince is concerned with results, but wrong if they equate *virtù* with the result rather than with deliberative skill and energy in action. *Virtù* is not completely technical because technical skill must result in a product

Machiavelli's vacillation simply conflates in a single term, *virtù*, an amoral version of the structural problem inherent in the classical and humanist concept of prudence—the problem of the relation of means to ends, of prudential deliberation to virtue or, in Machiavelli's case, to *virtù*.

This ambiguity or uncertainty about the status of deliberative skill and its relation to success is also reflected in the nature and function of examples in Machiavelli's texts. As I have suggested, a teacher who subordinates practical judgment to theoretical reason has only to present the student with general precepts and the logical rules of deduction, but a teacher whose theory of action equates judgment with the exercise of practical reason or the observance of decorum will have to educate such judgment through examples. Such examples will not have the status of mere illustrations of theory, as they would if they were subordinated to or subsumed under universally applicable abstract principles. They will not be expendable but necessary, since every judgment of decorum is a judgment of, and must conform to the exigencies of, a particular situation. If such judgment *merely* conformed to the particular, however, it would cancel itself out as a judgment, since it would involve no reference to a standard other than faithful representation (imitation) of the particular case. Judgment requires distance, and examples that educate such judgment must contain within themselves or dramatize this distance. Thus examples in humanist texts are to a certain extent problematizing since they are designed to provoke reflection. But their pedagogical aim also demands a limit to such problematizing: for if excessive identification with the particular leads to the collapse of judgment, excessive difference (the reflection on and putting in question of all possible standards of judgment—whether the standard of virtue or of *virtù*) does as well. Although Machiavelli lacked the humanists' faith in the ethical criterion of practical reason, he was not usually skeptical about the possibility of deliberation and action. Indeed, he insisted that such possibility could be realized only in a world purged of idealism. Machiavelli thus shares with the humanists a rhetoric of problematizing examples, and like the humanists he needs to limit such problematizing.[29]

(however much that product may reflect a compromise with one's original conception of the object), whereas *virtù* does not have to produce something else in order to be *virtù*. Or, as Ostwald observes (*NE*, 154, n. 20), "Practical wisdom is itself a complete virtue or excellence while the excellence of art depends on the goodness or badness of the product." Again, I am arguing only for the structural identity or homology of *virtù* and prudence or practical reason.

29. On problematizing examples, see Karlheinz Stierle, "L'exemple comme histoire, l'histoire comme exemple," *Poétique* 10 (1972): 176–98. Although Machiavelli was capa-

Virtù *and Agathocles*

The dilemma that Machiavelli faces is thus intrinsic to the problematic of imitation, but it is also tinged with a peculiarly Machiavellian irony insofar as the ethical claims for humanist imitation are a rhetorical topic contained within and thus ultimately undermined by the Machiavellian strategy of imitation. In this context, Agathocles' "overshooting" of morality is exemplary because, in both Machiavelli's strategy as author and Agathocles' as agent, it dramatizes and encourages the distanced reflection and thus the reflective imitation necessary for, if not sufficient for, success.

Irony and Allegory

Irony descends from the low mimetic: it begins in realism and dispassionate observation. But as it does so, it moves steadily towards myth, and dim outlines of sacrificial rituals and dying gods begin to reappear in it.
—*Northrop Frye*

As I have argued in the preceding pages, Machiavelli's reflection on the political uses of representation is tied to his revision of the humanist concept of prudential action. The prince is powerful to the extent that he diverges from a naive or moral concept of prudence, but he also maintains his power by "naively" imitating—or representing himself as faithfully reproducing—the conventional virtues. As in chapter 18, power is in part, if not entirely, the effect of the representational illusion of truth. But, as the case of Agathocles demonstrates, the exigency of representation, if representation is conceived of now as the means or the ability to generate the consensus and support of the people (chapter 8, 24 [44]); chapter 18, 51 [74]; *The Discourses*, book 2, chapter 23; book 3, chapter 19–23), also finally proves to be a forceful constraint on the abuse of power. Cruelty will be well used if "it is performed all at once, for reasons of self-preservation; and when the acts are not repeated after that, but rather turned as much as possible to the advantage of the subjects" (chapter 8, 27–28 [44]). The prince must in the long run please his audience if he is to maintain his rule. In the end, the rhetorical topic of truth proves to involve an ironic version of the ethical constraint that the humanists located in custom and consensus.

---

ble of using the same examples to illustrate different points (e.g., Giacomini's loss of favor in *The Discourses*, bk. 1, chap. 53; and bk. 3, chap. 16; cited in Felix Gilbert, *Machiavelli and Guicciardini*, 167), he needed, if his work was to have any practical effect, to stop short of the radical skepticism of a Montaigne, for whom examples could be used to illustrate almost anything. For if they are so used, then one has departed from the realm of *verità effettuale* and entered the realm of the unconstrained imagination, the realm of fiction.

This constraint also helps us to see how the analysis of power in *The Prince* logically gives way to that in *The Discourses*: the prince, to be successful in the long run, must found a republic because republics are capable of greater longevity and *virtù* than principalities. The "understanding reader" will see that when representation and force are mutually implicated, when representation becomes a means of power, and thus finally when power is mitigated by the exigencies of persuasion, the short-lived individual self-aggrandizement gives way to communal glory, and the prince must of necessity become a fellow citizen.[30]

This is the optimistic way to read the self-destructing rhetoric of *The Prince*. But, as most readers have noted, there is a more radical way in which the analysis of *virtù* undermines itself and Machiavelli's pedagogy in this text. As Machiavelli tells us over and over again, there are no general rules for virtuous behavior (e.g., chapter 20, 59 [85]), and there is no guarantee that the skill one practices in the interpretation of particular examples will enable one to respond appropriately in the next situation. This is, of course, as it should be. As Machiavelli writes in chapter 21, "No leader should ever suppose he can invariably take the safe course, since all choice involves risks. In the nature of things [*nell'ordine delle cose*], you can never try to escape one danger without encountering another; but prudence consists in knowing how to recognize the nature of the different dangers and in accepting the least bad as good" (65 [92]). But the essential emptiness of the concept of *virtù* receives a rather different and finally devastating articulation in chapter 25, where the role of fortune in the individual's ability to act virtuously finally seems to deprive the individual of any initiative whatsoever. As we saw, Machiavelli begins this chapter by discussing the relation of fortune and *virtù* in general terms. On this level he gives fortune a certain allegorical stability, as though fortune were something external to *virtù* that the latter had only to resist. When he descends to particulars, however, fortune has no stability whatsoever. The irony of politics and human action becomes so great—the possibility of action (as opposed to mere passivity) so compromised—that the distance constitutive of reflection finally collapses altogether. To recognize which situations require which kinds of imitation finally necessitates that the prince imitate the absolute flexibility of fortune itself. But one's ability to learn is itself, finally, a function of the *fortune*

---

30. Hulliung makes this point in *Citizen Machiavelli*, 56, 82, 231. See also Strauss, *Thoughts on Machiavelli*, 288–89; Manent, *Naissances*, 19–25; and *The Prince*, chap. 19, 53–54 [77–78], for Machiavelli's remarks on the origin of the French parliament. Nancy Struever has some interesting remarks about constraint in *The Prince* in *Theory as Practice*, 165–75.

of one's natural disposition, and is necessarily limited by it. In thus conflating the realm of necessity or nature with the agent of *virtù*, Machiavelli runs the risk of reducing *virtù* to the mere repetition—that is, the willed acceptance—of necessity: the mimetic representation of nature.[31] In so doing, he finally does substitute for the tautology of *honestas* and *utilitas* the tautology of *virtù* and success. It is not surprising, then, that Machiavelli should at this moment invoke the personified figure of Fortune (*Fortuna*) as a woman in a desperate, inconsequential attempt to redeem the possibility of action by relocating it in an interpersonal context.[32]

A few remarks about the allegorical tendency of *The Prince* may help to clarify this point. According to Angus Fletcher, the allegorical hero confronts a world of contingency, a world in which the individual has very little control over the consequences of his actions, and in which there often seems to be little causal connection between events.[33] Narrative sequence is threatened by parataxis but restored on the level of cosmic, often magical necessity.[34] As a result, the hero also seems to be not simply at the mercy of external events but in the control of some external power. In fact, the allegorical hero could be said to operate in a world of demonic powers, a world in which functions have been compartmentalized, personified. The result is that the hero himself becomes depersonalized; he is not a person but rather a personification of a function. In a world of *Fortuna*, in short, the hero becomes of necessity the embodiment of *Virtù*.

In such a world, then, the virtues no longer seem to be attributes of individual agents; rather, they recover their original sense of powers or forces, of *virtù*. As Fletcher remarks, "Like a Machiavellian prince, the allegorical hero can act free of the usual moral restraints, even when he is acting morally, since he is moral only in the interests of his power over other men" (68). To redefine virtue as *virtù* is thus "to rediscover a sense of the morally ambivalent power in action" (an advance, one might say, in the direction of "realism"), but it is also, ironically, to run the risk of doing away with free will. Although the intention behind Machiavelli's various exempla of *virtù* is to help the reader understand the formal, innovative character of this faculty, and the role of free will

31. See Manent, *Naissances*, 9–10, 35–39, for a more positive reading of the willing of necessity in *The Prince*.

32. Pitkin makes this point in *Fortune Is a Woman*, 292.

33. See Angus Fletcher, *Allegory: The Theory of a Symbolic Mode* (Ithaca, N.Y., 1964). All page references are given in the text of my essay.

34. On parataxis in *The Prince*, see Fredi Chiappelli, *Studi sul linguaggio del Machiavelli* (Florence, 1952), 40–42 (cited by McCanles, *The Discourse of "Il Principe*," 13; see also 13–15).

in determining what constitutes *virtù* in any particular situation, the quasi-allegorical status of the man of *virtù*, or of the prince as a *personification* of *Virtù*, suggests that the individual is not at all in control of his behavior—a suggestion that, as we have seen, becomes explicit in chapter 25. The way Machiavelli chooses to combat this demonization or personification of the person is to repersonalize what was becoming an increasingly abstract and *unmanageable* concept of fortune by introducing the figure of Fortune as a woman. In a kind of parody of humanist rhetoric *in utramque partem*, allegory is used to fight the allegorization or reification of the prince's *virtù*.

In light of these remarks, one can also see that the allegorical tendency of Machiavelli's "realism" is manifest in the sublime rhetoric of his concluding chapter.[35] Fletcher calls our attention to the structural similarity between allegory and the sublime. Simply stated, the experience of the sublime involves the inability of the imagination to comprehend sensuous experience, which leads to an awareness of the higher faculty of reason and to "reflection on man's higher destiny" (249). This discrepancy between sensuous experience and the higher claims of reason is analogous to the separation of sensuous representation and allegorical signified in the allegorical text. Furthermore, as Longinus reminds us, allegory is not only analogous to the sublime but can itself have a sublime effect, an ideological (249) or epideictic force when it "incites to action" (246). But, Northrop Frye, in the epigraph to this section, suggests, the structural incommensurability in the allegorical sublime can also have an ironic effect, by implying that the principle of authority or meaning (reason, God) is infinitely removed from the world of sensuous immediacy.[36]

Machiavelli obviously intends the sublime or divine rhetoric of his concluding chapter to function as the best of all hyperboles: to incite the Medici to action. Consider the following claim:

There is no figure presently in sight to whom she [Italy] can better trust than your illustrious house, which, with its fortune and its *virtù*, favored by God and the Church of which it is now the head, can take the lead in this process of redemption. (73 [102])

35. For some provocative interpretations of this concluding chapter, see Greene, "The End of Discourse"; and Sasso, *Niccolò Machiavelli*, 278–80.

36. Frye, *Anatomy of Criticism* (Princeton, N.J., 1957), 42. Fletcher is quoting Schiller: "For the sublime, in the strict sense of the word, cannot be contained in any sensuous form, but rather concerns ideas of reason, which, although no adequate representation of them is possible, may be excited and called into the mind by that very inadequacy itself which does admit of sensuous presentation"; *Allegory*, 251–52. See also Immanuel Kant, *Critique of Judgment*, trans. J. H. Bernard (New York, 1951), 88, 101 (pars. 25 and 28).

In these lines, Machiavelli conflates the fortune of the Medici with divine providence and the Church, and thus simultaneously debases religion and confers a certain grandeur upon the rulers of Florence.[37] In this light necessity, too, takes on a different and more positive appearance; it is no longer the necessity of fortune or of contingency or of (one's own) nature that resists *virtù* (as in chapter 25); rather, necessity is now the "providential necessity" that justifies the actions of the Medici. Describing men of *virtù*, he writes: "Their cause was no more just than the present one, nor any easier, and God was no more favorable to them than to you. Your cause is just: 'for war is justified when it is necessary, and arms are pious when without them there would be no hope at all'" (73 [103]). In its divine justification of the Medici as the redeemers of Italy, chapter 26 would be the final, brilliant example of Machiavelli's theatrical overshooting of the mark, of a rhetoric of representation that is neither constrained by logic to represent the truth nor guided by practical reason in its achievement of decorum, but that aims rather to produce the effect of truth—or to effect it. Yet the obvious alternative reading of the lines just quoted is that providential justification is conflated with the material realm of necessity. In this way, the collapse of the distance and difference necessary for action in chapter 25 turns out to anticipate the rhetoric of chapter 26, a rhetoric that, paradoxically, seems designed precisely to recoup the losses of the preceding chapter. In the end, exaggeration cannot free itself "from the weight of the factual, so that instead of merely reproducing being it can, at once rigorous and free, determine it" (Adorno; see the epigraph). In a final ironic twist, Machiavelli's providential rhetoric can then be seen to suggest that, to answer Schlegel's question, only (the hyperbolic figure of) God can save us from such ironies.

37. Pocock makes a similar point in *The Machiavellian Moment*, 171: "We must not say that divine inspiration is being lowered to the level of realpolitik without adding that realpolitik is being raised to the level of divine inspiration."

CHAPTER NINE

MACHIAVELLI'S GIFT OF COUNSEL

Albert Russell Ascoli

MACHIAVELLI'S *The Prince*, as we have known for some time now, is not quite the radically new document in the history of Western political thought that it has so often been represented as being. Allan Gilbert, and after him a number of others,[1] have pointed to important formal and thematic ways in which it participates in a specific and common humanistic genre: the educational treatise for the benefit of princes, itself part of a larger rhetorical, didactic mode that offers historical examples of ethical-political behavior for imitation (or avoidance) by its readers. The principal aim of my essay is to juxtapose this generalized didactic mission with another, closely related feature that the treatise shares with humanistic texts—its self-presentation as a "gift," of practical, prudential wisdom, of cogent political counsel, to a powerful patron—who, it is hoped, will reciprocate with patronage and em-

In writing this essay, I have benefited particularly from the reactions and suggestions of Victoria Kahn, David Quint, Constance Jordan, John Martin, John Marino, Ronald Martinez, and, first, Walter Stevens.

   1. Allan H. Gilbert, *Machiavelli's Prince and Its Forerunners: The Prince as a Typical Book De Regimine Principum* (Durham, N.C., 1938); see also Quentin Skinner, *The Foundations of Modern Political Thought*, vol. 1 (Cambridge, 1978), esp. 128–30; Peter Bondanella, *Machiavelli and the Art of Renaissance History* (Detroit, 1973). Felix Gilbert, in "The Humanist Concept of the Prince and the *Prince* of Machiavelli," *Journal of Modern History* 11 (1939): 449–83, argues that Machiavelli's use of the genre is satirical; see also his *Machiavelli and Guicciardini: Politics and History in Sixteenth-Century Florence* (Princeton, N.J., 1965), 324. Note the qualifications of Myron Gilmore, *The World of Humanism, 1453–1527* (New York, 1962, first published 1952), 135; Victoria Kahn, "*Virtù* and the Example of Agathocles," *Representations* 13 (1986): 63–83 [see the preceding essay in this volume]; Timothy Hampton, *Writing from History: The Rhetoric of Exemplarity in Renaissance Literature* (Ithaca, N.Y., 1990), 62–79.

ployment. In the space between these two obvious features of the text (its display of general precepts for princely behavior based on ancient and modern examples, and its address to a particular prince at a particular place and time), a third, hybrid project emerges that is perhaps more peculiarly Machiavellian, though still not unprecedented: the hoped-for intersection of those rules with that prince, plus the indispensable tertium quid of Machiavelli as counselor, leading to the implementation of a plan for dramatic action. That plan, I submit, was designed to resolve an ever-worsening political crisis that threatened to destroy, indeed did destroy, forever the fragile balance of power among the city-states and postfeudal fiefdoms of the Italian peninsula.

Thus, in addition to a general conveyance of knowledge, the treatise has two far more specific and contingent goals—one personal, one protonational, both "performative" in the sense of attempting to effect significant change, through the rhetorically persuasive deployment of language, by convincing the Medici: (1) to end Machiavelli's squalid exile by offering him employment as a counselor; (2) to adopt the visionary plan, the "nuovi modi e ordini" (new modes and orders), which Machiavelli foresaw as making possible the restoration of stability and a certain autonomy to Italy under the guidance of a new, secular prince whose family, by happy, indispensable chance, also controlled the papacy. To adopt this perspective is to take very seriously (although without loss of a certain irony) Machiavelli's stated desire to serve Lorenzo de' Medici, duke of Urbino. It is also to follow those readers who have claimed that Machiavelli's concerns in *The Prince* are not so much those of local Florentine politics, in which his preferences may well have been distinctly anti-Medicean and pro-republican, as they are, more broadly, "Italian."[2]

Put in this way, it would appear that my interest is in historicizing *The Prince*, treating it as the product of a particularly significant epoch in a specifically Italian history. That is not so, strictly speaking. I do assume the presence of "external" historical forces (or at least Machiavelli's belief that he was responding to such forces), which can be

2. E.g., Gilmore, *The World of Humanism*, especially 134; J. R. Hale, *Machiavelli and Renaissance Italy* (London, 1961), esp. 107–26; Federico Chabod, *Scritti su Machiavelli* (Turin, 1964), 40–46; Gennaro Sasso, *Niccolò Machiavelli: Storia del suo pensiero politico* (Naples, 1958), 260; and Sasso, *Studi su Machiavelli* (Naples, 1967), 34–35. Evidence of Machiavelli's continuing obsession with the disastrous peninsular situation can be found, for instance, in his letter to Francesco Vettori of August 26, 1513 (letter no. 138 in Niccolò Machiavelli, *Lettere*, ed. Franco Gaeta, 2d ed. [Milan, 1981]); *Decennale*, 2.181–93; and in the *Florentine Histories*, bk. 5, chap. 1.

considered efficient causes of the treatise's composition. My procedures, and my underlying interest, are more properly "rhetorical," however, in the sense that I am concerned less with historicizing Machiavelli than with showing how his text was attempting through linguistic action to "historicize" itself and its author—to transform both of them from marginality into dynamic agency in the historical process, notwithstanding formidable obstacles that stood between the exiled Machiavelli and the potent Medici, as between the words of his text and the deeds they alternately describe and recommend. And I will do this in part by elaborating my own extrinsic account of Machiavelli's historical circumstances, but to a greater extent by undertaking a close intratextual and intertextual analysis of the treatise.

My reading of *The Prince* is situated between two significant and apparently opposed tendencies in Machiavelli scholarship, which could, crudely speaking, be called "contentual" and "formalist." I am clearly in disagreement with those who feel that the task of reading *The Prince* is to deduce its theoretically generalizable *content*, whether it be absolutist or republican. Because all three of the aims (exemplary instruction, political reform, personal gain) that I ascribe to the treatise assign its language a "performative" function as rhetorical action, rather than simply a "constative" function of intellectual communication, one has to look at the strategic force of its utterances along with their "message" in every case. This is particularly true since the introduction of specific, local aims (rehabilitation of Machiavelli as a political operative, restitution of Italian unity and freedom) points to the patent interestedness and hence contingency of what is said in the treatise.[3]

I am also at odds, though to a lesser degree, with those whose focus is primarily "formal" (either "stylistic" or technically "logical"), that is, rhetorical in the modern (or more exactly, postmodern) sense of separating language as system from a "real" historical world to which it might refer and on which it might act. In particular, I am thinking of several recent essays and books that have quite appropriately placed in the foreground the "literariness" of *The Prince*—its use of myth, image, narrative, and trope—and have suggested that such literariness *in itself*

---

3. I would thus take issue with the claim of J. G. A. Pocock, *The Machiavellian Moment: Florentine Political Thought and the Atlantic Republican Tradition* (Princeton, N.J., 1975), 160, that "*Il Principe* . . . [is] a theoretical treatise, inspired by a specific situation but not directed at it." Perhaps more strongly than Pocock I would argue that the broader historical importance of *The Prince* and its innovative place in Western political thought derive quite specifically from the rhetorical and conceptual strategies it deploys in order to confront a "local" crisis.

subverts both the political knowledge of the treatise and its claims to political efficacy.[4] Although my reading shares many of the same formalistic tools of analysis that these readers deploy, I disagree with them on the same grounds that I disagree with the others: namely, that to understand the treatise rhetorically one has to look not at its content or its form (that is, its arsenal of rhetorical tropes and narrative devices), but rather at the hybrid and fundamental character of rhetoric in the Renaissance—at once a repertory of linguistic devices and a mode of verbal action—whose prestige depends upon its claims artfully to deploy language so as to transform knowledge into power, thought into action. In the same vein, one has to consider the possibility that the deployment of the "literary" in *The Prince* is, on the one hand, tactical (a means of making one's points more effectively), and on the other, defensive (a refuge from the intractable fact that one's auditors are as dangerous as they are obtuse).

In this perspective, again, the category of "contradiction," which from a late twentieth-century structuralist or deconstructive point of view reduces the logic of a text to sheer textuality itself,[5] becomes simply a necessary part of the temporal dynamic of a language that wants to move its readers (and its author) from point *A* to point *B* (or in this case, point *Z*). To state this in a reductively Machiavellian way, "the ends justify the means" and internal contradiction is always forgiven, if one is finally successful in getting what one wants. To put the question as one of either content or form, then, is to miss the point that the rhetorical action of the treatise is precisely that of mediating between form and content in order to effect goals that if achieved will (1) change the historical scene and hence repudiate the book's "content"; (2) liberate the author from the need to communicate his ideas in

---

4. See, for example, Giorgio Bárberi Squarotti, *La forma tragica del "Principe" e altri saggi sul Machiavelli* (Florence, 1966); Bárberi Squarotti, *Machiavelli, o la scelta della letteratura* (Rome, 1987); Ezio Raimondi, *Politica e commedia dal Beroaldo al Machiavelli* (Bologna, 1972); Michael McCanles, *The Discourse of "Il Principe,"* vol. 8 of *Humana Civilitas,* Studies and Sources Relating to the Middle Ages and Renaissance (Malibu, Calif., 1983); McCanles, "Machiavelli's *Principe* and the Textualization of History," *MLN* 97 (1983): 1–18; Thomas M. Greene, "The End of Discourse in Machiavelli's *Prince,*" in *Literary Theory/Renaissance Texts,* ed. Patricia Parker and David Quint (Baltimore, 1986); and Wayne Rebhorn, *Foxes and Lions: Machiavelli's Confidence Men* (Ithaca, N.Y., 1988).

5. McCanles, in "Machiavelli's *Principe,*" goes further and argues that for Machiavelli history is a text and that "physical power exerts no force unless it is textualized" (8); see also Ezio Raimondi, "Machiavelli and the Rhetoric of the Warrior," *MLN* Italian issue 92 (1977): 1–16; and the essay by Barbara Spackman in this volume. Although I do not underestimate Machiavelli's interest in and understanding of the powers of discourse and representation, I would agree with Rebhorn, in *Foxes and Lions,* 116, that "a rhetoric of words must sometimes yield to a rhetoric of violence."

writing and hence allow him to escape the impotent, exilic world of literary "form" and academic speculation altogether.

Evidence clearly shows that the treatise *was* written as a "gift" with very specific rhetorical purposes in mind. A famous letter of December 10, 1513, from Machiavelli to his friend Francesco Vettori, gives an account of the genesis and purposes of *The Prince*. The letter, like the treatise itself, is a product of the bleak period following the fall of the Florentine republic led by Piero Soderini and the reintroduction of the Medici into the city after a nearly twenty-year absence. Machiavelli, who had served Soderini and the republic as Secretary, was in exile at this time, having first been briefly imprisoned, and even tortured, by the Medici, who were quite reasonably suspicious of his ties to the old regime.

Machiavelli's friend Vettori had remained in the good graces of the Medici, and in 1513 was serving as Florentine ambassador to a Rome now under its new Pope, Leo X (the head of the Medici clan, whose election, following hard on the family's restoration in Florence the previous year, had completed their reversal of fortune). In a series of letters that year, Machiavelli discussed his plight with his friend and sought his intervention with the Medici (and above all with Leo) to give him the opportunity to practice again his political vocation, even in the meanest of capacities. The letter of December 10 reflects on the squalor and relative poverty of Machiavelli's postexilic life, culminating in an account of the composition of a short treatise on princes:[6]

> On the coming of evening, I return to my house and enter my study; and at the door I take off the day's clothing, covered with mud and dust, and put on garments regal and courtly; and reclothed appropriately, I enter the ancient courts of ancient men, where, received by them with affection, I feed on that food which only is mine and which I was born for, where I am not ashamed to speak with them and to ask them the reason for their actions; and they in their kindness answer me; and for four hours of time I do not feel boredom, I forget every trouble, I do not dread poverty, I am not frightened by death; entirely I give myself over to them.

And because Dante says it does not produce knowledge when

6. Letter no. 140, in Machiavelli, *Lettere*, ed. Gaeta; translation by Allan Gilbert from *The Letters of Machiavelli* (Chicago, 1988, first published 1961), 139–44. For a detailed reading of this letter, see the essay by John Najemy in this volume and his forthcoming book *Between Friends: Discourses of Power and Desire in the Machiavelli-Vettori Letters of 1513–1515* (Princeton, N.J., 1993).

we hear but do not remember, I have noted everything in their conversation which has profited me, and have composed a little work *On Princedoms.*

This letter, however, then moves beyond this traditional humanist topos of timeless communion among books: "And if ever you can find one of my fantasies [*alcuno mio ghiribizo*] pleasing, this one should not displease you; and by a prince, and especially by a new prince, it ought to be welcomed. Hence I am dedicating it to His Magnificence, Giuliano [de' Medici]." Later he adds: "The giving of [the work] is forced upon me by the necessity that drives me, because I am using up my money, and I cannot remain as I am a long time without becoming despised through poverty. In addition, there is my wish that our present Medici lords will make use of me, even if they begin by making me roll a stone [*voltolare un sasso*]."[7] Now the treatise appears to be a gift that should be particularly precious to a new Medici prince and whose primary purpose is not the advancement of "pure knowledge" but the obtaining of employment for Machiavelli as counselor—and with it the end of his exile and his humanistic *otium*.

When the final version of *The Prince* was completed some time before 1517, it was still dedicated to the Medici, although now the dedicatee was not Giuliano, who died prematurely in 1516, but rather Lorenzo, his successor as the secular limb of a Medici power that was rooted in Leo's papacy. Machiavelli addresses Lorenzo in a letter of dedication that echoes both the writer's claim of having a profound and unbiased knowledge of ancient and modern politics and his pursuit of preferment through gift:

It is a frequent custom of those who seek the favor of a prince to make him presents of those things they value most highly or which they know are most pleasing to him. . . .

Will your Magnificence . . . deign to accept this little gift [*questo piccolo dono*] in the same spirit that I send it? If you will read it over and study it carefully, you will recognize in it my most earnest desire that you may achieve that summit of grandeur to which your happy destiny [*fortuna*] and your other capacities predestine you. And if from that summit Your Magnificence will occasionally glance down at these humble places, you will

7. On the Sisyphean force of this locution, see Raimondi, "Il sasso del politico," in *Politica e commedia*, 165–72.

recognize how unjustly I suffer the bitter and sustained malignity of Fortune.[8]

Curiously enough, however, critics more often than not either have ignored these obvious indicators of the profoundly "interested" status of *The Prince* as gift of counsel to the Medici or have actively sought to explain it away, usually by affirming Machiavelli's adherence to a specifically anti-Medicean republican ideal, which finds its fullest expression in *The Discourses*,[9] which are openly republican. The underlying motive, of course, is the desire to see in Machiavelli the forerunner of an Enlightenment politics of democratically based secular liberty—and not the Elizabethan, or Straussian, personification of amoral, tyrannical evil. This desire has prompted such ingenious and intermittently persuasive accounts of the treatise's self-subverting ironies as those of Alberico Gentili, Ugo Foscolo, and Antonio Gramsci, which claim the treatise is meant to inform those who do not already know how power works (the oppressed peoples of Italy) rather than those who do (the princes themselves) so that they can better resist it; Garrett Mattingly's argument that the treatise is in fact a satire; and a recent variant that insists that the treatise deliberately gives bad advice in order to lure the Medici to their ruin.[10] The strongest arguments for not taking seriously Machiavelli's stated intent of counseling the Medici are basically three, the first two historical and extrinsic, the third logical and textual. I will

8. This and all subsequent translations of *The Prince* are taken from Niccolò Machiavelli, *The Prince*, trans. and ed. Robert M. Adams (New York, 1977); they have been checked against *Il Principe e le opere politiche*, introduction by Delio Cantimori (Milan, 1976).

9. On Machiavelli's republicanism, see Hans Baron, "The *Principe* and the Puzzle of the Date of the *Discorsi*," *Bibliothèque d'Humanisme et Renaissance* 14 (1956): 405–28; and Felix Gilbert, *Machiavelli and Guicciardini*, 155–56. Among those who *have* taken the claim seriously (some without abandoning the image of a "politically correct" Machiavelli) are Gilmore, *The World of Humanism*; J. H. Whitfield, *Discourses on Machiavelli* (Cambridge, 1969), e.g., 107–8; Chabod, *Scritti su Machiavelli*, 38; and Sasso, *Studi storici*, 14–15; see also Rebhorn, *Foxes and Lions*, 223–25. For a cogent analysis of Machiavelli's evolving understanding of and relationship with the Medici, from *The Prince* to the *Florentine Histories* (the latter work commissioned by the family), see John Najemy, "Machiavelli and the Medici: The Lessons of Florentine History," *Renaissance Quarterly* 35 (1982): 551–76.

10. Alberico Gentili, *De legationibus libri tres*, bk. 3, chap. 9, 171–72; Ugo Foscolo, "I sepolcri"; Antonio Gramsci, *Quaderni del carcere*, ed. Valentino Gerratana, 4 vols. (Turin, 1975), 3: esp. 1598–1601; Garrett Mattingly, "Machiavelli's *Prince*: Political Science or Political Satire?" *American Scholar* 27 (1958): 482–91; Stephen M. Fallon, "Hunting the Fox: Equivocation and Authorial Duplicity in *The Prince*," *PMLA* 107 (1992): 1181–95. The line of argument most frequently used is that the ruling class already knows how to

take the occasion of reviewing them to examine briefly the elements of the historical crisis that Machiavelli both confronted and attempted to describe.

In the first place, it has been argued that Machiavelli's intimate association with the republic and its ideals between 1498 and 1512 establishes beyond question his pro-republican anti-Medicean stance. This position is based on two hidden and suspect assumptions. The first is that democracy and autocracy were dialectically opposed alternatives for Machiavelli, when in fact for him, as for Aristotle, there was a third option—an aristocracy with oligarchical inclinations—that often turned the "people" and the "prince" from enemies into allies. More specifically, Florence, as is well known, was like Rome for Machiavelli in that it had attempted, but had often failed, to maintain a precarious balance between widely popular interests, the interests of a small class of wealthy aristocratic families, and the power that would coalesce around one autocratic individual representing a preeminent family. And although Machiavelli in *The Prince* specifically excludes discussions of republics (except insofar as they, and Florence in particular, present special problems of pacification to a "new prince"), he does make it clear that there is a natural and in some ways reciprocally profitable alliance to be made between the people and the prince against the *grandi* (chapter 9). The second assumption is that republicanism was for Machiavelli an essential and noncontingent preference, when in reality, as I have already suggested, there were strong historical forces at work in the Italian peninsula and in Europe as a whole that tended to offset local, Florentine considerations, even for Machiavelli. The main general point is his clear recognition, however qualified and incomplete, that contemporary Europe was dominated by unified nation-states.[11] The recurring figure of Ferdinand the Catholic, who had so recently unified Christian Spain, is relevant here (chapters 1, 13, 16, 18, and especially 21). And there is a pointed reference to the

---

acquire and hold power and thus does not need Machiavelli's advice. In my view, however, the dramatic failure of the Italian princes in this period to serve either their own best interests or those of "the governed" constituted prima facie evidence for Machiavelli that this was not so (see, for example, *The Prince*, chap. 24). In other words, although a few princes may well have already been following some of Machiavelli's precepts, particularly those concerning force and fraud, none at this time, not even Cesare Borgia, had achieved what the Italian peninsula so desperately needed of them.

11. Chabod, *Scritti su Machiavelli*, esp. 61. See Gramsci, *Quaderni del carcere*, on Machiavelli's attempt to develop "a national-popular collective will [*volontà*]" (my translation), 1559 (cf. 1563 and 1572); as well as Gramsci's *Lettere dal carcere*, ed. Sergio Caprioglio and Elsa Fubini (Turin, 1968), letters nos. 60 and 210. Felix Gilbert disagrees with the view that Machiavelli was the "prophet of the modern national state" (*Machiavelli and Guicciardini*, 182–84, 325–26).

gradual transformation of France from a loose connection of linguistically and politically separate provinces to a centralized government (chapter 3). Thus, Machiavelli's reader is constantly reminded both that Italy had failed to follow suit and that it was at risk from the adventurism of the French and Spanish monarchs, as well as from the vain ambitions of its own local princes who aspired to greater dominion.

Moreover, this trend had played itself out in a specific way in Machiavelli's historical imagination. The date to which he and many of his contemporaries, including Francesco Guicciardini, constantly return is 1494. Its significance is dual and deeply ambivalent for him. On the one hand, it is the year of the Medici's expulsion and the reinstallation of the republic, at first under the prophetic spell of Savonarola and later, after his demise, under the guidance of Soderini with the aid of his operative, Machiavelli. On the other hand, it is the year of King Charles VIII's *calata* and of his horrifying success in "taking Italy with chalk" (chapter 12), which for Machiavelli became the first signal of a tidal wave of French and Spanish invaders. Ironically (and this is an irony that runs deeply and divisively in Machiavelli's political thinking), the invasion by Charles made possible the expulsion of the Medici—just as later their restoration was made possible by the intervention of a foreign force under the Spanish viceroy.[12] The point is that however deeply Machiavelli felt his preference for republican rule in Florence, it was tempered by his awareness that neither Florence nor Italy was in charge of its own political circumstance in the post-1494 epoch—and that the "Florentine" problem was likely to be purely academic if the "Italian" question was not solved first.

The second major argument for discounting the dedicatory letter is that, even assuming that Machiavelli was serious in his recommendations concerning the behavior of a "new prince" operating outside the purview of the law and principles of legitimacy, Lorenzo was a thoroughly unworthy candidate for this job[13]—a fact reinforced by the easy substitution of Lorenzo for Giuliano on the latter's death. This argument has some merit, and part of my argument will be that Machiavelli's desire for collaboration with the Medici was tempered by a growing awareness of the inevitability of the failure of his projects, both personal and peninsular. Advocates of this position typically fail to take note of two basic facts, however—that any recommendations addressed to Lorenzo were ultimately addressed as well to the real

12. The events are narrated by Machiavelli in a letter of September 16, 1512 (letter no. 118 in Machiavelli, *Lettere*, ed. Gaeta).

13. See, for instance, Rebhorn, *Foxes and Lions*, 220.

leader of the Medici interests, Pope Leo X,[14] and that Machiavelli consistently saw the Church as *the* key to Italian peninsular politics, for good or for evil. The latter point can be made "extra-textually" if one reflects on the importance that Vettori, the Florentine ambassador to Rome and hence the copula between the Medici and themselves, had in Machiavelli's designs for self-rehabilitation. In *The Discourses* and the later *Florentine Histories,* the Church's special and determining role in Italian politics is stressed. The Church, lacking genealogical continuity from ruler to ruler (and being ruled, usually, by very old men who were not able to see their political projects from beginning to end), was unable to unify Italy by itself—but would not tolerate the emergence of any peninsular power that could effect unification, thus jeopardizing the Church's autonomy (*The Discourses,* book 1, chapter 12; *Florentine Histories,* book 1, chapter 9; cf. letter no. 138). In *The Prince* this point is also made, although in less obviously critical terms. In fact, Machiavelli offers some superficial bows in the direction of the Church's claims to a divine origin and authorization which exempts it (like Moses) from the rules that govern other, secular, states and their rulers (chapter 11, cf. chapter 6), even as he points again and again to its secular political role.[15] This is hardly surprising, given that it would be patently counterproductive to blame the Church for past and present failings when it was so central to his plans for the future, as will be seen later in this essay. One could argue that a rigorous analysis of the Church is absent from *The Prince* precisely in inverse proportion to Machiavelli's desire to resolve the problems he describes "hopelessly" in *The Discourses.* Nonetheless, the Church *is* subjected in the shorter treatise to a basic process of secularization and demystification—up to and including assigning it primary blame for a phenomenon that was (in Machiavelli's eyes) principally responsible for the ruin of Italy, namely, the employment of mercenaries rather than its own forces (chapter 11, cf. chapters 7, 12, and 13), and positing a direct and desacralizing analogy between the Church's particular form of rule and that of the paradigmatically pagan Soldano (chapter 19). Of course, two of the four contemporary political figures of greatest exemplary value for Machiavelli were the activist popes, Alexander VI and Julius II, with whom Leo X is specifically grouped as a third and climatic term (chapter 11).[16] (The other two are Ferdinand and Cesare Borgia, both closely identified

14. Felix Gilbert, *Machiavelli and Guicciardini,* e.g., 139.

15. Already in chap. 3 we learn that King Louis "was weakening himself . . . while strengthening the Church by adding vast temporal power to the spiritual power which gives it so much authority"; the story continues in chaps. 7, 11, 18, and 25.

16. Alexander VI is discussed in chaps. 3, 7, 11, and 18; Julius II in chaps. 7, 11, and 25.

with the Catholic Church.) Machiavelli clearly saw the newly "imperialist" papacy both as a dire threat and as an opportunity: a threat insofar as its political activities were in the service of its own traditional interests, which had no potential for being converted to the benefit of the whole peninsula; an opportunity insofar as they could be harnessed for the building of a separate, genealogically iterable, pan-Italian political entity. The overwhelming evidence for this, of course, is that *the* principal model of princely *virtù* that Machiavelli holds up for Lorenzo is Cesare Borgia, whose project was to carve out for himself a new and ever-growing state in the heart of Italy. His power depended, as does Lorenzo's, on the backing of a relative in the papacy—and his ultimate failure (according to Machiavelli) was determined exclusively by his loss of papal support on the untimely death of his father and his inability to control the selection of a successor (chapter 7; cf. chapters 8, 26).[17]

The last argument against the "seriousness" of Machiavelli's interest in the Medici is rooted in the long-standing, and oft-disputed, claim that there is a logical discontinuity between chapter 26, with its prophetic rhetoric of a redemptive, divinely inspired intervention by the Medici, deploying Machiavelli's "new modes and orders" in Italian history; and the pragmatic body of the treatise, which scorns recourse to all transcendental categories and overheated rhetoric, preferring what "is to what should be."[18] This claim has as an immediate corollary the idea that the chapter is an extrinsic and patently insincere piece of flattery tacked on to hustle the Medici, but is unrelated to Machiavelli's basic intellectual program. It is, however, possible to find a continuity, imaginative if not strictly logical, between the body of the treatise and this coda. Specifically, I would argue that chapter 26 takes up and completes the fundamental recourse to a secularized typology of exodus elaborated in chapter 6. This is not to deny that logical contradictions surface, here and elsewhere, within the treatise—but rather to assert that there is a partially submerged rhetorical economy that justifies the necessity or desirability of such contradictions. In

17. The importance of this parallelism to Machiavelli's project is noted by Gilmore in *The World of Humanism*, 77. Machiavelli, in a letter to Vettori of January 31, 1515 (letter no. 163 in Machiavelli, *Lettere*, ed. Gaeta), draws a clear analogy between Giuliano and Cesare Borgia.

18. Among those who argue for the extraneous nature of chap. 26 are: Felix Gilbert, *Machiavelli and Guicciardini*, 183, 325–26; and McCanles, *The Discourse of "Il Principe,"* 111. Among its many defenders as an integral part of the treatise are Chabod, *Scritti su Machiavelli*, 25, 69, 84–85; Gilmore, *The World of Humanism*, 135; Gramsci, *Quaderni del carcere*, 1556; and Eugene Garver, *Machiavelli and the History of Prudence* (Madison, Wis., 1987), 112–17.

other words, the problems Machiavelli causes for himself in chapter 26 are the logical outcome of his serious attempt in *The Prince* to offer counsel to the Medici and to install himself as counselor to them.

Turning now to a closer examination of the treatise itself, I take as my point of departure something that a number of structurally and logically attuned scholars have already shown[19]—that *The Prince* operates through shifting and yet interconnected oppositions (*virtù vs. fortuna*, autonomy *vs.* dependence, precept *vs.* contingency, prudence *vs.* impetuosity, and so on). Specifically, I will argue that the point of intersection between what Machiavelli is saying (the political-historical content of the treatise) and what he is doing (attempting rhetorically to translate his program into action and to transform himself into Medicean counselor) is located primarily in the treatise's continuing exploration of the tortuous relation of knowledge and power, and particularly of the importance of *autonomy*, that is, the combination in one individual of a synthesizing understanding of "new modes and orders" with the force, the arms, to impose them on a resisting populace and to defend them against intruders.[20] As we shall see, this dialectic of knowledge and power takes many forms and organizes many of the oppositions previously alluded to.[21] It also dictates the use of some of the most memorable images of the treatise: the armed *vs.* the unarmed prophet (chapter 6), the prince as soldier *vs.* the prince as lawmaker (chapter 12); the forceful lion *vs.* the crafty fox (chapter 18), the prince *vs.* his counselors (chapters 20, 22, 23); the two versions of *Fortuna* (chapter 25).

What holds all of these textual moments firmly together is an unfolding dialectic of two qualities, both of which the prince, especially the new, illegitimate prince, needs at various times to establish and maintain his power. Together these two qualities constitute Machiavellian *virtù*, the word that, of all those in Machiavelli's idiosyncratic vocabulary, has evoked the most commentary and caused the most confu-

---

19. Kahn, *"Virtù,"* 70; McCanles, *The Discourse of "Il Principe,"* e.g., 55–56.

20. On the theme of autonomy, see McCanles, *The Discourse of "Il Principe,"* xii and 51–54; and Hanna Fenichel Pitkin, *Fortune Is a Woman: Gender and Politics in the Thought of Niccolò Machiavelli* (Berkeley, Calif., 1984), esp. 3–22.

21. See, for example, chap. 7: Princes who acquire realms as a result of fortune "do not know how to hold what they have been given, and they could not do it if they did know [*non sanno e non possono tenere quel grado*]. They don't know [*non sanno*] because unless they are men of great shrewdness and vigor [*ingegno e virtù*], they cannot be expected to have the knack of command after living all their lives as private citizens [*in privata fortuna*]. And they cannot [*non possono*] because they have no troops [*forze*] of their own, which are devoted to them and trustworthy."

sion.[22] Indeed, some critics now argue that there is finally no logical and coherent definition to be found for it.[23] Part of the trouble is that the treatise elaborates its own definitions of the concept in relation to more traditional concepts of moral-political virtue, and sometimes offers the word in more conventional acceptations, if only to overturn them.[24] More important for my purposes is that the treatise often seems split between two operative definitions of *virtù:* (1) as sheer will power or personal force (which is the most common use of the word); (2) as a primarily epistemological category, more often indicated as *prudenzia* (which is the principal of the four "cardinal" *virtues* of ethical philosophy—the others being temperance, fortitude, and justice). The terms *virtuoso* and *prudente* are, in fact, consistently paired in ways that suggest in some instances that they are synonymous but more often that they are complementary qualities.[25]

22. For various interpretations of *virtù,* see Felix Gilbert, *Machiavelli and Guicciardini,* 179–200; Friedrich Meinecke, *Machiavellism: The Doctrine of Raison d'Etat and Its Place in Modern History,* trans. Douglas Scott (New Haven, Conn., 1957); Neal Wood, "Machiavelli's Concept of *Virtù* Reconsidered," *Political Studies* 15 (1967): 159–72; John Plamentatz, "In Search of Machiavellian *Virtù," The Political Calculus: Essays in Machiavelli's Philosophy* (Toronto, 1972), 157–78; J. H. Hexter, *The Vision of Politics on the Eve of the Reformation* (New York, 1973), 188–192 (chart, 203, gives all the uses of *virtù* in the treatise); Pocock, *The Machiavellian Moment,* esp. 156–82. On the question of Machiavelli's special vocabulary in general, see Fredi Chiappelli, *Studi sul linguaggio del Machiavelli* (Florence, 1952); and Chiappelli, *Nuovi studi sul linguaggio del Machiavelli* (Florence, 1969); Whitfield, *Discourses on Machiavelli;* and Hexter, *The Vision of Politics.*

23. E.g., Skinner, *The Foundations,* 138; Greene, "The End of Discourse," 72–74; McCanles, *The Discourse of "Il Principe,"* 56.

24. See Skinner, *The Foundations,* 133; McCanles, *The Discourse of "Il Principe,"* 59–65. The paradigm of this process is in chap. 8, where Machiavelli ostensibly excludes the repugnant brutality of Agathocles and Oliverotto from the definition of *virtù,* although he has just extended it to cover the violence of Borgia. Kahn, in *"Virtù,"* points out that the only obvious difference between Borgia and the other two is that his violence served a strategic purpose whereas theirs was in excess of what was needed. She argues that rather than focusing on an attempt to cling to moral respectability, chap. 8 emphasizes the inadequacy of the notion of virtue as an ethical absolute and demands the exercise of the reader's situational intelligence, his prudence (68–72). The irony is clearly highlighted by the inclusion of Oliverotto, who was one of Cesare Borgia's victims. I would also add that there is a temporal, narrative dimension to Machiavelli's redefinition of *virtù;* in other words, the equivocation about Agathocles' virtue or lack thereof is textually prior to, and prepares the way for, the systematic rejection of conventional moral virtues as politically unreliable in chaps. 15 through 18.

25. Rebhorn, in *Foxes and Lions,* 147, argues that Machiavellian *virtù* is the "conjunction of force and fraud"—but the two are not always so neatly reconciled in the text. Pocock, in *The Machiavellian Moment,* sees "prudence" as suggesting something like its modern sense of timorous caution and as the antithesis of the audacity proper to Machiavellian virtue (it *is* characteristic, however, of Guicciardini); see 268–70.

The two terms are coupled, for example, in Machiavelli's characterization of his prototype of the "new prince," Cesare Borgia, held up in chapter 7 as "uno *prudente* e *virtuoso* uomo" (a wise and able man), to be imitated by any new ruler who wants to "vincere per *forza* o per *fraude*" (overcome by force or fraud) and to "innovare con nuovi modi li ordini antichi" (revamp old [orders] with new [modes]).[26] I would suggest that not only are the first two adjectives meant to complement one another, each is also paired with a second, substantive, term: "virtuosity" with "force," "prudence" with "fraud." However, to understand fully what the virtue / prudence dyad means here and throughout, we need to go back to an earlier chapter, which links Machiavelli directly to the traditional understanding of prudence as a virtue at the boundary between intellectual and active domains.

This definitional use of *prudenzia* comes in chapter 3:

> The Romans did just what every wise ruler ought to do: you have to keep an eye, not only on present troubles, but on those of the future. . . . When you see the trouble in advance [*prevedendosi discosto*], it is easily remedied; but when you wait till it is on top of you . . . the disease is incurable. . . . That is how it goes in affairs of state: when you recognize evils in advance [*conoscendo discosto*] . . . (which requires some prudence to do [*il che non è dato se non a uno prudente*]), you can quickly cure them. . . .
>
> Thus the Romans, who could see troubles at a distance [*vedendo discosto*], always found remedies for them. . . . They never went by that saying which you hear constantly from the wiseacres of our day, that time heals all things. They trusted rather to their own character and prudence [*la virtù e la prudenzia loro*].

For Machiavelli, then, prudence is above all anticipatory foresight, and it is a basic necessity for governing in the temporal world, in combination with a *virtù* from which it will only later be fully distinguished.[27]

26. The same pairing of these terms can be found elsewhere in Machiavelli's work. See *The Discourses*, bk. 1, chap. 19: "Romulus . . . rel[ied] on prudence and on arms [*di prudenzia e di armi*]"; bk. 2, chap. 1: "virtue and prudence of a very high order"; as well as bk. 1, chap. 9; bk. 2, chap. 24. All translations are from *The Discourses of Niccolò Machiavelli*, ed. and trans. Leslie J. Walker, S.J., 2 vols. (London, 1975).

27. Other examples of Machiavelli's emphasis on the need for anticipatory foresight can be located in *Decennale*, 2.181–93; *The Discourses*, bk. 2, chaps. 18, 32. Sometimes, however, prudence appears as "practical wisdom" of a different sort: "prudence [*la prudenzia*] consists in knowing how to recognize the nature of the different dangers [*inconvenienti*] and in accepting the least bad [*el meno tristo*] as good" (*The Prince*, chap. 21; see also *The Discourses*, bk. 1, chap. 38). Mario Santoro, in *Fortuna, ragione, e prudenzia*

At this point I should make a brief excursus into the domain of intellectual history to recover a larger context for the notion of prudence, one linking it to the classical and humanist traditions of rhetoric and ethical philosophy that Machiavelli at once echoes and drastically transforms. The prudential tradition runs from Aristotle to Cicero and Macrobius, to Aquinas and Scholasticism, and to humanists from Petrarch to Machiavelli's near contemporary, Pontano.[28] In her pioneering study of that tradition, Victoria Kahn has illuminated a crucial aspect of the perennial humanist struggle to reconcile knowledge and power, by showing that rhetoric's attempts to imbue its language with wisdom converge with a mode of philosophy, prudence, which attempts to put knowledge into action.[29] The classical virtues are traditionally subdivided into the moral virtues, which govern behavior through "elective habits," and the intellectual virtues, whose province is abstract understanding of general principles rather than behavior per se. Only prudence is at once a moral and an intellectual virtue— since, as "practical wisdom," it functions to translate understanding into action and thus occupies an extremely prominent, and yet very unstable, place in classical and postclassical schemes. Its double valence makes it the perfect site for effecting a reconciliation between knowledge and power in human terms, even for a Scholastic like Saint

---

nella civiltà letteraria del Cinquecento (Naples, 1967), gives a useful catalog of occurrences of *prudenzia* and derivatives in *The Prince* (207–12) and other Machiavellian texts (215–31).

28. On the tradition of prudence and its Renaissance incarnations, see Santoro, *Fortuna, ragione, e prudenzia;* Victoria Kahn, *Rhetoric, Prudence, and Skepticism* (Ithaca, N.Y., 1985); Garver, *Machiavelli and the History of Prudence.*

29. Kahn, *Rhetoric, Prudence, and Skepticism.* The dilemma of reconciling knowledge and power, particularly in and through language, is, of course, perennial, but the specific terms in which Machiavelli defines the problem have been picked up and transformed from the debates and programs of Quattrocento humanism. It has long been recognized that the themes of "humanism" (will *vs.* intellect, active *vs.* contemplative) coalesce around the attempt of rhetoric to reconcile the constative and performative functions of language—in other words, both to *express* wisdom and to *act* accordingly. See, for example, Eugenio Garin, *L'umanesimo italiano* (Bari, 1952); Jerrold Seigel, *Rhetoric and Philosophy in Renaissance Humanism* (Princeton, N.J., 1968); Jack D'Amico, *Knowledge and Power in the Renaissance* (Washington, D.C., 1977). The importance of rhetoric for the humanists reflected a perceived crisis in (Scholastic) philosophy, which was unable to turn wisdom into ethical action and was thus seen by humanists as irrelevant. As I too argue in discussions of Quattrocento educational poetics in *Ariosto's Bitter Harmony: Crisis and Evasion in the Italian Renaissance* (Princeton, N.J., 1987), esp. chap. 2, Renaissance rhetorical theorists attempt to solve that problem by rejecting purely speculative thought in favor of a language of moral persuasion and political action, but they then face the inverse problem—that this language may be effective, powerful even, but still lack any provable grounding in truth.

Thomas.[30] At the same time, it is the perfectly problematic node at which the indeterminacy and instability of the relation between knowing and acting shows up and causes trouble. In Machiavelli's case, as we will see, prudence does hold out a tempting promise of bridging thought and action[31]—but only with the supplement of a forceful *virtù* that brings with it its own military arms. With that supplement, it is a defining attribute of a dynamic and visionary politics; without it, it slips passively toward the modern acceptation of the term as a timorous caution. And the very need for such a supplement is a de facto admission that traditional prudence, and the humanist ethical-rhetorical project that it grounds, are typically unable to carry out its mission of bridging theory and practice.

Machiavelli also draws upon at least three closely intertwined specifications concerning prudence that are commonly found in the tradition and that have a direct bearing on my concerns. The first was adumbrated in my reading of chapter 3. As the temporalized use of philosophical intelligence, prudence is itself always divided into three parts according to the basic temporal divisions—it is memory as regards the past; it is understanding as regards the present; and it is foresight as regards the future.[32] Arguably, however, these are not three equal partners—memory of the past and understanding of the present are presumably in the service of action that is based on foresight of possibilities and that attempts to (re)shape the future accordingly. This conceptual privilege of foresight is reflected etymologically insofar as "prudence" derives directly from *pro-videre*, to foresee; thus

30. Thomas Aquinas, *Summa Theologiae,* vol. 23, ed. W. D. Hughes (Oxford, 1969), 1.2ae, q. 58, art. 3–5; vol. 36, ed. Thomas Gilby (Oxford, 1974), 2.2ae, q. 47, art. 1–5. Aquinas draws on the distinction between moral and intellectual virtues in Aristotle and, like him, makes prudence an intellectual virtue though with ethical implications (see *Nicomachean Ethics* 1.13–2.1 [1103A] and 6.2–5 [1139A–1141B]; Cicero, *De officiis* 1.43.153; Macrobius, *Commentarium in somnium Scipionis* 1.8; Dante, *Convivio* 4.17). As Santoro, in *Fortuna, ragione, e prudenzia,* suggests (esp. 45), the most important humanist texts are Petrarch, *De remediis utriusque fortunae;* Coluccio Salutati, *De fato et fortuna;* Pontano, *De fortuna* and *De prudentia.*

31. See Gilmore, *The World of Humanism,* 132. Gilmore's definition of Machiavellian *virtù* is surprisingly close to the traditional definition of prudence: "the ability to carry out in practice an abstract scheme" and the "combination of intelligence and will, thought and action." On the theme of prudence in Machiavelli generally, see Santoro, *Fortuna, ragione, e prudenzia,* 179–231; Kahn, *Rhetoric, Prudence, and Skepticism;* Garver, *Machiavelli and the History of Prudence;* Pocock, *The Machiavellian Moment,* 24–25, 198, 232.

32. Cicero, *De inventione* 2.13.160; Aquinas, *Summa Theologiae* 2.2ae, q. 48 (ed. Gilby, 36:52–59).

the virtue as a whole takes its name from its third and most important part.[33]

The second specification is that *prudenzia* is closely linked precisely to the activity of giving counsel. Aquinas, whose entries on virtue and prudence in *Summa Theologiae* are in fact a compendium of topoi that arrive from the classics and persist into humanism, argues that prudence and counsel are intimately related.[34] He states specifically that "prudence is of good counsel about those things which pertain to the whole of a person's life and to the final end of human life."[35] And he pairs prudential counsel specifically with "precepts" (that is, with the teaching of rules), putting both directly under the auspices of "foresight [*providentia*]."[36] It is in accordance with this tradition, although in a very different spirit, that Machiavelli typically associates prudence with the counselor—as *virtù* and arms are the province of the prince.

The third specification is one that seems, at first, antithetical to Machiavelli's secularized, politicized definition of prudence, but that does have relevance for *The Prince*, as we will see. Prudence, as a human virtue, has a special relationship, in both the Scholastic and humanist traditions, to matters divine. Aquinas, again, is instructive. He makes the connection, obvious on linguistic grounds, between divine *providentia*, or Providence, and prudential *providentia*, or foresight, if only in order to distinguish them clearly: divine Providence takes into its omniscient field of vision "all things which are done for the sake of an end and *necessary*"; human prudence merely concerns the *contingentia operabilia* (contingent matters of human action), the operative distinction being between transcendent necessity and temporal contingency.[37] At the same time, however, he makes clear that human

---

33. Aquinas, *Summa Theologiae* 2.2ae, q. 49, art. 6 (ed. Gilby, 36:74–76). See also Boethius, *The Consolation of Philosophy*, 5.6; Isidore of Seville, *Etymologies*, bk. 10. An important modern reading of the problem of foresight in Machiavelli is in Gramsci, *Quaderni del carcere*, 1810–11.

34. Aquinas, *Summa Theologiae* 2.2ae, q. 52, art. 1–2 (ed. Gilby, 36:108–14). See also q. 49, art. 1, obj. 3 and resp. 3 (36:60); and q. 49, art. 4, obj. 2.

35. Aquinas, *Summa Theologiae* 1.2ae, q. 57, art. 4, resp. 3 (ed. Hughes, 23:53).

36. Aquinas, *Summa Theologiae* 2.2ae, q. 49, art. 6, resp. 3 (ed. Gilby, 36:76).

37. Aquinas, *Summa Theologiae* 2.2ae, q. 49, art. 6, resp. (ed. Gilby, 36:76). Pocock, in *The Machiavellian Moment* (28–30, 39), suggests the way in which a traditional theological politics supplemented prudence with a reliance on divine, providential guidance, associating the latter with a prophetic interpretation of history (e.g., 31–33); he does not, however, fully appreciate the conceptual connection between prudential and prophetic foresight, and hence tends to underestimate the importance of *prudenzia* in Machiavelli's text (e.g., 62, 238), even as he clearly indicates the vestigial presence of a Christian providential politics therein.

counsel, as part of prudence, is a *gift* of the Holy Spirit,[38] known doctrinally as *the Counselor*—and thus prudential counsel has an access to the wisdom of Providence that verges on the domain of prophecy.

This connection between prudence and Providence through the gift of the Holy Spirit is crucial because it guarantees not only that prudence as intellectual virtue is grounded in truth but also that as moral virtue it is grounded in goodness. Notwithstanding their polemical differences from Scholasticism, the early advocates of humanist ethics and politics—Coluccio Salutati, Leonardo Bruni, Lorenzo Valla—whose work most strongly asserted the possibility of a prudential politics, also grounded it and its associated rhetoric in theological and transcendent categories. In this Christian humanism, underlying human ethics, politics, and rhetoric is the Logos, God's Word, through which knowledge and power, truth and goodness, are perfectly united.[39] Without that grounding, as Aquinas shows himself to be all too aware, prudence is likely to degenerate into its opposing vice, *fraud* (*fraus, dolus,* and *astutia* are all given as the sinful counterparts of "practical wisdom"),[40] just as an unguided *fortitudo* is likely to decay into brute force.[41]

That this nightmare inversion does take place in Machiavelli we saw earlier in chapter 7, where *virtù* is aligned with force and prudence with fraud. But it is in chapter 6, "On New Principalities Acquired with One's Own Arms and Virtue," that the knowledge / power dialectic is given its fullest and most revealing treatment, and all the more so in light of the connections just established between prudence and prophecy, as well as between prudence and the counselor. This is the chapter in which Machiavelli turns to the great classical models of princes who successfully founded new states, based on "new modes and orders"—Moses, Cyrus, Romulus, Theseus—in preparation for the introduction of Cesare Borgia as contemporary exemplar for Lorenzo and his family. Moses, the prophet who was also a political founder is, despite Machiavelli's weak disclaimer, clearly the prototype of the visionary prince who imposes a new political order by means of his own resourceful *virtù* (as the chapter heading alone makes clear). In the same spirit Machiavelli will insist, using the hapless visionary priest Savonarola as a counterexample, that inevitably "i profeti armati vinsono, e li disarmati ruinorono" (armed prophets always win and unarmed prophets

---

38. Aquinas, *Summa Theologiae* 2.2ae, q. 52, art. 1 (ed. Gilby, 36:108–10).

39. On the Christian dimension of humanism, see Charles Trinkaus, *In Our Image and Likeness: Humanity and Divinity in Italian Humanist Thought,* 2 vols. (Chicago, 1970).

40. Aquinas, *Summa Theologiae* 2.2ae, q. 55, art. 3–5 (ed. Gilby, 36:152–58).

41. Kahn, *Rhetoric, Prudence, and Skepticism,* 186.

lose).[42] As I have already suggested, the visionary knowledge of the prophet clearly is a more powerful version of the "prudential" foresight advocated in chapter 3. But here to prophetic *provvidenzia* is added the ironic specification that without autonomous forces, vision will never impose itself. In other words, behind this equivocal image of the *profeta armato*, and beyond its evident irony, is the felt need to unite knowledge (prophecy) with power (arms) in one individual who can, as it were "counsel himself."

A curious double process—at once serious and ironic—unfolds in the chapter. By applying the word "prophecy" to temporal political concerns and by equating secular rulers, like Romulus and company, with a biblical patriarch, Moses, Machiavelli elevates worldly politics to a level of prestige traditionally reserved for matters divine[43]— effecting the very confusion Aquinas and others worked so hard to avoid. At the same time, he makes it perfectly clear that Moses, although he had God as his "preceptor" (*precettore*) was simply a lucky and talented ruler like the others, and that his success was based on the combination of his own political intelligence and autonomous arms. He thus turns "transcendence" from the (Platonic, Christian, humanist) ground of all human politics into a convenient political fiction. And with the sneering reference to the prophets who are "disarmati," Machiavelli completes the process of removing the political seer from the realm of transcendent vision and divinely instilled power to a purely secular level, thereby reducing prophecy itself to a role equivalent to

42. In *The Discourses*, bk. 1, chap. 11, Machiavelli gives a patently demystifying account of how Savonarola created "effects of prophecy" among his usually skeptical Florentine audience: "It did not seem to the people of Florence that they were either ignorant or rude, yet they were persuaded by Friar Girolamo Savonarola that he had converse with God. I do not propose to decide whether it was so or not, because of so great a man one ought to speak with reverence; but I do say that vast numbers believed it was so, without having seen him do anything out of the common whereby to make them believe; for his life, his teaching, and the topic on which he preached, were sufficient to make them trust him [*sufficienti a fargli prestare fede*]." (See also *The Discourses*, bk. 1, chaps. 45, 56 and *Decennale*, 1.154–65.) Letter no. 3 in Machiavelli, *Lettere*, ed. Gaeta, recounts in detail the rhetorical effects of two Savonarolian sermons of 1497. That the sermons in question took their texts from Exodus (and reiterated the friar's warning against the danger of a "tyrant" and his prophecy of a divine political mission for Florence) suggests that already in 1497, Machiavelli had linked Moses and Savonarola. In addition, Machiavelli records that Savonarola at one point quoted Aquinas on *prudentia* as practical wisdom and elaborated on the theme of serving God with "greatest prudence and observation of the times [*somma prudentia et observantia de' tempi*]." References to Savonarola also appear in letters nos. 138 and 184.

43. My argument here closely follows that of Pocock in *The Machiavellian Moment*, esp. 171 and 190, as well as that of Kahn in "*Virtù*," 79.

that traditionally played by *prudenzia,* an entirely human mode of vision. No wonder that in a later chapter Machiavelli takes the traditional topos of attributing the "scourge" of foreign invaders to the sins of the invaded and turns it on its head by making clear that the sins in question were those arising from an imprudent stupidity (in the use of untrustworthy mercenaries) rather than moral turpitude (chapter 12).

Here then is one of those fundamental Machiavellian paradoxes, perhaps the most fundamental: the theological conflation of power and knowledge in the divinely inspired prophet is both dismissed as the discarded, delusive substitute for a truly pragmatic politics and embraced as the structural model for Machiavelli's alternative—the secular *profeta armato.* The extent of the degradation that this "detheologizing" of prophecy and parallel "theologizing" of secular political categories implies is revealed in the following chapter, where, as we have already noted, the "modern prince's" *virtù* and *prudenzia* are translated into horrific violence and shameless fraud in the exemplary career of Cesare Borgia. And it is given its full and famous theorization in chapters 15 to 18, where the traditional moral virtues are systematically redefined, by inversion, to suit the new, detheologized reality of a world in which politics is based not on right but on pragmatic success.

Chapter 6, however, not only sets out the basic parameters within which the successful prince (any prince) must operate, it also establishes strong parallels between the circumstances of Machiavelli, who is offering "nuovi modi e ordini" for implementation by the Medici, and those of the armed, and especially unarmed, prophet. Machiavelli begins the chapter by ostentatiously calling attention to the examples that he is offering for imitation by his reader, an unspecified "tu," who, like Lorenzo, might be in the position of ruling "principati al tutto nuovi" (states completely new). The structural split between Machiavelli and his reader already predicts a failure on *both* parts to imitate the *profeti armati* who are such because they represent the union of knowledge and power in one individual. That anticipated failure is marked quite specifically by the equivocal terms in which the operation of imitation is described. Imitation, it appears, is actually a sign of weakness and of an inability to act autonomously and innovatively, and it can never be completely successful, precisely because the imitator is never the equal of the imitated: "Men almost always prefer to walk in paths marked out by others and pattern their actions through imitation [*imitazioni*]. Even if he [in fact: "tu"] cannot follow other people's paths in every respect, or attain to the merit [*virtù*] of his originals, a prudent man [*uno uomo prudente*] should always follow the footsteps of the great and imitate those who have been supreme."[44] This account of imitation as the last refuge of the mediocre is followed by the image of the prudent archer who hits his target by aiming much higher and farther than he can, in reality, hope to shoot, and then by the list of great men, biblical and classical, whose success depended on originality and autonomy rather than on the imitation of precepts offered by someone else. The contradiction is patent and potentially devastating for Machiavelli's openly thematized role as pedagogue: how can one "imitate innovation"?

The connection to Machiavelli can be seen most clearly, however, in the pathetic case of the would-be redeemer of Florence, Savonarola, whose fiery execution in 1498 roughly coincided with the date that Machiavelli entered the employ of the republican government. Savonarola, of course, was himself the author of a treatise on good government that was greatly indebted to Aquinas, a fierce critic of papal interference in secular politics, and a visionary advocate of a pan-Italian union to be constructed under Florentine leadership.[45] Thus although Machiavelli's treatment of Savonarola is obviously contemptuous, it is also evident that the *profeta disarmato* prefigures his own predicament as the possessor of "new modes and orders" who lacks arms of his own to put them into effect.[46] In chapter 6, the author thus performs a complicated operation—indicating the pragmatic necessity of combining vision and power in one individual, but at the same time

44. The subject of imitation is raised again in chap. 7, where Borgia, despite his failure, is offered as an example for imitation; chap. 14 ("a prince should read history [*leggere le istorie*] and reflect on the actions of great men [*li uomini eccellenti*] . . . so that he can imitate their successes and avoid their defeats"); chap. 18 (where the prince is urged to "imitate" both fox and lion). In chap. 19, however, Machiavelli points to the dangers of inappropriate imitation—imitating models that do not apply to your own circumstances is ultimately disastrous. Useful critics on the question of imitation in *The Prince* include Pitkin, *Fortune Is a Woman*, 268–73; Greene, "The End of Discourse," esp. 67–68; Kahn, "*Virtù*," 64–66; Garver, *Machiavelli and the History of Prudence*, 74; Hampton, *Writing from History*, 62–79.

45. On Savonarola's *Trattato*, see Donald Weinstein, *Savonarola and Florence: Prophecy and Patriotism in the Renaissance* (Princeton, N.J., 1970). On Machiavelli's possible debt to this text see J. H. Whitfield, "Savonarola and the Purpose of the *Prince*," *Modern Language Review* 44 (1949): 44–59, reprinted in Whitfield, *Discourses on Machiavelli*, 87–110. On the general question of Machiavelli's stance toward Savonarola, see Gramsci, *Quaderni del carcere*, 1578; Luigi Russo, *Machiavelli*, 3d ed. (Bari, 1949); Felix Gilbert, *Machiavelli and Guicciardini*, 144–52; Chabod, *Scritti su Machiavelli*, 267–73; Pocock, *The Machiavellian Moment*, especially 104–13; and Delio Cantimori's entry on Machiavelli in *Il Cinquencento*, vol. 4 of *Storia della letteratura italiana*, ed. Emilio Cecchi and Natalino Sapegno (Milan, 1966). See also n. 42 to this essay.

46. Chabod, *Scritti su Machiavelli*, 5–6, 81.

pointing indirectly to the probable failure of that union when it comes to the action of the prudent (if impotent) author on his powerful (if mediocre, or even stupid, reader[s]) and hence to Machiavelli's proposed symbiosis with the Medici.

An attempt to elide and even to resolve the tension between prudence and *virtù*, prophecy and arms, Machiavelli and Lorenzo, is carried out, rhetorically and dynamically, as the treatise unfolds. The first half of the treatise, following the explicit emphasis of chapter 6, stresses arms and their use, and hence the role of the prince himself. The process starts immediately in chapter 7, with Cesare Borgia as the "new prince" par excellence. Borgia, as I have already noted, is specifically said to unite prudence with *virtù*, fraud with force. But the emphasis clearly falls on the second term in each case, since his every labor during his short career was aimed at acquiring the independent arms that would stabilize his power and allow him to expand it.[47] Borgia thus not only is a model of the prince but also specifically figures the *treatise's* drive to ground its author's political intelligence in real, autonomous, power. This section of *The Prince* culminates in the crucial chapters, 12 to 14, which teach *the* lesson of the treatise: the folly of relying on mercenary or auxiliary troops—the absolute need for the prince, and for Italy in general, to rely exclusively on their own military resources.

Beginning with the pivotal chapter 15, however, a dramatic shift takes place that constitutes a de facto contradiction of what has gone before. From this point on, provident foresight of contingencies and the clever tricking of one's enemies become explicitly predominant over brute force and the autonomous possession of one's own arms. Moreover, at this point Machiavelli reintroduces himself into the text in order to stress the unique realism and pragmatism of his political vision—its capacity to identify things as they truly are and thereby to provide counsel that can effect significant change in the realities it identifies:

> I know the subject has been treated frequently before, and I'm
> afraid people will think me rash for trying to do so again,
> especially since I intend to differ in this discussion from what
> others have said. But since I intend to write something useful to
> an understanding reader [*utile a chi la intende*], it seemed better

47. The lesson of Cesare, however, is equivocal in this regard (as in every other)—since what is most striking is that he got so far without arms, simply on the strength of cleverness and foresight. Moreover, Borgia's downfall is specifically attributed not to the lack of his own army but to his inability to foresee the consequence of Julius II's election as Pope after his father's death.

to go after the real truth [*la verità effettuale*] of the matter than to repeat what people have imagined [*la immaginazione di essa*]. A great many . . . have imagined [*si sono immaginati*] states and princedoms such as nobody ever saw or knew in the real world, for there is such a difference between the way we really live [*come si vive*] and the way we ought to live [*come si doverebbe vivere*] that [those] who [neglect] the real [*quello che si fa*] for the ideal [*quello che si doverrebbe fare*] will learn how to accomplish [their] ruin, not [their] salvation.

Nonetheless, even though Machiavelli refuses the idealizing politics of Plato, Aristotle, and their heirs, reducing them to the status of imaginative fictions, this passage points obliquely to its own internal contradictions and to its probable failure to put its author's "new modes and orders" into effect. As I will soon show, "realism" ("come si vive" [how things are]) and "pragmatism" ("come si fa" [how one is to act]), despite their apparent affinities, do not necessarily coexist harmoniously in Machiavelli's text. In fact, the claim of dwelling exclusively in the empirical "here and now" is patently belied, most obviously in chapter 26, by the projection of a future significantly different from the present. And I would argue that Machiavelli surreptitiously elides the difference between realistic description and pragmatic exhortation through his use of the phrase *la verità effettuale,* which suggests with equal plausibility the "factual truth" of realism and the "truth with effects" of pragmatism.[48]

Even more immediately, the explicit reintroduction of Machiavelli as author-counselor and source of radically "new modes and orders" should remind us that the imperative of military autonomy (the need to possess one's own arms) sketched in chapters 12–14 had its roots in the even more fundamental autonomy of the *profeta armato,* one person in whom are united arms and vision (chapter 6). Inasmuch as this statement makes its effectiveness dependent on the contingent connection with a powerful reader who will both *understand* it and *use* it (its truth is only "utile a chi la intende"), it potentially belies its own claims to pragmatism and slides precariously into the utopian domain of the

48. Gramsci, in *Quaderni del carcere,* 1578, is clearly aware of the complexity of the term: "The politician in action . . . grounds himself on the 'effectual truth', but what is this 'effectual truth'? Is it perhaps something static and immobile? or rather a relationship of forces in continuous movement and mutation of equilibrium? To apply the will to the creation of a new equilibrium of really existent and operative forces . . . is always to move on the terrain of 'effectual reality' but only to dominate and overcome it. . . . The 'should be' is thus concrete—in fact, it is the only realistic and historicist interpretation of reality" (my translation).

profeta disarmato. Machiavelli's own *immaginazione*, then, is precisely the transparency of his text to a historical world from which he is excluded—an exclusion of which, to be exact, the text itself is both a product and an ostentatious sign.[49]

The sequence begun in chapter 15 culminates in chapter 18, "How Faith Should Be Kept by Princes." Superficially, the chapter seems to confirm that knowledge and power can be united in one person, who is doubly imaged as reconciling dual tendencies: those of the centaur, who is a combination of human and animal; and those of an animal that is doubly, monstrously bestial—capable of using both "the lion" of force and "the fox" of fraud. Although Machiavelli begins the chapter by advocating the use of both beasts, in fact the emphasis clearly falls not on forceful, autonomous *virtù* as it did in the first half of the treatise, but rather on fraud, traditionally, as it is for Dante in the *Inferno*, an intellectual sin, contrasted with the (lesser) sins of violence.[50] The importance of the chapter for my theme, however, goes considerably beyond this basic reversal. The allusion to Dante, as it turns out, is not mine but Machiavelli's.[51] John Freccero, in his essay entitled "Medusa and the Madonna of Forlì," included in this volume, shows that notwithstanding the classical precedents (especially Ciceronian) for the lion / fox pairing, Machiavelli is most specifically echoing these famous words put by Dante into the mouth of Guido da Montefeltro in *Inferno*, canto 27: "l'opere mie non furon leonine, ma di volpe" (my works were those of the fox, not of the lion).[52]

49. See the *Discorso sopra il riformare lo stato di Firenze* (ca. 1520), in Niccolò Machiavelli, *Tutte le opere di Niccolò Machiavelli*, ed. Francesco Flora and Carlo Cordié (Verona, 1950), 2:538. There Machiavelli speaks again of those who, "not having been able to make a republic in fact, did it in writing, like Aristotle, Plato, and many others, who wished to show the world that if they were not able to found a civic life [*un vivere civile*] as Solon and Licurgus had, it was not because of their ignorance but of their impotence to put it into action [*dalla impotenza di metterlo in atto*]" acknowledging that the problem is not the political ideas of these writers but their (and his own) lack of power to put those ideas into effect (my translation). The treatise is addressed to Pope Leo.

50. For Dante, interestingly enough, centaurs are the figures of bestial violence (*Inferno*, canto 12), although one centaur in particular is associated with fraud in the form of theft (*Inferno*, canto 25).

51. There are numerous analogies between the circumstances of the Machiavelli of *The Prince* and those of Dante. Both (1) are political exiles; (2) write treatises on the prince after participating in republican governments; (3) call upon princes who could realize their political projects; and (4) locate the cause of the Italian political crisis in the Church's meddling in temporal affairs. Machiavelli refers frequently to Dante—for instance, in the letter to Vettori of December 10, 1513 (no. 140) cited earlier; see *Asino*, esp. 2.20–22. See also his contestation of Dante's *De vulgari eloquentia* in the *Dialogo intorno alla nostra lingua* (whose authorship has been regularly questioned).

52. Cicero, *De officiis*, trans. Walter Miller, in the Loeb Classical Library (Cambridge, Mass., 1961), 1.13.41: "fraus quasi vulpeculae, vis leonis videtur; utrumque homine alien-

The most obvious points of overlap, as Freccero indicates, are that (1) Machiavelli, like Guido, uses the lion only to set up the fox, whose wiles are what really concern him; and (2) Guido, like Ulysses, his companion in the eighth "bolgia," and like Machiavelli, is a "counselor of fraud"—first because he specifically counsels Pope Boniface VIII to make promises that he will not keep, and then because what he counsels is ultimately fraudulent itself. (It cannot save either Guido or Boniface from eternal damnation.)[53] Along with these resemblances, there is an obvious difference: Guido, by his placement in hell, is shown to have violated a moral imperative grounded not in the contingencies of history but in a transcendent faith in God's absolute knowledge and power. Machiavelli, by contrast, has abandoned any notion of transcendent casualty and consequently valorizes as politically effective what Dante damned; Dante's ontological-ethical vision, like Plato's philosophical one in chapter 15, has become merely the utopian product of a human (poetic) imagination. Nonetheless, cantos 26 and 27 are just as concerned as Machiavelli's chapter 18 with the logical descent of classical ethics and metaphysics into animal violence and unscrupulous cunning. And, remarkably, those cantos too place the role of the ethical and political counselor in the context of degraded prophecy.[54]

---

issimum, sed fraus odio digna maiore" (fraud seems to belong to the cunning fox, force to the lion; both are wholly unworthy of man, but fraud is the more contemptible). On Machiavelli's use of the image see the essay by Ezio Raimondi included in this volume; see also Marcia L. Colish, "Cicero's *De officiis* and Machiavelli's *Prince*," *Sixteenth Century Journal* 9 (1978): 81–93.

53. More generally, on the shared question of fraud in Dante and Machiavelli, without reference to *Inferno*, canto 27, see Joseph Anthony Mazzeo, *Renaissance and Seventeenth-Century Studies* (New York, 1964), 90–116. Surprisingly, Sebastiano De Grazia, in *Machiavelli in Hell* (Princeton, N.J., 1989), fails to develop this connection.

54. Canto 27 and the episode involving Guido are the degraded aftermath of the Dantean Ulysses' fatally deceptive exhortation of his crew to "virtute e canoscenza" (virtuous action and intellectual knowledge) in canto 26. Beginning with the opening image of Phalarus enclosed within his bull, the canto is shot through with the imagery of men become beasts, as if the metamorphic powers of Circe had been relocated in contemporary Italy. In his long response to Guido's question about the current state of affairs in Romagna, Dante refers to the ill-fated and ill-advised *tiranni* of the region by their bestial *stemme*, preparing the ground for Guido's invocation of the man-beast topos in his fox/lion comparison (and anticipating Machiavelli's insistence on the failures of Italian leadership throughout the peninsula). Moreover, the flames that cover the "false counselors" specifically parody the Pentecostal descent of flames upon Christ's disciples, infusing them with the prophetic fervor of the Holy Spirit, the Counselor. The sinners' false prophecy is structurally contrasted with Dante's own potentially presumptuous assumption of a visionary prophetic role, since he compares himself to Elisha succeeding Elijah after the latter's transumption (canto 26, lines 34–36). In this regard, see James G. Truscott, "Ulysses and Guido: *Inferno* xxvi–xxvii," *Dante Studies* 91 (1973): 47–72; Giu-

Most to the point for my purposes is the way the hidden analogy between Guido's advice to Boniface and Machiavelli's to the Medici changes chapter 18 from an abstract precept ("Princes should never keep faith when it is to their advantage not to") to an oblique meditation on the historical predicament of its author, and specifically on his own hoped-for role as counselor. Ezio Raimondi has already suggested that if Chiron exemplifies the desirability of a fusion of humanity and bestiality in the prince himself, he also, as the teacher of Achilles, figures Machiavelli's vocation as educator of potentates.[55] The covert Dantean allusion, however, points to a much more specific dramatization of his potential connection with the Medici. As I have already argued, Machiavelli repeatedly stresses that the key to Borgia's temporary success, and the most promising sign for Lorenzo's future conquest, is the alliance they can effect between their own secular political resources and the power of the Church—one as son of Alexander VI, the other as nephew of Leo X. Alexander VI is in fact Machiavelli's sterling example of the power of deceit in chapter 18—and an obvious heir to Dante's Boniface in *Inferno* canto 27, a canto that, through its evocations both of the ill-fated donation of Constantine and of the Guelf/Ghibelline struggles, is clearly focused on the abusive role of the Church in the domain of secular politics.

The final piece of the puzzle is the recognition that if Machiavelli is analogous to the foxy guide, Guido, then his ultimate audience, his own Boniface, the one to supply the force to carry out Machiavelli's recommendation, is precisely a Lion in name, Leo X. In chapter 11 on ecclesiastical principalities, he had described Leo as the legitimate and legitimating heir to the imperial, expansionist papacy of Alexander and Julius: "his present holiness Pope Leo has found the papacy . . . strong; and we may hope that as his predecessors made it great by force of arms, he, by his generosity and countless other talents [*la bontà et infinite altre sua virtù*], will make it even greater and more to be revered." Here, in light of the systematic redefinition and ironizing of *virtù*, the real meaning of that wish is revealed: Leo, like all good princes, should merely possess the appearance of traditional, moral virtue, meanwhile making the best possible use of both the fox and the lion—including the employment of Machiavelli (who would then be the object of his "bontà"). But the evoked memory of the story of Guido also reveals Machiavelli's underlying fear of an unhealable split between himself and the patron he avidly pursues: betrayed by

---

seppe Mazzotta, *Dante, Poet of the Desert: History and Allegory in the "Divine Comedy"* (Princeton, N.J., 1979), 90–94.

55. See the essay by Ezio Raimondi in this volume.

Boniface's unkeepable promise of salvation, Guido earns only damnation for *his* gift of counsel.[56]

The possibility that the prince might betray his counselor, of course, is perfectly in keeping with the counsel that Machiavelli gives here (and throughout): that the prince, like Dante's Boniface, should promise anything and deliver nothing, if necessary to achieve his ends. One has only to look as far as the grisly end of Remirro de Orco, Borgia's ill-fated "executive officer" in Bologna, to verify the point (chapter 7). In fact, three of the next five chapters contain explicit meditations on the relationship of prince and subordinates which continue the displacement from power to knowledge, *virtù* to prudence.[57]

In chapter 20 Machiavelli discusses the general question of whom a new prince should trust after taking power: "Especially when they are new, princes have often found more fidelity [*fede*] and serviceability in men who were at first suspect than in men who originally enjoyed the royal confidence."[58] It is hard to deny the truth of Machiavelli's observation that those who assisted a new prince in displacing an old one are typically motivated not by love of the new but by discontent with

56. In letter no. 138, written to Vettori on August 26, 1513, Machiavelli pairs the fox and the lion, identifying himself as a fox at first in fear of the lion and then curiously observing him; see the Raimondi essay. See also *Asino* 6. 52–60; 7. 31–36. Pitkin, in *Fortune Is a Woman*, notes, without reference to the Dantean allusion, that the fox matches up with Machiavelli as counselor and the lion pairs with the prince (34).

57. J. H. Whitfield, in *Discourses on Machiavelli*, 25, notes the relevance of chaps. 20 and 22 to Machiavelli's circumstances, in the service of an interpretation rather different from mine. Pitkin, in *Fortune Is a Woman* (30–34, 46), and Rebhorn, in *Foxes and Lions* (82–83), both argue that Machiavelli stages his own condition through a series of counselor figures, including Ligurio in *Mandragola*. In *The Discourses*, bk. 3, chap. 35, Machiavelli notes the (mortal) dangers to the counselor who will be blamed if his advice is not followed by success.

58. Note the discussions in chap. 3 of the dangers to a new prince from those who helped bring him to power from within the city: "You cannot stay friends with those who put you in power, because you can never satisfy them as they expected"; and later on, "The man who makes another powerful ruins himself. The reason is that he gets power either by shrewdness [*con industria*] or by strength [*con forza*], and both qualities are suspect to the man who has been given the power" (Adams's translation). Compare them with the discussion in chap. 9 of what to do with the *grandi* of a newly conquered city: "Either they behave so as to be entirely obligated to you, or not. Those that obligate themselves, and are not greedy, must be honored and loved; those that aren't obligated to serve you, must be considered in two ways. If they do this from pusillanimity and a natural defect of the soul, then you have to make use of those that possess good counsel [*sono di buono consiglio*], because in prosperity they bring honor to you and in adversity there is nothing to fear from them. But when they artfully and ambitiously refuse to obligate themselves, it is a sign that they think more of themselves than of you [*pensono più a sé che te*]; and of these the prince must be wary and fear them as if they were open enemies" (my translation).

the old, and in the end are not likely to be satisfied by him. It is, however, equally hard to deny the tone of special pleading and barely disguised self-interest implicit in the insistent claim that "if the men who at the beginning of a regime are considered its enemies are in need of support to maintain themselves, the prince will have no trouble at all in winning them over. They are the more deeply obliged to serve him faithfully [*con fede*] because they know that only good service will cancel the bad impression [*opinione sinistra*] that he had of them." And the connections to Machiavelli become even more pressing if one compares these words to the protestations of habitual *fede* with which he closes the December 10 letter to Vettori.[59]

In chapters 22 and 23 Machiavelli tackles the question of counsel (and of its traditional, pernicious counterpart, adulation) directly, with the implicit secondary purpose of assuaging any fears that the brilliance of his intellect might rouse in Lorenzo or Leo. The first move in chapter 22 is to assign to the prince a special *prudenzia* precisely in the choice of his *ministri*. This leads to the well-known distinction between the "minds" ("cervelli") which see for themselves (the counselor—read Machiavelli), and those which discern what others understand (the prince—read Lorenzo/Leo). The theme is elaborated in chapter 23, which includes specific instructions as to how the prince can maintain control over his advisers (by, for example, accepting advice only when he himself solicits it) and avoid the hazards of lying adulation:

Many people think that a prince who is considered prudent [*dà di sé opinione di prudente*] gets that reputation, not on his own merits, but because he has good counselors around him [*li buoni consigli che lui ha d'intorno*]. That's completely wrong. For this is a general and unfailing rule: that a prince who is not shrewd [*savio*] himself cannot get good counseling [*non può essere consigliato bene*], unless he just happens to put himself in the hands of a single able man who makes all the decisions and is very knowing [*fussi uomo prudentissimo*]. In such a case, an ignorant prince might rule well, but it could not last, because in short order the counselor would take over the supreme power. If he consults with several different advisers [*consigliandosi con più di uno*], a prince without wisdom

---

59. Letter no. 140 in Machiavelli, *Lettere*, ed. Gaeta: "and of my honesty [*la fede mia*] there should be no doubt, because having always preserved my honesty [*avendo sempre observato la fede*], I shall hardly now learn to break it; and he who has been honest and good [*fedele et buono*] for forty-three years, as I have, cannot change his nature [*mutare natura*]; and as a witness to my honesty and goodness [*della fede et bontà mia*] I have my poverty."

will never get the different opinions coordinated [*consigli uniti*],
will never make a policy.

The irony here is that Machiavelli, in reassuring the prince that his own
intrinsic prudence will enable him to maintain control over his wily
adviser(s), at first verges on a form of deceitful adulation, but then
raises precisely the fearful specter of a symbiotic relationship gone
awry, one in which the dependent, yet ambitious counselor displaces
his overly trusting master (a circumstance common enough in the recent history of the Italian peninsula).[60]
The extent of Machiavelli's anxious concern with presenting himself
as a necessary and yet unthreatening supplement of knowledge to
princely force is most apparent in the criteria he gives in chapter 22 for
recognizing a faithful counselor:

> There is one way for a prince to judge of a minister [*ministro*] that
> never fails. When you notice that your minister is thinking more
> of himself than of you [*pensare più a sé che a te*], and that
> everything he does serves his own interest [*l'utile suo*], a man like
> this will never make a good minister; you cannot possibly trust
> him. The man who holds a prince's kingdom in his hand should
> think, not of himself, but of the prince.

This assertion of the counselor's, and by implication his own, selflessness flies directly in the face of a fundamental Machiavellian claim
about the innate evil and self-interestedness of human nature, on
which he had in fact founded his new politics of detheologized and
demoralized *virtù*.[61] And the extent to which this new position is merely tactical (one might say, "Machiavellian," in the spirit of chapter 18
itself) can be seen in the next chapter when it serves his rhetorical turn
to adopt the original, and antithetical, stance:

> Each of the ministers [*consiglieri*] will think of his own interests
> [*alla proprietà sua*]. . . . Ministers are bound to act this way, because
> men will always turn out badly for you unless they are forced to
> be good. Hence I conclude that the prince's wisdom [*buoni*

---

60. Notwithstanding this hint, it is hard to agree with Rebhorn, *Foxes and Lions* (esp.
224) that Machiavelli is a prince masquerading as a counselor.

61. E.g., chap. 17: "Love [of a subject for his prince] is a link of obligation which men,
because they are rotten [*per essere li uomini tristi*], will break any time they think doing so
serves their advantage," which leads to the famously cynical claim that "men are quicker
to forget the death of a father than the loss of a patrimony."

consigli] does not come from having good policies [*consigli*] recommended to him; on the contrary, good policy, whoever suggests it, comes from the wisdom [*prudenzia*] of the prince.

The gap between what Machiavelli counsels (a princely autonomy that preserves itself through constant suspicion of betrayal by others and the readiness to betray them in turn) and his own projected role as counselor (grounded in his own faithfulness and selflessness) is clear. Just as clear are the damaging implications of that gap for the project of bringing together Machiavelli's knowledge and Medici power.

This sequence of chapters betrays Machiavelli's anxious awareness that his aspiration to serve his former master's enemies is virtually inconceivable *on his own terms*. Nonetheless, he has clearly been willing to run the risk of open self-contradiction in order to achieve the final purpose of the treatise, carried out over its last three chapters. In tracing the complete failure of Italian princes, heirs of the bestial *romagnoli* tyrants indicted in *Inferno*, canto 27, both to foresee dangerous changes away from present good fortune and to acquire independent arms to guard against such changes, Machiavelli in chapter 24 zeros in on the universal absence of and desperate need for the intersection of prudent foresight and autonomous force in contemporary Italy. He here transfers the principal lesson of the treatise to the plight of the Italian princes: "only those defenses are good, certain, and lasting that depend on yourself and on your own ability [*da te proprio e dalla virtù tua*]." Then in chapter 25 he attacks in "theoretical" terms the possibility of shaping historical contingency by relying on personal *prudenzia* and *virtù*. This chapter therefore acts as a pivot between the diagnosis (what *is*) offered in chapter 24 and the remedy (what *should be*) prescribed in chapter 26. That remedy in turn calls specifically for the intervention of Lorenzo and the Medici family to heal the more serious woes of the whole peninsula. Machiavelli also insists, in language that specifically recalls the archery image [*per mira*] of chapter 6, on the part he himself must play in applying the new modes and orders elaborated in the treatise: "there can be no great difficulty, if you [*la casa medicea*] imitate the methods [*ordini*] of those I have proposed as examples [*per mira*]" (chapter 26). This sequence of three chapters thus aims to convert the treatise from a collection of written precepts into a course of action to be followed in definite historical circumstances. If successful, it would effect both of Machiavelli's practical goals—the resolution of the Italian crisis and his own reintegration into the structures of power.

Unfortunately, even as these chapters project the union of knowledge and power at the dynamic intersection of text and history,[62] they also point allusively but unmistakably to the likely failure of all of Machiavelli's projects. Chapter 25 indeed sets forth a final test of the proposition that human *virtù*, in spite of such obvious failures as those chastised in chapter 24, can dominate the shifting tides of history, that is, *Fortuna*. In doing so, however, it effects a definitive separation of the two aspects of virtue—prudence and force—whose intersection had been postulated as essential from chapter 6 on. Two dialectically opposed images of human domination of *Fortuna*, first by foresight and then by main force, are offered: initially, *Fortuna* is imaged as a seasonally torrential river whose floods are foreseen (through "provvedimenti") and can be contained ahead of time by the digging of channels and building of embankments; subsequently, *Fortuna* is seen as a helpless woman who is mastered not by prudence but by the brutal violation of a blind, overtly phallic *virtù*.[63] The two are clearly presented as mutually exclusive alternatives: either one has foresight or one uses arms, and there seems to be no room left for the *profeta armato* who combines both.

More specifically, Machiavelli admits in chapter 25 that *Fortuna* is so uncertain that no general precept for action could possibly cover all possible circumstances—that in fact the same action can have diametrically opposed results in only slightly different situations. This sense of contingency, increasingly present in the latter chapters of the treatise, has lately been seen as symptomatic of a profound epistemological crisis, because it implicitly subverts *The Prince* itself qua rule-giving treatise on the reign of princes.[64] Although I do not discount the epis-

---

62. See McCanles, *The Discourse of "Il Principe,"* 136–37.

63. Pitkin, *Fortune Is a Woman*, 148–52.

64. Greene, in "The End of Discourse," argues that the attempt to install precepts gives way to a "surrender before pure contingency" (70) in the last third of the treatise (70–74). See also McCanles, *The Discourse of "Il Principe,"* 47; J. J. Marchand, "Machiavelli e il determinismo storico (dai primi scritti al *Principe*)," in *Machiavelli attuale,* ed. Georges Barthouil (Ravenna, 1982), 57; Kahn, "*Virtù,*" 75–77; Garver, *Machiavelli and the History of Prudence,* 92; Hampton, *Writing from History,* 70–73. But the problem had not escaped the attention of Italian critics earlier; see Chabod, *Scritti su Machiavelli,* 385. Relevant passages are found in chap. 20: "There is no formulating a definite rule about these many alternatives without knowing the particular circumstances [*di tutte queste cose non vi possa dare determinata sentenzia se non si viene a particulari*]." Also, "Fortresses may be useful or otherwise, according to circumstances [*secondo e' tempi*]." Discussion of this tendency begins already in chap. 19, where Machiavelli points to an apparent discrepancy between his rules and the example of late Roman emperors, which can be resolved only by noting that imitation of historical examples will not work unless one imitates exclusively those aspects of the past that are specifically appropriate to one's own situation. Note, by the way, that the underlying thread of chap. 19 is a counterexample to the basic thesis of the

temological dimension of the problem, I would argue that the primary reason for stressing both the necessity of adapting one's behavior to local conditions and the incompatibility between precepts and contingencies is to make clear the continuing need for a prudent adviser who can adapt his "new modes and orders" to the changing "times" (in the well-known dialectic of *mutazione e riscontro* treated by, among others, Giulio Ferroni in his essay in this volume). From the beginning of *The Prince*, Machiavelli thus hypothesizes a human supplement, himself, to compensate for the inadequate precepts, one who can *foresee* changing circumstances and adapt his counsel accordingly.

What *is* really damaging, however, is Machiavelli's acknowledgment in the same chapter that even if one did foresee changes and made plans to change with them, human nature, especially that of princes, is not able to effect such changes. Instead we are left with an image of (leonine) force that is successful only because its author, Pope Julius II, died before circumstances changed; it is a force from which prudence—the prudence that a counselor (Machiavelli himself, for instance) could provide—is specifically excluded. ("And thus Julius carried, in his rash and adventurous way [*la sua mossa impetuosa*], an enterprise that no other pope, who exercised the greatest human prudence [*con tutta la umana prudenzia*], could successfully have performed.") This admission, in fact, is made in the space between the two images of *Fortuna* mastered and determines the shift from the one to the other—if foresight cannot be translated into historical adaptations, then only a blind and desperate violence is left.[65]

A closer look at the unfolding logic of chapter 25 shows how systematically it compromises not only Machiavelli's basic ideas but his own projected position as counselor. It also reveals that these failures are veiled in an aggressive, and aggressively literary, rhetoric of dominating violence. In the first image, *Fortuna* is the violent attacker and the prudently "virtuous" man thwarts it not by countering its force but by containing it within an essentially passive receptacle. In the second, human *virtù* reverts to sheer aggressive violence and it is Lady *Fortuna* who waits passively.

This recourse to imagery is clearly designed to conceal the empirically ungrounded sleight of hand by which *Fortuna* is changed from

---

book, since it points to the radically destabilizing effect of the standing Roman army, which is, apparently, what Machiavelli wants for "unarmed" Italy. It also points to the purely relative notion of "autonomy," which invariably includes reliance on "others" in some form. This sequence culminates in chap. 25, as we shall see. See also the end of chap. 21.

65. Sasso, in *Niccolò Machiavelli*, 265, 275, notes that the second half of chap. 25 contradicts not only the first half but most of the rest of the treatise as well.

irresistible force to compliant victim. Moreover, the use of literary figures helps to conceal the real and perilous position of the Machiavellian counselor. The logical consequence of the first, adaptive, "passive" concept of virtue is, the reader learns, a man whose foresight allows him to change every time circumstances change ("if he could only change his nature with times and circumstances [*con li tempi e con le cose*], his fortune would not change")—who, in other words, becomes structurally identical with *Fortuna* as change personified, since his alterations mirror hers exactly. We are not given an explicit example of this kind of person, although we *are* offered one of a prince unable to change his violent ways, namely Julius II. But, as I have shown, Machiavelli himself has been consistently identified with prudent foresight. And in his attempt to win over the Medici as patrons—that is, in the very act of writing *The Prince*—he is clearly trying to change "con li tempi e con le cose." In chapter 25, Machiavelli identifies prudential virtue—and himself as counselor of foresight—tacitly yet strongly with *Fortuna* herself.[66] Thus when Lady Fortune is newly imaged as submitting to the brutal violence of young men (the youthful Lorenzo is substituted for an aged Julius), Machiavelli has quietly placed himself and his counsel on the side of the acquiescent female victim rather than on that of the overmastering prince.[67]

The image of *Fortuna* as a woman just waiting to be raped, usually assumed to be prototypically Machiavellian, is instead the sign of a total exclusion of prudence, and hence of Machiavelli's vision, from the

66. Throughout the treatise, as we have seen earlier, *virtù* is defined not absolutely but in relation to an opposite (*Fortuna*) or a complement (*prudenzia*). At this point we are treated to the possibility that the two most common dialectical partners of virtù (fortune, prudence) might coincide in unexpected ways.

67. Not only is the first image of *Fortuna*, as a flood, opposed to the second image of *Fortuna*, as a woman, on the grounds of being active rather than passive and impersonal rather than personified, it also anticipates the sexualizing of power in the image of violent possession. The raging flood of *Fortuna*, which prudent virtù tames by bringing it within a containing channel, is potentially analogous to an image of coitus. That potential could not legitimately be activated, one concedes, were it not for the explicitly, violently sexualized image that follows—and for the pattern of graphically sexualized moments here and there throughout Machiavelli's oeuvre: for example, *Belfagor*; various passages in *Mandragola* and *Clizia*; letter no. 108 in Machiavelli, *Lettere*, ed. Gaeta; *The Discourses*, bk. 3, chap. 6. See also Pitkin, *Fortune Is a Woman*, and the essays by John Freccero and Ronald Martinez in this volume. In these terms, then, the reversal from one image to the next is even more striking. In the first, *Fortuna* is the "male" aggressor [*il torrente*] and the "virtuous" man is implicitly cast in the role of receptive woman; in the second, these roles are obviously inverted. (N.b.: This is not to be taken as a claim that Machiavelli identifies or empathizes with the political subjugation of women. Far from it—he appropriates the traditional reductive identifications of the feminine as subordinate and passive simply to bemoan his own condition.)

historical domain of politics, and can even be said to dramatize in the most brutal terms the author's sense of his own vulnerability to princely violence (which for him has the unbridled force of *Fortuna* as it appears in the *first* image). If the passage is "Machiavellian" in some sense, it is so only insofar as it reflects a quasi-pornographic fascination with the violence that he sees everywhere around him (and that has even been turned briefly against his own body) but that he does not himself have the power to inflict.

At this point of utter defeat—with this tacit recognition of the overwhelming likelihood that Machiavelli will not become the Medici's counselor and that his precepts, and his vision of Italian history, will likely fall on deaf ears—Machiavelli lapses into the utopian rhetoric of political prophecy that fills chapter 26, in a last desperate attempt to resuscitate a project collapsing under its own internal contradictions and its author's hopeless understanding that it is fundamentally impractical and idealistic according to his own pragmatic logic. Machiavelli begins chapter 26 by asking if the times are right for a "new prince" in Italy, one "prudente e virtuoso," like Borgia, like the *profeta armato*, like the hybrid centauresque monster to be composed of Machiavelli's counsel and Medicean power. And he does so specifically by returning to the terms and imagery of the sixth chapter, the one that more than any other defines the treatise's values and aspirations:[68]

> And if, as I said above [in chapter 6], it was necessary, to bring out the power [*virtù*] of Moses, that the children of Israel should be slaves in Egypt; and if, to know the magnanimity of Cyrus, it was necessary that the Persians be oppressed by the Medes; and for Theseus' merit to be known, that the Athenians should be scattered—then, at the present time, if the power of an Italian spirit is to be manifested, it was necessary that Italy be reduced to her present state; and that she be more enslaved than the Hebrews, more abject than the Persians, more widely dispersed than the Athenians; headless, orderless, beaten, stripped, scarred, overrun, and plagued by every sort of disaster.

Italy, like *Fortuna* personified as a helpless woman ready for the taking, indeed as one who has been violated many times before, now awaits the salutary embrace of a redeeming prince.

As in chapter 6, Machiavelli plays here on the relatively short conceptual distance between a visionary human prudence and a transcen-

---

68. Whitfield, *Discourses on Machiavelli*, 27; Garver, *Machiavelli and the History of Prudence*, 115.

dently grounded prophecy, as he imagines Lorenzo under Leo's sponsorship as the "redeemer" of Italy—an improbable Christ figure, successor to Borgia's unholy John the Baptist:

> And though one man recently showed certain gleams, such as made us think he was ordained by God for our salvation, still we saw how, at the very zenith of his career, he was deserted by Fortune. Thus Italy, left almost lifeless, waits for a leader who will heal her wounds. . . . Behold how she implores God to send someone to free her from the cruel insolence of the barbarians. . . . There is no figure presently in sight in whom she can better place her trust than your illustrious house, which, with its fortune and its merits [*virtù*], favored by God and the Church of which it is now the head, can take the lead in this process of redemption.

In a shocking about-face from the tone of chapter 6, however, the unarmed Machiavelli here openly employs *as his own* a prophetic rhetoric (the name of God, virtually unmentioned in the preceding twenty-five chapters, appears six times in a few paragraphs) that seems utterly incompatible with the desacralization of a prophetic politics, as of all theological, philosophical, and poetic idealism, begun in chapter 6 and extended through the rest of *The Prince*.[69]

If chapter 26 opens with a return of prophecy, the barely repressed "other" of pragmatic political discourse, it closes with the even more startling and stirring intersection of Machiavelli's treatise with the banished language of poetry. As he calls upon the Medici to enforce the "nuovi modi e ordini" that are so clearly his own, thereby projecting the imminent intersection of text and history, counselor and prince, knowledge and power, he frankly acknowledges that "those who know what they are doing cannot enforce obedience [*coloro che sanno non sono obbediti*]." These words plainly echo Dante's description of Aristotle ("maestro di *color che sanno*" [*Inferno*, canto 4]) and his fellows suspended eternally in the "noble castle" of virtuous pagan thinkers.[70] Machiavelli thus enrolls himself allusively in the same imaginative limbo of poets and idealist philosophers (not to mention *profeti disarmati*) to which he earlier consigned Dante and Plato—without hope he too lives in desire. And it is clearly no "mere contingency" that leads Machiavelli and his treatise at the close to words taken from a vain

---

69. Greene, in "The End of Discourse," 77, notes the shift and links it to the passage in chap. 6, but he sees no disabling contradiction within Machiavelli's own role.

70. Compare *Asino*, 8.37–44, where the locution *color che sanno* is used in close connection with the virtue of prudence.

political prophecy made 160 years earlier by a poet, Francesco Petrarch:
"virtù contro a furore / prenderà l'arme; e fia el combatter corto: / Ché
l'antico valore / nelli italici cor non è ancor morto" (virtue against
furor will take up arms, and the battle will be short: because the ancient
valor has not yet died in Italic hearts [my translation]).[71]

Oblique confirmation of Machiavelli's realization of the unhappy
destiny of his "gift of counsel" comes in the dedicatory letter to *The
Discourses*, likely composed after the multiple failures of the other treatise.[72] There Machiavelli defines a different readership for his work
and in doing so clearly offers a palinodic reassessment of the role he
had so recently attempted to claim for himself in offering *The Prince* to
an unpromising young scion of the house of Medici:[73]

> I know that I have made no mistake at any rate in this, that I have
> chosen to dedicate these my discourses to you in preference to all
> others; both because, in doing so, I seem to be showing some
> gratitude for benefits received, and also because I seem to be
> *departing from the usual practice of authors, which has always been to*
> *dedicate their works to some prince*, and, blinded by ambition and
> avarice, to praise him for all his virtuous qualities when they
> ought to have blamed him for all manner of shameful deeds. So,
> to avoid this mistake, I have chosen not those who are princes
> [*quelli che sono principi*], *but those who, on account of their*
> *innumerable good qualities, deserve to be* [*quelli che per le infinite buone*

71. See Bárberi Squarotti, "*Il Principe,* o il trionfo della letteratura," in his *Machiavelli,*
150; and Greene, "The End of Discourse," 74–77. Still, quoted in the context of Machiavelli's work, Petrarch's words take on a meaning very different from their original one.
Virtù, which for Petrarch is a quality that unites political energy and moral righteous-
ness, has been systematically stripped of that meaning by Machiavelli in chaps. 15
through 18, as we have already seen. Thus the knowledge that Petrarch's prophecy has
remained unfulfilled during the intervening century and a half since it was written is
countered by the prediction that a different sort of *virtù*—the one that takes up its *own*
arms and freely uses the weapons of the very "furor" it combats and from which it is
ultimately indistinguishable—might have better success.

72. On the vexed question of the date of *The Discourses* vis-à-vis that of *The Prince,* see
Felix Gilbert, "The Composition and Structure of Machiavelli's *Discorsi,*" *Journal of the
History of Ideas* 14 (1953): 136–56; Baron, "The *Principe*"; Chabod, *Scritti su Machiavelli,*
32 n, 34–35 n; Roberto Ridolfi, *The Life of Niccolò Machiavelli,* trans. Cecil Grayson (Chicago, 1963), 174–75 and 294–95 n. 10; Sasso, *Niccolò Machiavelli,* 211–19. *The Prince* itself
(chap. 2) suggests the prior existence of a treatise on republics, and I do assume that the
two works were composed together over a period of time—but I firmly believe that the
letter to Cosimo Rucellai and Zanobi Buondelmonti deliberately positions *The Discourses*
as being written after *The Prince.*

73. Ridolfi, in *The Life of Niccolò Machiavelli,* 170, also reads this letter as an attack on
Lorenzo.

parti loro meriterebbono di essere]; not those who might shower on me rank, honors, and riches, but those who, though unable, would like to do so. For, to judge aright, one should . . . admire those who know [*quelli che sanno*] how to govern a kingdom, not those who, without knowing how, actually govern one [*quelli che, sanza sapere, possono governare un regno*]. (My emphasis)

In addressing Zanobi Buondelmonti and Cosimo Rucellai, his young patrons, interlocutors, and disciples from the Orti Oricellari circle, Machiavelli specifically echoes and inverts the letter to Lorenzo in which he himself follows the practice of those who always "dedicate their works to some prince." Moreover, he clearly reverses his earlier claims to be writing not about what "should be" but about "what is."

The palinode of *The Discourses* constitutes neither a simple rejection of the lessons taught in the shorter treatise, nor a bad case of sour grapes; it is instead the resigned, "realistic" acceptance of a double failure, marked by the ineluctable division between those who "know" (*sanno*) and those who have power (*possono*, from *potere* [power]) in words that echo from chapter 26 ("coloro che sanno non sono ob-bediti"). On the one hand is the inability of the savvy but "unarmed" Machiavelli to effect a transfer of what he knows to those who are ignorant in themselves but have the power to effectively use that knowledge; on the other, the recognition, anticipated by the rhetoric of chapter 26, that this failure itself means that Machiavelli's rules for princely conduct, however rooted in the interpretation of the "facts" of past and present politics, constitute not the prudent representation of "what is" but a prophetic vision of "what should [but will not] be."

In the dedication of *The Discourses,* as in chapter 26, Machiavelli acknowledges that *The Prince* is likely to prove no more effective than Petrarch's canzone in reshaping history and far less so in promoting the welfare of its author, who notoriously prospered through the pa-tronage of *grandi* and even of tyrants. This is not, however, simply a feature of "language itself" as some of the recent "formal" readers of the treatise have suggested—rather it is a melancholy calculation of the empirical improbability that the Medici, or some other prince, might read and act on Machiavelli's words of advice. Nor does he in fact offer a *complete* renunciation of the dual project of referential realism and pragmatic intervention. There remains the contingent possibility that a particularly astute "principe" *might* accept Machiavelli's "gift of coun-sel," as well as the historical reality that the treatise has shaped, in fundamental ways, modern political theory and may even have influ-enced political action, even by those who most profess to abhor the Machiavellian doctrine (as they have defined it). And even Machiavelli himself found his way, gradually, back into the employ of the Medici (notably in the commission to write the *Florentine Histories*) and into the political arena (as the friend and adviser of the one reader of the age most able to appreciate his political intelligence, Francesco Guicciardini), although it may well be that Machiavelli's *literary* writings had much more to do with this modest success than *The Prince* or even *The Discourses*.

The real message of the final clash between prudent pragmatism and utopian prophecy in *The Prince*, however, is none of these but another, as I have already begun to suggest. Once the wide gap between Machiavelli's foresight and the Medici princes' power has been recognized, once his own hidden identification with the Savonarolian *profeta disarmato* has become apparent, once he admits that "what is" matters to him far less than "what (could and) should be," a fundamental mystification inherent in his conceptual and rhetorical pragmatism is made apparent. At this point, the recourse to a transcendental order, however hopeless and "imaginary," is apparently the only option left to Machiavelli. In fact, Machiavelli's gift of prudential counsel is at its *most* pragmatic and realistic precisely in its prediction that it will be accepted and implemented only if it is indeed also a truly prophetic gift of the Holy Spirit—however unlikely that may appear to be in the terms of *The Prince*.

The reemergence of a discredited rhetoric of prophecy and the descent into a "poetic" utopia in chapter 26 are thus not a sign of delusion and self-deception but rather the last and most persuasive manifestation of a weary realism that enabled Machiavelli to foresee his text's and his own historical subjection to a tortuous destiny of misinterpretation and emargination. As Machiavelli's keenest interested reader, Antonio Gramsci, clearly knew, the open lapse into poetic prophecy constitutes the pragmatic recognition that utopian vision is also the province of the prudent politician—that however "realistic" our grounding in the present and the past may be, the future is accessible always and only in the imagination as the "could be" and "should be" that leads us blindly onward toward the "things unseen" that a transcendent faith alone can discover.[74]

In this light, we see that hard-headed "pragmatism" is itself profoundly utopian and shot through with an implicit transcendental

74. See the passage from Gramsci, *Quaderni del carcere*, quoted in note 48 above. See also Gramsci, *Quaderni del carcere*, 1555: "The fundamental character of *The Prince* is not that of a systematic treatment, but rather that of a 'living' book, in which ideology and political science are fused in the dramatic form of 'myth'" (my translation). And he associates "the utopian character of *The Prince*" (1556) precisely with chap. 26: "Even the conclusion of *The Prince* is bound to this 'mythic' character of the book" (1555).

faith, because it pretends to know and to act on an empirical basis, even though the futurity toward which that knowledge and those actions are oriented is always, necessarily, imaginary, and thus literary, in Machiavelli's own conception of that domain. Conversely, the prophetic mission of Moses masks the practical conjunction of prudent foresight with one's own arms. Thus Machiavelli's book of counsel is a gift in the truest and rarest sense, since it is given gratuitously, if longingly, without any real hope of reciprocity. And long after its disappointed author's death, *The Prince* goes on insisting, to whoever will listen, on the necessity, as on the impossibility, of gesturing toward history and the human community, and toward a future whose darkness it has so brilliantly illuminated over the centuries.

CHAPTER TEN
MACHIAVELLI
AND VICO

Giuseppe Mazzotta

THE most cursory glance at the history of ideas shows that Machiavelli's political thought makes him the point of origin and reference of much modern speculation on political philosophy. With varying degrees of circumspection, theorists of the modern state, from Bacon to Hobbes to Spinoza, acknowledge Machiavelli's founding role in the modern political debate. Hobbes's *De cive*, which is thoroughly shaped by the proposition, drawn from Justinian's *Digest*, that "what pleases the Prince has the force of law," is a text that could have been written by Machiavelli himself. Unsurprisingly, the treatise had the effect of making the epithet "Hobbist" a term of abuse, in the same tradition as the epithet "Machiavellian."[1]

Spinoza's *Tractatus theologico-politicus,* the chief burden of which is to reflect on the imperatives of reason and on the desirable shape of government in the world of immanence, cautiously seeks to rescue

1. Thomas Hobbes, *De cive or The Citizen*, ed. S. P. Lamprecht (New York, 1949), 1.4.1. All quotations from Machiavelli are taken from Niccolò Machiavelli, *Tutte le opere di Machiavelli,* ed. Mario Martelli (Florence, 1971). English translations are taken from Niccolò Machiavelli, *The Prince*, trans. Robert M. Adams (New York, 1977); and *The Discourses of Niccolò Machiavelli*, ed. and trans. Leslie J. Walker, S.J., 2 vols. (London, 1975). I have modified Adams's translations to make them more literal. The Italian quotations of Giambattista Vico, *La scienza nuova,* are taken from the edition of Paolo Rossi (Milan, 1977). The English quotations are taken from Giambattista Vico, *The New Science of Giambattista Vico,* trans. Thomas G. Bergin and Max H. Fisch (Ithaca, N.Y., 1970). An English translation of the autobiography is available: Giambattista Vico, *The Autobiography of Giambattista Vico,* trans. Max H. Fisch and Thomas G. Bergin (Ithaca, N.Y., 1944). The references to the other works of Vico are taken from Giambattista Vico, *Opere,* ed. Roberto Parenti, vol. 1 (Naples, 1972).

Machiavelli's thought from the commonplace conviction that his is merely a doctrine of absolutism and of coercive power:

> What means a prince whose sole motive is lust of mastery should use to establish and maintain his dominion, the most ingenious Machiavelli has set forth at large; but with what design one can hardly be sure. . . . He perhaps wished to show how cautious a free multitude should be of entrusting its welfare absolutely to one man, . . . and I am the more led to this opinion concerning that most farseeing man, because it is known that he was favorable to liberty, for the maintenance of which he has besides given the most wholesome advice.[2]

It is especially in the political debates of our own days that Machiavelli has never ceased to be an obligatory point of reference. Benedetto Croce, Giovanni Gentile, and Antonio Gramsci, three thinkers whose political theories span the spectrum of the twentieth century's ideologies, have variously interpreted Machiavelli's ideas on absolute sovereignty, his musings on the nature of political society and of the state, his judgment about the place of the rule of law in the realm of politics, and so forth, in order to construct and justify their particular designs of the human polity.[3]

Entrenched anti-Machiavellianism, which includes the likes of Tommaso Campanella, Innocent Gentillet, and Jean Bodin, displays a downright revulsion at what it construes as the most frightening elements of Machiavelli's vision: his ideas about the nature of power; his assumption that the world is not exactly the handiwork of God; his belief that words have no necessary relationship to what they name and that it is therefore hazardous to take the prince at his word. Nonetheless, it still casts him as the source and epitome of modern political praxis. When taken together, these two contradictory strains in the interpretation of Machiavelli exemplify the persistent, bewildering ambiguities of a thought that seems to preclude the very possibility of understanding.[4]

This pattern of viewing Machiavelli's thought as a hermeneutical and moral scandal shifts radically when we come to Giambattista Vico.

---

2. Benedict Spinoza, *A Theologico-Political Treatise and a Political Treatise,* trans. R. H. M. Elwes (New York, 1951), 5.5.

3. See Benedetto Croce, *Elementi di politica* (Bari, 1925); Giovanni Gentile, *Studi sul Rinascimento* (Florence, 1923); Croce, *Studi vichiani* (Florence, 1968); and Antonio Gramsci, *Note sul Machiavelli, sulla politica e sullo stato moderno* (Turin, 1949).

4. See, on this subject, Friedrich Meinecke, *Machiavellism: The Doctrine of Raison d'Etat and Its Place in Modern History,* trans. Douglas Scott (New Haven, Conn., 1962).

As we shall see, for Vico Machiavelli is not merely the originator of a modern political science. Vico certainly believes, as *De mente heroica* (Of the Heroic Mind) makes clear, that a single heroic and innovative personality such as Columbus, Descartes, and Galileo can open up new worlds of knowledge. But in *The New Science* he valorizes the power of events more than that of individuals in the making of history. From this perspective and in this context it ought to be clear that the name "Machiavelli" is to be taken as the event of a thought, the way Vico's own name is understood, for instance, in his *Autobiography*. All of this is meant to suggest that Vico delineates in *The New Science* a compelling and rigorous archeology of the lines of force within which he inscribes Machiavelli's thought.

Vico thus departs from the tradition of moralistic judgments of Machiavelli's political theories. To be sure, in the proem which dedicates *On the Most Ancient Wisdom of the Italians* to Paolo Mattia Doria, Vico still refers to Machiavelli as a teacher of "the most evil art of government"; but in *The New Science* he seeks to penetrate to the center of Machiavelli's discourse, to the metaphysical underpinnings of his doctrines. There, Vico shares Machiavelli's analysis of society, but he places that analysis in the framework of his own broader educational concerns. Vico responds to Machiavelli's role as educator, for he believes, as Plato did, that the heart of a rigorous philosophical discourse, such as his own, can be nothing less than a theory of education; the practice and theory of education were, it turns out, Vico's lifelong passion.

Vico's career at the University of Naples; the *Inaugural Orations;* the sense of the necessity of a daring and imaginative knowledge presented in *De mente heroica;* his systematic attempts to challenge Cartesian paradigms of education and to reorganize the curriculum in *The Study Methods of Our Time;* the casting of the self as Socrates in the story of self-education that is his *Autobiography;* the notion, put forth in *The New Science* in an open polemic with Plato's dismissal of Homer, of the educational role of poetry in shaping the encyclopedia of knowledge—these are the elements that show how Vico's interest in myths, politics, rhetoric, history, law, social institutions, and literature is profound and innovative, and yet it is subordinated to the ideal of a spiritual and moral paideia.

It is my argument that Vico operates a shift in the common understanding of Machiavelli, but this shift is clearly not abrupt. Despite the prejudices that inspired a negative assessment of Machiavelli's theories, some thought had already been given to the methodological foundation of those theories. Bodin, for instance, denied the epistemic validity of Machiavelli's political analysis, complaining about the narrowness of the historical examples he studies (as in the *Florentine Histories*). By contrast, however, Francis Bacon's *The Advancement of Learning* reflects on the politics of knowledge—how it is geared to the interests of the state—and thus views Machiavelli's theories of statecraft as theories of knowledge devised to escape the abstract tendencies of universalizing historiographers. Simply put, Machiavelli's writings provide Bacon with the exemplary configuration of knowledge derived from the particulars of history: "And therefore the form of writing, which of all others is fitted for such variable argument as that of negotiation and scattered occasion, is that which Machiavelli most wisely and aptly chose for government; namely, Observations or Discourses upon Histories and Examples. For knowledge drawn freshly and in our view out of particulars knows best the way back to particulars again."[5]

The suggestion that Vico operates a shift in the understanding of Machiavelli to some degree unsettles a commonly cherished assumption that there is a "continuity" in Italian speculative tradition. Giovanni Gentile, who self-consciously stands in the tradition of Machiavelli, Giordano Bruno, and Benedict Spinoza, recapitulates the earlier arguments of Bertrando Spaventa and sketches the outline of a specifically Italian philosophy (including Leonardo, Machiavelli, Bernardino Telesio, Campanella, Bruno, and Vico). The specificity of this national tradition, for Gentile, would lie in its pursuit of the natural world of immanence and in its will to abide within the confines of that world. By the same token, Benedetto Croce maintains that Vico's thought places on a moral plane, and thereby fulfills, Machiavelli's insights into what is politically useful.[6]

The positing of an unbroken connection and progress between Machiavelli and Vico is not altogether without justification. The evidence for Vico's consciousness of Machiavelli and for his assimilation of much of Machiavelli's thought is overwhelming. The wide range of views they share about man's nature and history is sometimes explained by stressing their common historical roots, but generally Vico's thought is mediated by Machiavelli's. Their common point of departure may well be the Augustinian concept of the fallen human condition as well as their acknowledgment of the inherent bestiality at the core of man's most civilized projects. The remarkable degree of ideological continuity between Machiavelli and Vico is also shown by their

5. Francis Bacon, *The Advancement of Learning*, ed. Thomas Case (London, 1951), 2.22.4 and 6; 2.23.8.

6. Benedetto Croce, "Machiavelli e Vico: la politica e l'etica," in *Elementi di politica*, 59–67.

belief that the world of history is made by man; their rejection of utopian constructions; their conviction that man is defined by historical-cultural experiences (institutions, beliefs, language); the dependence of their respective methods of analysis on the vast reservoir of cultural and mythical memories; and their conceptions of historical cycles.

The theory of historical cycles, which in Machiavelli harks back to Plato and Polybius, becomes in Vico one of *corsi* ("courses") and *ricorsi* ("re-courses")—terms that describe the repetitive patterns in history's unfolding. Vico's cycles can be best represented by a spiral, which figures the simultaneous movement of the circle and the line, and thus defines the pattern of identity and difference between the past and the present. Not that Machiavelli is really unaware of the existence of differences and complexities in the scheme of historical recurrences. In *The Discourses*, he reveals with utmost clarity his belief that history's repetitions should not be understood as merely mechanical stagings of the unvarying drama of the same human passions and tendencies; rather, these occurrences are always characterized by the intrusion of irreducible particularities:

> Prudent men are wont to say—and this not rashly or without good ground—that he who would foresee what has to be, should reflect on what has been, for everything that happens in the world at any time has a genuine resemblance to what happened in ancient times. This is due to the fact that the agents who bring such things about are men, and that men have, and have always had, the same passions, whence it necessarily comes about that the same effects are produced. It is true that men's deeds are sometimes more virtuous in this country than in that, and in that than in some other, according to the type of education from which their inhabitants have derived their mode of life. (Book 3, chapter 43, p. 575)

The many conceptual similarities between Vico and Machiavelli cannot hide the profound differences between them, however. Some of these differences are attributable, no doubt, to the diverse tempers of their times and of the thinkers themselves as well as to much that Vico finds incomplete in Machiavelli's thought. Machiavelli tends to reduce the rich inventory of history's differences to unalterable and homogeneous laws. Vico, who is an eclectic thinker, seeks the principle of correlation among different registers of historical experience. This characterization needs further clarification. Eclecticism, which is the cornerstone of the major seventeenth-century philosophical edifices (Descartes, Spinoza, Leibniz), acknowledges and upholds the objective existence of differences. Unlike the syncretism of Pico, for instance, which aims at harmonizing conceptual differences in order to uncover the underlying unity of all knowledge, Vico's eclecticism refutes the notion that various traditions essentially say the same thing and can thus be linked to a grand scheme of harmonious correspondences. For Vico, the unity of knowledge can be restored by patching up, and at the same time highlighting intersections between, the very differences that make up a system of thought.

The differences between Machiavelli and Vico certainly go beyond the enunciation of abstract principles such as these; they color both the perspectives and the semantics of the two thinkers. Vico both browses in and peruses what he calls "the museum of credulities"; and he revels in the world of relics, magic, and superstition because to him they are the archaic vestiges of the foundation of all knowledge. For Machiavelli, religion is a passive force, or an instrument of political power (*The Discourses*, book 1, chapter 12); for example, Friar Timoteo in *Mandragola* is the skeptical curator of what to him is nothing more than a lifeless museum of hollow beliefs and practices. From a semantic point of view, one could draw up a long list of instances to show the extent to which Vico redefines Machiavelli's lexicon. The use of the term *virtù* in *The Prince*, for instance, is to be understood as virtue in the sense of "power." A brief review of the values conferred on the word by the philosophical tradition will convey the sense of the differences between Vico and Machiavelli. Aristotle, in the *Nicomachean Ethics* (1106a), casts virtue as a disposition to the good, but the Roman personification of *virtus* is one of warlike courage. Saint Thomas Aquinas unites the two traditions in defining virtue as "some perfection of power" (*Summa Theologiae* 1–2, q. 55, a.2) and as the potentiality to achieve a perfection. For Vico, however (and this distinction is of capital importance), virtue is not an intrinsic personal quality as it is for Machiavelli, but rather is achieved by the operation of the free will: "L'uomo abbia [ha] libero arbitrio, però debole, di fare delle passioni virtù" (Man has free choice, however weak, to make virtue of his passions).[7] In short, virtue is for Vico the conatus by which the force of passions can be bent and given new directions.

The list of semantic differences between the vocabularies of Machiavelli and Vico could be further extended to cover such key terms as fear, pity, the "religious," and order. A few remarks about a couple of these concepts will suffice to illustrate some concrete features of these two distinct structures of understanding. Machiavelli, for instance, speaks of the "stato ben ordinato" to characterize a functional institu-

---

7. Vico, *The New Science*, ed. Bergin and Fisch, bk. 1, sec. 2, "Elements," par. 134–36.

tion and a stable political structure; for Vico, by contrast, order entails method, and thus his central principle of investigation—namely that "L'ordine dell'idee dee procedere secondo l'ordine delle cose" (The order of ideas must follow the order of institutions [*The New Science*, book 1, section 2, "Elements," 64: 36])—echoes a long line of speculative thought, which stretches from Giacomo Zabarella to G. C. Scaliger and Francis Bacon.[8]

The question of fear, on the other hand, brings to a head the radical difference in the concerns of Machiavelli and Vico. For Machiavelli certainly understood the politics of fear and intimidation (as one of his most memorable sentences runs, it is far better for the prince to be feared than to be loved). He sees fear as a strategy of power, a realistic mode of controlling the imminent dangers and real or imaginary threats besetting the security of one's world. For Vico, fear is an internalized passion. In one of his most radical formulations concerning the nature of the passions, Vico says that fear is objectless in that it does not originate from the outside world, but is generated from within. The Cartesian constitution of the self is rooted in the cogito; Descartes would consider fear as the sign of a rationally undisciplined mind. In *The New Science*, fear is the ground of the obscure consciousness of a self divided from itself; this terrifying vertigo of self-apprehension leads man to idolatry, divination, and poetry—activities that are (though not directly) "political." If anything, Vico's reflections on fear are intended to echo and transform the insights of Epicurus and Lucretius on the origin of religion: "it was fear which created the gods in the world; not fear awakened in men by other men, but fear awakened in men by themselves" (*The New Science*, book 2, section 2, "Poetic Metaphysics," par. 382; cf. "Elements," par. 191).

These conceptual differences are too regional and even too predictable to give a true sense of the originality of Vico's critique of the

8. "Just as the order of beings follows the order of intelligence, so our intellect follows the order of being"; G. C. Scaliger, *Exotericarum exercitationum libri XV de subtilitate ad Hieronymum Cardanum* (Hanau, Germany, 1634), 6. The most influential thinker on this subject (concerning Bacon, above all) is Giacomo Zabarella, who writes in the treatise *De methodis* contained in the *Opera Logica . . . quorum seriem, argumentum, & utilitatem versa pagina demonstrabit*, 6th ed. (Frankfurt, 1604): "Order, in so far as it is order, does not have the force of drawing together, but only of arranging; method, however, has an inferential force [*vim illatricem*], and gathers one thing from another" (*De methodis* 3. 1 and 2). See also Bacon's formulation: "Knowledge that is delivered as a thread to be spun on, ought to be delivered and intimated, if it were possible, in the same method wherein it was invented" (*The Advancement of Learning*, 2, 14, 4, [p. 162]). The whole issue is masterfully treated by Leroy E. Loemker in *Struggle for Synthesis: The Seventeenth-Century Background of Leibniz's Synthesis of Order and Freedom* (Cambridge, Mass., 1972), 157–76.

foundations of Machiavelli's thought. Part of the critique Vico levels specifically at Machiavelli reflects his broader critique of the central tenets of Renaissance thought. The proposition that effectively sets in motion *The New Science* seeks to redefine the pivotal doctrine of humanism: "Because of the indefinite nature of the human mind, wherever it is lost in ignorance man makes himself the measure of all things" ("Elements," par. 120). Leaving aside momentarily Vico's critique of the Cartesian assumption of the stability of the mind, I should stress that this humanistic principle, which is conventionally attributed to Protagoras (and which, for instance, shapes Pico della Mirandola's belief in the centrality of man), is dismissed by Vico at the start of his work in the conviction that it is a reductive appropriation of the heterogeneous domains of a world of which man, far from being the center, is only a part.

Consistent with this critique, Vico first points out the limits of Plato's ideal republic ("Elements," par. 131); second, he sketches the dynamics at play in the making of the polis. "Legislation," writes Vico, "considers man as he is in order to turn him to good uses in human society. Out of ferocity, avarice, and ambition, the three vices which run throughout the human race, it creates the military, merchant, and governing classes, and thus the strength, riches, and wisdom of commonwealths. Out of these three great vices, which would certainly destroy all mankind on the face of the earth, it makes civil happiness" ("Elements," par. 132). The founding vices of the Machiavellian political theory and posture are simultaneously presupposed and transcended from Vico's perspective of historical becoming. Machiavelli's much vaunted political realism, it would seem, produces a frozen picture of man's natural existence and thereby robs man of the thought of historical alternatives to the naturalistic course of events; by contrast, Vico's historical consciousness asserts possible alternatives to man's natural conditions.

Vico's confrontation with the tenets of humanism and with some aspects of Machiavelli's thought confirms what many scholars have believed: that Vico broadens the domain of Piconian (and Cartesian) subjectivity and assigns a vast scope to Machiavelli's narrow experience of the inner dynamics of the polity. But to show Vico's comprehensive account of the "archeology" of Machiavelli's thought—its buried origin, extensions, and purposes—one must turn to the striking reflections in the concluding section of *The New Science*. In what is known as "Conchiusione dell'Opera" (Conclusion of the Work), Vico begins by evoking the idea of an eternal natural commonwealth ("un'eterna repubblica naturale") ordained by divine Providence. Within this context Vico then juxtaposes the belief in the providential order of history with theories of political philosophy shaped by beliefs in chance and fate:

> Adunque, di fatto è confutato Epicuro, che dà il caso e i di lui seguaci Obbes e Macchiavello; di fatto è confutato Zenone, e con lui Spinosa, che danno il fato: al contrario, di fatto è stabilito a favor de' filosofi politici, de' quali è principe il divino Platone, che stabilisce regolare le cose umane la provvedenza. Onde aveva la ragione Cicerone, che non poteva con Attico ragionar delle leggi, se non lasciava d'essere epicureo e non gli concedeva prima la provvedenza regolare l'umane cose: la quale Pufendorfio sconobbe con la sua ipotesi, Seldeno suppose e Grozio ne prescindè; ma i romani giureconsulti la stabilirono per primo principio del diritto natural delle genti. Perchè in quest'opera appieno si è dimostrato che sopra la provvedenza ebbero i primi governi del mondo per loro intiera forma la religione, sulla quale unicamente resse lo stato delle famiglie; . . . Laonde, perdendosi la religione ne' popoli, nulla resta loro per vivere in società: nè scudo per difendersi, nè mezzo per consigliarsi, nè pianta dov'essi reggano, nè forma per la qual essi siano affatto nel mondo. Quindi veda bene Bayle se possan esser di fatto nazioni nel mondo senza veruna cognizione di Dio! (706–7)

Hence Epicurus, who believes in chance, is refuted by the facts along with his followers Hobbes and Machiavelli; and so are Zeno and Spinoza, who believe in fate. The evidence clearly confirms the contrary position of the political philosophers, whose prince is the divine Plato, who shows that providence directs human institutions. Cicero was therefore right in refusing to discuss law with Atticus unless the latter would give up his Epicureanism and first concede that providence governed human institutions. Pufendorf implicitly denied this by his hypothesis, Selden took it for granted, and Grotius left it out of account; but the Roman jurisconsults established it as the first principle of the natural law of the gentes. For in this work it has been fully demonstrated that through providence the first governments of the world had as their entire form religion, on which alone the family state was based; . . . Hence, if religion is lost among the peoples, they have nothing left to enable them to live in society: no shield of defense, nor means of counsel, nor basis of support, nor even a form by which they may exist in the world at all. Let Bayle consider then whether in fact there can be nations in the world without any knowledge of God. (*The New Science*, par. 1109)

This paragraph primarily hinges on the distinction between philosophical-political atheism and a theology of Providence. But the passage displays such a web of conceptual resonances that it can be taken as a miniature emblem of Vico's style of thought. It is an imaginative compression of associations that recapitulate parallel reflections from earlier fragments of *The New Science* and that together constitute a brilliant tour de force: interacting and mutually self-implicating discourses on cosmology, ethics, and politics. The broad sweep of Vico's historical consciousness exemplifies Vico's understanding of the history of thought and of ideas (as opposed to the Platonic belief in eternal ideas), of the persistence of traditional strains of philosophy throughout history, of the corollary that individual events can be understood only within the furrow of traditional lines of thought. The political philosophy of Plato (and of Cicero and Vico himself)—which can be summarized, as Vico summarizes it in paragraph 342 of *The New Science*, as a rational civil theology of divine Providence—is viewed as a radical alternative to the tradition of Epicureanism, which for Vico extends to the political theories of Machiavelli and Hobbes (and which also includes Lucretius).

The metaphysical premises of Epicurean cosmology are delineated earlier in *The New Science*. In book 1, section 4, "Method" (par. 340), Vico discusses the passions and impulses of the first men and explains the impulse proper to human choice and free will as the power to control the motion of the bodies and the bestial passions. Vico illustrates this idea by referring to the law of motion in classical mechanics and in modern mechanics: "And what the theorists of mechanics call powers, forces, impulses, are insensible motions of bodies, by which they approach their centers of gravity, as ancient mechanics had it, or depart from their centers of motion, as modern mechanics has it." But Epicureanism, which is based on Democritean atomism, is tantamount to an antiteleological, materialistic conception of the universe: "For the philosophers have either been altogether ignorant of it [i.e., of civil theology of divine Providence], as the Stoics and Epicureans were, the latter asserting that human affairs are agitated by a blind concourse of atoms, the former that they are drawn by a deaf chain of cause and effect" (par. 342). This Democritean-Epicurean cosmology, vehemently opposed by Plato (as Diogenes Laertius reports), posits the world as matter in endless motion without the intervention of free choice to affect the movement of atoms, and without purpose or providential order.

Such an assessment of Epicurus's universe of chance and determinism, which stifle the freedom of the will, shapes the realm of politics and ethics; for Vico, it constitutes nothing less than a mechanistic picture of the world. In the Epicurean physics of the natural world, the elements comprising matter interact by collision; nonetheless, there is what Lucretius calls the *clinamen*, which is to be understood as the atom's power to swerve off its own mechanical, inert path of motion, thus averting the catastrophe of colliding forces. The moral equivalent of such a swerve is the Epicurean sage's withdrawal from the public arena to the "garden of Epicurus," where the philosopher can abide in the pursuit of the mind's pleasures. Given these cosmological and moral premises, the Epicurean political theory comes forth, paradoxically, as fundamentally nonpolitical, if one takes "political" to mean the economy of one's interaction with others. The central flaw of Epicureanism is its atomistic individualism, the lack of a sense of the organic unity of the whole. Moreover, Epicureanism comes to stand for a concept of subjectivity, for an individuality no longer anchored in a recognition of authority, and for a world of individual lordship crystallized by the libertinism of seventeenth-century Epicureans such as Pierre Bayle and Pierre Gassendi.

Hobbes's world picture is shaped by principles that are not far removed from Epicurean scientific materialism. The laws of Hobbes's natural philosophy are those drafted by Galileo (whom he met at Padua) and by William Harvey, Galileo's student. If in Plato's *Republic* the model for politics is music, Hobbes's politics and ethics are a direct extension of Galileo's physics of motion and inertia. The body politic—we are told in *Leviathan*—is a mechanical engine in which "every joint and member is moved to performe his duty."[9] That man is a machine in motion, driven by imagination and appetites, is overtly stated by Hobbes in language that rephrases Galileo's law of uniform motion: "when a body is once in motion, it moveth, unless something else hinder it, eternally . . . so it also happeneth in that motion, which is made in the internal parts of a man, then, when he sees, dreams, etc." (chapter 2, "Of Imagination"). Human desire, fear, anger, and other passions derive from what Hobbes takes as immutable laws of nature, and from them he deduces that the state of nature "is nothing else but a mere war of all against all."[10] In such a natural state of reciprocal fear and antagonism, all individuals are isolated entities distrustful of one another. Political society is not given as an organic whole; rather, the construction of the covenant of political obligations depends on the exercise of a coercive power and on the will to establish boundaries for what C. B. Macpherson calls "possessive individualism."[11]

9. Thomas Hobbes, *Leviathan*, ed. A. D. Lindsay (London, 1962), introduction.

10. Hobbes, *De cive or The Citizen*, ed. Lamprecht, preface.

11. C. B. Macpherson, *The Political Theory of Possessive Individualism: Hobbes to Locke* (Oxford, 1969).

One meaning of Vico's placement of Machiavelli in the tradition of the radical individualism of Epicurus and Hobbes comes to the fore in the reference to Bayle and the atheism of the libertines. In point of fact, the philosophical libertine (such as Bayle, Raimond de Sebonde, Peter Scarron) is a skeptic who claims moral freedom, which is understood as the power to do what one likes. He thereby makes the self, and not God or other transcendent authorities, the only norm by which reality can be known and judged. Philosophically, the skeptic, above all the Cartesian skeptic whom Vico repeatedly attacks, holds that the only indubitably certain assertion is that "I am" and entertains doubts as to the existence of the outside world. For Vico, the division between the inner and outer worlds cannot be neatly drawn. Historically, the skepticism of the libertine has been identified with the atheism of Machiavelli, rather than with Cartesian philosophy, and Vico falls within this tradition. Tommaso Campanella's *Atheismus triumphatus*, a text that belongs to the spiritual climate of the "anti-Machiavel," probes the links between the skepticism of the "heresiarchs" (by which Campanella means the theology of the Reformation) and the political idolatry of Machiavellian princes. The suspicion of bonds between Machiavellism and atheism characterizes the polemics triggered by the works of, among others, Geoffroi Vallée (*Ars nihil credendi*), G. C. Vanini, and Jean Bodin.

It is not difficult to see that Vico's critique of philosophical naturalism is at one with his critique of Renaissance Neoplatonism, in that these two strains of thought (as well as Cartesianism) both presuppose and ratify a common concept of subjectivity, a notion of an autonomous self that depends on the representation of the world as a series of passive, disintegrated objects waiting to be arranged according to the designs of one's own imperial self. In practical terms, this assumption of a gulf between subject and object leads to a politics of absolute power: the entities of the world are there to be controlled by the subject. It also leads to Vico's logically prior insight into the paradigm of Machiavelli's thought, to his reduction of knowledge to a static framework. In point of fact, *The Prince* is the text that can shed light on Vico's assessment of, and distance from, Machiavelli's vision.

As is widely known, *The Prince* belongs to the rhetorical genre of educational treatises.[12] That the text fully belongs to the tradition of the education of the prince (which includes works by Saint Thomas Aquinas, Vittorino da Feltre, Erasmus, and Rabelais), has often been remarked by scholars. They have also stressed some pervasive themes of

---

12. Allan H. Gilbert, *Machiavelli's Prince and Its Forerunners: The Prince as a Typical Book De Regimine Principum* (Durham, N.C., 1938).

The Prince, such as the counsel it offers, its ceaseless probing into the exemplary possibilities of history, and its focus on the dubious possibility that the prince can learn from history. In effect, Machiavelli's educational concern is rooted in his double assumption that, first, politics is an art that can be taught and that, second, a unified, single meaning can be disentangled from the discourses and plots of history. Such a concern emerges most clearly from Machiavelli's adoption of a double rhetorical stance in *The Prince.* Right from the start (chapter 2), Machiavelli announces his intent (namely, to leave behind any discussion of republics and to turn to the theme of principalities) by deploying the rhetoric of weaving ("andrò tessendo gli orditi"), as well as the rhetoric of erudite philosophical debate ("e disputerò come questi principati"). The treatise, in effect, presents itself as a mixture of the mechanical art of weaving (almost an extension of the material activity of Florentine textile workers) and of the logical, rational art of the *disputatio.* This double metaphor shapes and characterizes the ambiguous status of *The Prince,* which oscillates between being an esthetic construction and being a manual of political science. The double metaphor, finally, accounts for the rhetoric of political "remedies" that the text abundantly prescribes.

The Prince is punctuated by this medical language. Chapter 3, for instance, recommends, as a way of circumventing the difficulties of new principalities, a number of remedies: "E uno dei maggiori remedii e più vivi sarebbe che la persona di chi acquista vi andassi ad abitare" (One of the best and most effective remedies is for the new possessor of territories to go there and live); we are also told that when disorders are about to break out, "vi puoi rimediare" (you can remedy them); and that when these disorders get out of hand, "non vi è più rimedio" (there is no longer a cure); later in the same chapter we are reminded that "L'altro migliore remedio è mandare colonie" (Another, and even better, remedy is to set up colonies). Examples of the presence of such rhetoric could be multiplied, but what matters most is that Machiavelli here deploys the traditional association between medicine and rhetoric.[13]

Historically, such a link is available in Thucydides' study of the science of history (written as it was under the influence of the Hippocratic school); in Plato's *Phaedrus;* in Petrarch's *Invective against a Certain Physician;* and even in Boccaccio's *Decameron.* What this historical link between the two arts primarily suggests is that physicians and rhetoricians are educators because their respective aims are to teach health

---

13. Ronald L. Martinez, "The Pharmacy of Machiavelli: Roman Lucretia in *Mandragola,*" *Renaissance Drama* 14 (1983): 1–43.

and to teach virtue; it also implies that medicine is a model for eloquence, in that rhetorical language has the power to persuade its audience to achieve what is perceived as virtue and to cleanse and heal the diseased body politic. At the same time, medicine, far from being a pure science yielding certain knowledge, is the art of conjectures and of probabilities that forever elude definite determinations. *Mandragola* stages a parodic version of the links between medicine-magic and rhetoric. In *The Prince,* on the other hand, medical rhetoric is the paradigm of Machiavelli's epistemology; the language of this text is punctuated by a number of repeated key words (such as *virtù*), whose meanings vary according to their context and whose semantic shiftiness can be remedied by the will of the prince to control the drift and instability of words and signs, to extrapolate and construct a world, however precarious it may be, of order and sense.

Vico's distance from this epistemic paradigm is self-evident. *The New Science* (which—as the title itself suggests—redefines all forms and principles of knowledge and presents knowledge as history) features a theory of knowledge radically opposed to Machiavelli's. For Machiavelli, as we have seen, rhetoric is a force and the prince must learn how to bend it into a strategy to increase his power. Vico offers a critique of the Machiavellian and Cartesian definition of subjectivity, according to which the isolated self hopes to shape and control the heterogeneous world of history. Moreover, language is for Vico not just an instrument of power and a tool of persuasion. Rather, it is "constitutive," in that it constitutes the world and the horizon of its possible fables, in the same way that atoms constitute material reality. In brief, language, which is both rhetoric and poetry (which cannot be simply equated), not only describes the heterogeneous entities of history but, above all, serves as the model for the polity and is the ground that makes the knowledge of entities possible. Finally, language is for Vico the all-inclusive shared idiom of culture, and it is capable of providing the basis for a unified science (in which all the differences are preserved) because it is capable of achieving ultimate intelligibility. Within this perspective, poetry plays a paramount role. Whereas Machiavelli ends *The Prince* by expressing the poetic excitement and energy of Petrarch's "Italia mia," with its political rhetoric of a wished-for war between virtue and fury, Vico views poetry in *The New Science* as the "place" where the prodigies and monstrosities of the imagination are both tamed and kept alive—where the clichés of rhetoric are alienated into new and sublime inventions.

This overarching structure of language and poetry cannot be construed as leading to the elimination of individualities in the objective, transcendent generality of language. As I have argued throughout this essay, Vico redefines Machiavellian and Cartesian subjectivity, but he never nullifies it. A reading of the *Autobiography,* which deliberately alludes to and takes to task Descartes's construction of the self, would show the extent to which Vico's own idea of nonautonomous selfhood is best understood in terms of the framework of language he elaborates. The meaning of words, as Vico argues throughout *The New Science,* is found by connecting each word to a network of related words, for the syllables of language are, for Vico, forces, equivalent to the atoms of classical physics. In the section "Poetic Economy," for instance, Vico reflects on "families" (book 2, section 4, par. 554) and writes: "Thus marriage emerged as the first kind of friendship in the world; whence Homer, to indicate that Jove and Juno lay together, says with heroic gravity that 'they celebrated their friendship.' The Greek word for friendship, *philia,* is from the same root as *phileo,* to love; and from it is derived the Latin *filius,* son. *Philios* in Ionic Greek means friend, and mutation to a letter of similar sound yielded the Greek *phyle,* tribe."

For Vico, who in many ways is the philosopher of the legality and arbitrariness of boundaries, boundaries between words are fluid, serpentine, active and never static. What is true for the determination of words is equally true for the articulation of different disciplines: there are no conceivable autonomous disciplines such as "politics," "ethics," "esthetics," and "religion," such as one finds in the fragmentary practices of the Renaissance cult of individuality, at least as this cult is nowadays understood from a Cartesian and Hegelian standpoint. But for Vico, each discipline always entails and is assimilated to the other; overlaps with the other, though they are never fully coincident. The epistemological model Vico has in mind, as I have said, is language. This fundamental model finds its contingent realization in notions such as the "republic of letters" (*res publica litterarum*) and its related construct, the encyclopedia. This concept, which Vico uses in a text such as the *Seconda risposta,* has a long history that begins with Cicero and goes through Petrarch and Scaliger to Johann Alsted and Leibniz.[14]

The concept also includes institutions such as universities, academies, and courts. The existence of such a republic was made possible by the availability of printing and guaranteed by scientific publications, journals, and private correspondences that immediately had a public resonance. The aim of the republic of letters is the pursuit and dissemination of new knowledge for the education of self and others.

14. Loemker, *Struggle for Synthesis,* 28–52. See also Giuseppe Mazzotta, "Vico's Encyclopedia," *Yale Journal of Criticism* 1 (Spring 1988): 65–79.

Its members are the likes of Petrarch, Erasmus, Juan Luis Vives, Bruno, Campanella, Marin Mersenne, Descartes, Paracelsus, Girolamo Cardano, Robert Fludd, and Bacon. The erudition these intellectuals proclaim finds its embodiment in the new encyclopedism of Alsted, Johann Comenius, and Leibniz. What the republic of letters and encyclopedism together symbolize is the moral conviction of the necessity of a cosmopolitan map of knowledge, beyond the self-centered conceits of both savants and nations. More poignantly, they symbolize the revival of a transnational chart of the intellect that had been the dominant feature of the Middle Ages. They also enact the totality of knowledge as a dynamic, fragmented unity of multiple parts and viewpoints.

Vico's thought lucidly grasps that, just as in language sentences are made by endless groupings and regroupings of syllables, so each entity (such as politics, religion) needs other entities in order to reveal itself. He thus belongs fully to the republic of letters. His work, in fact, must be understood in the light of these traditional and yet radical educational practices of a republic that is both utopian and real. It is likely that Vico would also extend the right of citizenship in this non-Platonic republic to Machiavelli, especially to the author of *The Discourses*. Machiavelli's grand tragic vision, that values are established by freedom and by discourse, is indeed the ethical principle of the republic of letters. This hypothetical inclusion of Machiavelli in the republic simply means that "Machiavelli" is also found in "Vico," but that the name "Vico"—although it designates a potentiality or a disguise of "Machiavelli"—blazes the trails of a thought whose blurred contours we finally begin to discern.

CHAPTER ELEVEN

PURITY AS DANGER: GRAMSCI'S MACHIAVELLI, CROCE'S VICO

Nancy S. Struever

IN his essay "Machiavelli e Vico," Benedetto Croce wrote:

> Il successore del Machiavelli non bisogna cercarlo nè fra i machiavellici, che continuano la sua casistica e precettistica politica e scrivono sulla 'ragion di Stato,' sovente mescolando a quei precetti trivialità moralistiche; nè fra gli antimachiavellici, banditori di fusione e identificazione della politica con la morale e ideatori di Stato costruiti su puri dettami di bontà e giustizia. . . . Il successore vero fu un altro italiano. . . , il Vico, non benevolo al Machiavelli, eppure pieno del suo spirito, che egli chiarifica e purifica, integrando il suo concetto della politica e della storia, componendo le sue aporie, rasserenando il suo pessimismo.

One should not search for the successor of Machiavelli among the Machiavellians, who continue a casuistic and preceptive politics and write on "reason of state," often mixing with these precepts moralistic trivialities; nor among the anti-Machiavellians, dispensers of fusion and identification of politics with morality, and idealists of a state which assumes goodness and justice as "pure givens." . . . The true successor was another Italian, Vico, who was not benevolent toward Machiavelli, yet he was full of his spirit, which he clarified and purified, integrating his concepts of politics and history, composing his *aporia*, and coming to terms with his pessimism.

Croce is, I believe, precisely right in pointing to pessimism as genius; it is Machiavelli's "austere and dolorous moral sense" that gives his investigation its edge.[1] Bernard Williams has termed it a "pessimism of strength."[2] It is, however, a pessimism badly, infelicitously received. In his *Storia dell'Età Barocca*, Croce specifies an Italian identity and an Italian achievement, but he specifies difficulty as well: Machiavelli can neither be lived with nor lived without, neither ignored nor accepted.[3] Croce outlines three programs in seventeenth-century Italian political theory and historiography: (1) a program that restores the medieval unity of politics and morality, a restoration that will emphasize a Christian, Tridentine unity (or, perhaps a classical, civic humanist one similar to that existing in seventeenth-century England as described by J. G. A. Pocock in *The Machiavellian Moment*),[4] and that will try to colonize and subordinate Machiavellian truths; (2) a program that considers Machiavelli as simply the negative of moral law, Christian or classic; (3) a program that defines Machiavellian politics as positive, but distinct from moral law, yet in a determined relation with it (90). It is the last initiative that Croce finds fruitful; its well-motivatedness lies in its development of Machiavelli's notion of a difficult yet intimate, problematic but powerful relation between politics and ethics. Machiavelli, in short, has raised the issue of political morality in a way that demands an answer. To be sure, Croce points to a contemporary ambiance of hypocrisy—a covert Machiavellism that accepts Machiavellian formulations if masked as Tacitean (a partial explanation of the vogue

1. Benedetto Croce, "Machiavelli e Vico: la politica e l'etica," in *Elementi di politica* (Bari, 1925), 64–162. I shall argue that Giambattista Vico purified and strengthened Machiavelli's strategies of impurity. The title of my essay, of course, invokes Mary Douglas's brilliant study of the repudiation of polluting danger by the strategies of purity, *Purity and Danger* (Harmondsworth, 1970).
   I have suggested connections or parallels between Renaissance and Vichian practices in "Vico, Valla, and the Logic of Humanist Inquiry," in *Giambattista Vico's Science of Humanity*, ed. Giorgio Tagliacozzo and Donald Verene (Baltimore, 1976), 173–86; "Fables of Power," *Representations* 4 (1983): 108–27; "Vico, Foucault, and the Strategies of Intimate Investigation," *New Vico Studies* 2 (1984): 41–70; and "Rhetoric and Philosophy in Vichian Inquiry," *New Vico Studies* 3 (1985): 131–45.
   2. Bernard Williams, *Ethics and the Limits of Philosophy* (Cambridge, Mass., 1985), 171.
   3. Benedetto Croce, *Storia dell'Età Barocca in Italia: Pensiero, poesia e letteratura, vita morale* (Bari, 1925), 90.
   4. J. G. A. Pocock, *The Machiavellian Moment: Florentine Political Thought and the Atlantic Republican Tradition* (Princeton, N.J., 1975). Pocock's primary strategy is to claim that Machiavelli carried the strain of fifteenth-century Florentine civic humanism to the Anglo-American political world; the strain is, of course, the one that Hans Baron described in *The Crisis of the Early Italian Renaissance* (Princeton, N.J., 1966). However, an earlier expression of the paradigm is significant. In "Religion and Politics in the German Imperial Cities during the Reformation," *English Historical Review* 52 (1937): 405–27, 614–33, Baron describes the civic virtue of Strassburg and its fate with, I would argue, the Weimar Republic in the background as its contemporary correlate. It links fifteenth-century Florence with sixteenth-century Strassburg and twentieth-century Weimar and

of Tacitus in the late sixteenth and seventeenth centuries).[5] Croce also deplores the distressingly strong seventeenth-century current of casuistry. Here political and moral theory were contaminated in the enormously detailed, lengthy texts and by the heavy diffusion of the genre, a genre developed to aid the confessional trade in its dealings with new socioeconomic and political-religious changes. For Croce, the popularity of long, tangled chains of argument that relate general principles to particular cases, argument heavily illustrated by often outré exempla, is at the same time the popularity of legitimizing tactics of an exceptionally thin sort—producing, among other things, a legalistic, meretricious Machiavellism.

Croce relates in considerable detail the fortune of Machiavellian ideas. He maintains that Machiavellism was recognized by seventeenth-century theorists as intrinsic in the actions themselves; Machiavellian strategies were present, acknowledged or not, in the political practices of the century. Traiano Boccalini notes that the Ottoman Turk used the tactics without having read either Machiavelli or Jean Bodin (81). All princes, ecclesiastical and secular, Machiavellized (80–81). And, in political theory there were certain accommodations to Machiavelli's "austere and dolorous" account; Giovanni Botero rationalized Machiavelli by first distinguishing between prudence, practical moral wisdom, and "astuzia" (attention to interests), then admitting that the difference was only in degree and tone (87). Botero, in short, found himself unable to repudiate Machiavelli's notion of the structural difficulties of politics, his prejudice against moralistic prescription for political protagonists. He recognized that political talents do not automatically produce moral good; moral virtues do not automatically produce political values.

At the end of this "baroque" and exasperating seventeenth-century development, Giambattista Vico masters Machiavelli; he succeeds in raising the argument to a higher level. Croce employs a rather peculiar turn of phrase to characterize the relation: Machiavelli is an unconscious exponent of Vico, Vico an unwilling exponent of Machiavelli.[6] Yet certainly Croce is correct again to focus on pessimism as strength;

---

attempts to combine Greek and Roman formulas, in both rhetoric and politics, but the optimistic reading of a Ciceronian program is actually beset by historical difficulties. The paradigm could be attributed to fifteenth-century Florentines, but not to Machiavelli, who retains classical definitions of moral and political values but focuses only on historical actions, of which he gives a pessimistic account. His real interest is in dysfunction, rather than "good" government.

5. On the resort to Tacitus in the late Renaissance, see Marc Fumaroli, *L'âge de l'éloquence: Rhétorique et "res literaria" de la Renaissance* (Geneva, 1980), 153.

6. Benedetto Croce, *Elementi di politica* (Bari, 1925), 66.

Vico replaces the centaur (half man, half beast) symbol of Machiavelli with his stipulation of "la parte belluina" of man as fundamental; without "quella barbarie generosa" there would be no civility (65). But Croce's aestheticism colors his explanation; he underlines this insight into the stiffness and obduracy of overrefined civility compared with the plasticity of barbarism, its responsiveness to fresh political strategies, with a figure: a sculptor can more easily form a statue from a raw, unmanipulated block of marble than from a spoiled, previously worked one. Croce appeals not simply to sculpture, but to literature as well. Vico, in another of Croce's "aesthetic" namings, adds temporicity, makes a dramatic plot of *corsi* and *ricorsi* out of the steady insights into the extreme structural difficulty of Machiavelli (66). Vico's notion of *ricorsi* stipulates that plots do not simply "thicken" the account, they reiterate; later plots resonate with and revise earlier stories.

Although Croce is correct to link Machiavelli and Vico, a better argument to justify such a linkage can be found in Antonio Gramsci's account of Machiavelli's theoretical practice. Gramsci understands the powerful intrication of abstractness of mode and impurity of topic in the Machiavellian program; the combination of the choice of an abstract mode or approach with the premise of the intrinsic impurity and untidiness of the political object. Pessimism in Machiavellian inquiry is defined as existing in a network of multiple possibilities; the hypothetical captures the rough choices of political alternatives—real alternatives. Gramsci begins a section of "notes" on Machiavelli in the *Quaderni del carcere* by referring to the "prince" as a "myth."[7] The capacity of the Machiavellian text to continue to explain politics to us in the twentieth century stems from the potential of the central protagonist to be read as the concretization of the collective will, "will as working consciousness of historical necessity, as protagonist of a real and effective historical drama" (*QC*, 1559). The prince is a "doctrine," an empty carapace that can be used to cover the endless array of possibilities, radically diverse, in political history. The prince is certainly not a foundational myth in the classicizing, Ciceronian vein—a heroic protagonist embodying and preaching fundamental virtues, obligations, rights, duties. This would be the narrative equivalent of foundationalism, the ethical objectivism that motivates Pocock's *Machiavellian Moment*. In the Pocock/"Cambridge School" approach, there is an easy movement from the philosophical task of defining a list of virtues and rights as fundamental, timeless, to the historical task of "configura-

---

7. Antonio Gramsci, *Quaderni del carcere*, ed. Valentino Gerratana, 4 vols. (Turin, 1975) (hereafter cited as *QC*). The notes on Machiavelli are concentrated in Quaderno 13, 1555ff.

tion," of demonstrating the patterned unfolding of virtuous plots in time.

Gramsci's reading, it seems to me, distinguishes the extraordinary energy and care Machiavelli took to establish a new "philosophy of praxis" (*QC*, 1598). Machiavelli's steady focus on praxis, a focus that gives rise to the multitude of short, skeletal narratives of past and present actions in his texts, justifies and compensates for his strenuous efforts to proceed hypothetically, addressing a hypothetical audience, the *uomo della provvidenza* (1618), about a prince who is a *pura astrazione dottrinaria* (1556). Further, Machiavelli does not ever intend to "change reality," according to Gramsci (*QC*, 1578). At every point, politics, which deals not simply with the possible but with specific possibilities, scenarios, defines the constraints and limits of activities. Theory, in one strong sense, makes no difference; Gramsci acknowledges that there may be a blockage between thinking out possible alternatives and putting alternatives into practice. On the one hand, no hope is offered of relaxing in the achievements of theoretical purity; on the other hand, the promise of practice is delayed.

The Gramscian explanatory edge lies in his appreciation of the power of Machiavelli's theoretical or hypothetical program. Compare, for example, the inconsistency of other readings. Pocock's *Machiavellian Moment* rather tediously insists on a literal reading of Machiavelli's interest in the reform of a civilian militia, but this reading confounds Machiavellian *virtù* with classical virtues and thus contradicts the strong exclusionary definition of *virtù* as bare capacity, which, according to Pocock, is an accomplishment of Renaissance theory. But Gramsci replicates Machiavellian theoretical purity in confronting praxis. He views the citizen militia as another concretization of the collective will, this time in opposition to the aristocracy; indeed, it is a form of *Iacobinismo!*[8]

---

8. See *QC*, 1560: "Ciò intendeva il Machiavelli attraverso la riforma della militia, ciò fecero i giacobini nella Rivoluzione francese." Pocock, of course, views the militia as the vehicle of civic (bourgeois?) humanism, but it is intriguing that Gramsci accuses Croce of a fear of Jacobinism (*QC*, 953). Pocock needs Machiavelli's explanation of the militia as a link between fifteenth-century Florence and seventeenth-century English theorists, such as James Harrington. But I regard the interest in a civilian militia as an obsession of Machiavelli's, a reaction to a thorn in the flesh. Florentine incompetence is a burden, an embarrassment, and this betrays Machiavelli. He knows better; most certainly he must have observed that the Florentine militia's victory in Pisa in 1509 was followed by its defeat at Prato in 1512. He knows, most of the time, that the problem is intractable; Gramsci notes that Machiavelli's military thought is inadequate; he regards his exclusively political focus as causing errors in judgment (*QC*, 9, 1573). The last responsibility, however, we must attribute to Machiavelli is that of anticipating the National Rifle Association in its appropriation of Harrington. Recall that for Gramsci, the militia is an

The important similarity between the Machiavellian and Vichian investigational programs lies in the intrication of abstractness of mode and impurity of topic. Their work seems to acknowledge that it is dangerous for an elegant theory to propose purity, to displace the rigor of the mode onto the results of the investigation. It is no accident that one of the most sensitive modern readings of Machiavelli is also one of the most disheveled; Sebastian De Grazia's *Machiavelli in Hell* communicates very well the basic impurity in the investigative result. In a major effort of historical contextualization of Machiavelli, De Grazia depicts in absorbing detail the many Florentine obligations, often conflicting, that invest the texts.[9] Intrication, however, begins inside the investigative strategies. Here it may be useful to refer to a peculiar, almost opaque, statement by Louis Mink, in one of his many defenses of narrative: "Narrative is a primary cognitive instrument—an instrument rivaled, in fact, only by theory and by metaphor as irreducible ways of making the flux of experience comprehensible."[10] But both Machiavelli and Vico need two cognitive instruments; neither exhibits a simplistic faith in the comprehensibility of narrative alone or metaphor alone. Theory—strong arguments that establish the interactive status of separate investigative elements—justifies narrative and metaphorical modes. In Machiavelli, theory dominates narrative, and thus reads without reducing political plots; indeed, the very large number of "alternate courses of events which are rather short in duration," Hintikka's notion of "possible worlds," indicates hypothetical or theoretical zeal. In Vico, theory situates metaphor and explicates cognitive accidents. In Machiavelli's case, it is a matter of speaking hypothetically, persevering in an almost subjunctive mode, of a large array of nasty choices in truncated stories. Croce claimed that Vico's *The New Science* was one great substitution of profound for superficial classification; a new taxonomy that deals in wrenching differences.[11] Vico's bizarre, subtle, and absolutely central investigational strategy is to use etymology to reveal language as a tissue of the strong metaphors of the past, a network of begged civil questions. Every rich, expressive etymon used to make connections is already the site of previous connections. The theoretical framework for etymological research, then, the philosophical philology, ensures not only the intrication of purity of

---

incarnation of Jacobinism, but Jacobinism is another incarnation of the prince (*QC*, 1559).

9. Sebastian De Grazia, *Machiavelli in Hell* (Princeton, N.J., 1989).

10. Louis O. Mink, "Narrative Form as Cognitive Instrument," in Louis O. Mink, *Historical Understanding*, ed. Brian Fay, Eugene O. Golob, and Richard T. Vann (Ithaca, N.Y., 1987), 185.

11. Benedetto Croce, *La filosofia di Giambattista Vico* (Bari, 1911), 152.

mode and impurity of object, but the inextricability of barbarism and civility. Theory will not purify practice. Vico's peculiar genius is to explain how, in etymology, we can trace the weight of barbarism in our shared language, laws, and institutions, how we can discover the means by which barbarism is encapsulated in civility.[12]

The chronology of Machiavellian initiative, the mixed reactions to Machiavelli described by Croce, and the Vichian appropriation of Machiavelli suggest that the serious historical work of the sixteenth and seventeenth centuries was the final effacement of civic humanism. *The New Science* was the culminating effort, in both form and content. In the fragmentary form, the broken arguments, of the text we can read the repudiation of the Renaissance humanist historiographical model, the heroic narrative that teaches morality by example. There are no plots of edification, and there are few heroes. Indeed, there are few proper names in *The New Science;* Cicero, for example, appears only as an authority on legal semantics. Cicero's historical usefulness is to explain the usage of the terms of his times–the drift of custom and the formulas of institutions.

Still, it could be argued that Vico was more "civic" than the humanist Ciceronians. Vico would claim, of course, that he was more civic than Machiavelli, whom he censured as one of the "solitary" philosophers,[13] since he regarded as ineluctable the connection between an emphasis on materialism, on chance, and an emphasis on self-enclosure, solipsism. In the explanation of his frontispiece, Vico repudiates private illumination in his quest for civic light; moral learning is solipsist, and thus the formula of humanist historiography, the instruction of individuals by reference to exemplary heroes, becomes a form of self-indulgence. Yet the most telling and instructive contrasts can be found, not just in the writing of history but in the uses of Roman history—by the civic humanists of Florence of the Quattrocento; by Machiavelli, particularly in *The Discourses;* and by Vico. I would argue that each successive stage represents a differentiation and deepening of insight into the untoward nature of political activity, the risks of civility. The simple equation of virtues with *virtù* is eventually supplanted

12. Not that Vico diminishes the difficulties of historical work; the Vichian approach is best characterized by Leszek Kolakowski's perceptive statement: "Every sentence we utter presupposes the entire history of culture of which the language we use is an aspect. No word is self-transparent. None may pretend to hand over to the hearer the unadulterated world to which it is supposed to refer. Whatever reality the word conveys, it is a reality filtered through the thick sediments of human history we carry in our minds, though not in our conscious memory" (*Metaphysical Horror* [Oxford, 1988], 58–59).

13. Giambattista Vico, *Autobiography,* trans. Max H. Fisch and Thomas G. Bergin (Ithaca, N.Y., 1946), 138.

by the depiction of the mandatory struggle with the barbarism within, with an internal potential of political protagonist and political structure for gross incivility.

This description does not quite accord with Croce's notion of a "generous" barbarism. But Croce's perspicacious plot, his stipulation of Vico as successor to Machiavelli, makes an important point about the Vichian development of the Machiavellian malign. I would argue that such a connection does not merely describe an addition, a useful revision; rather, the connection, once made, settles that there is no return. We cannot, as ethical and political inquirers, retreat to some classicist harmonization of a foundationalist ethic and an optimistic politics. It is not that there have been no civic humanist attempts and texts, particularly in seventeenth- and eighteenth-century Anglo-American theory as Pocock and his colleagues have described it. But the early attempts seem askew, unconvincing in their accounts of political behavior, and the modern civic humanist readings of Machiavelli diverge from the Machiavellian plots that seem most perspicuous. In a very strong sense, Machiavelli's novelty is irremediable; it is simply impossible to go back and beyond Machiavelli and reassert a "medieval," unproblematic system of politics and morality.

An Impure Modernity

What does it mean to say that modernity has no remedy for Machiavellian politics? What are the implications for modern ethical inquiry? First, if we follow Gramsci's explication of Machiavelli, and Croce's argument for Vico as Machiavelli's successor, we conclude that the insight that founds the Machiavellian and Vichian moments is the sense of purity as danger. Perhaps, then, modernity needs a program of impurity. Second, the concatenation of the names Machiavelli and Vico, Croce and Gramsci, suggests a specifically "Italian" initiative, a strand of investigative activity that not only assumes impurity but refuses to reduce it to purity.

The Italian edge, the accomplishment, is a certain power in confronting political necessities, the corrosive nature of political acts. The vital element funding Machiavelli and Vico's seriousness is the consideration of necessity. Certainly the interest in necessity is a recurrent theme of an anthology of Italian philosophical papers, *Recoding Metaphysics*, edited by Giovanna Borradori.[14] One of Borradori's philoso-

---

14. Giovanna Borradori, ed., *Recoding Metaphysics: The New Italian Philosophy* (Evanston, Ill., 1989). I incorporate here parts of my review of Borradori in *New Vico Studies* 8 (1990): 56–61. Several of the essays in the collection single out the relation of metaphysics

phers, Emanuele Severino, claims, as have Nietzsche and his followers, that we must go back before Socrates to the *right* pre-Socratics to re-found Western philosophy. Severino, however, opts for Parmenides: necessity is the now unremarked, but central problem of meta-physics.[15] In the same collection, Aldo Gargani opposes the aesthetic bent, the playfulness or frivolity of Francophone philosophy. For Gargani, the unending playfulness, the unlimited construction of "versions" of the world, leads to unendurable boredom—to an "unendurable regime of simply possible thoughts."[16] Our weighty witnesses, the scientists, writers, and painters, were looking not for their images, or vision, in the intellectual mirror, but for "the weight of necessity that had moved them, made them investigate, write and paint" (78). Gargani claims that "the only thing I cannot give myself is necessity" (79). It is, therefore, "counter-intuitive to concern oneself with something whose meaning is in principle proved to be no different than that of adding a further version of the world to the collection of already existing ones" (77); "giving, attributing meaning" is an activity of an unendurable regime (80).

What is intriguing, of course, is that the modern Italian fascination with necessity works from an entirely different set of presuppositions than did the Italian Renaissance moment. Machiavelli and Vico's accomplishment was the acute, intense description of the nature of necessity: in Machiavelli, the ineradicably untoward in politics; in Vico, the barbarism that is encapsulated in civility. For Machiavelli and Vico chose history over fiction, activity over precept, the public or civil over the private or the individual—basing their choice, I would argue, on what was, in its original form, an Augustinian argument. In the *De doctrina christiana*, Saint Augustine claims that

> although human institutions of the past are described in historical narration, history itself is not to be classed as a human institution,

---

to technology, and of antimetaphysics to our distressing technocratic pillages. Although Borradori asserts parallels between contemporary Italian and French thought, I would argue that this Italian concern is in contrast to Francophone philosophy, which is fasci-nated by an aesthetics of free play, frivolity as duty. Frivolity motivates the French reading of technological event as literary text, a reading that is the result of a "literari-ness" that invests the location of inquiry. To be sure, there is no privileged perspective, no Archimedean point outside the text; but there is a form of privileged address, preten-tious in its pretense. The address pretends fun, but has an unacknowledged un-literariness; it hides its objective skills. This is a peculiar malfunction.

15. Emanuele Severino, "Time and Alienation," in Borradori, *Recoding Metaphysics*, 167ff.

16. Aldo Gargani, "The Friction of Thought," in Borradori, *Recoding Metaphysics*, 77ff., esp. 80.

for those things which are past and cannot be revoked belong to the order of time, whose creator is God. It is one thing to describe what has been done, another to describe what should be done. History narrates what has been done faithfully and usefully; but books of haruspicy and all similar books seek to show what should be done or observed with the audacity of the author, not the faith of a guide.[17]

It is relatively unproblematic to relate Vichian Providence to Augustinian Providence. It is more interesting to claim, as Gramsci does, that Machiavellian necessity finds its historical profundity in Vico's Providence (*QC*, 1089, 1481); or that Vichian Providence replicates Machiavelli's *Fortuna*, for both are constructs of postclassical necessity.[18] To be sure, Vico disassociated Providence from the simplicity of Christian redemptive myths as moral ordering structures. In *The New Science*, however, the Christian argument supports the status of history in a peculiarly strong way. What is done, *factum*, has the status of truth, *verum*; Providence has selected deeds, and deeds select insight.

Machiavelli and Vico provide, then, irremediable insights into irrevocable deeds. In the Augustinian and post-Augustinian argument, history is as serious as the accumulation of necessities. And for Machiavelli and Vico, necessity means that politics necessarily fails. The necessity of politics is untoward; it is, in Bernard Williams's phrase, constituted as "dirty-handed."[19] The validity of politics does not derive from its intrinsic value. It is counterintuitive but correct to claim that Machiavelli de-essentializes politics; thus, for example, continuity of political identity is, simply, the historical achievement, the concrete stratagems, of Rome. In Augustinian terms, Machiavelli is not an auda-

17. Augustine, *On Christian Doctrine*, trans. D. W. Robertson, Jr. (Indianapolis, 1958), 2.28.44.

18. Gramsci connects Machiavellian necessity and Vichian Providence in *QC*, 1089, 1481; he discusses Machiavellian necessity in *QC*, 658, 687. Croce is aware of the importance of Tommaso Campanella and Vico's "discovery" of Providence in the seventeenth century (*Storia dell' Età Barocca*, 231). On necessity in Machiavelli and Providence in Vico, see Gennaro Sasso, "La lettura degli autori antichi," in *Il guardiano della storiografia* (Naples, 1981), 280. Vico's Providence, of course, invokes Leibnizian possibility as well as Machiavellian necessity. It is important, but very difficult, to describe the subtlety of their antideterminism, which takes account of a peculiar range of necessity, most obviously the irony of unintended consequences.

19. Bernard Williams, "Politics and Moral Character," in *Moral Luck* (Cambridge, 1981), 54ff. Williams speaks of politics as "specially liable to produce an uncancelled moral disagreeableness" (61). "Even the moral ends" of the politician seem to subsist in a rather dangerous, unsecured way in the political domain (60). Machiavelli would state this more radically.

cious haruspex, divining essences, stipulating the "ought," but a faithful guide delineating the "is." A parallel study of Saint Augustine's account of Roman politics in the *City of God* and the Machiavellian account in *The Discourses* would be rewarding. Machiavelli gives an exclusive, powerful definition of politics—powerful in part because it excludes linkages with classical values. The unitary national state may be necessary on occasion, but it is itself not defined in terms of final moral value. Politics consists of the various public acts of maintaining or ruining (to use Roland Barthes's verbs) the unitary order. The Roman lesson for Machiavelli, and to a certain extent for Vico, is that sheer continuity, or maintenance, is the only criterion of political success; order, as in the phrase "law and order," is rudimentary, necessary for mere survival, without—and this seems a clear theoretical gain— even the support of the authoritarian ideology of "law and order."[20] De Grazia perhaps links Machiavelli's approbation of Cesare Borgia's "useful cruelties" too closely with Machiavelli's assertions of "the common good" as value. Machiavelli certainly did not attribute "civic humanist" intentions to Borgia, nor does he tie cruel means to transcendent common-good ends in a general and unsubtle way. Gramsci is correct in insisting that Machiavelli "does not recognize transcendent/immanent elements, but bases everything on concrete actions of man, who works and transforms reality through historical necessity."[21]

The brilliance of Machiavelli and Vico is in their reconsideration of the status of history. History is no longer the treasury of philosophical exempla of the civic humanist paradigm; historiography is the record of the operative constraints on future (yet past) contingents. History deforms moralistic philosophy when it takes account of the encapsulation of barbarism in civility, of the untoward or malign in politics. For Vico, dysfunction is normal in the process; Vichian historical irony explains the efficiency of the malign. And the stronger the assertion of the seriousness of history, the stronger the denial of the status of the historian as simply an interpreter, merely a creator of versions. Machiavelli and Vico select history but reject the historian's role as a hermeneuticist, who matches interpretative version to human fiction—an exerciser of haruspicy, in Saint Augustine's words. The denial reso-

---

20. Vichian *corsi* and *ricorsi* represent still another tactic of de-essentializing. On Machiavelli's *mantenere/ruinare*, see Roland Barthes, "Le discours de l'histoire," *Social Science Information* 6 (1967): 65–75. One could argue that Saint Augustine again preceded them; *The City of God* contains lengthy descriptions of politics as *only*, merely, a Roman achievement. And Gramsci twists the tale again: the Italian Renaissance intellectual, such as Machiavelli, was a cosmopolite, not a nationalist (*QC*, 133, 1361–62).

21. De Grazia discusses Borgia in *Machiavelli in Hell*, 302ff. The citation from Gramsci is from *QC*, 657.

Nancy S. Struever

nates in Gargani's lack of interest in a theory of versions, with its theoretical slide to the self-importance of the version creator.[22]

What is of central interest is the connection between serious history and perspicuous ethics. The contingent and factitious are the proper focus of speculation; necessity is simply, purely historical. The propriety lies in the focus on completed actions as specific limits; deeds are the foundation of our lives. These may be the assumptions of the argument that in the careers of Croce and Gramsci, the vital intervention was that of the Marxist philosopher Antonio Labriola.[23] If Labriola urged them to adopt a "philosophy of praxis," what is the significance of this practical turn for our consideration of theory as practice?

Croce's "absolute historicism" seems at first to be a simple, useful continuation of the Italian moment.[24] But Gramsci criticizes Croce's philosophy of praxis as inadequately practical: if Marx translated Hegelian abstraction into actuality, Croce retranslated praxis back into an ideal, abstract philosophy. What Gramsci finds absent in Croce, he finds usefully present in Machiavelli. First, he contrasts Machiavelli as politician, and therefore strong theorist, with Francesco Guicciardini as diplomat, and therefore skeptic. Then he contrasts Machiavelli, with his theoretical devotion to grim practice, and his grim devotion to theory, with Croce as "bookish, erudite, intellectualist." He deplores Croce's self-enclosure in a Germanic version of Vico, a circular argument in which history defines liberty, and liberty justifies history. Croce observed necessity, but disguised it with an "ethico-political" history (QC, 1208)—precisely the thin, moralistic history Machiavelli and Vico rejected.[25]

22. Compare F. R. Ankersmit's claim that the function of historical narrative is not to describe, explain, or interpret, but to "represent"; history is more like art, painting, than like the history of art—indeed, more like postmodernist art with its self-reflexivity. But this, again, places at risk necessity, justifies frivolity as a version ("Historical Representation," History and Theory 27 [1988]: 205–28).

23. David Roberts, Benedetto Croce and the Uses of Historicism (Berkeley, Calif., 1987), esp. 34–35, 41–42. See Croce's Materialismo storico ed economica marxistica, 7th ed. (Bari, 1944); and his Contributo alla critica di me stesso (Bari, 1945). It is significant that the latter text (Oxford, 1927), as well as The Philosophy of Vico (New York, 1913) was translated by R. G. Collingwood.

24. Roberts points out that Croce's conception of history as radically de-essentialized is anti-Hegelian: "For Croce, in contrast to Hegel, there is no higher form governing the process, no telos whereby reality, or the universal spirit, comes back to itself, becomes conscious of itself, or discovers itself. . . . Everything that happens is historical, is necessary for reality to be as it is . . ."; "[Croce] did his best to portray his own task as historically specific" (Benedetto Croce, 53, 95).

25. Gramsci's remarks on the philosophy of Croce are concentrated in Quaderno 10, 1207ff. On Croce's retranslation from practice to abstraction, see QC, 1233; on Machiavelli and Francesco Guicciardini, see QC, 760, 781–82; on Croce as "bookish," see QC, 1241–

286

Gramsci certainly contemplated the "end of history" and the end of necessity; his hypothesis of a final absorption of politics into civility as telos, goal, can be viewed as failure of historical nerve, the kind of totalizing strategy that Croce's "absolute historicism" was designed to resist (*QC*, 662, 1691). It is, perhaps, less damaging than the fusion of moralism and politics of the civic humanist paradigm, which still tempts Croce, even though he defines such a fusion as irretrievable medievalism. For Gramsci, Croce's fear of Jacobinism is a rejection of impurity, of the disobliging, messy, structured or unstructured violence of political operations that involve massive popular participation (*QC*, 1220). It implies a general gentility, very like a civic humanist prissiness, which makes no place for—but neither does it resist, head-on—radical change either from the left aiming for hegemony or from an authoritarian right.[26]

The inadequacies of civic humanism, Croce, and Gramsci can be defined by comparison with Machiavellian efforts. His elegant, spare political project gives rise to an elegant, spare ethical project—spare, and exigent, for his tactics of address assume an estranged, unfamiliar audience. His address does not lecture an audience of practical men but forces practical men to theorize. It is coupled with a hard, incredulous estimation of his reader's competence and dispositions to imitate, and this explains the nonexemplary nature of his examples. Vichian inquiry, of course, has a similar, powerful stratagem in "internalizing barbarism." The coefficient stories of phylo- and ontogenesis locate the barbaric actions of nations in the individual's own developmental plot; it is an intimate, damaging way of asserting the unforgettable persistence of bestiality in civility. Both purvey an experience of necessity.[27]

The new investigative edge of Machiavelli and Vico can be traced to the new status of history. The domain of useful knowledge is that of hypothesis, argument, possibility, and the historical work that pro-

---

42. Croce's notion that Vico was anticipatory of *all* of nineteenth-century German philosophy is surely wrong ("Il Vico e lo svolgimento posteriore," in *La filosofia di Giambattista Vico*, 241ff.).

26. We may balance Gramsci's "end of history" fantasy against Croce's timidity. Yet civic humanism in any form, Crocean or Baronian, is surely an inadequate protection against the untoward and its seductions; think of the enchantment of Anglo-American post-liberals with realpolitik in its more awkward forms.

27. One could argue that the Italian moment appeals to the "right" Nietzsche as opposed to the "wrong," aesthetic Nietzsche; it requires a general "strong" pessimism as opposed to a general gentility. And it requires particular refusals, especially of the unwitting "purity" of the aesthetic program, which has an argumentative structure that is pure because it is thin; it stretches its claims far beyond its stated capacity, while appealing only to an intellectualist sodality. It is poignantly elitist.

duces configurational patterns of possibility and necessity. It is the historical work, in particular, that nourished their ethical interests. There are several obvious advantages to their program. First, it imposes a limited referential liability. Gramsci's two statements (that Machiavelli was a political scientist only for his own time [*QC*, 1572]; and that historical solutions have their genesis only in actual situations [*QC*, 758]) suggest that historians' "versions" are of limited value; historical work is continuous and unending.[28]

Second, Machiavelli and Vico developed alternative, intriguing ways of describing necessity. The function of the Machiavellian tissue of possible plots, as well as of his web of hypothetical argument, is to map necessity, and thus impose a range of constraints on politics. Vichian historical irony, the insistence on unintended consequences, gives another version of necessity by connecting desirable achievements of civility with their (merely) providential origins. Vichian irony explicates the extraction of the beneficial from the untoward. Machiavellian narratives may show how necessity feeds virtue; the greater the necessity, the greater the virtue in the act.[29]

Third, their program eliminates invidiously distinct stages of inquiry. History is not a catalog of exemplary events, followed by an excogitation of results; rather, historical inquiry produces a series of nondetachable, "ingredient conclusions"—conclusions stuck to their stories.[30] Useful knowledge is neither about events, nor about results in propositional form; it is neither about events in their specificity, nor about succeeding statements of results in their independence. Since all particulars are grasped as being attached to modalities, all results are inseparable from experience.

This definition of history is rich in ethical yield. Necessity, for both

28. Recall Aldo Gargani's strictures on the "unendurable regime" of versions; he also claims that "truth is this interest in the necessity of what is defined as 'true'" ("The Friction of Thought," in Borradori, *Recoding Metaphysics*, 79). A history that claims that it is merely a "version" of the French Revolution self-destructs. The appreciation of historical work requires a shift of focus from the attributions of "subjective" or "objective" to a concern with the delineations of possibility and necessity. Or, to return to Saint Augustine: "subjective" and "objective" are terms appropriate to authors of books on haruspicy, not to historians.

29. De Grazia, as usual, cites the appropriate texts; in his brief discussion of necessity (*Machiavelli in Hell*, 195ff.), he uses "Gli uomini non operano mai nulla se non per necessità" (Men work nothing well except through necessity), from the *Discourses*, bk. 1, chap. 3 (*Machiavelli in Hell*, 198); and "Necessità fa virtù, come . . . abbiamo detto" (Necessity makes virtue, as we have often said), from the *Discourses*, bk. 2, chap. 12 (*Machiavelli in Hell*, 198).

30. The phrase "ingredient conclusions" is an important element in Louis O. Mink's "The Autonomy of Historical Understanding," in *Historical Understanding*.

Machiavelli and Vico, is always historical. And all possibilities are historical descriptions; only careful description of possibility illumines necessity; possibilities exist in a domain of complete historical symmetry; all past possibilities can be future possibilities, for the hypothetical is omnicompetent.[31]

The program imposes two independent but simultaneous constraints—a double constraint. First, the inquirer may not reject out of hand the historical definitions of virtues and civil goods; second, he may not ignore, he must become versed in, historical plots of political necessity. This is not De Grazia's "new ethical philosophy," which he attributes to Machiavelli. The ethical lesson of submitting to both frameworks at once is a demanding one. I have argued that the Machiavellian-Vichian succession sharply focuses on impurity and, in so doing, questions easy community practices, jolly academic solidarities. In a Machiavellian community of inquiry, longitudinally defined, the tendency is to devalue slight tasks: proper practice is not hermeneutics, not redescription, not conversation, and certainly not moralism. It is significant that both Bernard Williams and Machiavelli, with strong notions of the politically useful, deny that a simple utilitarianism, an algebra of use, is a solution. Williams, indeed, seems to think that the best we can hope for from our politicians are "habits of reluctance" in the conduct of politics.[32] But the challenge, for Machiavelli, and for a modern Italian effort, lies in the perfect awareness of necessity.

31. Again, De Grazia notes that for Machiavelli, all historical possibilities are possibilities still: "Tutte le cose che sono state io credo che possano essere" (All of the things that have been can, I believe, be again); from the letter to Francesco Vettori of December 20, 1514; cited in *Machiavelli in Hell*, 116.

32. De Grazia occasionally indulges in paradox: Machiavelli is both a moralist (*Machiavelli in Hell*, 367) and an antimoralist (316). See Williams, "Politics and Moral Character," in *Moral Luck*, 59, 63. This may be the insight that is lurking in Gramsci's remarks on Machiavelli's pessimism of intellect, optimism of will (*QC*, 762).

CONTRIBUTORS

Albert Russell Ascoli is Associate Professor of Italian and Comparative Literature at Northwestern University. He is the author of *Ariosto's Bitter Harmony: Crisis and Evasion in the Italian Renaissance* (Princeton, N.J., 1987) and of essays on Petrarch, Dante, Boccaccio, and others.

Carlo Dionisotti is Emeritus Professor of Italian Literature at the University of London. He is the author of *Geografia e storia della letteratura italiana* (Turin, 1967), *Europe in Sixteenth Century Italian Literature* (Oxford, 1971), *Machiavellerie* (Turin, 1980), and *Appunti sui moderni* (Bologna, 1988), as well as numerous critical editions and essays on a wide range of topics.

Giulio Ferroni is Professor of Italian Literature at the University of Rome, "La Sapienza." He is the author of, among other works, *Mutazione e riscontro nel teatro di Machiavelli* (Rome, 1972), *Il testo e la scena* (Rome, 1981), and *Storia della letteratura italiana* in four volumes (Turin, 1991).

John Freccero is Professor of Italian Studies at New York University. He is the author of *Dante: The Poetics of Conversion* (Cambridge, Mass., 1986) and of essays on Petrarch, Machiavelli, Svevo, Donne, and others.

Victoria Kahn is Professor of English and Comparative Literature at Princeton University. She is the author of *Rhetoric, Prudence, and Skepticism in the Renaissance* (Ithaca, N.Y., 1985), and of the forthcoming *Machiavellian Rhetoric: From the Counter-Reformation to Milton* (Princeton).

Ronald L. Martinez is Associate Professor of Italian at the University of Minnesota, Minneapolis. He is co-author (with Robert M. Durling) of a study of Dante's rime petrose, *Time and the Crystal* (Berkeley, Calif., 1990) and of articles on Dante, Boccaccio, and Machiavelli. He is currently engaged in a study of

Dante's Stazio in the *Purgatorio* and is doing research on the subject of Italian Renaissance theater and statecraft.

Giuseppe Mazzotta is Professor and Chair of Italian at Yale University. He is the author of *Dante, Poet of the Desert* (Princeton, N.Y., 1979), *The World at Play in the Decameron* (Princeton, 1986), *Dante's Vision and the Circle of Knowledge* (Princeton, 1992), and *The Worlds of Petrarch* (Durham, N.C., 1993). At present he is writing a book on the poetic philosophy of Giambattista Vico.

John M. Najemy is Professor of History at Cornell University. He is the author of studies in Florentine political history, including *Corporatism and Consensus in Florentine Electoral Politics, 1280–1400* (Chapel Hill, N.C., 1982). He has also written essays on Renaissance political ideas and a book on Machiavelli's letters, *Between Friends: Discourses of Power and Desire in the Machiavelli-Vettori Letters of 1513–1515* (Princeton, N.J., 1993).

Ezio Raimondi is Professor of Italian Literature at the University of Bologna. He is the author of many books, including *Metafora e storia* (Turin, 1970), *Scienza e letteratura* (Turin, 1978), *Il silenzio del gorgone* (Bologna, 1980), *La poesia come retorica* (Florence, 1980), and *Intertestualità e storia letteraria* (Bologna, 1991).

Barbara Spackman is Associate Professor of Comparative Literature and Italian at the University of California, Irvine, and author of *Decadent Genealogies: The Rhetoric of Sickness from Baudelaire to D'Annunzio* (Ithaca, N.Y., 1989). She has published essays on Machiavelli, Folengo, D'Annunzio, and Marinettti and is currently working on a study of the rhetoric of Italian fascism, entitled *Figuring Realism: Rhetoric, Ideology, and Social Fantasy.*

Nancy S. Struever is Professor of History, with a joint appointment in the Humanities Center, at Johns Hopkins University. She is the author of *The Language of History in the Renaissance* (Princeton, N.J., 1970) and *Theory as Practice: Ethical Inquiry in the Renaissance* (Chicago, 1992).

INDEX

Index

Index

Library of Congress Cataloging-in-Publication Data

Machiavelli and the discourse of literature / edited by Albert Russell
    Ascoli and Victoria Kahn.
        p.   cm.
    Includes bibliographical references and index.
    ISBN 0-8014-2870-X (alk. paper). —ISBN 0-8014-8109-0 (pbk. alk. paper)
    1. Machiavelli, Niccolò, 1469–1527—Criticism and interpretation.
    I. Ascoli, Albert Russell, 1953–   . II. Kahn, Victoria Ann.
    PQ4627.M2Z74   1993
    852'.3—dc20   93-11804